In the High Yemen

Scott gives a fascinating account of an expedition that took place in 1937 to the Yemen when the country was closed to Europeans by order of the Imam. Ostensibly a scientific expedition, it possesses great political, cultural, and anthropological interest. The tense negotiations which preceded the expedition and the ultimate success assured that this work remains perhaps the most important account ever written of that forbidding land that occupies the southern half of the Arabian shore.

FRONTISPIECE.
North-east from the summit of Jebel Jihaf towards the mountains of the Yemen: terraced fields of tall green dhurra.

IN THE HIGH YEMEN

Hugh Scott

Routledge
Taylor & Francis Group

LONDON AND NEW YORK

First published in 2002 by
Kegan Paul International

This edition first published in 2011 by
Routledge
2 Park Square, Milton Park, Abingdon, Oxfordshire OX14 4RN

Simultaneously published in the USA and Canada
by Routledge
711 Third Avenue, New York, NY 10017, USA

First issued in paperback 2016

Routledge is an imprint of the Taylor & Francis Group, an informa business

© Kegan Paul, 2002

All rights reserved. No part of this book may be reprinted or reproduced or utilised in any form or by any electronic, mechanical, or other means, now known or hereafter invented, including photocopying and recording, or in any information storage or retrieval system, without permission in writing from the publishers.

British Library Cataloguing in Publication Data
A catalogue record for this book is available from the British Library

ISBN 13: 978-1-138-97245-2 (pbk)
ISBN 13: 978-0-7103-0786-6 (hbk)

Publisher's Note
The publisher has gone to great lengths to ensure the quality of this reprint but points out that some imperfections in the original copies may be apparent. The publisher has made every effort to contact original copyright holders and would welcome correspondence from those they have been unable to trace.

PREFACE

PROVISION has been made for the appearance of the technical reports of the British Museum (Natural History) Expedition to South-West Arabia, 1937–8, in a special publication to be issued in parts by the Museum. Despite the war it has been possible to produce a first part of this publication early in 1941.

Outside the purely technical results of the Expedition there remained much that is worthy of publication, both of general natural history and relating to the country itself and its people, based on our memories and impressions and on very full notes written on the spot, as well as hundreds of photographs. This led me and my fellow-traveller, Everard B. Britton, M.Sc. (a colleague with me on the Museum staff), to contemplate writing jointly an account more general and popular than could be included in the official publication. But the months immediately following our return to England were occupied with the preliminary task of preparing and sorting the thousands of specimens and hundreds of photographs brought back. By the time a joint scheme for a book had been drafted and work started thereon, the war had broken out and, shortly after, my collaborator was called away. I can only thank him cordially for his ardour, helpfulness and hard work during the Expedition, and for the later work which greatly assisted me in planning this book.

As it now appears, with the framework reshaped, the book is in three parts. In the first I have tried to explain simply the scientific questions which prompted us to undertake the journey, and the methods used in carrying out our work. Though new to travel in South-West Arabia, I was not entirely a stranger (either in personal experience or reading) to countries abutting on the southern end of the great Red Sea rift, and my interest in the problems which they suggest was not new. Readers must not, however, expect a complete answer to the scientific riddles here. Even in normal times some years of labour are needed to work out in detail the results of such an expedition. Under present conditions, with colleagues, collections and libraries scattered and intercourse with scientists in many countries cut off, the task promises to be even longer.

The second part, the bulk of the book, is a personal narrative of our journey in two Arabian countries. The Western Division of the Aden Protectorate (as opposed to the Hadhramaut in the Eastern

Division) is still far from familiar to the general reader. The Kingdom and Imamate of the Yemen is a closed mysterious country, its ruler is a sacred personage, holder of a centuries-old office, combining in himself spiritual and temporal sovereignty. The routes we traversed are known to very few living Europeans (or Americans) and to only a handful of British. There is no up-to-date book by any English writer on these countries, the former an important part of a very large British Protectorate, the latter an independent realm of much consequence politically and otherwise owing to its common frontier with British territory. Indeed these lands ought to be better known to readers at home. Thus it seemed worth while to record the observations of two travellers primarily naturalists, but also intensely interested in many other aspects of the country, its peoples, customs and architecture, and its several ancient civilisations. Much relating to these matters is woven into the narrative. Personal experiences, small or trivial in themselves, and intercourse with individuals, will also often shed light on a strange and little-known land.

In the third part I have tried to summarise briefly the present state of knowledge of the tribes inhabiting this part of Arabia, of the dawn of human history there and the subsequent history before and since the coming of Islam. This portion is a compilation of facts and opinions to which I do not claim to have added anything original. But no book, least of all in English, exists in which even an outline of these subjects is brought together under one cover. Many aspects of the narrative will be better understood if the historical sections are read. Finally a very short chapter is added on some of the products and possibilities of development of this corner of the vast Arabian peninsula.

HUGH SCOTT.

HENLEY-ON-THAMES,
   1942.

CONTENTS

	Page
PREFACE	vii
NOTE OF ACKNOWLEDGMENT	xi
NOTE ON TRANSLITERATION AND DATES	xii
LIST OF PHOTOGRAPHS	xiii
NOTE ON PHOTOGRAPHS	xvii
LIST OF MAPS AND FIGURES	xix

PART I. INTRODUCTORY

Chapters
- I. Outline of the journey: difficulty of entering the Yemen . 3
- II. Our scientific quest . 6
- III. What we sought, and how our collections were made . 10
- IV. Previous exploration of the Yemen by naturalists . 13

PART II. THE JOURNEY

- V. Aden and Lahej . 21
- VI. Gateway to the highlands: Aden to Dhala . 29
- VII. Dhala, capital of the Amiri highlands . 33
- VIII. Life on Jebel Jihaf . 42
- IX. Recesses and heights of Jebel Jihaf . 53
- X. The upper Wadi Tiban and Jebel Harir . 63
- XI. The hot springs of Huweimi. Entry to the Yemen . 76
- XII. Ta'izz, chief city of the Southern Yemen, and its Amir . 82
- XIII. Through the central highlands to San'a . 98
- XIV. Many-towered San'a . 117
- XV. Treks in San'a district: our farthest north . 142
- XVI. The Great Festival: we meet the Imam at last . 163
- XVII. Last days in San'a and exit via Hodeida . 178

PART III. HISTORICAL—AND THE FUTURE

Chapters		Page
XVIII.	The peoples of South-West Arabia, and beginnings of their history	195
XIX.	History before the coming of Islam	204
XX.	Remains of the pre-Islamic civilisation	214
XXI.	Since the coming of Islam	222
XXII.	Products and possibilities	233
	Notes	238
	Bibliography	239
	Index	243

Note of Acknowledgment

ACKNOWLEDGMENTS of the generous support and help which I received both in England and Arabia in carrying out the Expedition have been expressed elsewhere. It is now a pleasure to thank the institutions and persons who have assisted me during the writing of this volume. Sincere thanks are tendered to Sir Bernard Reilly, K.C.M.G. (Governor of Aden at the time of the Expedition), for kind help and advice regarding many matters; to the Trustees of the British Museum for sanctioning publication of the Map of San'a District; to the Royal Geographical Society for kindly allowing inclusion of the route-map and the plan of San'a, and certain other illustrations which appeared in the *Geographical Journal* for February, 1939; to the Royal Central Asian Society for permitting inclusion of four text-figures and other illustrations published in their *Journal* in January, 1940; to Major C. T. P. Bailey of the Victoria and Albert Museum, who obtained for me permission to have a drawing made of an Abyssinian Cross belonging to H.M. the King; to Colonel E. L. Hughes, Librarian of the Royal United Service Institution, for full information about the "Jingling Johnny" figured on page 167, and to Mr. E. F. Britton (father of my fellow-traveller), who first called attention to the nature of this object.

I am indebted to Dr. G. M. Morant of the Royal Anthropological Institute for valuable help in drawing up the summary of anthropological views on the peoples of South-West Arabia (Chapter XVIII), and to Miss G. Caton-Thompson for information and suggestions bearing on the short account of the pre-Islamic history (Chapter XIX). While many colleagues have helped me in the naming of the animals and plants mentioned in the narrative, I would specially express my indebtedness to the late Mr. George L. Bates and to Mr. W. L. Sclater regarding the birds, and to Messrs. J. E. Dandy and C. Norman of the Botany Department of the British Museum (Natural History). Dr. K. P. Oakley of the Geology Department also kindly explained and discussed certain points. The special debt owing to my fellow-traveller, E. B. Britton, has been mentioned in the Preface. Mr. M. Aurousseau and Miss A. B. Carson, of the Permanent Committee on Geographical Names, have aided me about the meaning of certain words. Miss Brenda Hudson, Miss Margaret Mackay and Miss Dorothy Hillcoat have devoted great care to making the drawings for the maps and figures in the text.

NOTE ON TRANSLITERATION AND DATES

TRANSLITERATION of Arabic words presents many pitfalls to one whose knowledge of the language is very small. I have, frankly, not tried to be quite consistent. In the spelling of place-names I have, as far as possible, followed the *First List of Names in Arabia (N.W. and S.W.)* issued by the Permanent Committee on Geographical Names (Royal Geographical Society) in December, 1931, and the pamphlet *South-West Arabia: Transliteration of Names* published by the Government of Aden in January, 1937. Names of persons are also generally spelt according to the latter pamphlet.

These lists agree in representing the "choking sound" *ain* by the conventional ', which I have therefore inserted in names and other words where required. But there is a difference between the two lists in transliteration of vowels. In the 1931 List *a* and *u* are preferred to *e* and *o* except in a few conventional spellings, and in particular the diphthong *fatha ya* is transliterated *ai* rather than *ei*. In the Aden List, on the other hand, it is attempted to render closely the local pronunciation of the southwest, therefore *ei* is used. After my return I followed the 1931 list in using *ai* in several place-names, e.g., BAIT BAUS and other names in which BAIT occurs, GHAIMAN, JEBEL RAIYANI. These names appear thus on the maps and in the published official "List of collecting stations", but in the text of this book I have used *ei* (e.g., BEIT BAUS, GHEIMAN) as more nearly representing the local pronunciation—the sound being much like the second syllable of *obey*. There are (I know) other inconsistencies in my choice of vowels. In some cases a purely phonetic rendering is deliberately preferred, or one is given in addition to the standard spelling. In a few instances old-established conventional English renderings of words are used. But the form MUHAMMAD is adopted throughout, except in referring to certain persons of European education (in one case a Turk) who spelt their name MOHAMMED when writing French or English.

A sign is printed over long vowels in some less-known words; thus, in 'ĪD and WADI NATĪD the long *i* is sounded like English *ee*; in MAHMŪD and MANSŪR the long *u* is almost like the English *oo*. But it has not been thought necessary to insert this sign in well-known words, e.g., over the second syllable of the oft-repeated word IMAM.

Lastly, the form AL YEMEN (as opposed to AL YAMAN), clearly representing the sound to English ears, is the spelling adopted in both the published lists cited, and also on the postage stamps issued in that country.

All *dates* mentioned are in terms of the Christian Era, unless it is otherwise stated.

LIST OF PHOTOGRAPHS

FACING PAGE

North-east from the summit of Jebel Jihaf towards the mountains of the Yemen: terraced fields of tall green dhurra   *Frontispiece*

1. *Aden: the old city in the Crater, at sunset* } 24
2. *In the older part of the town of Lahej*
3. *The crags of Aden across the bay, over the* dūm-*palms on the sand-dunes of Hiswa* 25
4. *Tribesmen, houses and brushwood huts at Al Milah* } 32
5. *The route over the bed of Wadi Hardaba*
6. *Dhala: the principal mosque* } 33
7. *Dhala town from the castle-hill, backed by Jebel Jihaf*
8. *Central building of the castle at Dhala* } 36
9. *The smaller castle at the top of Jebel Jihaf*
10. *A grove of thorny ʿilb trees near Dhala* . . . 37
11. *A pool in Wadi Dareija* 40
12. *Children and sheep on Jebel Jihaf* } 41
13. *Tall-stemmed aloes in Wadi Dareija*
14. *Volcanic mountains in the afternoon haze, from Jebel Maʿfari* . 42
15. *Top of Jebel Jihaf; the cultivated plateau and the mountain-castle* } 43
16. *A summer afternoon rainstorm on Jebel Jihaf*
17. *A house on Jebel Jihaf, with hedge of tall tree-euphorbias* . 46
18. *Naji, chief tribal guard of our escort in the Amiri highlands—a humorist* } 47
19. *Amiri women and girls on Jebel Jihaf*
20. *Sling, pipe, gourd food-vessel, and door-lock from the Amiri highlands* 48
21. *North-west edge of Jebel Jihaf, with thunderclouds over the Yemen mountains* } 49
22, 23. *Threshing wheat and ploughing on Jebel Jihaf*
24. *Building dykes before irrigating fields at Dhala* } 50
25. *Ploughman followed by three men turning the soil with a heavy shovel, near Sanʿa*
26. *Raising water at Dhala* } 51
27. *The water from the hide bucket is directed into a channel*
28. *The pale lilac purple-throated trumpets of a prickly* Barleria-*bush* } 58
29. *The dwarf rock-pink of the Yemen*
30. *Gorge at the head of Wadi Leje; wild-fig trees lighted by the setting sun* } 59
31. *A battery of bee-hives in Wadi Leje*
32. *From the summit of Jebel Jihaf towards Jebel Hesha and the brown ramparts of the Yemen* 62
33. *Descent of the north-west face of Jebel Jihaf* . . . 63

xiv   *List of Photographs*

                                                                                                     FACING PAGE

34. Camp at Al Muriah, near the Tiban river
35. Striking camp at Al Muriah; Jebel Hesha in the background   68
36, 37. The two sons of Sheikh Shaif and their servant
38. A tribesman of Jebel Halmein brings a live puff-adder in a cleft stick   69
39. View east over the Halmein and Yafa country, from the summit of Jebel Harir
40. Tomb of a saint on the summit of Jebel Harir   76
41. Ta'izz from the north, with Jebel Sabir in the background
42. View from the roof of the 'Amil's Guest-house in Ta'izz   77
43. Qubba of Husein Pasha in Ta'izz; banana and pawpaw trees in the foreground
44. Ta'izz: one of the large mosques, in the Turkish style   84
45. A water-sprite in the recesses of Jebel Sabir
46. On the road to Mocha near Ta'izz; a cistern and fountain for ablutions near a large wild-fig tree   85
47. Approach to Ibb over the pass, on a cold evening in December   98
48. Looking north from the Wadi Thabad in Jebel Sabir
49. The old walls and city of Ibb, from the east   99
50. Ibb: minaret with roofed gallery
51. Ibb: the crowd, and the apparatus for raising water for the mosques   102
52. Outside the principal gate of Ibb   103
53. The Amir of Ibb at his door, with the Qadhi and chief men of the city.
54. The Amir's house (right) at Ibb, on the ancient walls   104
55. Makhadar in the afternoon light
56. The sergeant (in middle) and soldiers of our escort from Ta'izz to San'a   105
57. View from the Sumara pass; village of Menzil Sumara in the foreground   108
58. On the highest point of the Sumara pass, before our descent to the plain of Yarim
59. In the city of Yarim, after sunset   109
60. An ancient cemented cistern, south of Dhamar
61. Arrival of our heavy baggage in San'a   114
62. Qadhi Mohammed Raghib, the Imam's foreign secretary   115
63. San'a: the Arab city in the afternoon light, from the housetop in Bir al 'Azab   122
64. San'a: soldiers drilling on the parade-ground outside the palace
65. Outside the palace precincts, the main building in the background   123
66. San'a: in the Arab city   126
67. San'a: mosque of Mahdi Abbas, 16th Century Turkish style; shops of lapidaries on left
68. San'a: courtyard of Great Mosque, showing small rectangular local ka'ba in the open court   127

List of Photographs xv

FACING PAGE

69. Mosque of Al Madressa, San'a, built in the Yemeni Arab style . 128
70. A street in San'a leading to the mosque of Al Abhar . ⎫ 129
71. A " square " close to the same mosque . . . ⎭
72. An interior in the suburbs of San'a . . . ⎫ 130
73. Plaster-work and double traceried windows in an upper room ⎭
74. Minaret of the mosque of Salah ad Dīn at San'a . . 131
75. One-storied shops in the suqs of San'a . . ⎫ 132
76. Children in the lucerne-fields outside the city walls . ⎭
77. Raising water in Bir al 'Azab . . . . ⎫ 133
78. View in Dhamar . . . . . . ⎭
79. A street in the Jewish quarter of San'a . . ⎫ 134
80. A brickfield and kiln, San'a . . . ⎭
81. Meysha al Abyadh, the leading Jewish silversmith of San'a, and his ⎫
   son . . . . ⎬ 135
82. Scrolls of the Jewish scriptures in a synagogue . . ⎭
83. Silverwork . . . . ⎫ 136
84. A silver-gilt necklace made by the silversmith in Phot. 81 . ⎭
85. Weaving at Beit Baus . . . . . ⎫ 137
86. A spinner (wearing sleeveless sheepskin coat) at Wadi Dhahr ⎭
87. San'a plain from the hills above Hada . . . ⎫ 144
88. Bare walnut-trees in the orchards at Hada, in January ⎭
89. Beit Baus : the walled town on its slab of volcanic rock (trap) ⎫ 145
90. Houses at the foot of a cliff of trap, Beit Baus . ⎭
91. Beit Baus : looking in through the town gate . ⎫ 146
92. Beit Baus : woman feeding a camel . . ⎭
93. East from Wadi 'Asr 147
94. The Imam's new country-house in Wadi Dhahr . . 150
95. A cliff at Wadi Dhahr, with the entrance to a pre-Islamic tomb ⎫
96. The cactus-like spurge, Euphorbia officinalis, growing at 9,000 ⎬ 151
   feet, near Haz . . . . . . ⎭
97. Approaching the extinct crater of Jebel al Kohl, in the Harra of ⎫
   Arhab . . . . ⎬ 156
98. Red cinder-cones and black lava-flows seen from Jebel al Kohl ⎭
99. Sheikh Husein of Gheiman 157
100. Boys of Gheiman want a place in the picture . ⎫ 162
101. Mother and children at Al 'Asr . . . ⎭
102. San'a : outside the Bab al Yemen . . . ⎫
103. San'a : crowd outside the Meshhed during prayers at the 'Id al ⎬ 163
   Kabir . . . . ⎭
104. On the edge of the Yemen highlands : looking west down Wadi
   Masnah 182
105. The rough dwellings used by visitors to the hot springs at Hammam ⎫
   'Ali . . . . ⎬ 183
106. The last of the mountains, in the Wadi Siham . ⎭
107. Grass-thatched huts in the Tihama . . . ⎫ 188
108. A doorway at Hodeida . . . . . ⎭

List of Photographs

FACING PAGE

109. *Hodeida : houses, mat-walled huts, bundles of hides* }
110. *Our embarkation in the sambuq at Hodeida* } 189

FOLDING PANORAMAS

111. *North-west face of Jebel Jihaf, from Al Muriah in Wadi Tiban* }
112. *Southwards towards Ma'bar from Naqil Isla, 9,600 feet* } 192
113. *San'a from the east* }
114. *Wadi Dhahr from the south. In centre, the Imam's house shown in Phot. 94* } 193

NOTE ON THE PHOTOGRAPHS

ALL the photographs reproduced are our own, with the single exception of No. 68. For this view of the courtyard of the Great Mosque at San'a, a subject of which we could take no photograph, I am indebted to Herr Robert Deutsch, an engineer who was surveying for a railway under the Turks in 1911–12.

More than eight hundred photographs were taken, of which over a hundred are reproduced here. Some of those not technically the best are included to render the photographic survey of the country and the occupations of the people more nearly complete. After our return in 1938 our results, taken as a whole, won the high approval of experts. It may therefore be helpful to give some details of apparatus and exposures. We had three cameras. I worked either with an Ensign quarter-plate (f/4·5), or with a Rolleiflex (f/3·5) which takes pictures $2\frac{1}{4}$ inches square. Britton also used these cameras, but more usually a Voigtländer (f/6·3), taking an intermediate size, $3\frac{1}{4} \times 2\frac{1}{4}$ inches, with which some excellent results were obtained. Fine grain panchromatic film was used throughout; Agfa I.S.S. ("Super-special") film-packs for the Ensign camera, Agfa Isopan (ultra-rapid) rolls for the Rolleiflex, Selo rolls for the Voigtländer. We attributed much of our success to the use of a photo-electric exposure meter (the Weston Universal). No exposure was made without first registering the strength of the light, excepting snapshots taken when there was no time for such preparations. The index-figure on the meter had of course to be changed to correspond with the type of film in use (it was 16 for the Selo rolls, 20 for the Agfa rolls, and 24 for the Agfa film-packs).

We kept records of many exposures, though many photographs had also to be taken hurriedly and under circumstances which rendered the recording of details impossible. Speaking generally, moving objects in the bright hours of the day were photographed with stop f/11 and $\frac{1}{50}$th second, or f/8 and $\frac{1}{100}$th second. But all panoramas and distant views and many average views of scenery and buildings were obtained by setting the Ensign or the Rolleiflex camera on a stand and using the smallest stops, f/20 to f/29 (usually f/22 or f/25), with a correspondingly longer exposure, such as $\frac{1}{10}$th second; moreover, as a yellow light-filter was very often used to gain increase of con-

Note on the Photographs

trast in tones for these subjects, the time was then doubled to $\frac{1}{5}$th second, or in weak light even to a half or a whole second.

We were working in Latitudes between 12° 45′ and 15° 50′ North, and usually at high altitudes (between 4,000 and 9,000 feet, occasionally higher). A few examples are given of exposures and the particular conditions in each case. The letters *y.f.* are added when the yellow light-filter, approximately doubling the time, was used. The middle part of the day is meant when no definite time is stated.

Frontispiece (distant view from mountain, 7,800 feet, September): f/22, $\frac{1}{10}$th sec., y.f.

Phot. 3 (at sea-level, November, near sunset): f/25, 1 sec., y.f.

Phot. 9 (castle and village, 7,100 feet, late September, 5 p.m.): f/25, $\frac{1}{5}$th sec., y.f.

Phot. 17 (near view at 7,000 feet, early October, 4.30 p.m.): f/22, $\frac{1}{10}$th sec., y.f.

Phot. 26, 27 (quickly moving objects, 4,800 feet, October): f/8, $\frac{1}{100}$th sec.

Phot. 39 (distant view from mountain, 7,700 feet, late October, cloud and sun, 1 p.m.): f/22, $\frac{1}{10}$th sec., y.f.

Phot. 48 (distant landscape from nearly 6,000 feet, late December, midday): f/22, $\frac{1}{5}$th sec., y.f.

Phot. 61 (street scene, early January, nearly 8,000 feet): f/11, $\frac{1}{50}$th sec.

Phot. 63 (view over city, nearly 8,000 feet, early March, 2–4 p.m.): f/22, $\frac{1}{5}$th sec., y.f.

Phot. 72 (room interior, February): f/16, 1 sec.

Phot. 74 (near view of buildings, nearly 8,000 feet, February): f/22, $\frac{1}{5}$th sec., y.f.

Phot. 88 (near view, 8,000 feet, January, 3 p.m.): f/22, $\frac{1}{2}$ sec., y.f.

Phot. 94 (average view, nearly 8,000 feet, January, midday): f/22, $\frac{1}{5}$th sec., y.f.

Phot. 104 (distant view from over 8,000 feet, March, midday): f/25, $\frac{1}{10}$th sec., y.f.

Phot. 112 (distant panorama from 9,600 feet, March, 3–4 p.m.): f/29, $\frac{1}{10}$th sec., y.f.

LIST OF MAPS AND FIGURES

MAPS

MAP		PAGE
1.	The major political divisions of the Arabian Peninsula	2
2.	Part of Aden Protectorate and the Yemen, showing the author's route	20
3.	Plan of San'a	122
4.	San'a and district . . . . facing	142

FIGURES

FIG.		PAGE
1.	Plan of the Jami' al Kabir (The Great Mosque) at San'a	127
2.	Much-weathered sculptures built into the outer wall of the Great Mosque, San'a	128
3.	Jingling Johnny carried by a soldier in the procession at the 'Id al Kabir	167
4.	Impression of triangular seal stamped in red pigment on the envelope containing our summons to a private audience with the Imam	173
5.	Column from the temple at Huqqa	215
6.	Bull-headed waterspout from the temple at Huqqa	217
7.	Abyssinian processional cross with horn-like projections from the base	218
8.	Flag of the modern state of the Yemen	223

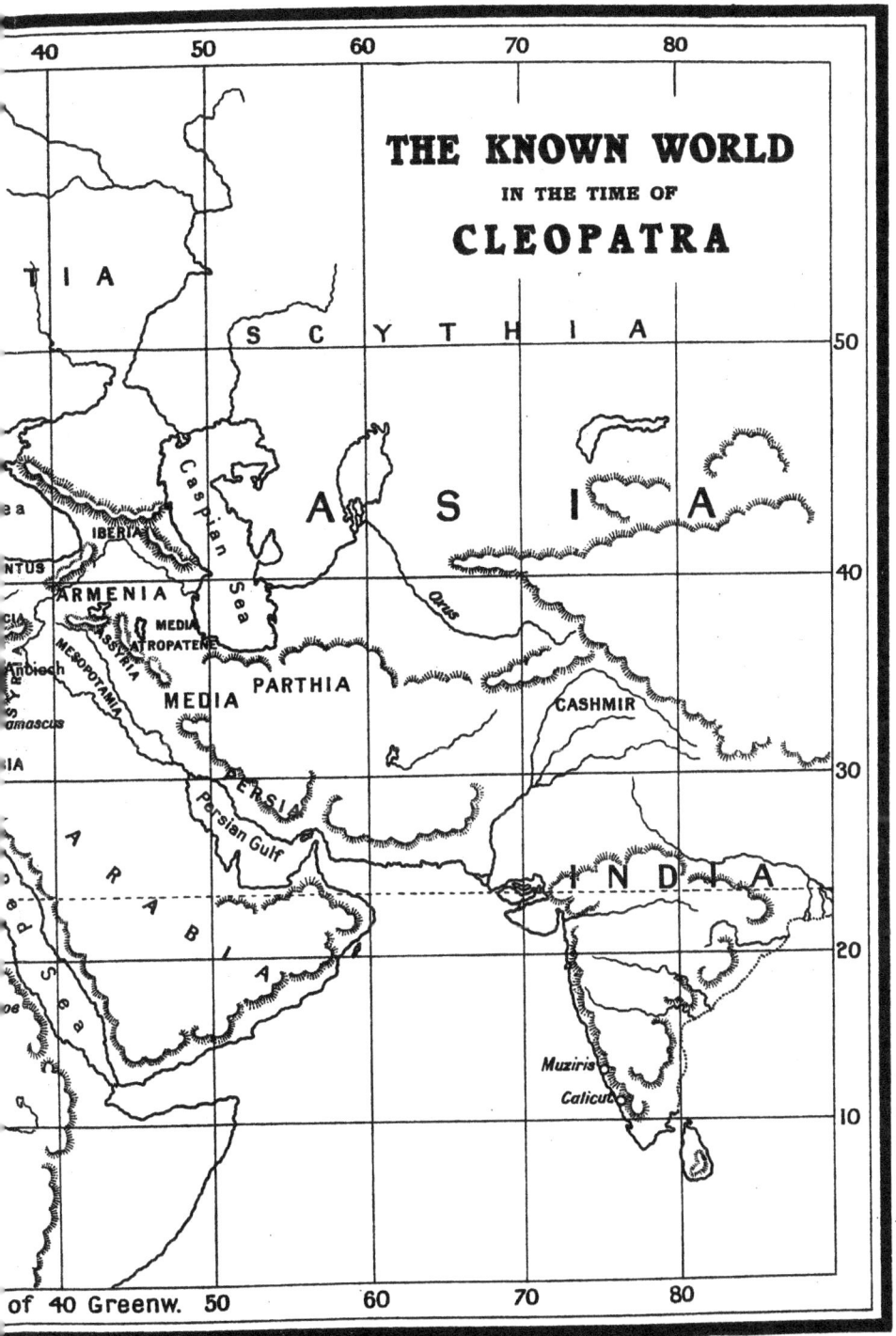

PART I
INTRODUCTORY

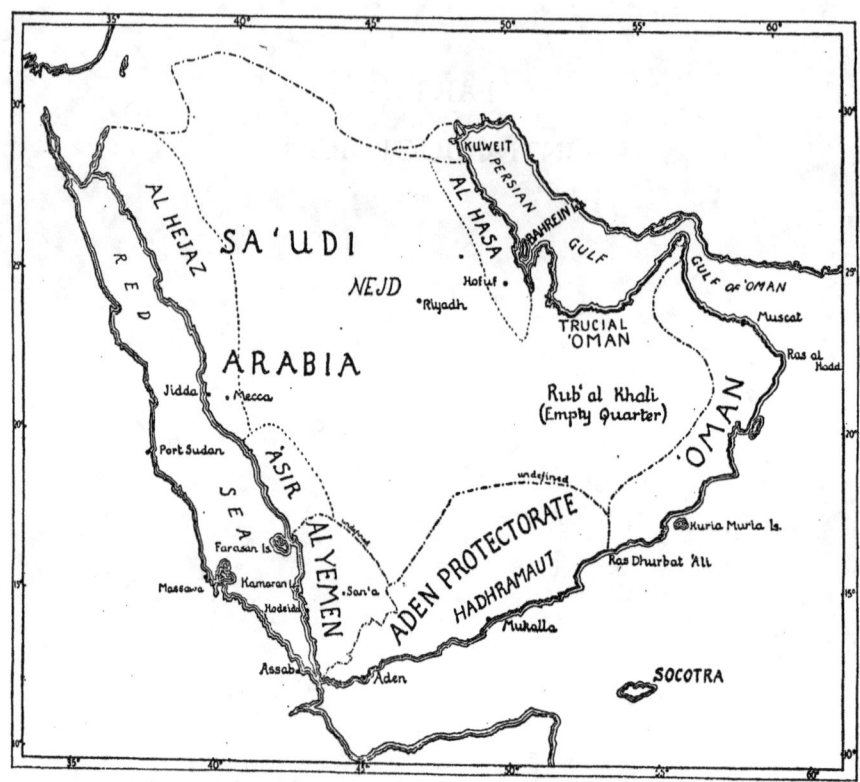

MAP 1. *The major political divisions of the Arabian Peninsula: international frontiers (approximate) indicated by alternate heavy lines and dots. Within the Kingdom of Sa'udi Arabia the former provinces of Al Hejaz, 'Asir and Al Hasa are indicated by broken lines. Besides the Sa'udi Kingdom, the principal states and territories are the Sultanate of Kuweit; the Sheikhdom of Bahrein; the Sultanate of 'Oman (Trucial 'Oman excluded); the Colony of Aden and the Aden Protectorate (including Socotra I.); and the Imamate and Kingdom of the Yemen. The block of highlands which were the object of the Expedition extend from 'Asir in Sa'udi Arabia through the whole length of the Yemen into the south-western part of the Aden Protectorate.*

CORRIGENDA

P. 84, line 23 : for " Mufadhal " read " Mufadhdhal " (as the letter *dh* is doubled).

Pp. 123, 171, 181, 226, 227 : the title of the present Imam and of several of his predecessors " Al Mutawakil Allah " should strictly read " Al Mutawakkil 'al' Allah ", since the participle *mutawakkil* (waiting, relying) must in this phrase be followed by the preposition *'alā* (on, upon).

P. 187, line 2 from bottom : " ajeeb ! " should be transliterated *'ajīb* ! (" remarkable ! ").

P. 222, bottom line : " Khulifah " should read " Khulafa " (plural of Khalīfa).

P. 226, line 14 from bottom of text : " 12th century " should read " late 11th century " ('Abbās, father of Zurei', attained (jointly with his brother) the lordship of Aden about 1083, and the descendants of Zurei' ruled the principality till the Eyyubite conquest in 1173).

Chapter I

OUTLINE OF THE JOURNEY: DIFFICULTY
OF ENTERING THE YEMEN

ALONG the southern half of the Arabian shore of the Red Sea rises a great mountain mass. Its tablelands average 8,000 feet in height, while the higher peaks, as yet incompletely surveyed, tower to more than 12,000 feet above the sea. These highlands stand in the track of the saturated winds of the south-west monsoon, which during the summer months blow from the Indian Ocean towards the heated land masses of Asia. Consequently a heavy and regular summer rainfall renders this the most fertile of all that part of Arabia named, centuries ago, Arabia Felix. In sharp contrast are the deserts and steppes of the interior and the barren coastal strip known as the Tihama.

A great block of these mountains lies in the Yemen, a land on the high-road to the East, yet a closed and hidden land whose very existence is unsuspected by most travellers passing along the Red Sea. To penetrate these fertile highlands of the Yemen Britton and I set out for Aden in August 1937.

We are both entomologists, and members of the staff of the British Museum (Natural History) at South Kensington. We had been given leave of absence to make an expedition into the mountains of South-West Arabia, principally to form representative collections of the insects of the region. The causes which led us so ardently to wish for this are outlined in the second chapter.

For political reasons the Expedition was no easy matter, and for the last month before leaving England we had been beset by the gravest doubts as to whether we should succeed in our ambitious project. The highlands which we longed to reach have their northern extremity in the south-western corner of the Kingdom of Sa'udi Arabia, that is, the province of'Asir, a land to which it was impossible to gain admission. The mountains and tablelands continue through the whole length of the Kingdom of the Yemen, and extend beyond its southern frontier into the western division of the Aden Protectorate north and north-west of Aden. One of our principal motives was to investigate the insects, plants, and other forms of life at very high altitudes, say above 9,000 feet. Though the northern part of the British Protectorate is certainly high, its mountains nowhere exceed 8,000 feet. It was, therefore, essential that we should—ruling out 'Asir as impracticable—enter the Kingdom of the Yemen. Herein lay the difficulty, for the Yemen is a state closed to Europeans except with the express permission of its ruler, the Imam, who as King wields absolute authority and is most jealous of European penetration. Could he be convinced of the innocence of our purpose?

The Imam of the Yemen has no permanent representative in Britain, and can only be approached through the Colonial Office and the Government of Aden. Sir Bernard Reilly, Governor of Aden, while on leave in England in 1935, discussed the subject with me sympathetically, but warned me of the difficulty of getting permission to enter the country. He had, in 1934, headed a Mission to San'a, the capital, and carried through the delicate negotiations for the Treaty of San'a, by which the British Government officially recognised the Imam as King of the Yemen. Nothing, therefore, must be done to imperil the existing friendly relations with the Imam. The proposal that I should be allowed to enter the country could only be broached at a propitious moment. This did not occur till the end of 1936, when the Imam consented, under certain restrictions, to our visit.

In July 1937, however, the Imam withdrew the permission given six months earlier through his Foreign Secretary, saying he would prefer the Expedition to be " postponed ". But in the meantime our preparations were complete, and we decided to travel to Aden and work in the mountainous parts of the British Protectorate until consent to our entry into the Yemen could be obtained.

On arrival at Aden, acting on the advice of our friend, Captain B. W. Seager, the Frontier Officer, we travelled nearly ninety miles northwards to Dhala, capital of the Amiri highlands. In this territory, under the friendly protection of the Amir of Dhala, and with the guidance of the British Political Officer, we worked for two months. We camped for over a month at 7,000 feet on Jebel Jihaf, a mountain massif to the north, which reaches 7,800 feet, and also explored parts of the Wadi Tiban and ascended Jebel Harir, a 7,700-foot mountain at the eastern limit of the Amir's principality. This first journey into the interior proved of the greatest interest. The Dhala highlands, though politically separated, are geographically a continuation of the Southern Yemen. The collections made there, though on the whole from slightly lower altitudes, are equal in value with what we subsequently found in the Yemen itself.

At the end of November, soon after our return to Aden, the Aden Government at length got permission from the Imam for us to visit

Ta'izz, in the Southern Yemen. Setting out from Aden early in December, we reached that city, where, after a stay of three weeks, our permit was extended to the capital. We then travelled to San'a through the central highlands, by way of Ibb, Yarim and Dhamar. After a sojourn of more than two months, and smaller journeys round the capital, we travelled down to Hodeida, on the Red Sea coast.

So at length, after long periods of waiting and hope deferred, we covered in this second journey a large part of the highlands of the Yemen, the country " on the right hand " or, as some would derive it, the land of happiness and prosperity.[1]

[1] Regarding the meaning of the name, see p. 204.

Chapter II

OUR SCIENTIFIC QUEST

THAT we should have persisted in carrying out our expedition despite delays and disappointments presupposes an ardent desire to visit the country. I shall, therefore, try to explain why an expedition to the fertile highlands of South-West Arabia was to me a long-cherished project. It is necessary to outline, as simply as possible, how the countries bordering on the southern end of the Red Sea came to have their present geological structure; also how this affects their climate to-day, and the climatic changes which have taken place before and since early historic times. In the third chapter is told what kind of collections we made and our ways of collecting specimens, while the fourth is devoted to a short review of earlier exploration of the Yemen by naturalists.

The south-western corner of the Arabian peninsula is of peculiar interest, because its fauna and flora link on to and overlap those of three great biogeographical regions—the Northern or Palæarctic, the Oriental, and the Ethiopian or Tropical African. The interest which I and my colleague felt in the geographical distribution of its animals and plants had arisen independently. To both of us South-Western Arabia presented large areas almost entirely unexplored from our standpoint. While, however, Britton was keenly interested in the possibility of finding links with the countries to the north and east, the motive which led me to work so ardently for an Arabian expedition was mainly a desire to compare the fauna and flora of the South-West Arabian highlands with those of the Abyssinian highlands on the opposite side of the Red Sea, which I had visited eleven years before.

There exist, as said, two great blocks of highlands, one on either side of the southern end of the Red Sea. Their core consists of ancient crystalline rocks on which have been superimposed, in very remote epochs during which the area was submerged below the sea, huge thicknesses of several successive formations, corresponding mainly to the Jurassic and Cretaceous of Europe. The latter period, when our chalk was formed, is represented in Ethiopia and South-West Arabia chiefly by sandstones about 1,100 feet thick. After their deposition the whole area was, at the end of the Cretaceous or in early Tertiary time, uplifted far above sea-level, and a phase of faulting, the formation of cracks in the earth's crust, set in. This was accompanied by a mighty outpouring of molten volcanic rock which solidified into enormously thick layers of " trap " (in central Yemen they have been estimated at over 2,000 feet thick) ; the trap to this day constitutes great areas of the high tablelands, and has been subsequently eroded, so that in places it ends in sheer cliffs or stands in gigantic detached slabs (Phot. 89). The cracking of the earth's crust mentioned above, continuing in successive phases over a vast period of time, resulted in the sinking in of three great trough-faults or rifts, namely the Red Sea, the Gulf of Aden, and the northern extremity of the complicated system of East African rifts. These three great trough-faults, meeting at the narrow Straits of Bab el Mandeb, have cut across the formerly continuous uplifted block and separated the Abyssinian from the Yemen highlands.

The process of cracking, the pushing up to thousands of feet above sea-level of some blocks of the earth's crust and the sinking in of others, occurred in successive phases. Three great systems of faults are distinguishable, one running north-north-west and south-south-east, or parallel to the length of the Red Sea, a second running due north and south, and a third almost at right angles to the first, parallel to the Gulf of Aden. The succeeding phases gave rise to step-like formations, so that we now have the Red Sea lying in its deep trough, a narrow belt of lowlands along the coast on either side, and the great mountain ramparts rising in steps to the high plateaux. The high plateaux of the Yemen are, however, not merely the bent-up and broken-off edge of the land-mass constituting the peninsula, but are a block which has been uplifted along lines of faulting on both sides, so that it falls away (though less precipitously) on the east towards the deserts of the interior, as well as on the west towards the Red Sea. The isolated high tablelands thus formed lie at 7,000 to 9,000 feet above sea-level. From them peaks and ranges soar to far greater altitudes.

In the later part of the period of faulting, comparatively recent volcanic outbursts occurred. These eruptions, separated by a very long interval from the earlier outpourings of trap, probably began in the first part of the Tertiary period and have continued in successive phases down to historic times. Some of the works of man were probably overwhelmed by the later outpourings, and the whole area is one in which dying volcanic activity is still manifested by the presence of vapour-emitting fissures and numerous hot mineral springs. To this recent volcanic period belong many extinct cones and craters in Abyssinia and South-West Arabia. On the Arabian coast it comprises the Aden peninsula itself and other craters west of it, and many of the grim, barren islands in the Red Sea, such as Perim, the Hanish Islands, the Zubair group and Jebel Tair. In the interior it has given rise to the areas known as " Harra ", such as the Harra of Arhab, north of San'a, a desolate-looking tract of red cones and grey-black, scarcely weathered, lava-flows (Phots. 97, 98), reflected in the use of black lava-blocks for building houses and walls round fields.

Finally, the most recent formations are alluvial and æolian deposits, according as they have been accumulated by the action of water or wind. Such are, first, the narrow strips of coastal lowlands or desert country known as Tihama, and, second, the thick beds of wind-accumulated dust (a coarse-grained kind of " loess ") forming the plain surrounding San'a, not far short of 8,000 feet above sea-level. On these latter deposits the largest city in Southern Arabia depends for its very existence. Rain-water, sponged up by this extremely porous substance, is tapped by numerous deep wells, and the bricks of the city's ancient encircling walls and of the greater part of its houses, old and new, are made of the same material.

What sort of climate the country may have enjoyed during the earlier phases, after its uplift and separation from Africa by the Red Sea rift, is too complex a question to discuss here. But there is evidence that great changes have occurred in more recent geological times, within the Pleistocene period. Within this limit (perhaps a million years) South-West Arabia has been subjected to alternating wetter and drier episodes. The cooler and wetter phases (" pluvials ") were probably contemporaneous with those of which evidence has been discovered in East Africa, and which are believed to have synchronised with periods of glaciation farther north. In Pleistocene times there appear to have been two major pluvial episodes, separated by a drier phase during which occurred the earlier outbursts of recent volcanic activity. Much later there has apparently been a new wet phase, continued into the early centuries of the Christian era.[1] Since its cessation, the gradual process of drying has extended outwards towards the coast, a change referred to again in the historical summary, Chapters XIX and XXII.

The natural processes outlined above, extending over long epochs of time, affect present conditions as follows. The high plateaux and lofty mountains catch the summer monsoon and have abundant rains from June to September. Streams, waterfalls and rivers, many of which flow perennially, exist at medium and high altitudes in the interior. Those flowing outwards do not normally reach the sea, but are lost in the sands of the Tihama. They shrink greatly in the

[1] See Dr. S. A. Huzayyin, " Egyptian University Scientific Expedition to South-West Arabia ", *Nature*, Vol. 140, p. 513, 1937.

winter months, when the boulder-strewn water-courses of the wadis are usually almost dry. In summer, however, the rivers are liable to rise suddenly and rush down as torrents. Deep and steep-sided valleys, canyons and gorges have thus been scored in the ranges and the edges of the tablelands. Other streams flow inwards, descending more gradually from the watershed formed by the high mountains fringing the outer edge of the highlands. The waters of this latter series may peter out in the arid interior; but the wadis in which they flow may join great valleys, formed in moister periods but now dry, running far east across the peninsula.

The combination of high altitude and abundant perennial streams results in temperate conditions, in which the animals and plants of temperate latitudes flourish. Some forms of life the same as or nearly related to those of the Mediterranean, and even of Central and Northern Europe and Asia, exist on the high plateaux and mountains of the Yemen and of Abyssinia. There are flowers such as primulas, irises and potentillas, and among butterflies, clouded yellows, graylings and wall-browns—not always identical with the familiar European species, but near enough to be at once recognised. Some of these may have only recently spread across the hot intervening deserts and lowlands to the island-like blocks of fertile, temperate highlands. Others may be relics of the former periods when the climate of the whole region was cooler and wetter than now. On the other hand, the hot coastal lowlands and deep valleys are at present inhabited by tropical (largely African) plants and animals, while tropical and temperate species mingle in the middle altitudes.

Though the separation of the South-West Arabian and Abyssinian highlands occurred after the remoter geological epochs, it took place quite long enough ago for some of the animals and plants on either side to have diverged in the course of evolution. We may therefore expect, and we do in certain cases find, closely related but slightly different representatives of the same groups on opposite sides of the Red Sea. Moreover, the Red Sea rift has acted as a barrier to the distribution of some forms of life. For instance, the giant lobelias of the Tropical African mountains reach as far north as the Eritrean highlands, but are not found across the Red Sea in the Yemen. Conversely, some European and Asiatic plants such as the iris reach as far as the Yemen but are not established on the African side.

When our large collections have been studied in detail, it is hoped that a contribution will have been made towards solving these questions concerning the past history of this part of the earth, and the rate at which new species and varieties are evolved.

Chapter III

WHAT WE SOUGHT, AND HOW OUR COLLECTIONS WERE MADE

WE were interested, in the first place, in insects of every kind. Entomologists, however, have to deal with a class more numerous than all other living things put together. For insects are the dominant form of animal life on the earth. At a conservative estimate about half a million distinct kinds are known and vast numbers still await discovery. Nevertheless most people are quite unaware of the existence of the great majority of the creatures we were seeking; forms usually inconspicuous, often dull-coloured and with hidden ways of life; mostly small or minute, even as minute as one millimetre (about $\frac{1}{25}$th inch) long. Thus in practice we could not collect all orders of insects equally. Attention was therefore concentrated on the groups most likely to throw light on questions of geographical distribution. Such, in particular, are grasshoppers and locusts, beetles—especially certain groups associated with particular plants or restricted to very high altitudes—bees, wasps and related forms, as well as butterflies and moths.

Our collection eventually numbered about 27,000 insects. Hundreds of land and fresh-water shells, of spiders, scorpions, centipedes and related creatures, and of woodlice were also collected, while even vertebrate animals in the shape of bats, reptiles and frogs were not entirely neglected. We did not try, however, to collect the better-known larger animals, birds and beasts. Out botanical work resulted in our getting together about 600 specimens of flowering plants and ferns. What with collecting and preserving all these specimens, taking more than 800 photographs and writing copious notes on all we saw, our hands were kept very full.

As to the apparatus needed for the highly specialised work of insect collecting, I was guided largely by experience, both at home and on previous expeditions, especially in Abyssinia. We swept great numbers of insects of all kinds from herbage with large strong nets made of the heaviest quality of " Swiss Silk " (bolting cloth) with broad edges of strong unbleached calico, fitting on to jointed iron rings or strong wooden hoops, which in turn are fixed to short, stout, wooden handles.

Nothing less than these nets and frames, which I have had specially made for each of my expeditions, would withstand the tough and thorny vegetation and the constant blows against sharp stones and tree-trunks. We had lighter nets of standard pattern, with bags of mosquito-netting, for catching butterflies and other delicate insects on the wing, but these light nets were usually soon broken. Next, we had provided ourselves with special sieves of different meshes, and white waterproof sheets on which to sift dead leaves and other debris. We usually carried an axe and chisel for cutting decaying wood or tearing off bark, and sometimes a crowbar for wrenching up boulders in order to search for the insects which live beneath. Special nets of extra fine mesh were used for collecting aquatic creatures from ponds, pools and streams.

Killing-bottles and tubes charged with potassium cyanide had to be in readiness. For rapidly collecting very small insects out of the net, or from siftings, Britton used an aspirator, a wide-bore glass tube, into which the insects are sucked by means of a length of rubber tubing, and from which they cannot escape. When a large number of insects have accumulated in the glass tube, they are anæsthetised by sucking the vapour of ethyl acetate through the tube, after which they can be shaken into a killing-bottle. I preferred to pick up the minute insects one by one on the point of a moistened camel's hair brush. On our daily excursions, therefore, our satchels held all these things, as well as a stock of glass-bottomed pill-boxes in which delicate flying insects could be brought home alive, and tubes of spirit for soft-bodied specimens. We were glad to have our Somali servants (of whom more is to follow) at hand to help and to carry some of the apparatus !

In the evenings or at other times between the collecting excursions, we were at work packing and labelling the insects we had taken. Butterflies have to be placed singly in triangular paper envelopes and packed away in tins. Moths, bees, wasps and flies are pinned through the thorax with fine stainless steel pins into cork-lined boxes. The more robust insects—grasshoppers, beetles and plant-bugs—are quickly and safely packed between layers of smooth cellulose wool in strong cardboard boxes. Smaller specimens were placed in fine sifted sawdust, in small cardboard boxes about the size of a matchbox, an old and tried method by which tens of thousands of tiny specimens have been sent home by famous expeditions from distant parts of the world. Some of the smallest insects of all, a millimetre or less in length, were gummed at once to small pieces of card, to prevent their being lost. We instituted a detailed system of numbering the separate lots, recording date, place of capture, altitude, and any special notes on their habits. The boxes of specimens amounted, before our journey was out, to hundreds. They were sent or brought home, and the task of unpacking and mounting, begun at the Museum while we were still overseas, continued for well over a year after our return. Spiders and other soft-bodied creatures were preserved in tubes of spirit, snails' shells were packed in cotton-wool in matchboxes, and plant-specimens dried and pressed.

With dry weather in all but the first month, we were not troubled by mould, which so often spoils insect specimens collected in the moister parts of the tropics. Nevertheless, as a precaution, we painted the inside of every box before use with a solution of naphthalene in chloroform. Ants, at first, did some damage; their scouts would invariably discover any box not completely closed, and soon a living stream of ants would be pouring in and out. The only safeguard was to seal the boxes, when full, with adhesive tape, while boxes in process of filling were kept on a table, the legs of which stood in tins of water.

It can easily be realised that all this apparatus, with plenty of "spares" to replace breakages, filled many cases. Together with boxes of stored food, tents and other camp-outfit, and our personal belongings packed in steel mule-trunks and canvas-covered mule-panniers, they amounted to well over thirty packages. On journeys where motor-transport was possible the heavy gear filled a lorry. But no bale or box must exceed a certain size and weight, as camels, mules and donkeys had to be used in the most interesting parts of our route.

Chapter IV
PREVIOUS EXPLORATION OF THE YEMEN BY NATURALISTS

THE South-West Arabian highlands have been comparatively seldom penetrated by travellers whose object was primarily natural history. Our expedition can, indeed, claim to be the first of which the official purpose was exclusively natural history, and mainly entomology. In the earlier explorations of the country, botany on the whole received far more attention than zoology. But several of the best-known explorers of the Yemen highlands, such as Arnaud, Halévy and Glaser (all mentioned in the Bibliography), were almost solely intent on archæological and historical discovery.

Archæological, ethnological, geographical and natural history investigations were combined in the classic expedition headed by Niebuhr in 1763—the mission composed of six members, of whom only the leader lived to return to Europe and give its invaluable results to the world. Again, the four members of the Egyptian University Expedition of 1936 devoted themselves to several widely different branches of science, as detailed near the end of this chapter. The same applies to the German savants, Rathjens and von Wissmann. Though their results are of the highest value, composite expeditions are not always best suited to the modern specialised methods demanded by entomology in the field.

In this chapter it is not attempted to give an exhaustive summary even of natural history exploration, but only to mention the more important missions and travellers. Nor have I tried to outline fully the routes of investigators as well known as Niebuhr and his companions. Epitomes of their experiences can be read in several books, if those interested have not access to the original.

At least one record of certain natural products of the country dating from long before the Christian era is well worthy of mention. Then, omitting perforce the great medieval travellers in Arabia, Oriental and European, we must pass to the naturalist-travellers of the 18th Century and later.

We may here except from ancient exploration of the Yemen the plant-collecting expeditions of the Egyptians to the land of Punt.

Undertaken largely to introduce into Egypt trees yielding incense, these expeditions are recorded or graphically depicted on the walls of Egyptian temples from about 2500 B.C. onwards. But it does not seem certain whether the journeys lay in South-West Arabia or (more probably) in some part of Ethiopia. "Punt" may have referred to both sides of the Southern Red Sea, though some of the animals shown in the wall-pictures could probably have been brought only from the African shore.[1]

With this exception, the earliest reference (as far as I can discover) to the natural history of South-West Arabia occurs in the famous "History of Plants" written by Theophrastus about 300 B.C. This writer, the successor of Aristotle as head of the Peripatetic School of Philosophy, mentioned the vanished kingdom of Qataban (see below, p. 208). He was, however, primarily concerned with the aromatic plants yielded by different countries, and did not himself visit South-West Arabia. The information given by Theophrastus is considered to be very accurate. He did not, as did some classical writers, confound the natural products of the country with wares such as cinnamon, brought thither from India or Ceylon by Arab traders. Arabia was only the mart for merchandise of the latter kind.

In modern scientific exploration first place must be accorded to the expedition organised by King Frederick V of Denmark in 1762, and sent out under the leadership of Carsten Niebuhr. The results can be read in Niebuhr's own great works. In his "Beschreibung von Arabien", published at Copenhagen in 1772, the topography of the country, the manners, customs and religion of its people, and other subjects, are treated in the "First Part" under separate sections, while the different parts of Arabia, either visited by the Expedition or described at second-hand, are dealt with in the "Second Part". So far as the Yemen is concerned, this work remains indispensable to the present, showing in word and illustration how little the daily life of the country has changed in 175 years. The companion volumes, entitled "Reisebeschreibung nach Arabien", etc. (Copenhagen, 1774), contain the actual itinerary of Niebuhr's journey. Only the later part of the first volume of the *Reisebeschreibung* is concerned with the Yemen; but this itinerary supplements the *Beschreibung*, containing additional facts about particular places and describing the reception of the party by the Imam at San'a.

Of the six members of Niebuhr's party only the leader survived to return to his country and publish the story. The party arrived in the Yemen at the end of December, 1762. Von Haven, Arabic

[1] A recent article by R. E. Cooper, "The first record of plant introduction", appeared in the *Journal of the Royal Horticultural Society*, lxv, pp. 334–7, 1940.

scholar and philologist, died at Mocha in May, 1763; his body was carried to the European cemetery by sailors from an English ship, and all the British community resident in Mocha attended the funeral. Peter Forskål, botanist and pupil of Linnæus, died at Yarim in July, 1763, on the journey up to San'a; Niebuhr relates dispassionately the grim difficulties encountered in arranging the interment. After the remaining members had left the Yemen, Baurenfeind, an artist, and a Swedish servant named Berggren died later in 1763 on the voyage to India, and finally Christian Cramer, surgeon-zoologist, passed away at Bombay in February, 1764.

Probably some, if not all, of those who died contracted the virulent form of malaria still indigenous to the lowlands and hot valleys of the foothills in the Yemen. A fortunate result of the advances since made in tropical medicine is seen in our own fate. Britton, having unluckily contracted malaria at Ta'izz, was in the first serious stages of the illness when we reached that same town of Yarim. We had, however, both stored up powers of resistance by regular dosing with atebrin. Consequently he was able to complete the journey to San'a where, though seriously ill, he was quickly cured by further treatment.

The labours of Niebuhr's colleagues were not lost. Forskål, in particular, described many of the species of plants he had collected, and his work was published twelve years after his death.[1] Many of his specimens found their way into the herbarium of Sir Joseph Banks, with which they passed to the Natural History Museum after 1820. In many cases no examples of these species from Arabia were received at the Museum from that time until we brought home fresh material in 1938.

The results of the travels of the next traveller-naturalist, Ulrich Jaspar Seetzen, botanist and orientalist, were lost to science. This explorer in the Russian service had been under suspicion in the Hejaz and, after entering the Yemen about 1810, he was murdered, under circumstances never since cleared up, in the district of Ta'izz.

In 1836, P. E. Botta, on behalf of the Muséum d'Histoire Naturelle at Paris, carried out an important botanical journey from Hodeida, through parts of the lowlands *via* Beit al Faqih and Hais to Jebel Sabir, south of Ta'izz. His exploration of Jebel Sabir, the 9,800 feet summit of which he climbed, is an outstanding part of his work. Owing to illness he did not reach the central high plateaux or San'a, and left the country by Mocha. His narrative appeared in 1841.

A botanical journey was undertaken by A. Deflers in 1887. His " Voyage au Yemen ", published in Paris in 1889, contains (besides

[1] Flora Aegyptiaco-Arabica, 1775. Besides editing his " Flora ", Niebuhr brought out three other posthumous works of Forskål.

lists of the plants collected) some general information and descriptions of parts of the country. During a five-months' journey (late March to late August) Deflers travelled eastward from Hodeida over the mountains *via* Manakha. He visited San'a and districts north of it (some of them rather farther north than any we reached). On leaving the capital he followed the route between San'a and Ta'izz in the reverse direction from that described in Chapter XIII. Finally he returned to Hodeida from Ta'izz through Zabīd and Beit al Faqih, a route we did not cover. His work includes a bibliography and a summary of explorations previous to his time, fuller than that here given.

When Deflers was completing his book, the botanist G. Schweinfurth, already renowned for his studies of the flora of Ethiopia, travelled for several months in the Yemen, exploring the country between Hodeida and Manakha. One result was an important comparison [1] of the plants of South-West Arabia with those of Northern Abyssinia. It was shown that, while the two floras have much in common, there are some striking differences. Schweinfurth stressed that some plants characteristic of South and East Africa extend as far north as Eritrea but have not crossed the Red Sea into Arabia. Conversely, some Indian plants reach as far west as the Yemen but are not found in Africa.

I can barely mention Cruttenden (1836) and Millingen (1873) who, besides travelling in the interior, made observations on natural history or collected specimens. The published account of Passama, a French naval officer who travelled in the lowlands from Mocha to Zabīd in 1842, contains (among much else) a list of medicinal or other useful plants and their products. These three travellers are mentioned in my Bibliography. Ehrenberg and Hemprich in 1825, and the botanist Bové in 1830–31, visited several parts of the Arabian Red Sea coast, including a few places in the Yemen, as well as Kamarān Island and the Farasān Islands. They made collections, but the two former apparently wrote no narrative, while the travels of Bové were only published in an abridged form many years afterwards.

The late G. Wyman Bury, besides writing two books of great value on South-West Arabia (see Bibliography), included an account of an ornithological journey to the Yemen in a paper entitled " The Birds of Yemen ", by W. L. Sclater.[2] The latter, in the same paper, summarised some earlier explorations, mainly ornithological, carried out largely in the Aden hinterland.

The German explorers Rathjens and von Wissmann, whose archæo-

[1] *Verhandlungen der Gesellschaft für Erdkunde*, Berlin, Vol. xviii, 1891, pp. 531–50.
[2] *The Ibis*, April 1917, pp. 129–86.

logical explorations are cited several times in the following pages, also collected many plants, a list of which by Dr. Oskar Schwartz is included in Volume III of their " Südarabien-Reise " (1934). Dr. Rathjens, moreover, collected insects, some of which have been acquired by the British Museum and amalgamated with our collection. These two writers have made very important contributions to the geology of the country, a rather neglected subject.

Lastly, the Egyptian University Scientific Expedition to South-West Arabia in 1936 [1] was a composite mission of four members, who carried out researches in several fields, geology, archæology, anthropology and entomology. We look for much help from the detailed results of this mission ; meanwhile the more general views already expressed by its leader, Dr. Huzayyin, are quoted in these pages.

Reading the stories of the earlier naturalists, from Niebuhr (1763) to at least as late as Deflers (1887), one is struck by the freedom of movement which they enjoyed, whether under the reigning independent Imam of the day or during the second period of Turkish dominion. Suspicion of ulterior motives, political or commercial, had not been aroused in those happy days as it has later been ! Thus Botta in 1836 ascended and explored Jebel Sabir (south of Ta'izz), denied to us in all but its lower slopes. Deflers, while at San'a in 1887, as a mere excursion climbed Jebel Nuqūm, which we dared not even mention ! On the other hand, tropical medicine was far less advanced. Two of Niebuhr's companions died in the Yemen, the other three died later on their journey. Serious illness (malaria or dysentery ?) contracted in the lowlands forced Botta to abandon his projected visit to San'a and to return to Europe. Deflers complained of other forms of ill-health. Our experiences may be compared with theirs.

[1] General account in *Nature*, Vol. 140, pp. 513–14, 1937.

PART II
THE JOURNEY

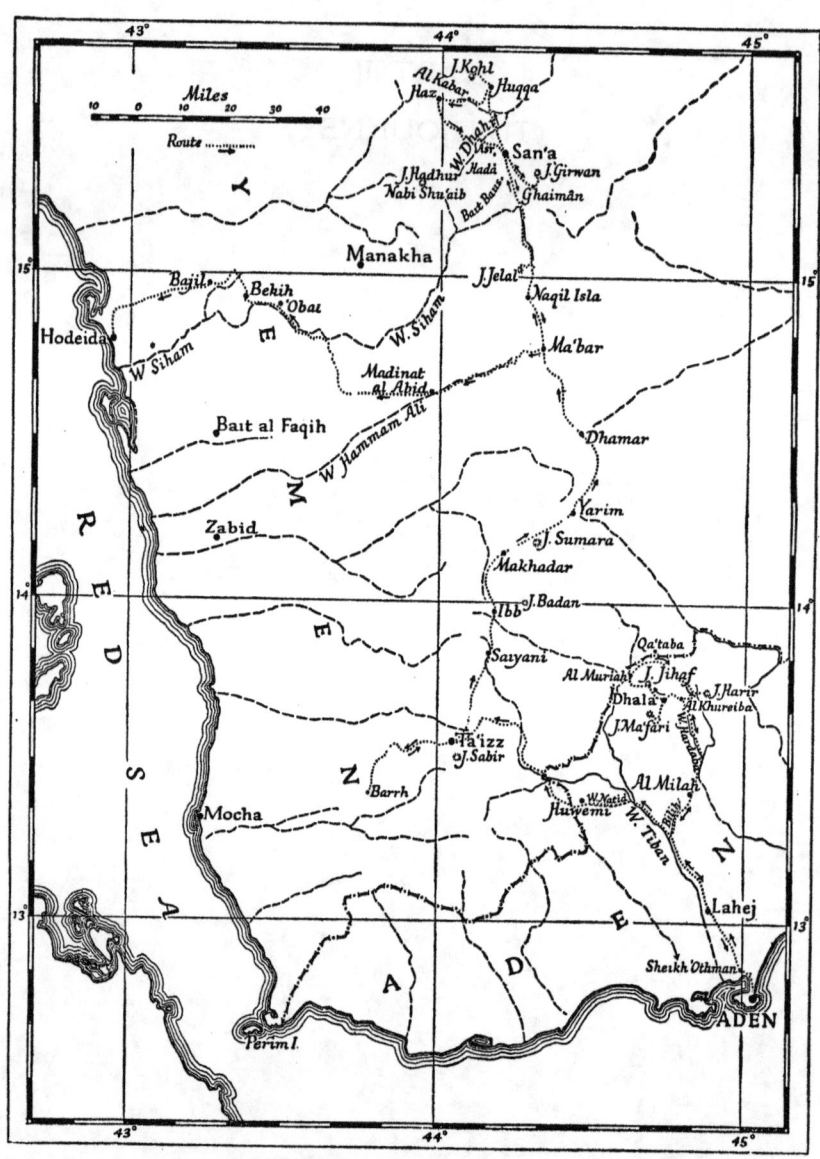

MAP 2. *Part of Aden Protectorate and the Yemen, showing the author's route.*

Chapter V

ADEN AND LAHEJ

WHEN the British India steamship *Mulbera* anchored at Aden, off Steamer Point, early on September 3rd, 1937, we were taken in charge by a short fat Somali policeman, accompanied by another Somali, very tall and thin, with an engaging smile. The latter, Jam'a 'Ismail, a man under thirty, was destined to play an important part in our wanderings. To picture the country as we found it on those journeys is the purpose of the following personal narrative.

During a week spent in Aden before our first journey to the interior, we stayed, by his kind invitation, at the house of the Frontier Officer, Captain Seager. This is one of a group of new houses at Khormaksar, on the narrow sandy neck joining the volcanic crater of Aden to the mainland. On the verandah, in the welcome coolness of our first evening, our host explained the impossibility of re-opening with the Imam at that moment the question of permission for us to enter the Yemen—which (as explained) the Imam had previously given, but withdrawn about a month before our departure from England. To have broached the subject again immediately after our arrival would probably have ended our hopes of ever reaching our promised land. On Captain Seager's advice, therefore, we quickly decided to spend the time, till a propitious juncture should occur, in visiting the high and fertile Amiri country, in the Western Division of the British Protectorate, where we could reach altitudes of nearly 8,000 feet.

While preparations were hurried forward, we saw what we could of our base and its surroundings. Here, therefore, are gathered together our impressions of Aden itself and its immediate hinterland. Here also the town and oasis of Lahej, and their ruler, find a place. Since the base for both our journeys to the highlands was Aden, the highlands can be better pictured by contrast with its barren volcanic peninsula and coastal lowlands.

Our arrival in one of the two hottest months, September (the other being May), was intentional. Our journey was timed so that we should reach the mountains just at the end of the rains, when insects and flowers would be appearing in abundance. But it was not the best season for sight-seeing in Aden itself. The temperature in houses was sometimes close on 100° F., and water drawn from cold-water taps often reached that point. If we went to Steamer Point or into the old town in the Crater during any but the coolest hours, the blast of air from the scorched rocks was decidedly fierce. Nevertheless I found the climate much less trying than my last experience of the Middle East, a summer in the plains of 'Iraq. Life at our host's house at Khormaksar, with its wide open upper verandah and plenty of daylight, was infinitely preferable to being shut in a darkened, tightly closed, house from 7 a.m. till 6 p.m. We were again in Aden for several weeks from mid-November till early December. Then, though temperatures were much lower, we were often buffeted, on the exposed flats of Khormaksar, by a fatiguing hot easterly wind. Our final visit was late in March, before our departure for England.

During our first crowded week we were glad to have Captain Seager's car often at our disposal, and the services of his driver Saad, a small, lively Aden Arab. Saad had been a taxidriver and consequently was full of the most varied information about Aden.

Whatever the disadvantages of climate, and the extreme scantiness of vegetation on the volcanic crags—where, however, bulbous plants, herbs and shrubs can be found in flower in the gulleys at some seasons —we found Aden a most interesting and likeable place. Many British people who are stationed there share this view, though Aden is often maligned by passing travellers who land only for a few hours.

The Colony (as distinct from the Protectorate) comprises two small mountainous volcanic peninsulas connected by a narrow strip of hinterland. The peninsulas are separated by a wide bay which they nearly enclose like the two claws of a pincers, leaving an opening some five miles across. Each peninsula is connected with the mainland by a flat sandy isthmus. The "Little Aden" peninsula on the west, inhabited only by fisher-folk, is about seven miles wide. Its black volcanic crags rise to 1,200 feet from slopes of yellow sand. Seen from Aden itself they form a fantastic silhouette against the setting sun.

The eastern peninsula, Aden proper, is about six miles across and its barren peaks reach a height of 1,725 feet. The several parts of the Settlement are more widely separated than is often imagined. From Steamer Point, where the Government Secretariat, some large stores kept by Indians and other business houses stand close to the waterfront, it is more than four miles to the old historic Aden, usually spoken of simply as "Crater". The chief road between the two is by way of the impressive "Main Pass" cut through the crater-rim on the northwest; to the north-east a second road leads into Crater through a tunnel. The view of the old city shown in Photograph 1 was taken at sunset, from a path winding up the inner side of the crater-wall, past the Tower of Silence of the local Parsee colony, to the quarries where pumice-stone is dug and loaded on to donkeys. The valley containing the famous Tanks is not visible, but lies below on the left. From this point, a little farther to the right, the Gulf of Aden is seen, opening out to the Indian Ocean on the east side of the peninsula. Close to Seerah Island, an islet with an old Portuguese fort, connected with the shore by a causeway—and, at low tide, by wet sand—was the point of the British landing in 1839. All round the peninsula, too, there are headlands separated by sandy bays, where the vivid colours of the tropical sea contrast with the grim hues of bare volcanic rock.

The *suqs* of the old town are thronged with Aden Arabs dressed in turbans, short coats, and sarong-like silken " futas " of many bright colours, Somali policemen in khaki uniforms and tarbūshes, various Indian people and many other nationalities. Among these townspeople tribesmen from the Tihama or the broken foothills look the more primitive, wearing, as they do, little but high-crowned broad-brimmed straw-hats and kilt-like white cloths reaching from waist to knee ; each has the curved sheath of his short dagger (*jambiya*) fastened to his girdle, but the sheath is empty, for the weapon has been left at the police-post on entering the Colony from the Protectorate.

The great antiquity and past glories of Aden can barely be touched in this short sketch. The old Crater town has architectural features of interest even now. In past centuries, even down to the 18th, it would appear to have possessed considerable architectural splendour. A few lines descriptive of the Tanks, most impressive and best known of Aden's ancient monuments, are left till Chapter XX, where the Aden Tanks are compared with the many kinds of tanks and cisterns seen in the highlands of the interior.

For the history of Aden stretches back into the remote past. Whether it is identical with the " Eden " mentioned by Ezekiel (chap. xxvii, v. 23) is a question for Biblical scholars. It seems clear that this Eden has nothing to do with the Garden of Eden (to which reference is made as " the garden of God ", in quite a different context, in Ezekiel's later chapters). At least one well-known commentator regards this Eden of Ezekiel's twenty-seventh chapter as identical with Aden, unless it be a third place named Eden, the state of Beth-Eden in Mesopotamia, mentioned in inscriptions and in several books of the Old Testament. But this latter possibility appears to be ruled out by the fact that Ezekiel significantly associates his Eden with places in South Arabia. Inveighing against the Kingdom of Tyre, " the merchant of the peoples unto many isles ", the prophet passes in review the countries to which the people of Tyre made long trading voyages. "Eden" is bracketed with "the traffickers of Sheba" (east of the modern Yemen) and with Canneh, believed to be the "Cana" of Pliny and the chief port of the incense country.

There seems little doubt—indeed, there has long been little in the minds of some [1]—that this Eden was simply Aden. If so, the crater-girt city was well known as a port at least as early as the 6th Century B.C., when Ezekiel wrote. In any case Aden is named by many later writers from the early centuries of the Christian era, through the Middle Ages down to later times. But enough here of reflections on the far past.

If, instead of turning up-hill and through the Main Pass to Crater, we go from Steamer Point along the inner side of the peninsula, on the shore of the bay of Aden, we pass through the ship-building quarter, Ma'alla, where dhows and other local craft are under construction. Some four and a half miles of metalled road lead this way from Steamer Point to Khormaksar. Along this road move cars, people coming in from the hinterland with produce, and heavy two-wheeled wooden carts drawn by camels, used for transport of building-stone and other materials. The narrow sandy isthmus supports a low sage-green scrub of maritime plants. The metalled road continues another six miles along the inner side of the isthmus, passing lagoons haunted by wading birds and flamingoes, where sea-water is evaporated and beside which stand gleaming piles of salt.

The metalled road ends at the little town of Sheikh 'Othman, surrounded by its oasis and with shady public gardens on one side. Close by are the buildings of the Keith Falconer (Church of Scotland) medical mission. Our memories of Sheikh 'Othman are of a clean, well-kept town, where, during Ramadhan, in November 1937, the lighted *suqs* after sunset were full of bright-coloured eastern life, as the people broke the long day's fast. Again, early in December, on the Id al Fitr ("festival of breaking the fast"), the little Id (or Bairam) marking the end of Ramadhan, crowds thronged the coffee-houses and the stalls and side-shows of a fair. All the men were decked out with brilliant new turbans, futas and shawls. Gay little new flags, red or green, often with a white crescent, flew on the mosques and on the graves of *welis* (saints) in the cemeteries outside the town.

Beyond Sheikh 'Othman, a police-post and barrier mark the entrance into the Protectorate. But we need not yet take the desert track northwards towards Lahej and Dhala. Turn to the left (westward) towards the north shore of the bay of Aden, along the sandy track to Fukam and the Little Aden peninsula. It leads through a

[1] For instance, W. B. Harris, "A Journey through the Yemen", 1893, p. 126.

PHOTOGRAPHS 1 AND 2.

Aden: the old city in the Crater, at sunset.
In the older part of the town of Lahej.

PHOTOGRAPH 3.

The crags of Aden across the bay, over the dūm-palms on the sand-dunes of Hiswa.

country of sand ridges and maritime scrub, then past small oases and thick patches of the curious branching dūm-palms,[1] each branch of which bears a crown of fan-shaped leaves.

Near Hiswa the dry channel of the Wadi Kabir, the western branch of the Wadi Tiban, reaches the shore. (The Wadi Tiban, after descending from far in the interior and receiving several tributaries, forks curiously about thirty miles north of Aden into a western branch, the Wadi Kabir or Great Wadi, and an eastern branch, the Wadi as Saghir, or little Wadi, which peters out in the lowland sands.) Close by (Phot. 3) the bare crags of Aden are seen across the bay. Even in the drought, which is rarely and irregularly broken, little clouds of condensed moisture hang over the highest points at evening. In the green foreground, on the sandhills, are dense thickets of dūm-palms, some date-palms, and low maritime scrub. Had we wished to search among the roots and stems for coastal insects, we should have needed to beware of venomous horned vipers, plentiful here. As it was, the only one we saw had been caught by an Arab in a garden at Sheikh 'Othman.

Beyond the green belt of vegetation, the long stretch of wet shell-covered sand, over which at low tide scurried numberless crabs, was the haunt of grey or purple herons, white egrets, various small long-billed wading birds, and duck.

If we pass the barrier at the police-post just north of Sheikh 'Othman, quitting the Colony of Aden proper and entering the Protectorate, a sandy track leads northward to the large oasis and the town of Lahej. This is the capital of the 'Abdali Sultan, the premier Arab ruler in the Western part of the Protectorate. Duties levied on merchandise passing through his territory from the interior to Aden form an important part of the Sultan's revenue.

Between fifteen and twenty miles, with a very gradual ascent of about 400 feet, separate Sheikh 'Othman from Lahej. This strip of lowland desert has no vegetation but dwarf scrub, and there are patches of loose sand to be crossed. A little south of Lahej oasis some large mounds of sand and refuse invite exploration by archæologists. Many of the countless sherds of red pottery strewn over the surface are ornamented unlike any earthenware now made in the district. They appear to be of medieval Arab workmanship.

After passing the southernmost green fields and date-palms of the oasis, cars usually halt in the centre of the town beside a bare parade-ground. At the nearer end, raised above the dusty plain in a large garden, stands the modern palace of the Sultan, a white two-storey building with rectangular outlines and flat balustraded roofs, with a

[1] A species of *Hyphæne*.

pyramidal roof rising over the central part. The far end of the parade-ground is faced by some other large buildings belonging to the ruling family, rather older, but still modern ; three-storeyed mansions with rows of large round-headed and latticed windows in the upper floors. Lahej is open and unwalled, and in its older parts (Phot. 2) are some great houses of dun-coloured brick, in the old Arab style of these lowlands. Their roof parapets are set at intervals with triangular elevations of the wall, rising in several little steps and each surmounted by a pinnacle. These large buildings rise above the one-storeyed shops in the *suqs* and the humbler dwellings of the people. The lanes and *suqs* of Lahej are associated in my memory with plenty of fruit and vegetables, but also with a plague of flies.

A very fertile and pleasant part of the oasis lies a few miles north of the town, just below the fork in the Wadi Tiban. A long avenue of broad-leaved Terminalia-trees casts a welcome shade over the dusty road. On either side groups of tall date-palms raise their plumed crowns amid irrigated fields of bright green millet. At Al Huseini, where is a summer pavilion of the Sultan, he and other members of his family have undertaken tropical agriculture on a considerable scale, and many products of the eastern tropics are gathered together. At the end of November, after our first journey to the interior, we camped for some days in an empty house belonging to a brother of the Sultan. It was approached by a winding dusty lane, between large plantations of bananas bordered by rows of pawpaw trees, with their crowns of hanging palmate leaves as large as any I have seen. Huge screw-pine trees (*Pandanus*) stood in dense spreading clumps, sending down aerial roots from their branches to form new stilt-like stems. The masses of dark-green foliage of tall mango-trees contrasted with many other shades of green. There was little fruit at the time of our visit, except bananas, bunches of which were being cut and loaded into lorries for Lahej or Aden. The gardens close to the house contained plantations of citrus and custard-apple, pomegranates and sugar-cane, beds of sweet-potatoes, roses, cannas, and many ornamental tropical trees and flowers. This place was the most tropically exuberant of any that we saw. To us, visiting Al Huseini after two months of trekking and camping in the rough Amiri highlands, it seemed restful and luxuriant indeed. We took a fine sampling of lowland insects to compare with those of the highlands, largely by shaking and beating the rich foliage of the plantation and the wild flowering shrubs in the Wadi Kabir. For the house stood on the edge of the earthen cliffs bounding the wadi-bed, from which it was separated by a flowing, raised irrigation-channel and by a network of deep crevasses dissecting the banks into earthen hummocks and pinnacles.

We slept each night on the house-roof, untroubled by mosquitoes, though we had been warned to beware of malaria. We suffered much from the attentions of sand-flies, hordes of which penetrated the meshes of our mosquito-nets, till we took to spraying the latter with " Flit ". Temperatures at night fell to about 63° F. From midday till three o'clock the sun was fierce, even in late November, and these hours were spent in preserving the morning's " catch ", in an upper room where the thermometer only touched 84°. The varied bird-life of the oasis was a source of delight. Bright green bee-eaters abounded, perching on the wires of the telegraph-line leading northwards to the mountains; Arabian bulbuls, grey with the head black, quite unafraid, uttered their melodious whistling, especially about dawn; white storks, a black stork, and flocks of white egrets walked in the fields and gardens; the bushes seemed alive with warblers and other small birds; paradise fly-catchers displayed their reddish-brown plumage and black heads as they flitted occasionally out and back among the densest parts of the plantation, the males spreading their long tails fanwise when they rested. In beating foliage for insects, I flushed a pair of startled nightjars from a tamarisk-bush in the bed of the wadi.[1]

We had social diversions too, at Al Huseini. When European visitors from Aden unexpectedly appeared one evening and I had ordered the best meal that we could provide, I was astonished to find the table set with glasses, china plates, coffee-cups and other articles certainly not included in our camp equipment. These had all been raided by Jam'a from the Sultan's summer pavilion half a mile away, by collusion with the servants there; needless to say, they were all returned after the feast.

Only after our stay was ended were we able to visit and thank the Sultan of Lahej, His Highness Sir 'Abdul Karīm ibn Fadhl ibn 'Ali al 'Abdali. Our call, arranged beforehand from Aden, was timed for ten o'clock on the morning of the principal day of the 'Id al Fitr (December 6th, 1937). The Sultan, meeting us at the top of the steps leading to the first floor of his new palace, overlooking the parade-

---

[1] In the parts of this narrative where birds are mentioned by name, their identity has been verified, as far as is possible without specimens, by the expert on Arabian ornithology, the late George L. Bates. He took great trouble in discussing my notes with me. In the present instance, the bee-eaters were the only resident Arabian species, the Little Green Bee-eater (*Merops orientalis cyanophrys*). The nightjars were one of two resident species, probably a form of *Caprimulgus nubicus*. The Arabian Bulbul (*Pycnonotus xanthopygos*) and the Paradise Fly-catcher (*Tchitrea viridis ferrati*) are named without doubt. The white storks were the well-known species, on passage. The black stork must have been Abdini's Stork (*Sphenorhynchus abdinii*); no other is known from Arabia.

ground, led us to a room furnished with armchairs and sofas covered with gold brocade. We found our host a tall man in the sixties, dignified and handsome, wearing a moustache and a closely-trimmed pointed beard. His garments, partly Arab, partly adapted from European fashions, consisted of a bright coloured turban, a black morning-coat buttoning up to the neck, striped morning trousers, and over all a flowing black gold-edged 'aba of a very fine fabric. The resulting effect was certainly imposing. Our reception was cordial and informal. While we drank coffee out of gold-porcelain cups, the Sultan questioned us about our journey—one of his nephews interpreting, for several younger members of the ruling family speak excellent English—and showed amusement over the difficulties we had experienced in getting permission from the Imam to enter the Yemen. In fact, the Sultan smiled broadly and meaningly, for the tenacity and strong will of the redoubtable old monarch of the Yemen are well known to the neighbouring rulers in the Aden Protectorate. The Sultan also asked for information about certain insect pests infesting the citrus trees at Al Huseini, whither his heir, Sultan Fadhl, had come to supervise spraying operations during our stay. As we left the palace, men of every sort and condition, all wearing new and bright coloured garments, were passing up the steps to pay their respects to the Sultan at his public reception on the festival day.

Chapter VI
GATEWAY TO THE HIGHLANDS: ADEN TO DHALA

OUR departure from Khormaksar for Dhala, capital of the Amiri country, took place in darkness, at 4.15 in the morning of September 10th. The distance as the crow flies is only sixty-five miles north, but by road about ninety, with rough ground to be covered and an ascent of 4,800 feet. The start was made early in the hope that we should reach Dhala easily within the day. But in the event the journey occupied nearly two days.

Captain Seager's house having now become our base for the whole expedition, some of our thirty cases of equipment were left stacked in the spacious ground-floor verandah. What we needed had been loaded into a lorry and a small car overnight. The owner-driver of the lorry, 'Ali Ahmed, was a well-known Aden Arab. If his vehicles were not always in the best condition, he certainly showed skill at repairs. Our provisions and medical stores had been supplemented, and a thousand rupees in silver and small change had been packed.

Besides the tall Somali, Jam'a, who had met us on the steamer, two other Somalis had been engaged. On our host's advice all three servants were of this nationality, to avoid any chance of friction such as might occur if Arabs and Somalis were mixed. Some of the best servants obtainable at Aden are Somalis; moreover I had noticed a peculiar nimbleness and aptitude, possibly not all fortuitous, for natural history collecting in one or two of this nation whom I had met years before in Abyssinia. On our present journey, Ahmed Mahmūd, a rather short slight young man, with sharp features, was to be my personal servant; 'Omar Isma'il, a taller man, was attached to Britton. Both became valuable collectors. All three spoke Arabic and English besides their native Somali, to which Jam'a and 'Omar added a working knowledge of Hindustani, while Ahmed could also write Arabic. Their agreeable characters and lively sense of humour added greatly to the amenities of the Expedition, of which they deserve to be regarded as full members. We owe much to Captain Seager's wise help in their selection.

In spite of a delay at daybreak, needed to extricate the heavily laden small car from a stretch of loose sand, we were quickly past Lahej and

Al Huseini. North of the point where the Wadi Tiban forks into its two branches, the track crosses to its eastern side. Some miles farther, at Nobat Dakim, the valley of the Tiban is left behind and the track leads north-east along the Wadi Bilih. Here too the tropical luxuriance ceases and the grim stony foothills and sparse thorn-scrub begin, soon giving place to higher mountains, the first of which, Jebel Munif, rises to 4,000 feet on the right. Some miles of rough track crossing a watershed lead down into a broad open valley, surrounded by jagged mountains, ridge behind ridge, in which lies the Wadi Milah.

We had been over five hours on the road when we halted at the village of Al Milah, for breakfast in the little whitewashed, windowless upper room of one of the few mud-built houses (Phot. 4). By far the greater number of the dwellings are rectangular huts having a rough framework covered with brushwood or thatch. This village of the Haushabi tribe differs from either the stone-built mountain dwellings or the circular, African-looking, grass-thatched houses of the Yemen Tihama.

Trouble with the engine of the lorry necessitated repairs, not completed till mid-afternoon. By this time lowering cumulus clouds had piled over the mountains. To go on meant the risk of being overwhelmed by a rapidly rising spate of water in the narrow wadi-bed which is the only road inland. Rather regretfully we resigned ourselves to a night at Al Milah. We slept on the little roof terrace outside the upper room of the same mud-house where we had breakfasted. Next morning we had a pleasant experience of the natural courtesy of even the poorer people. The wife of the householder, who was working in a hut near by, deprecated the suggestion that we had ejected the family from their sleeping apartment, saying she wished our quarters had been better.

Our stay at Al Milah had its compensations, for before the rain started we were able to make our first " bag " of insects on the broad bush-covered floor of the wadi. The insects, mostly common African species, served as a sample of the lowland fauna, useful for comparison with those taken later at higher altitudes. After sunset, when the rain had passed, more insects arrived, attracted by the light of the paraffin pressure-lamps reflected from the white walls of the house. Among these night-flyers were moths, cockchafer beetles, large-winged female ants, and a few huge rhinoceros-beetles, so called from the curved horn which projects from the thorax. In some parts of the East these last commit serious depredations by eating into the rolled-up young leaves of banana trees, while their fleshy, curved larvæ damage roots of sugar-cane or leaf-stalks of coconut-palms.

We were off next morning at six-thirty, but this time the clutch of the small car began to slip, and eventually we were forced to transfer to the lorry. The empty car was driven on in a series of short spurts, till 'Ali Ahmed could leave it in the care of the headman of a hamlet. Next day it was picked up on the return journey and taken back to Aden in the empty lorry.

Meanwhile the lorry, with ourselves crowded into it, bumped and crashed on, with sharp turns to avoid trees and rocks, up the narrow bed of the Wadi Hardaba (Phot. 5). At ten-minute intervals the water in the radiator boiled furiously and we had to stop to replace it from supplies carried in tins. The time was, however, far from wasted, for during the halts we collected insects in parts of the wadi where water was running and in the thickets of feathery tamarisk fringing its banks. Blue tiger-beetles (in their larval stages fierce predators on other insects) ran and flew with extreme swiftness over the wet gravel, while red-bodied dragon-flies cruised to and fro along the streams. In the scrub of thorny acacias on the steep rocky slopes behind the tamarisk, grasshoppers displayed their brilliant scarlet or yellow hindwings as they leapt and flew, but disappeared abruptly when they landed on the volcanic rocks, the dark shade of which they exactly matched when the hindwings were hidden.

Down in the wadi large, grotesque-looking Arabian Grey Hornbills,[1] with mottled dark grey-brown and white plumage, flew in groups from tree to tree, while from the tamarisk the cicadas kept up a ceaseless shrilling.

Here and there in the wadi-bed grew a shrub (*Calotropis procera*) of the Asclepiad family, with large grey glaucous leaves, clusters of maroon-coloured flowers, and large inflated seed-vessels packed with seeds and silky hairs; it is a small tree characteristic of the lower altitudes in Abyssinia and Somaliland, as well as on the Arabian side of the Red Sea.[2] In the upper part of the Wadi Hardaba, between 2,000 and 2,500 feet, begin narrow terraced fields, the first of a system far more developed higher up. These little fields bore crops, still bright green, of *dukhn* or " bulrush-millet " (*Pennisetum*), a low-growing millet with a long compact cob or ear rather like a bulrush-head.

At the head of the Wadi Hardaba the winding rocky defiles of Al Khureiba pass lead steeply up to the Dhala plateau. The track was made by British troops at the period of demarcation of the frontier between the Protectorate and the (then) Turkish Yemen, nearly forty

---

[1] *Lophoceros nasutus forskalii*.
[2] The charcoal obtained by burning the wood of *Calotropis procera* was used in making gunpowder (Passama, 1842, cited by Deflers, " Voyage au Yemen ", p. 13). The silken floss from the seed capsules of a related species (*Calotropis gigantea*) is used elsewhere, like kapok, for stuffing mattresses and similar purposes.

years ago. We walked up this road with the lightened lorry bumping its way up after us. Across a chasm to our right we saw our first Arabian waterfall cascading down a cleft among rank vegetation. At the top of the 2,000-foot ascent, by one of those transformations familiar to the traveller who climbs the mighty ramparts of the highlands, either in Abyssinia or in South-West Arabia, we suddenly found ourselves, at an altitude of about 4,800 feet, on one of the lower steps of the high plateaux. We were in a new country, an undulating tableland dotted with large trees and covered with green fields of *dhurra*, the tall highland millet (*Sorghum*), which at this altitude and upwards replaces the more lowly *dukhn*. More jolting over the tableland, among low rocky hills crowned with villages of stone towers, brought us at last to Dhala in mid-afternoon. Thirty-five hours' travelling from Aden, and we had reached the capital of the Amiri principality.

PHOTOGRAPHS 4 AND 5.
*Tribesmen, houses and brushwood huts at Al Milah.
The route over the bed of Wadi Hardaba.*

PHOTOGRAPHS 6 AND 7.
Dhala: the principal mosque.
Dhala town from the castle-hill, backed by Jebel Jihaf.

Chapter VII

DHALA, CAPITAL OF THE AMIRI HIGHLANDS

DHALA had for several reasons been chosen as a centre from which to begin our work in the highlands. The country within a day's excursion is interesting and varied. Jebel Jihaf, the great mountain-mass on which we camped for weeks, is within easy reach. We were free to use a stone-built two-storeyed Government Rest-House, on a hillock within a mile of the town, before and after our treks to the mountains, and usually when one or other of us descended from the mountain-tops to replenish stores. And, not least important, a high level of law and order is kept within the principality by its rulers—a happier state of things than that then existing in some of the tribal territories a few miles away, where many small warring chieftains held sway among the wild mountain-ranges.

The Government of the Amiri country was in the hands of two Amirs, Nasr ibn Shaif and his son, Haidara. In troublous times, comparatively recently past, the family has owed its security, and even its rescue from aggression by the " powers that be " north of the Yemen frontier, to British intervention. This is amply repaid by the loyalty of the Amirs to the Aden Government. During our two months in their territory we received every possible kindness at their hands.

Though Amir Nasr was away from Dhala in September, our arrival at the Rest-House was observed from the castle above the town, a mile away, and within a few minutes Amir Haidara was riding down to greet us on a little chestnut horse with six men running before and after. We, anxious to make a good impression at our first meeting, hastily unpacked camp-chairs as he approached, and ordered coffee to be prepared. He dismounted and, after exchange of greetings, entered the Rest-House with us. We then saw Amir Haidara to be a rather short and slightly built man of about thirty-five. His lively expression bespoke intelligence and a keen sense of humour. The poor health from which he unhappily suffered was manifested in his appearance, though (as we afterwards found) he was very wiry and could be both energetic and determined. He wore a bright pink embroidered turban, a grey cloth coat, coloured shirt, and silken futa reaching to the knee, while his legs and feet were bare. In his belt was the big curved dagger or *jambiya* (locally pronounced " gumbia "), carried by every man of standing. At this interview, the first of many, we sat round a small table and, over coffee and cigarettes, after the usual polite inquiries concerning each other's health, we explained to the Amir our purpose in visiting Dhala and our wish to go to the top of Jebel Jihaf. Amir Haidara answered that he would gladly welcome us on the mountain, as he intended going to his smaller castle (Phot. 9) there in a few days. He then took his leave, but meanwhile a violent afternoon squall of wind and rain, sweeping across the plateau, reminded us that the summer rains were not yet over. From the Rest-House verandah the Amir and his men watched the torrents of muddy water rushing down the slopes, till the storm abated, and he rode away, holding up a black umbrella.

Amir Nasr, whom we met later, on his return to his capital, is also short, of slight build, and of lighter complexion than most of the Amiri people. His face is deeply lined and strongly featured ; his expression is kindly, his speech blunt and direct. He is on the most fatherly terms with his people. Indeed, the relations existing between both Amirs and their subjects are simple and open, an example of the monarchic-democratic state of society typical of the country. The rulers hold absolute sway but are easily accessible to the humblest of those beneath them. Amir Nasr had, in fact, been persuaded to reside at Lahej for a time because his inability to refuse the requests of petitioners was impoverishing his treasury, since the Amirs are not rich for a family of hereditary rulers. I imagine it would be hard for Amir Nasr to say " no " to any poor tribesman, whether deserving or not.

The younger Amir, though equally kind to the law-abiding, could deal sternly with criminals. Some men convicted of offences were confined in a prison attached to his small castle on Jebel Jihaf. Another example of his methods of administering justice came under our personal notice later, when we were camped close to the Yemen frontier. There had been a theft of money by a tribesman, hired as a porter, from our servants' baggage. The circumstances and the culprit were not in doubt. Amir Haidara, informed of this incident, first sent the man (decidedly one of the less agreeable-looking) back to us, in the hope that we could induce him to make restitution. He, however, though his looks and manner clearly indicated guilt, repeatedly protested his ignorance of the whole matter, with many invocations of Allah. Afterwards he disappeared and made a dash across the frontier. Amir Haidara then compelled the whole of the man's particular section of his tribe to refund the sum ; at length we received an amazing collection of small currency, mostly pieces of a few annas' value, with a few whole rupees and one *riyāl* (Maria-Theresa dollar). Eventually we persuaded the elder Amir to take back an equivalent sum in notes, as a contribution towards a new school then building at Dhala.

Amir Nasr dressed in the same style as his son, with the large bright-coloured turban, cloth coat, broad belt, *jambiya*, and silken futa worn kilt-fashion, but in addition he wore European woollen stockings and shoes. These mountain chiefs, dressed thus, and having their bright futas ornamented with a tartan-like pattern, seemed like an Arab version of the Highland chieftains of bygone times. Ordinary tribesmen and peasants on the other hand wear short skirts of plain white cotton material, and white or indigo-dyed turbans. The upper part of the body is clothed in a short white coat or swathed with white material. During the heat of the day, when working in the fields, the peasants are stripped to the waist, and their feet and legs are bare (Phots. 22, 23, 27). Every man wears a bulky girdle, in which is stuck, in the middle in front, the *jambiya* or dagger, with short broad curved blade and ornamented handle. The sheath too is ornamented, and tapers to a point much longer than is necessary to hold the blade, and in some cases it is curved right up into a U-shape. The *jambiya*, though a weapon, is even more an ornament and sign of social standing. Behind it is worn a small sheath-knife for domestic purposes.

In the cold months and at greater altitudes (in the Yemen) the cultivators are glad of short sleeveless sheep-skin coats, with the wool turned in or outwards. The indigo dye runs from the tribesmen's turbans on to their perspiring foreheads. In fact, running from the turban or other garments seemed to be the cause of the blue-green smears on the faces and bodies of men whom we met at different times during our journey. Some tribes, however, may deliberately smear the upper part of the body with the pigment.

Altogether these dwellers in the mountains and on the high tablelands of the south-west are very unlike the tall, bearded, aquiline type of Arab. They are dark skinned, of only medium height, with short straight noses and scanty beards, or no beard at all. Their dress removes them still further from the conventional view of an Arab. (Readers who wish to know what anthropologists think of them, see Chapter XVIII.)

Naturally, little could be seen of the womenfolk in the town of Dhala. Occasional glimpses might be caught of ladies of the Amir's household in the castle precincts. Their dresses, mostly of bright red, struck a note of vivid colour against the dark tones, greys and browns, of the high tower-houses and the encircling castle-walls. But away in the country women and girls go about, and work in the fields, free and unveiled, and there was no difficulty in noting the style of their dress and ornaments. On Jebel Jihaf, for instance, most of the women were dressed in a loose ankle-length one-piece garment, usually with a round neck, heavily embroidered, with three-quarter-length bell-shaped sleeves. The whole garment was finished off with a wide sash tied in front. These dresses were either brightly striped or indigo-dyed. The headdress consisted of an indigo-dyed cloth worn either as a cowl or as a loosely tied turban. Turmeric is used as a cosmetic by the younger women, so that their faces are often stained bright yellow. In addition their faces are sometimes decorated with designs in *kohl* or black antimony powder. The patterns may be in the form of horizontal lines across the forehead, with a median line down the middle of the nose and chin, and occasionally large asterisk-like marks are drawn upon either cheek and on the forehead above the nose (Phots. 12, 19).

Dhala itself lies at the foot of the castle hill, a little unwalled town, a crowd of rectangular, tower-like houses two and three storeys high, with flat roofs and low parapets (Phot. 7). Built of roughly squared blocks, often nearly cubical, of the local igneous rock, very dark brown or grey, sometimes almost purple, they have a slight " batter ", the walls sloping inwards from base to parapet. Doorways and windows, the latter mostly small and plain, are picked out in whitewash. There is otherwise little ornament outside. Some houses, especially the larger ones, have ornamental string-courses constructed by setting a course of stones diagonally or in other ways, and the windows set back in round-headed arched recesses, each with an unshuttered opening in the head and a larger window beneath, furnished with roughly carved shutters (Phots. 8, 17). These houses impress the beholder as of great massiveness and solidity. Their walls are very thick and the stairs are built of heavy stone blocks, often of unequal height. The ground storey, given up to storerooms and stalls for domestic animals, is very dark, and on entering from the bright sunlight the visitor has to feel his way round trusses of hay and often a recumbent cow. At the foot of the staircase there is usually a wooden gate, to stop the cow or other domestic animals from walking up. The visitor ascends, groping in darkness round many right-angled corners, until, after passing the kitchen and the women's apartments, he emerges into the men's living-room, usually spacious, lofty and well-lighted.

These stone towers are, with little variation, characteristic of the mountain villages right up into the Yemen, but in the town houses there is much more diversity. In the cities of the Yemen they are often much larger and higher, with more storeys and a wealth of exterior and interior ornament. The nature of the building material, the plentiful use of brick and plaster as well as stone in the cities, has no doubt been a great factor in bringing about this difference. But

PHOTOGRAPHS 8 AND 9.

Central building of the castle at Dhala.
The smaller castle at the top of Jebel Jihaf.

PHOTOGRAPH 10. *A grove of thorny 'ilb trees near Dhala.*

there is food for thought as to how Europe and the nearer East may have reacted on one another in their styles of medieval architecture. While the more severe styles of ornament in the Dhala highlands recall Norman architecture, the highly decorated interiors in the Yemen town-houses bring to mind some phases of late Gothic (Phot. 73).

The same simplicity, massiveness, and roughness are reflected in the mosques of Dhala itself and the larger villages in the Amiri highlands. Those at Dhala (Phot. 6) are plain rectangular stone buildings, with pinnacles at the corners and at intervals along the walls, and squat minarets. The roof is flat or consists of a series of small whitewashed cupolas. In the tiny mountain hamlets the mosque is simply a little low oblong building, flat-roofed, with a rough pinnacle at each corner. It has no minaret and no ornament, and is lighted only through the doorway, while outside there is a little rough-walled enclosure, open to the sky. Some of the lonely shrines of *welis* (saints), on mountain-tops and elsewhere, have much the same form (Phot. 40), while others have the added dignity of a small cupola.

It fell to us to see something of the interior of the castle at Dhala, when we stayed there, by invitation of the Amir, from September 23rd to 26th, during the festivities which marked a visit of the Governor of Aden. The castle consists of a large old stone tower-house (Phot. 8) standing, like a keep, in a courtyard surrounded by lower buildings and walls, with several flanking towers, apparently of later date. Arriving on horseback at the main entrance, an archway in the outer wall, we found the rough stone steps lined by Tribal Guards. Amir Haidara came down to welcome us with a friendly smile, and led us up the steps, which turn sharply to the right at the top, through a rather narrow doorway into the courtyard. We did not enter the central tower, which contains the women's apartments, but were taken up another flight of stone steps to the first floor of the outer buildings, into a long whitewashed room with a shuttered window opening immediately over the main entrance. Our room had two sets of plain arched niches in the walls, into which we put our lamps, cameras and other gear; the floor was covered with plain matting; unshaped tree-trunks lay as beams across the top of the walls, supporting the rough rafters; both beams and rafters were plastered in and whitewashed.

On the same floor, beyond the flight of stairs, was a large room in which the Amir and his male relatives sat and smoked their water-pipes. Outside their door was a small kitchen, in the apse-like projection formed by one of the flanking towers in the outer wall, and beyond it the bathroom and lavatory, sufficiently primitive to recall arrangements in a medieval castle. But the rooms were clean, part of the passage-way on this floor was open to the sky, and the flies, though annoying, were less numerous than is sometimes the case in England. The ground floor beneath our room consisted of a dark undercroft, used for stores and stables.

The visit of the Governor of Aden (Sir Bernard Reilly), an important event in the Dhala Amirate, brought together a very large concourse of tribesmen, and gave us the opportunity to witness many local ceremonies and customs. Amir Nasr returned to his capital by car from Lahej for the great occasion. Amir Haidara met him at the foot of the castle hill and together they rode up on horses. Dismounting at the top, they walked to the entrance between two lines of their troops, preceded by a band of drums and wooden pipes.

The following morning, the Governor having arrived from Aden by air, with the Air Officer Commanding, the Amir's troops paraded, and tribesmen lined the sides of the road leading to the Parade Ground, discharging their rifles into the air as the Governor's car approached. The Amir's regular troops appeared for the first time in new khaki shirts and shorts, in place of their white native dress. The several companies were distinguished by turbans respectively khaki, white and indigo. In this smart turn-out we saw the results of training on modern lines by qualified instructors under the control partly of the Amir and partly of Captain (now Major, the Hon. R. A. B. Hamilton (the Master of Belhaven), then Political Officer in the district.

Regular tribal armies approved by the Government, such as the one we saw at Dhala, were intended to act as an internal security force. Apart from the Royal Air Force there were then almost no British forces in the Protectorate, but the more important Arab rulers maintained these regular troops, known as Tribal Guards. Started some years ago, they are maintained by their respective chiefs as far as the resources of the latter permit, but the Aden Government helps in cases where the chief cannot bear the whole cost. In return, the Tribal Guards are supervised by a British Officer appointed by the Government and, while adding to the authority of their own chief, they must be used by him in a way approved by the Government. Later, but some time before the outbreak of the world war, the Tribal Guards were supplemented by a force of Government Guards under direct Government control.

The Parade Ground at Dhala was afterwards given up to an Agricultural Show, the first ever held in the Protectorate. There were classes for donkeys, cattle, sheep, goats, camels, and chickens, the last entered by members of the Jewish community. The Political Officer (Captain Hamilton) had tried for six months to explain the idea of an agricultural show to the tribesmen. A large measure of success was achieved, but nevertheless some of the simpler folk entered their animals because they were told to, and kept back their best, fearing that they would be expected to give them to the "Wali Sahib", as they called the Governor. When they found that His Excellency, instead of claiming the exhibits, distributed prizes in money for the best of each class and sex, these unsuccessful competitors indignantly complained that they had a much better animal at home!

Next day the keen sense of humour of the people showed itself in the events at a sports meeting. There were tugs-of-war and donkey races, while the boys ran sack races and played ring games. One boy stood on his head for a long while before the Governor and the Amir, while another beside him, swathed in sacking and made up like a huge fowl with an enormous beak, preened himself in a most birdlike manner, evoking roars of laughter from the crowd.

The festivities ended that night with a display of tribal dances before the Governor and the two Amirs. The scene was lighted by a great bonfire near the Rest-House, and by flaring balls of earth and ashes soaked in paraffin. The band of drums and wood-pipes took its place within the ring of spectators and began a monotonous plaintive music. Men and boys danced in pairs, facing each other, or in rows with linked arms. The dancing at first was not very energetic, but after a while the performers began to warm to their work and as each couple tired and fell out, two more men leapt into their place. Unsheathed *jambiyas* were flourished in the air above the dancers' heads as they stamped and turned, all in perfect time to the rhythmic beat of the drums. In an apparently impromptu comic dance, a man held a white skull-cap between his teeth while others in turn tried to snatch it away with their teeth, keeping their hands behind their backs. Whatever strain the resulting tugs-of-war put on the dancers' jaws, their feet never ceased to follow the complicated steps of the dance.

The Arab dances were interrupted when the Jews of the town approached in procession, carrying lanterns. To us, seeing them for the first time, these South Arabian Jewish men and boys looked very strange, with their shaven heads, long ringlets on either side of the face, and little skull-caps.

The ground was cleared. Rabbis with red kerchiefs round their heads opened long narrow books and led wailing choruses, while tall, heavily bearded Jews danced slowly and decorously in pairs—a weird sight in the flickering light of the fires. Finally the Jews departed in procession as they had come, with their lanterns, leaving the ground once more to the Arabs.

All the principal tribes of the Protectorate have their own dances, alike in their main features but differing in detail. Those in which *jambiyas* are flourished aloft no doubt originated as war-dances, but are not necessarily war-dances now. They are associated, rather, with occasions of public rejoicing, such as that at Dhala, or they form part of the festivities at weddings. In the Yemen too, the Imam himself and the great Amirs governing outlying districts are preceded in ceremonial processions by bodies of soldiers who dance as they move forward. Though the steps of the dances that we saw varied, the feature common to most was the holding aloft of the gleaming, unsheathed short dagger, with its point directed downwards.[1]

In the mind's eye Dhala town and its people, and all the activities in which we took part, are seen in their own special setting. There is the rolling plateau on which, when we arrived in mid-September, almost every cultivable spot was covered with tall green crops of ripening *dhurra*; later, when the plumes of grain had been gathered and the stems cut and stacked in bundles, these countless little fields were dry and dusty stubbles. Near the town they are interspersed with plots of vegetables and some gardens of young *qat* trees—the tree, holding in its young shoots stimulating or intoxicating drugs, of which we were to see and hear much more in the Yemen. Scattered here and there between the little fields of *dhurra* stand large spreading acacias and thorny '*ilb* trees.

Low rocky hills rise from the general level; too rough for cultivation, they are waste ground, or grazed over by sheep or goats; covered with sharp-edged blocks of volcanic rock, and dotted with succulent cactus-like euphorbia bushes about three feet high, with clumps of trailing fleshy wild vines (*Cissus quadrangularis*) and other plants. On these hillocks we first learnt the great difficulty of collecting on such ground. The abundant grasshoppers, of which we had to secure large numbers, leapt and flew very swiftly in the hot sunshine, settling in places where their protective colouring rendered them almost invisible and where the jagged stones often made it impossible to get a net over the insect. Huge blue Pompilid wasps also cruised over these low hills, making a curious loud rattling buzz in their flight; carrying, too, the spiders which they capture and then paralyse by stinging them in the nerve-centres, so that the wasps' cells may be stocked with fresh meat for the larvæ which hatch later.

Higher hills, capped by crowded villages, rise from the plateau.

[1] In Nejd and the Hejaz, on the other hand, the waving of swords, or smiting of sword-blades on shields, would seem, judging from descriptions, to be characteristic. Doughty describes young Bedawi men dancing at a circumcision feast " a-row, every one his arm upon the next one's shoulder " ("Arabia Deserta," Vol. i, Chap 12), and he also graphically narrates how young men in Kheybar in Nejd danced, " smiting sword to buckler ", in the light of a bonfire (Vol. ii, Chap. 5). Apart from these classical descriptions I have found little about men's tribal dances (as opposed to those of women and girls) in standard works on Arabia.

PHOTOGRAPH 11.
A pool in Wadi Dareija; prickly acanthus bushes and roots of wild-fig trees on left.

PHOTOGRAPHS 12 AND 13.
Children and sheep on Jebel Jihaf.
Tall-stemmed aloes in Wadi Dareija.

The background in every direction is formed by mountains, some table-shaped, others more jagged. Reaching heights between 6,000 and 8,000 feet, they are coloured in many shades of tawny and darker brown, according to the nature of the rock, and show a haze of greyish-green where scrub-vegetation maintains a foothold on their stony sides. Nor is the contrast wanting of brilliant sunlight and deep shade in the early and late hours of the day, and, particularly before the rains had ended, the moving shadows cast by great masses of cloud.

Within a few miles lie spots of surprising luxuriance, hidden narrow clefts, or gorges where cliffs give shade during much of the day and where perennially running water favours a rank growth of trees and vegetation of all kinds. Above all Wadi Dareija, a few miles to the south-west, on the old track still used by camel caravans between Aden and Dhala, proved for us a very rich hunting-ground. The track leads away from the town behind the castle hill over fields and through a wood of old spreading 'ilb trees (*Zizyphus spina-christi*, Phot. 10). These gnarled veterans recall ancient olive-trees by their growth, till closer inspection reveals their thorns and little cherry-like edible fruits (the 'ilb is related not to olive but to buckthorn). Beyond this wood a gorge is entered. Its cliffs echo the barks of the baboons which frequent the place in troops. The defile is divided by a sudden drop, and the descent to the lower gorge is made by a steep zigzagging path, beside an overhanging cliff of calcareous rock. Shallow caverns at the bottom are filled with stalactitic formations. On one side, in a narrow recess, a waterfall tumbles into a pool (Phot. 11) over which the spreading foliage of large wild-fig trees casts a welcome shade, while their roots cover the face of the cliff with serpentine windings and penetrate the joints of the rock. A tangle of prickly-leaved branching acanthus bushes [1] and other plants surrounds this rock-basin. Aloes [2] of unusual form, with tall pole-stems (Phot. 13), rise among the dense thickets on the talus slopes of the lower gorge. Such a diversity of wild plant life is generally only found in sheltered places at medium altitudes. In the hot steamy valleys of the Yemen, running west, the vegetation is even more luxuriant.

These memories of Dhala itself and its immediate surroundings must be brought to a close. I must pass to the story of the weeks of trekking and camping undertaken, with Dhala as " advanced base ", on the mountains and in the valleys of the outlying parts of the Amir's territory. But when the time came for us finally to quit the Amiri highlands, after the experiences recounted in the following chapters, we felt a genuine regret at leaving the little town, its hospitable Amirs and the friendly mountain-folk.

[1] *Acanthus racemosus.*   [2] *Aloe sabaea.*

Chapter VIII
LIFE ON JEBEL JIHAF

IN the early morning of September 16th we left the Rest-House at Dhala to establish a camp about 2,500 feet higher, on Jebel Jihaf, the highest of the mountains which encircle the Dhala plateau, rising to over 7,800 feet. On the mornings after our arrival at Dhala a thick cloud-cap hid the summit of this great mountain, but when clear it stood out as a fine rocky mass with a long jagged outline, rising to a peak at either end. Seen from the town its south-easterly slopes, steep, stony and uncultivated, give little indication of the surprises in store on the top.

Britton, Jam'a and I set off on three horses lent by Amir Haidara, followed by Ahmed and 'Omar on hired donkeys. Amir Haidara kindly put one or other of his horses or mares at our disposal each time we went up or down the mountain. Sure-footed, rather tall or of medium height, and brown or chestnut-coloured, some of them became good friends of ours. In particular, " Amir ", so named because he was a present from the Amir of Ta'izz to the Amir of Dhala, and " Rassas " will be remembered by a few other Europeans besides ourselves. Our baggage train consisted of nine hired camels. As an example of transport-costs, the hire of each camel was $2\frac{1}{2}$ rupees (3s. 4d.) and the total cost of the journey from Dhala to the top of the mountain, including hire of donkeys and presents to boys and men, 34 rupees (£2 5s. 4d.).

Seven miles of stony track, winding in and out among the spurs and gulleys of the mountain, had to be covered. The only difficult part was a long stretch of bare rock, steep and smooth, near the top. Though at first tempted to dismount and walk over this " glacis ", on subsequent ascents and descents, knowing the horses better, we trusted them to carry us across.

As our first ride up Jebel Jihaf fell on a Thursday, market-day at Dhala, we met many parties of tribesmen descending. These indigo-turbaned, white-kilted, wiry hillmen carried produce for sale in the town, vegetables and young kids, while one man had a tiny calf in a bag slung over his back ; some carried little gourds full of ghee (liquid butter). Many men had their tobacco-pipes. The pipe most used

PHOTOGRAPH 14.

Volcanic mountains in the afternoon haze, from Jebel Ma'fari.

PHOTOGRAPHS 15 AND 16.
Top of Jebel Jihaf; the cultivated plateau and the mountain-castle.
A summer afternoon rainstorm on Jebel Jihaf.

by the peasantry of these mountains has a stem made of a straight stick, bored, with the bark left on, and about three feet long. The end-piece and bowl are carved out of a single lump of greenstone found on the mountain and ornamented with simple patterns. The heel of the pipe is flat, and the bowl, bent up at a sharp angle to the end-piece, is rendered more capacious by a broad iron lip, supported by chains attached to a ring round the stem.[1] Resemblances between this corner of Arabia and the parts of Africa opposite are many, and not least in some of the homely objects of daily use. The gourd food-vessel and the pipe shown in Photograph 20 have a distinctly African look. In fact, tobacco-pipes of this pattern seem most nearly to approach Nubian and East African types, though the latter have not (at least not always) the metal rim.

The tobacco grown in small fields in the Amiri highlands consisted of a variety with stems about six feet high and small, pale pink flowers.

The descending stream of tribesmen aroused wonderment as to how so many people found a living on a barren mountain. But, after crossing the bare rock-glacis and climbing a ridge whence we looked westwards over a chaos of grotesquely shaped mountains (shown from a different view-point in Phot. 14), we again found the scene transformed rather as we had when reaching the edge of Dhala plateau at the top of Al Khureiba Pass. For the top of Jebel Jihaf is a bowl-like table-land (Phot. 15), closely cultivated and girdled with rocky hills up which terraced fields are carried wherever human ingenuity has been able to contrive. We rode along narrow paths winding between fields of tall green *dhurra* with plumes of ripening seed, of short-strawed wheat and barley, lucerne and chick-peas, and irrigated beds of onions. Villages of stone towers and houses are perched fantastically on hilltops. Other groups of houses surround little greens of short turf on more level spots, where wild-fig trees throw patches of shade.

With the change in vegetation many wild flowers came into view. The low cactus-like euphorbia-bushes of the rocky hillocks near Dhala are less in evidence, but tall candelabra-like tree-euphorbias,[2] ten or

---

[1] The wood used for the pipe-sticks appears to be cherry. Scarcely from the high Yemen, but imported? The immortal Hajji Baba, when setting up as a vendor of pipe-sticks, contracted with a woodcutter, who was to go to the Lur and Bakhtiari mountains of Persia, where he would cut sticks of specified sizes in the forests of wild cherry-trees. These sticks were afterwards to be bored in Baghdad and made up into parcels for export (James Morier, " Hajji Baba of Ispahan," Chap. lxv).

[2] These are ʻamq-trees (*Euphorbia Ammak*). The varied forms of cactus-like plants so characteristic of this part of Arabia, as well as of the drier parts of Africa, sometimes miscalled cactuses, are members of an entirely different order, the *Euphorbiaceæ*, to which belong the spurges of Europe. There are no wild cactuses

twelve feet high, abound, and form stout prickly hedges round these "village greens" (Phot. 17).

The Amir's mountain-keep, recalling a border peel-tower, crowns a conical hill on the farther edge of the bowl-shaped plateau. One of the larger villages is huddled on the steep slope beneath this small castle (Phot. 9). At our first arrival we were met at the foot of the hill by the Amir himself, mounted on a tall horse, and followed by sixteen tribal guards on foot, bearing rifles. At a level place we dismounted and advanced to greet each other with salaams and handshakes. The Amir insisted on my heading the procession up to the keep on his horse, while he followed on the horse that I had ridden. Clambering on to the large padded saddle was not the easiest thing, since European boots would not go into the narrow Arab stirrups. However, with the sixteen guards marching in front in double file, we proceeded to the top and dismounted. We went through a high narrow portal furnished with heavy wooden gates into a narrow courtyard. The guard presented arms and we entered the keep itself. A servant with a lantern lighted us up the dark stairway, over the raised ridges at the foot of each flight, to a long, narrow, well-lighted room at the top of the building. The keen mountain air entered through a number of unglazed windows set in the immensely thick walls. These windows, small and close to the floor, had each a pair of roughly carved shutters, while above were arched niches which served for the stowage of small articles. The floor was covered with matting and two layers of rugs. The walls had been recently whitewashed, though fresco designs in red, representing motor-cars and other rather surprising objects, showed through. A table and folding chairs had been placed for us at one end; the other was occupied by a high bed with brilliant coverings. We talked with the Amir about the mountain (like all the local people he called it "Gihaf", since this is one of the parts of the Arabic-speaking world where j is sounded hard), and he pointed out its far limits from the windows of his eyrie. Tea was then served by the Amir's servants, but he excused himself from partaking. He then left us to a substantial lunch provided by himself

in Arabia, nor (with a single exception) anywhere outside Tropical America. But in dry countries many euphorbias have developed a fleshy, succulent, prickly form, storing up water in their tissues to resist the long dry season, and thus they have come by convergence to resemble cactuses closely in growth. Their little flower-heads, greenish or yellow, are quite unlike the large, brightly coloured flowers of cactuses. The only cactus in Arabia is the imported prickly pear (*Opuntia*), now naturalised round the Mediterranean and in dry parts of Africa, Asia and Australia. There were some thickets of this on Jebel Jihaf, and it is grown in other districts of the Aden Protectorate and plentifully in the Yemen. The prickly pear is easily recognisable by its flattened jointed stems.

but served by our own servants; soup, chicken, custard pudding in a large round dish, and finally flat chupatties of *dhurra*-flour and local honey, crystalline and solid.

After thus sampling Amir Haidara's hospitality we went down the castle hill, on the opposite side to that by which we had approached, to a little plain where a space for our tents had been cleared. The site was the edge of an old cemetery. As we afterwards found, burial-grounds are often the only available level space for a camp. The graves are marked by groups of rough stones on the flat surface, and the older ones become almost obliterated by displacement of the stones. Nevertheless we always tried to avoid walking on graves, though the local tribesmen did not appear to show any great respect for these cemeteries.

Jebel Jihaf is far more than the wide, cultivated shallow cup which opened itself to our delighted gaze on that first day. The great massif of igneous rock, for such it is rather than a single mountain, extends about fifteen miles from north-east to south-west (Phot. 111). Deep winding valleys are carved in its north-eastern, western and south-western edges, but they leave unbroken the cultivated bowl-shaped plateau and its encircling hills. Within walking distance of our camp we had country varied enough to occupy us for a month. Our camp, however, was almost on the western edge of the plateau, and our activities were sharply bounded in that direction by the brink of the great outer wall of the mountain. This falls precipitously more than 3,000 feet into a wide undulating plain, where lies the upper part of the Wadi Tiban. Beyond this rise the brown ramparts of the highlands of the Yemen.

All the cultivation and intricate terracing, carried in places up the outer walls of the mountain for two thousand feet (Frontispiece) and occupying every possible square foot of the top, and the human life which they support, depend on the plenteous supply of water. Springs and wells seem countless; of the latter the mountain is said to have more than three hundred. We experienced the ending of the summer rains which replenish this copious supply. On the day when we camped our tents were pitched only just before a furious storm of wind and rain swept up (Phot. 16). We held on to the main poles, but here, as I had found in the Abyssinian highlands, the double-fly tents withstood the wind and kept out the rain.

The violent afternoon rain and hail squalls stopped after the first few days. Though the rains were ending earlier than in some years, great mushroom-shaped clouds still piled up over the Yemen mountains to the north and west (Phot. 21) and lightning still flickered there, even after the end of September and long after the storms had ceased on Jebel Jihaf. Some have thought that the cloud-caps on the mountains, the rushing winds and reverberating thunder of the summer storms in this, the Land of Uz, caused the writer of the Book of Job to picture " the Lord speaking to Job out of the whirlwind ". But my Somali servant and friend, Ahmed Mahmūd, has taken a gentler poetic view of the rains. Over a year after our return to England, and when he had become a sergeant in the Mounted Government Guards, Ahmed, with the help of an Arab quartermaster who knew English well, wrote me one of several letters. This one was from Summer Headquarters at Dhala, where (he said) the horses recently bought locally and in the Yemen were being trained. Ahmed had been relating the incidents of our journey to his friend the quartermaster till late at night, " under the golden drops of rain showering on our heads in the darkness, watering the lovely flower-garden of our Summer Headquarters at Wadi Safra, and listening to the roaring of the running water falling from the mountain, feeding the thirsty wadi-bed and trees on its flanks, awaiting the summer months to nourish her after the long dry winter of Dhala ".

During the transition to dry-weather conditions our tents were buffeted every afternoon by a strong wind from the south-east, and between five and six o'clock swift-moving cloud, raw and chilly, enveloped the camp. But by the beginning of October the late afternoons and nights were still, while wind usually got up from the east before dawn and blew during most of the day, so that papers and specimens could only be safely handled inside the tents, which had purposely been pitched facing west. Minimum night temperatures ranged between 51 and 57 degrees Fahrenheit, though the day maximum in our tents sometimes reached nearly 90 degrees.

Our Somalis established themselves in an empty isolated stone house, standing about fifty yards from our tents, put at our disposal by Amir Haidara. This low tower had a dark and uneven staircase, into the corners of which large earthenware vessels for food were built with mud and plaster. The men slept on the flat roof, where they constructed a shelter for the kitchen fire. During the first few days, while rainstorms continued, cooking had to be done in the low dark rooms, whence smoke could not escape. Jam'a apologised for the smoked meals, owing to the difficulties of cooking in " that bungalow ". Trained as a servant to Europeans in Somaliland and Aden, he regarded all houses as " bungalows ", though no houses could be less like a bungalow than the grim stone towers of the Amiri highlands.

As almost every crag and eminence had its cluster of houses, the people habitually converse from house-top to house-top. Remarks are bawled from one hamlet to the next across the intervening ground.

PHOTOGRAPH 17.
A house on Jebel Jihaf, with hedge of tall tree-euphorbias.

PHOTOGRAPHS 18 AND 19.

Naji, chief tribal guard of our escort in the Amiri highlands—a humorist. Amiri women and girls on Jebel Jihaf.

Messages are thus passed quickly from village to village over long distances. The stentorian tones of our chief 'askari, Naji, shouting frequent requests from the roof of the servants' house to a man named Obādi stationed in the village beneath the Amir's tower, were a regular accompaniment to life in our camp on Jebel Jihaf. Obādi's duty was to see that firewood, water and other necessaries were supplied to the camp.

Besides Naji (pronounced Nagi), three other 'askaris or tribal guards, told off by the Amir as our escort, stayed with us throughout our two months in the Amiri country. The small wages which they earned in the Amir's service were supplemented by " presents " from us at a regular rate of about ten rupees per man per month. One or two of these guards, equipped with rifles and *jambiyas*, accompanied us on every walk. They were extremely willing and gifted with a keen sense of fun. Naji, in particular, was a humorist, whose often whimsical expression is conveyed to some extent in Photograph 18. Ahmed Hādi, the next, besides being a wag was a musician. By the camp-fire during Ramadhan he sang in the characteristic high-pitched voice of the tribesmen. He accompanied himself with perfect rhythm by thrumming on the bottom of an empty paraffin tin. 'Ali, the third *'askari*, was a tall pock-marked man with a hooked nose, usually called " 'Ali al 'Askari " (to distinguish him from the fourth guard, " 'Ali as Saghir " or " Little 'Ali ", who was small in stature and mentally rather simple).

'Ali al 'Askari had been a soldier of the Imam. While in the Yemen he had been stationed in San'a, the attractions of which he used often to describe in glowing terms. After being sent back to his own Amiri country he had taken part in military operations in 1928 by which the Yemenis were driven out of the north-western part of the Protectorate. One of his traits was an intense dislike of snakes. This terror was, however, partly feigned. He would utter awful howls when shown even an entirely inoffensive reptile. He would scarcely go on watch one night when a very young snake, sent up by messenger from Dhala in a torpid state and a long Government envelope, had revived and escaped. Every stone in the rough wall which the guards had erected to shelter their fire must be moved in a vain search for the snake. 'Ali vowed that he would be unable to sleep that night, a naïve admission on the part of a sentry ! Another instance of his naïveté occurred when we visited Jebel Harir after our stay on Jihaf. Being a native of one of the small villages on Jebel Harir, 'Ali asked to go on leave to his family, which we gladly granted, as he had then accompanied us about six weeks. He returned, however, before his leave of absence had expired, complaining that his family wanted him *to work* !

One duty of the guard on watch was to drive off the village dogs. They, however, were not the only disturbers of the night, for hyænas often howled close by, evoking a pandemonium among the dogs in the village. Otherwise there was little evidence of larger wild animals on Jebel Jihaf, excepting large grey baboons [1] and an occasional hare. The baboons frequently descended by day in troops from rocky inaccessible places to rob the *dhurra* fields, and small boys armed with slings were employed to chase them off.

To hyænas and baboons may be added a strange animal, possibly mythical, spoken of by Amir Haidara and mentioned in Chapter XIX, p. 206 (footnote). At one of our conferences with the Amir, when he used to ride down from his tower to have tea with us and discuss our future plans, we showed him a series of picture post cards of the Natural History Museum. Subsequently almost all the great personages met on our journey saw these cards, and like Amir Haidara all were very interested in the skeletons of enormous extinct animals. The Amir was particularly amused at the huge skeleton of *Diplodocus*. He remarked, with a twinkle in his eye, that it would have made a fine camel. He appeared, however, quite to grasp that it must have lived in shallow water. These extinct titans led him to speak of a *dufaira*, a man-eating monster said to have lived formerly near Ta'izz, in Yemen, but we could not determine whether this animal had ever really existed.

The snakes so feared by our friend 'Ali al 'Askari were not uncommon on Jebel Jihaf. Two five-foot African Cobras were killed close to the servants' house. More entertaining (and not venomous) reptiles were the large chamæleons [2] often met with, with their crested heads and independently moving eyes, their changes of colour, and their long awkward legs with two-toed feet.

On our mountain-top, where so many living things were different from those met with in the lowlands, or even at the intermediate altitude of Dhala, this difference naturally extended to the birds. Arabian Bulbuls, however, still uttered their melodious whistling at dawn, as in the lowlands at Al Huseini, disporting themselves in the tall hedge of tree-euphorbia round our servants' house. The numerous kites and ravens [3] which scavenged round the village and camp were also of the same kinds as those seen lower down. The house-sparrows [4] which hopped and cheeped about the stone towers were very like our little town birds at home, for in this part of Arabia the house-sparrow is only a variety of the typical form, unlike its opposite number in

---

[1] *Papio hamadryas.*   [2] *Chamæleon calyptratus.*
[3] *Milvus migrans ægyptius* and *Corvus corax ruficollis.*
[4] *Passer domesticus* var. *indicus.*

Photograph 20.

Sling, pipe, gourd food-vessel, and door-lock from the Amiri highlands; the wide metal rim fitted to the stone bowl of the pipe holds charcoal on top of the tobacco.

PHOTOGRAPHS 21, 22 AND 23.
North-west edge of Jebel Jihaf, with thunderclouds over the Yemen mountains. Threshing wheat and ploughing on Jebel Jihaf.

Abyssinia, which is a distinct species. Most characteristic of the mountain were several kinds of chats and wheat-ears, among which the Arabian Pied Chat,[1] rather smaller than a common wheat-ear, was conspicuous by its black and white plumage and dusky whitish cap. The Little Yemen Rockthrush,[2] slate-coloured above, with slatey-blue throat and tawny red underparts, by its movements and its sweet brief song recalled a rather large robin; while farther from the camp, among cultivated fields, an oriole[3] displayed its black and yellow plumage.

Early in October a pair of Red-winged Glossy Starlings,[4] glossy blue-black with orange-brown in the wings, appeared in the tree-euphorbia hedge, and in December birds of the same kind flew in small flocks, uttering their whistling note, over the roofs of Ta'izz in Southern Yemen. Swifts and swallows, the latter probably the same kind as our British summer migrant, put in an appearance on Jebel Jihaf towards the middle of October, on their southward journey from northern lands.

Small brightly coloured turtle-doves[5] frequented trees and thickets; while nests of the only Arabian weaver-finch[6] hang in numbers from trees in the Amiri highlands, but were untenanted during our visit (September to early November). Hawks, larks, finches and many other birds which cannot be named, abounded.

Photographs 22–27 tell something of the agricultural occupations which proceeded around us during our stay on the mountain. With the early setting in of the dry weather, the tribesmen were busy harvesting *dhurra*, barley and wheat. Men and boys worked in gangs along the terraced fields, hand-picking the plumes of grain from the tall *dhurra* plants. For days, at the end of September, the countryside echoed from morning to night with a chorus sung by the harvesters, a haunting melody drawn out into quavering notes, which, unfortunately, we found impossible to memorise or record.

After the *dhurra* grain is plucked each field is worked over again. The tall stems, sawn off with a sickle a few inches above the ground, are either used for green fodder or piled in bundles in conical stacks to dry, and used later as dry fodder and litter. In many fields the stubbles were ploughed up immediately, but in other places they were left. We found *dhurra* stubbles in the Yemen and ploughing in pro-

[1] *Œnanthe lugubris lugentoides*.   [2] *Monticola rufocinerea sclateri*.
[3] Probably a form of *Oriolus monacha*, the Black-headed Oriole common in Abyssinia and other parts of Africa.
[4] *Onychognathus tristramii hadramauticus*.
[5] *Streptopelia senegalensis*, a dove very widely distributed in Africa and called the Laughing Dove or Little Brown Dove.
[6] *Ploceus galbula*.

gress as late as January and February. As there is usually only one *dhurra* crop a year, fields may lie fallow four or five months before the next sowing. The number of crops reaped annually and the season of sowing, however, vary considerably at different altitudes and in different districts. As this applies to other crops as well as *dhurra*, I can do little more than describe what we saw.

The ploughs used on Jebel Jihaf (Phot. 23) were of a kind met with throughout our journey, primitive wooden instruments drawn by a yoke of small humped oxen. In this form of ploughing the earth is broken by the simple driving forward of an iron-capped spike, there being no curved ploughshare to turn the soil. Near San'a afterwards we saw the actual turning laboriously done by a separate operation (Phot. 25); a team of three men wield a heavy shovel for this purpose, one clasping its long wooden handle while the other two hold cords attached to the upper corners of the blade. This tool, as well as the apparatus of pole and boards dragged by a yoke of oxen, used for building up dykes round fields before irrigation (Phot. 24), seem to be peculiar to South Arabia. They are the "smaller shovel" and "bigger shovel" of the modern German explorers of the Yemen, and both were described and illustrated by the great Danish explorer, Niebuhr, about 170 years earlier.[1]

On Jebel Jihaf the ploughman was sometimes followed by his womenfolk, who broke the clods with mattocks (Phot. 23). These were wooden instruments with the shorter limb at an acute angle to the handle, and only the point capped with an iron spike. A different form, with a long curved iron spike nearly at right angles to the wooden handle, was seen in use for deep trenching of fields near San'a.

Men, boys and girls reaped the wheat and barley, not by dragging them up by the roots (as is sometimes done), but by grasping a handful of the stems and sawing through them with a sickle. This tool has not the full curve of a European sickle, but the blade runs straight from the handle and is only curved round, almost at a right angle, towards the tip. The little bundles of wheat and barley were laid in rows on natural threshing-floors of bare rock, and threshed with a flail, in the form of a long curved unjointed stick (Phot. 22). We saw in several places, though never in use, large sledge-shaped stones which are drawn by camels over the ears of corn to crush out the grain.

The grain was winnowed by the simple process of pouring it and the chaff out of any convenient receptacle, too often a paraffin tin, held high above the head, so that the chaff is blown away as the grain falls. The winnowers here do not stand on raised wooden platforms.

---

[1] See Rathjens and von Wissmann, "Südarabien-Reise," Vol. ii, pp. 28, 29, 1932; and C. Niebuhr's "Beschreibung von Arabien," pp. 156 *sqq.*, and Plate 15.

PHOTOGRAPHS 24 AND 25.

Building dykes before irrigating fields at Dhala.
Ploughman followed by three men turning the soil with a heavy shovel, near San'a.

PHOTOGRAPHS 26 AND 27.
Raising water at Dhala.
The water from the hide bucket is directed into a channel.

Some large stones outside our servants' house marked the entrance to subterranean vaults. Jam'a and others hinted at sinister tales regarding them, but they were simply cellars for storage of grain.

It is tempting to digress on the methods of threshing and winnowing used in different countries, such as the wooden sledges set beneath with rows of sharp flints, and drawn by mules and oxen round and round over the threshing-floors of bare hard earth in Northern Spain; or the wooden sled, containing a revolving wooden cylinder set with axe-heads, pulled over the threshing-floor by donkeys in 'Iraq. By the two latter methods the straw is cut into short pieces and the grain pressed out of the ear at the same time. On the plains of Castile and in 'Iraq, too, I have watched men tossing the mixed grain and chaff into the air with wooden winnowing forks, but no implements of this kind were met with in the places visited on our Arabian journey.

All through the day, at each of the innumerable wells, a boy drives a yoke of the humped oxen down an inclined plane, thus hauling up a large bucket made of a single ox-hide, by a rope passing over a wooden pulley. At the well-head a man stands ready to direct each bucketful into the irrigation channel (Phots. 26, 27). In the cities of the Yemen the wells are much larger, with longer inclined planes excavated deep into the earth, to meet the much greater depth of the wells; several buckets are drawn up side by side, and are emptied automatically at the well-head by a trip-cord attached to the bottom of each bucket (Phot. 77).[1]

During the harvest on Jebel Jihaf the only crops irrigated were onions. At regular times men opened with a rough wooden implement the little earthen banks blocking the ends of the furrows, to let the water run between the rows of plants. In mid-October bigger banks were being made round fields needing to be irrigated later. The dry dusty soil was heaped up by the great, broad, wooden shovels already mentioned, dragged by a yoke of oxen and directed by means of a pole attached to the planks.

While these agricultural operations are the normal work of the Arab tribesmen, various forms of craftsmanship are the exclusive reserve of the Jews, of whom there are small colonies even in the villages on the top of the mountain. All metal-work is in their hands. They make, among other things, the small light tomahawk-like axe-heads, fixed on long thin wooden handles, with which the people chop wood for fuel. No disposition to do any unnecessary chopping

---

[1] This kind of well is general in the Aden Protectorate and the Yemen. The *saqiya*, or large wooden wheel over which passes an endless chain of earthenware water-vessels, so widely used in Egypt and other Mediterranean lands, is apparently not used in South Arabia.

was, by the way, noticeable ! We had to pass time after time in single file along the same narrow paths through scrub, but our tribal guards, willing enough in other ways, would not cut away branches of thorny acacia encroaching on the path. I thought regretfully of negro woodmen I had known in the luxuriant forests of tropical islands, men with wonderful skill in slashing a way with long broad-bladed knives through the densest jungle.

Local craftsmen also make the wooden keys and the massive wooden locks for house doors (Phot. 20). The keys look rather like wooden tooth-brushes, with little pegs arranged differently in each case. When the key is pushed into a slot in the heavy bolt, the pegs fit into corresponding holes in the wood. In each hole is a little wooden pin, with a head to prevent it from dropping down too far. Each pin is pushed upwards by the corresponding peg on the key. The bolt is then freed and can be slid sideways to open the door. When the bolt is shot home, the wooden pins fall into their holes by their own weight, and the door is locked. This allows of a different arrangement of pins and pegs for every lock ; a door can therefore only be unlocked with its own accurately fitting key, as is the case with a Yale lock. This form of wooden lock is widely distributed. It is a rough version of that generally used in ancient Egypt, and a similar form was, within living memory, used in some northern countries, for instance, the Faroe Islands.

Chapter IX
RECESSES AND HEIGHTS OF JEBEL JIHAF

IT is time to say something of the wild parts of Jebel Jihaf, the uncultivated, rough and stony places of the greatest interest to us in our work. The deepest recess explored, Wadi Leje (pronounced " Leggy "), lies towards the south-western end of the mountain, and the highest point near its north-eastern extremity (see again the panorama, Phot. 111). Our camp lay roughly midway between the two. But, though long all-day excursions were made on foot to these distant parts of the mountain, the immediate surroundings of the camp provided plenty of stony wild land, covered with scrubby vegetation, small trees, flowering bushes and herbs. So, when less arduous walking and collecting were needed we worked close at hand, or along the narrow strips of waste ground at the back of the little terraced fields. There, at the foot of the stone terrace of the field above, was shade and moisture enough to allow a rank growth of grass and flowering weeds.

On all expeditions such as ours it is, moreover, occasionally necessary to stay in camp all day, dealing with accumulated specimens, writing up notes, or putting plant specimens between fresh drying-papers, laying out the used sheets of paper in the hot sun to dry, held down by stones, lest they should be carried away by the gusty winds.

The uncultivated places were just as difficult to work on as the stony hills near Dhala. The chasing of flying insects put even the nimbleness of our Somalis to a severe test. Every movement of a sweep-net was hampered by the extreme prickliness and wiriness of the vegetation. My experience of the prevalence of thorns of every shape and size in other tropical countries was here quite surpassed. We often thought that the Romans should have named this part of the peninsula Arabia Spinosa rather than Arabia Felix. On such exacting ground the number of specimens secured in a short time was decidedly less than in more luxuriant tropical countries, and very much less than in a favourable summer at home. But there was a wide diversity and, with hard work, our collections steadily increased. Special methods of collecting had to be used for such purposes as, for instance, the sifting of debris from dead parts of the tree-euphorbias. In the Canary Islands and Morocco many insects live exclusively on these peculiar plants, and we were anxious to discover if any corresponding association exists in South-West Arabia.

A few hundred yards from the camp the opaque brown water of a fairly large village pond was alive with " fairy shrimps ". These transparent creatures, about three-quarters of an inch in length, which paddle along on their backs, are classed by zoologists as the most primitive of all small crustaceans. Each sweep of the water-net in this pond brought up scores of the shrimps at a time, and with them a smaller number of ostracods, small crustaceans enclosed in a double shell like that of a mussel. Both kinds were found again in shallow rain-water pools on other parts of the mountain, even on the very summit. As the pools dry up, the fairy shrimps (or branchiopods) and the ostracods produce resistant " winter eggs ", which remain dormant in the dried mud until they are stimulated to hatch by the rains of the following year. The winter eggs also serve as a means of distributing the species, for they may easily be blown about in dust, or carried from the mud of one pool to another on the feet of birds.

The very steep western face of the mountain was scored with gullies full of rank vegetation. We occasionally climbed down these ravines for a thousand feet or so, for there flew butterflies which never appeared on the top of the mountain, notably a species of *Acræa*, a long-winged, rich brown butterfly with a most graceful gliding flight. The most inaccessible parts of the western side were the homes of troops of baboons. At our intrusion into their territory they would race away up the rough slopes, shrieking and barking to each other.

Our moth-screen was set up at night near the camp, but as the rains came to an end fewer insects were attracted to the lamp, until we finally gave it up as unprofitable. At nightfall the long-horned grasshoppers began their high-pitched singing from the dense clumps of euphorbia and from the *dhurra* fields, a sound produced only by the males, and, in this family of insects, caused by the rubbing together of specially strengthened ribs at the bases of the wings on each side. In daylight these insects (*Tettigoniidæ*) are very hard to see, owing to their protective green colour, but at night the males can be captured by cautiously tracking the sound to its source, and running down the grasshopper with an electric torch.

At our altitude of more than 7,000 feet, on the windy plateau-edge, and with low night temperatures, we were untroubled by malarial mosquitoes and little pestered in our tents at night even by ordinary gnats. Scorpions were common enough, and I had a narrow escape when Britton brushed one from my collar only just in time. Solifugids, a group of animals related to scorpions and spiders, have powerful shears on either side of the mouth, with which they kill insects and other prey; though they are harmless to man, I particularly dislike them, and it was a strange perversity which led small individuals to appear night after night on the inside of the roof of my, not Britton's, tent. One after another they went into tubes of spirit, but next night another solifugid would be on the tent roof.

Flowers, interesting and often lovely in themselves, as well as attractive to insects, abounded. Taking these as one of my special provinces (for we had to divide our labours), I made haste to collect as many kinds as I could before the dry weather had set in too long. Some of the most showy were species of *Barleria*, very prickly bushes of the acanthus order, with large trumpet-shaped blooms. Two kinds flourished in every waste place. One with prickly leaves had lilac-coloured flowers shading to deep purple in the centre (Phot. 28). The other,[1] with thorns in groups of three on the stems, had peach-coloured blossoms shading to deep orange. A beautiful orange gladiolus, yellow in the throat, grew along the waste strips at the backs of the terraced fields, among prickly plants related to nightshade, with fruits like little hard tomatoes. The scarlet blooms of a low-growing hibiscus,[2] four feet high or less, made brilliant points of colour in many a wayside thicket. Clumps of *Vernonia*, with flower-heads rather like small knapweeds, showed as patches of vivid magenta among a mixture of labiate herbs on a steep slope north of our camp. These are only a very few of the rich diversity of blossoms.

Every kind of wild flower was not, however, blooming at the end of the rains. Some were only in bud and opened with tantalising slowness weeks afterwards; for instance a plant (*Kalanchœ*) of the family *Crassulaceæ* with fleshy leaves and heads of orange flowers, and a bushy *Senecio* with clusters of little yellow flower-heads. The latter, a striking object, related to groundsels and ragworts, and also to the great tree-*Senecios* of the East African mountains, reaches a height of from four to eight feet. Thickets of a clematis much like "traveller's joy" sprawled over some of the stone terraces, but its foam of creamy flowers did not appear until December, when we saw it again in Southern Yemen. It was in this respect unlike another trailer over rocks and terraces, the sweet white jasmine,[3] which always displayed more or less blossom throughout our stay in Arabia. There were plants which we were destined never to see in bloom, such as an orchis with rosettes of spotted leaves. Probably the early summer months, about the opening of the rains, are the season when its flower-spikes brighten the patches of close turf on Jebel Jihaf.

Wadi Leje, the deep narrow valley south-west of our camp, which we explored near the end of our stay on Jebel Jihaf, is quite different

[1] *Barleria trispinosa.*   [2] *Hibiscus meidiensis.*   [3] *Jasminum officinale.*

from any of the other valleys in the mountain. In the middle it narrows to a gorge only about twenty feet wide, with almost vertical walls of bare rock. This ends abruptly in a sheer drop into a broader lower gorge, so that the whole valley is sharply divided into an upper and a lower part (as in the Wadi Dareija near Dhala). The precipice was impassable and the upper and lower parts of the wadi had to be visited separately on different days. Comparatively little sun penetrates the upper valley owing to its narrowness, and consequently there is scarcely any cultivation of grain. The few terraces, all near the head of the valley, are very small and irregularly shaped, but extremely neatly made. These little fields, where the long grass had just been mown, seemed like miniature alpine pastures in late summer.

The stream, apparently perennial, falls down a succession of rock slides and precipitous steps, on two of which, to our great surprise and delight, clumps of yellow primulas grew beside the stream, with their roots in the running water or in very damp soil. Later we found the plant at many places, extending as far north as the environs of San'a. We were, however, unprepared to see primulas in South-West Arabia, so that our first find is vividly impressed on the memory. In mid-October the main flowering was over, but the dead stalks showed that they bear five or six tiers of flowers, while the smaller lateral stalks still bore slender-throated deep yellow blooms. The stalks rise from rosettes of long narrow leaves, the younger of which are white with a mealy waxen efflorescence.[1]

A difficult scramble over boulders down the third and lowest step in the upper valley brought us to a rock face covered with maidenhair fern, down which the stream falls into a deep pool. Some large whirligig beetles (*Dineutes*) were gyrating on the surface of the water and caddis-flies were swept from the bushes and herbage at the sides. Wadi Leje was the first place at which any of this latter group of insects were taken, and the three kinds found there are among the very few hitherto collected in Arabia.

Beyond this pool the narrow gorge was dry on the surface, choked with boulders and bushes. From the edge of some huge rocks wedged into the extreme lower end of the upper ravine, a waterfall could be seen splashing down hundreds of feet of precipice into the lower valley. Britton descended a rock chimney on our alpine rope till he reached a

---

[1] This plant, *Primula verticillata*, was one of the many discoveries of Forskål, the botanist member of Niebuhr's expedition, who died in the Yemen in 1763. Some of the tiny black seeds collected by us germinated and so renewed the stock in several Botanic Gardens in Britain; where, however, this primula is a plant for the greenhouse, not the open.

lower projecting ledge, but could get no further. He was hauled up again, clutching a bunch of fronds, several feet long, of a fern [1] found hanging from a crevice beneath the overhanging rock-edge.

The few people working in the upper valley seemed to be secluded even from the other inhabitants of the mountain. On one of our visits a very small boy, who had gone into the fields with his father, dissolved into tears at the sight of two Europeans who tempted him to try chocolate. An older boy, a cowherd named 'Ali, was alarmed for the safety of his charges when Jam'a and the other Somalis fired at a target with Naji's rifle. We assured the boy that his cows were not the mark for our ammunition, while his small brother, seated on a ledge on the steep ravine-side, shouted shrill comments and warnings. While we lunched under a large acacia after our tiring scrambles in the narrow gorge, the wider, but deep, green valley above was the scene of various diversions. The three Somalis practised high-jumping over a turban cloth. Ahmed afterwards war-danced with 'Ali the askari, the two facing each other, each holding a *jambiya* aloft, till their gravity broke down in fits of laughter. Britton borrowed a sling from another boy, but sling practice ended in an accident. The boy's forehead was cut with a stone, but he bore no malice, and the damage was patched up with adhesive plaster and a rupee.

The slings (Phot. 20) used by these young goatherds and cowherds, and by those who protect the *dhurra* from the marauding baboons, are strongly and neatly plaited with strands of black and white goat's hair arranged in patterns. One which I have is a cord over six feet long, expanded in the middle into a curved pouch three inches wide. Other slings were made of a very tough white plaited cord, the fibre of which, we are told, is prepared from the leaves of aloe.

The visit to the lower gorge of Wadi Leje was our most arduous excursion on Jebel Jihaf. In altitude it lay only about 1,500 feet below our camp, but a long détour was needed to find any way of approach. First, a descent of about 700 feet led into the head of another terraced valley, watered by streams running from some pretty little falls overhung by bushes, maidenhair and other ferns. A long walk thence southward, up and down over stony ground and terraced fields, brought us to a place where the earth seemed to end abruptly in space. Looking down about 800 feet of very steep scree, covered with boulders and low thorny plants, I saw the lower Wadi Leje, and Britton, with 'Omar and 'Ali al Askari, seated at the bottom under a tree. They had gone in advance, while I climbed down more slowly with Ahmed and Naji; for the shouts of 'Ali, from below, to my men, not to bring the " sahib " down such a place, made us the more determined to reach

[1] *Pteris vittata.*

the valley-bed. We passed through a wide belt of low bushes [1] with hairy grey leaves, still showing some bright blue trumpet-flowers, though their blooming was nearly over. These were not prickly, but below them stretched thorny acacia scrub, and at length a few fields of *dhurra*, millet and onions, and the boulder-strewn stream-bed, nearly dry. Here our two parties reunited close to a solitary stone house.

At the head of the lower valley, between grand craggy cliffs and peaks, is a narrow cleft, marking the lip of the upper gorge where our rambles had been abruptly ended a few days earlier. The waterfall that we had seen descends, not from the upper gorge, but from a much greater height down the cliff-face on the south of the cleft. The angular head of the lower valley is filled with tall trees, wild-figs and acacias, forming almost a patch of high forest (Phot. 30).

Near at hand some brilliant sunbirds [2] darted from flower to flower round a thicket. The iridescent plumage of the males flashed like gems as they wheeled and turned in the hot sunshine, displaying amethyst or coppery-violet on the head, emerald and sapphire on the back and throat, and ruby across the lower breast. The females, on the other hand, are small and of a dull grey hue. This lonely valley-head, at about 5,600 feet, was evidently a favourite haunt of the sunbirds, for in the evening four or five of them had settled to roost in a single bush on the steep talus-slope. They were again met with in several places, as far north as the pass beyond Saiyani in Southern Yemen, nearly always in lonely rocky valleys in the middle altitudes.

The dwellers in the solitary house in lower Wadi Leje were bee-keepers. In their small garden stood a " battery " of seventeen hives, raised a few feet from the ground on a wooden platform, in a building consisting of three rough stone walls, the fourth side being open, and the whole roofed with brushwood (Phot. 31). The hives, long hollow cylinders laid horizontally and filled in at the ends with clay or plaster, were in four tiers, comprising respectively five, five, four and three hives, from the lowest to the highest tier.

These hives were strongly reminiscent of the type used in Egypt from at least as far back as 2600 B.C. till the present day. I cannot say whether the hives in Wadi Leje were long mud cylinders like the ordinary Egyptian hives, which are built up into batteries of seven or

---

[1] *Barleria Hildebrandtii*, a near relative of the bush shown in Photograph 28.

[2] A variety of the Abyssinian sunbird, *Cinnyris habessinicus*. The lovely birds of this family eat small insects as well as sucking the juices from flowers with their long bills and tongues ; in the latter habit, and in their iridescent colours, they are (despite the absence of any really close relationship) Old World counterparts of the humming-birds of America.

PHOTOGRAPHS 28 AND 29.
The pale lilac, purple-throated, trumpets of a prickly Barleria-*bush.*
The dwarf rock-pink of the Yemen.

PHOTOGRAPHS 30 AND 31.
*Gorge at the head of Wadi Leje; wild-fig trees lighted by the setting sun.
A battery of bee-hives in Wadi Leje.*

eight tiers, with sometimes twenty hives or more in the lower rows; or shorter, chimney-pot like cylinders of baked earthenware, such as are used for bee-hives in Cyprus. I think, rather, that they were made out of hollow tree-trunks, like those used in parts of Abyssinia, where they are hung in trees or under the thatched eaves of houses.

During our stay on Jebel Jihaf we sampled excellent local honey contained in gourds, given us by our friend Amir Haidara. The consumer has to overlook the dead bees, larvæ and other objects which pour with the sweet fluid from the little opening made in the gourd, which is stoppered by pushing a small, neatly excised square piece of the rind tightly into its place.

After our lunch-halt under a tree near the lone house and our survey of the hives, we set off light-heartedly in the afternoon for the waterfall. We underestimated the time needed to climb up the steep slopes of smooth bare rock down which the stream slid, and to cross the rougher rock and the stony grass-grown screes. But at length the head of the lower valley was reached, and we stood at the foot of the fall, where the water tumbled down sheer cliffs on to a very steep boulder-strewn slope. Flying spray made it difficult to examine the rock-face, where we had vainly hoped to find certain rare insects inhabiting waterfalls. The cliff was bare but for some wild-fig trees clinging to crevices, and sending down serpentine roots of great length.

At the bottom of the waterfall many leaves were covered with a calcareous deposit from the water, and near by was a small limestone cave.

Now, at about four o'clock, the other side of the valley was falling into deep shadow. Ahmed and 'Omar scaled the cliff and ran along ledges of the precipice like goats, to seek a shorter way back to camp. With the same object the askaris led me some way up an awful scree, for we had no wish to be benighted in this inaccessible ravine. There was, however, no practicable path, and nothing to do but reunite in a party and make our best pace down the valley, back to the lonely house. Then followed a race against the fast failing daylight, up the long rough talus-slope down which we had come at midday. I submitted to be partly pushed and dragged up by the Somalis, and none of us recked anything of garments rent by the innumerable thorns. Though dead tired when we reached the terraced fields at the top, we had still several miles of rough country to cover. Luckily we managed to hire donkeys, on which we rode to camp in the light of a full moon. Their saddles, without stirrups, tilted precariously to one side and the other, as our mounts ran along the very outermost edge of the high stone terraces, with a drop on one side of many feet to the next field below. We had to hold our legs out straight in front, native fashion, to avoid rocks and thorns. But we reached camp safely, and we had achieved our purpose of seeing the beautiful lower Wadi Leje and its waterfall.

Towards the north-eastern end of the mountain lay the dome-shaped summit which is its highest point, 7,840 feet. To reach it from the camp meant a long walk, though the difference in height was little more than 700 feet. Beyond the cultivated land, and after crossing the shoulders of some of the rocky peaks encircling the plateau, lay the most interesting parts of the ascent, along the foot of the sheer cliffs which top the north-western face of Jebel Jihaf (Phot. 21). Below these cliffs stretch steep slopes traversed by paths at an unpleasantly sharply tilted angle. At our first climb the tribal guards insisted on leading us round the outer face of a precipitous crag crowned by a small village. They assured us that this route was shorter and better. But the real reason of their preference was manifest when their continued shouts to the village above brought several of the villagers running nimbly down a cliff path, bearing cups and a pot of steaming coffee. Naturally, for so important a reason, a halt had to be made! Farther on, the path descended a rough natural rock-staircase between walls of rock, evidently a passage formed by erosion of a dyke of rock of softer consistency than the walls on either side. In the wet grit at the foot of these cliffs, where shade and moisture are greatest, among patches of green Selaginella, nestled some of the real alpine plants of South-West Arabia. Here we found for the first time a white stone-crop [1] and a pretty creeping gentianaceous plant,[2] with white wide-open flowers tinged beneath with purple. Here also were patches of the creeping campanula with mauve-blue flowers, which its original discoverer, Dr. Forskål, named the edible campanula [3] because its thick succulent roots were eaten by boys. (Though we did not hear of this custom, it is well-known, and a related species, the rampion,[4] from Mediterranean lands, was formerly cultivated in England for its thick roots, used either as a cooked vegetable or salad). In more sunny places, crevices in bare rock were brightened by the Yemen rock-pink [5] (Phot. 29), a compactly tufted plant with deep pink flowers on extremely short stalks. All these alpines were met with again on the mountain passes of the Yemen.

Beyond the rock-staircase the path to the summit curved round the uppermost field-terraces, which cling to the sides of a steep gully up to about 7,500 feet. Rank herbage beside the track was full of a tall meadow-rue [6] with little greenish flowers, almost over in late September and early October. A great spreading acacia on the top-

---

[1] A true *Sedum*.   [2] *Swertia polynectaria*.   [3] *Campanula edulis*.
[4] *Campanula rapunculus*.   [5] *Dianthus uniflorus*.   [6] *Thalictrum schimperianum*.

most terrace threw a shade most welcome during the hottest hours of a day spent working there.

Above the topmost terraces again, farther along the north-west face, lay a deep pool, far back in a very narrow cleft in the rock. Here the women from the highest mountain village drew their water, crossing a bare sheet of rock at a steep angle with vessels balanced on their heads. In this moist deep cleft we enriched our collection with two more kinds of ferns and a flower new to us, a kind of bugle,[1] white tinged with pale blue; also with delicate land-shells of a long narrow spiral shape.

To reach the extreme summit another path must be taken, round the inner, less precipitous, side of the dome. The top itself is a rough stony expanse, with low scrubby plants, bare patches of rock, and, on the north slope, stretches of close short turf. Few living things were visible; the only birds were a wheat-ear or two, the only butterflies a wall-brown and a small copper. On September 20th, however, some pools of rain-water still lying on the sheets of bare rock yielded to our nets water-beetles, water-bugs, fairy shrimps and certain fly-larvæ—one of those interesting catches of aquatic insects, all of which must either colonise these evanescent pools anew every monsoon season, or lie dormant, in one of their stages of development, in the dried-up mud during the winter months.

A few men and boys were watching the terraced fields of *dhurra* below, ready to drive off marauding baboons. These people led our servants and askaris to a rough stone shrine close to a sacred spring on the very edge of the stupendous mountain face which falls away between three and four thousand feet.

Deep chasms wind down from the summit to the north and north-east extremities of the mountain. The one lying in the latter direction presented a most wonderful sight, terrace upon terrace of tall, bright green *dhurra* stretching up its almost precipitous sides for a thousand feet or more, and clusters of stone towers crowning point after point of its jagged ridges (see Frontispiece). Beyond the foot-spurs of the mountain to the north and north-west lay, three to four thousand feet below, a great broad depression with an undulating floor; and beyond it again the mighty rampart of the Yemen highlands, with Qa'taba, a little dark brown frontier town, at their feet. The wide plain lying between, taken as a whole, appears to have no name; it is plateau country surrounded by mountains and through it runs the Wadi Tiban.

To the west the most striking and nearest of the Yemen mountains is Jebel Hesha (Phots. 32, 35). At the northern end of its huge mass

[1] *Ajuga bracteosa.*

there are lofty cliffs and three rounded peaks. On the middle summit glistens a little whitewashed shrine, venerated locally by the Arabs as the tomb of Eyyub, in other words the Old Testament Patriarch Job, for local Arab tradition claims this region as the Land of Uz.[1]

As this same great depression, separating us from the Yemen, could be seen from the edge of Jebel Jihaf quite close to our camp, we gazed longingly almost every day across it to the Yemen mountains. Jebel Hesha and its neighbours seemed, indeed, so near and yet so far away. For throughout our stay on Jihaf, and even when, in late October, we were in the Wadi Tiban within a mile of the frontier, we were still quite uncertain if we should ever enter the Yemen. No further word about our projected journey thither was received during our two months in the Amiri country. One morning on Jebel Jihaf, however, Jam'a told me that he had dreamed in the night. "Sahib," he said, "I dreamt you were in San'a and were talking to the Imam." I have no reason to think he merely fabricated the dream to cheer our drooping spirits, for during his seven months with us the excellent Jam'a never gave cause to doubt his word. In any case, the dream came true.

[1] See Chap. xix, p. 207. It may be added that the local Jews do not, apparently, agree with the Arabs in venerating the building on Jebel Hesha as Job's tomb.

PHOTOGRAPH 32.
From the summit of Jebel Jihaf towards Jebel Hesha and the brown ramparts of the Yemen.

PHOTOGRAPH 33.
Descent of the north-west face of Jebel Jihaf.

Chapter X

THE UPPER WADI TIBAN AND JEBEL HARIR

THE end of our stay on Jebel Jihaf meant the break up of the camp where we had lived nearly five weeks, and which we had come to regard, affectionately, as home. Our work on the mountain was finished, as far as such work ever can be on an expedition lasting only a few months. After final discussions with Amir Haidara, we had decided to descend the 3,000-foot precipice forming the north-west face of Jebel Jihaf, into the " great depression " between us and the mountains of the Yemen proper ; to camp near the upper waters of the Tiban, thence to trek round the base of the north-eastern end of Jebel Jihaf and to penetrate into the mountains east of Dhala, to the extreme eastern limits of the Amirate at Jebel Harir.

When long periods have to be spent in stationary camps, purchase or long-term hire of pack animals (the latter being the method I had employed years before when " on safari " in Abyssinia) is too costly. In the Amiri highlands, therefore, we simply hired for each move such means of transport as could be assembled locally. When we left the top of Jihaf our baggage, swollen by the collections made during our stay and by additional supplies brought up from Dhala, needed eleven camels, four pack-donkeys and ten porters.

Accordingly, on October 19th, the caravan straggled off. Four riding-donkeys were to be used, turn and turn about, by our Somalis and the Arab tribal guards. Amir Haidara again lent Britton and myself a horse and a mare, the latter with a foal running beside her. But, as these wise animals absolutely refused to budge with us on their backs when we reached the precipitous part of the descent, we took the hint, and walked till we reached the foot-spurs at the bottom of the precipice (Phot. 33).

What a climb down ! The point for which we were making is a thousand feet lower than Dhala, on the opposite side of the mountain, and the track leading up from Dhala is an easy incline by comparison. From our camp, first a drop of a few hundred feet into a little valley of small murmuring waterfalls, then up a ridge to the real brink of the mountain-wall. Then hundreds and hundreds of feet of very steep zigzag, in parts built up into rough steps with large stone blocks. The loaded camels, donkeys and men all came down without mishap, but it astonished me that there were no mules in the district, when they are so much used a little to the north, in the Yemen. A brief halt at the foot of the sheer cliffs enabled a " bag " of beetles to be hurriedly taken from wet grit, where spring-water oozed from the rock. A delicate little pink flower, never seen again on our journey, was found near by.[1]

There had been delays in starting, and, when the steep spurs at the foot of the sheer cliffs were reached, our new camping-ground was still some miles away, unattainable before nightfall. A hurried scamper on horses and donkeys, up and down over ridges and through thin scrub of thorny acacias, in the light of a rising full moon, brought us to a small village. The head-man, Sheikh Shaif, forewarned of our coming, led the way to a low building at the back of his tower-house, containing a large low room where the men of the village meet to smoke and talk. It was furnished with mats and carpets, and rough wooden stands intended for water-pipes served as tables for our evening meal. We were glad of the *kishr* provided by our host, the beverage made from coffee-husks by the poorer Arabs, who can seldom afford to use the actual coffee-beans; though rather watery compared to strong coffee, especially Arab coffee, it is pleasant enough. The heat, however, seemed so great after the keen air of the mountain-top that we were glad to sleep on the roof, wakened occasionally by the periodic loud braying of a donkey, and each time momentarily conscious of the brilliant moon hanging farther towards the west.

Next morning a short ride brought us to a site where camp was pitched, close to the village of Al Muriah. This was a poor place by comparison with the mountain hamlets we had left, a collection of low one-storey dwellings, clinging to the sides of rocky hillocks (Phot. 34). The country immediately round is stony semi-desert with sparsely scattered bushes, now almost leafless, and a little cultivation in the hollows between the stony ridges. At this much lower altitude, 3,800 feet, the heat in our tents reached 95° Fahrenheit. Moreover, during two out of our three days' stay a strong easterly wind blew, filling the afternoon air with dust-haze and obscuring the sharp outlines of Jebel Jihaf, besides covering all small apparatus and other articles with fine dust. As the village provided no suitable place for servants' quarters or kitchen, we gave up the second tent for that purpose. We were careful to use our mosquito-nets, as Anopheline mosquitoes, though not numerous, bit actively; they were visitors from one of the moister hollows, the floor of which, besides cultivation, contained patches of rank green scrub. Malaria is evidently prevalent, and the local

[1] A species of *Erythræa* (Centaury), possibly new to science.

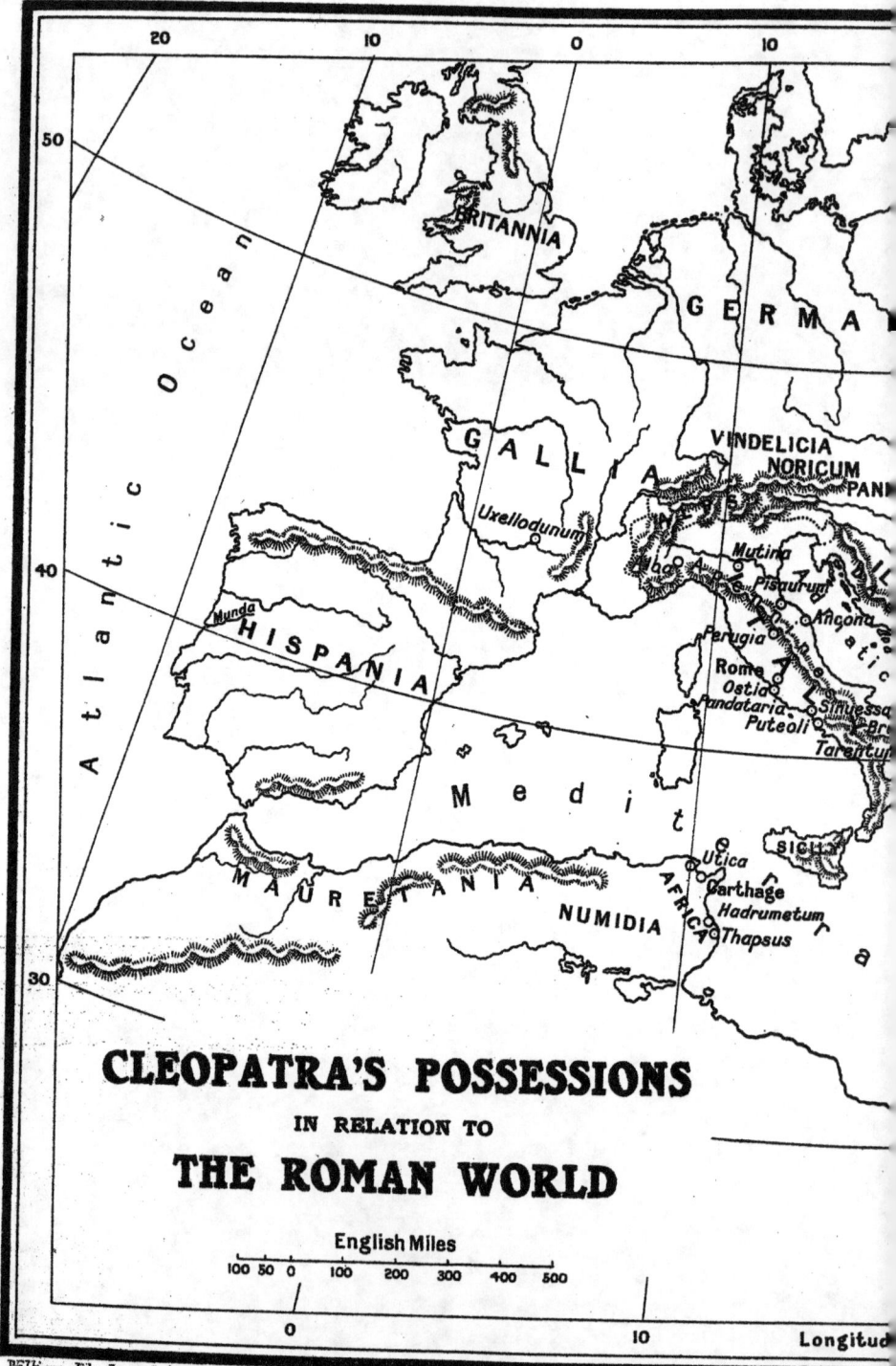

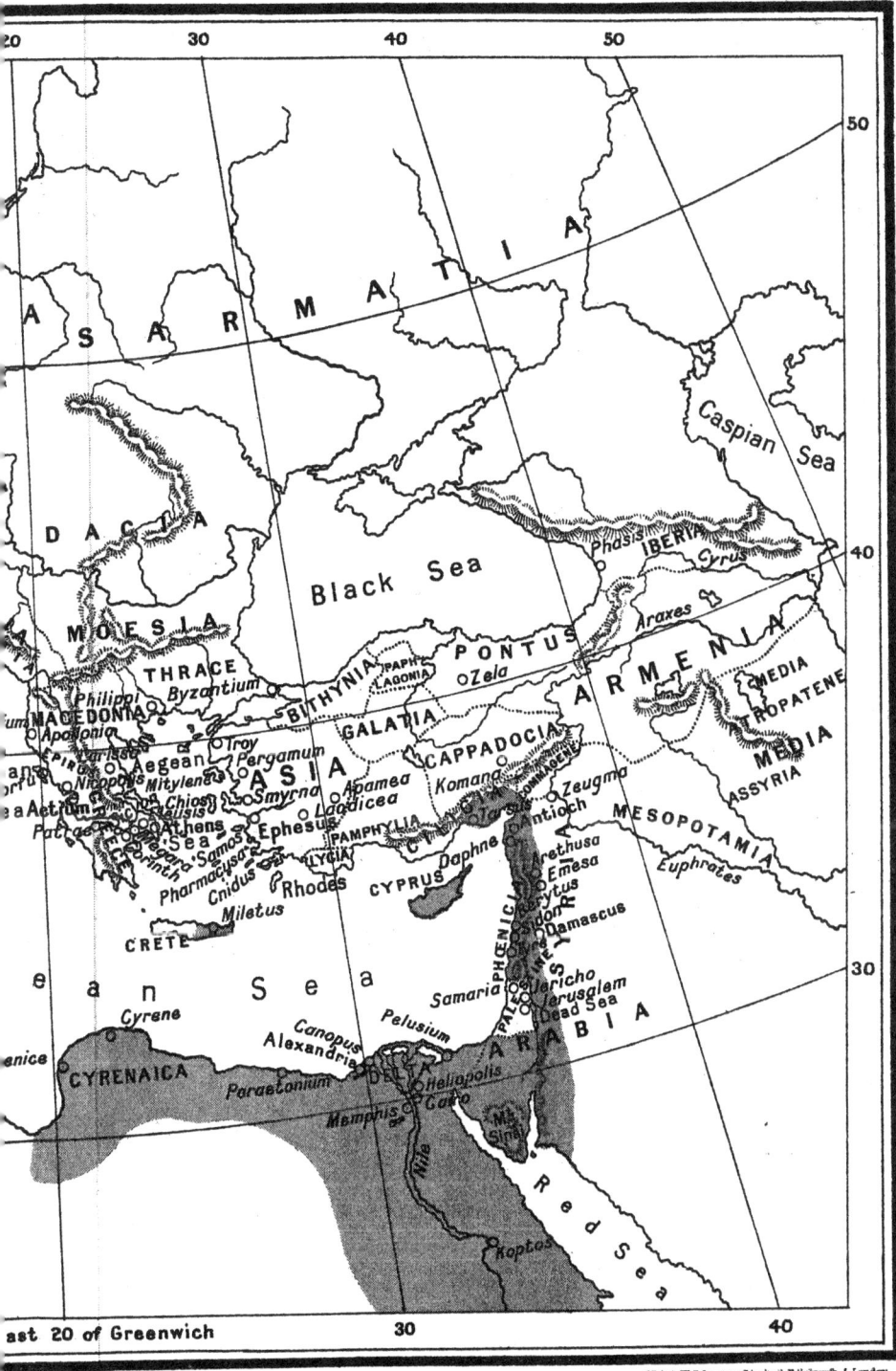

tribesmen look less healthy than those of the mountains. Altogether an unpleasant contrast to the bracing heights of Jihaf!

The only level place for a camping-ground was again the edge of a graveyard, while a little to the east stood the whitewashed tomb-mosque of one Weli Isma'il (seen in the middle-distance in Phot. 111), a saint of local fame. This shrine, sometimes the object of pilgrimages from the surrounding district, has a cupola, and conventional designs and Arabic words round its walls. The walled enclosure outside has a deep tank for ablutions, and a smaller, rougher building in one corner. Outside is a second *qubba*, smaller and plainer. From 3,000 feet above, on Jebel Jihaf, this group of little buildings, which we had seen almost daily, looked curiously like an aeroplane standing on the ground.

Sheikh Shaif came from his own village to see us at Al Muriah. Though a rather grubby little man, he wished to do everything possible for our comfort. He brought with him his two little boys (Phot. 36), very brilliant in variegated turbans and girdles, fringed and tasselled. The elder, though only about ten or eleven, carried a rifle. The boys had in attendance a little servant (Phot. 37), much darker-skinned and curly-headed, whose face bespoke a cheerful impish disposition. Over tea I showed the Sheikh's sons illustrated papers several weeks old ; military subjects, pictures of the war in China and parades of German soldiers, excited most interest.

The real object of our stay at Al Muriah was far more agreeable than the immediate surroundings of our camp. About half a mile west, a steep descent led to the Tiban river, flowing in a valley between earth cliffs somewhat under a hundred feet high. Here the running water tempered the heat, and a refreshing coolness was noticeable on coming down from the hot stony dusty ground above. The valley contained few trees, but tall reeds, long grass and other herbage fringed the banks, and dense thickets of low bush date-palm [1] stood a little back from the water's edge. The river itself recalled a trout-stream, murmuring among stones and flowing past shingly patches. In the water waded one or two brown birds of that strange-looking species, the hammerhead,[2] so named from the form of the tuft of feathers projecting at the back of the head. Related to herons and egrets, it ranges widely over Arabia and large parts of Africa.

Like the hammerheads, we also waded in the Tiban. I had to ford and re-ford the river several times (though on some crossings, Ahmed Mahmūd insisted on carrying me, amid much merriment). I was afterwards glad that I had not remained barefooted when working on the banks between the crossings ; for my companion, who

[1] *Phœnix reclinata.*   [2] *Scopus umbretta.*

waded for a long time nearly up to the knees, turning over stones in his search for aquatic insects, later suffered rather badly from sunburn about the knees. His perseverance was, however, rewarded by the capture not only of insects but of a number of small fish, with no better bait and hook than cheese and a bent pin. These fishes proved to be a species, previously undescribed, of the barbel family, with short whisker-like appendages above and below the mouth. They belong to a genus (*Garra*) with many representatives extending across the Orient from Southern China to Abyssinia. Britton later discovered another new form of *Garra* in a cistern south of San'a, at the head of a stream draining towards the deserts of the interior. Isolation in different valley-systems may well have contributed towards the evolution of a number of closely-related but distinct species in South Arabia.

Near the river I experienced for the first time how rich a yield of insect booty could be obtained from low, grey-foliaged, broom-like bushes of *Indigofera*, wild indigo (then in pod), by shaking over the net. The same treatment was used with success on thickets of tamarisk, till a hasty retreat had to be made from swarms of large angry wasps, which were chewing the bark off the stems as material for their nests. I had already been chased and stung by one of these wasps [1] on Jebel Jihaf, but, applying neat brandy from a pocket-flask immediately, I found the sting of the wasp, as large as a medium-sized hornet, much less painful than I expected.

During all our stay in this valley we were hoping to throw light on the presence or otherwise of an African tsetse fly [2] which was discovered in the Wadi Tiban more than thirty years earlier, at the time of the Anglo-Turkish Boundary Commission. The capture of the fly then was the solitary recorded occurrence of any of these devastating insects outside Tropical Africa. We found no trace of the fly, but our penetration for this purpose of the rather dense dry scrub on the far (west) side of the river brought us for the first time into contact with the monstrous 'adan [3] in full flower. This bush or small tree—for, though usually about four feet high, some were seen in the Yemen lowlands reaching twelve feet—has hideous swollen stems, as though afflicted with elephantiasis. At this season it was leafless, but here and there a bush was covered with handsome crimson or deep pink trumpets, paler in the middle, and with long fruits filled with seeds and silken hairs.

No natural history object, however important, could be allowed to make us stray far on that west side of the Tiban. A few hundred yards might have had serious consequences, for the Yemen frontier was very close. The triple dome of Jebel Hesha (Phot. 35) was more

[1] *Vespa orientalis*. [2] *Glossina tachinoides*. [3] *Adenium obesum*.

tantalisingly near than ever. Our camp at Al Muriah was visited by Yemeni tribesmen desiring medical treatment, and Britton's skill was called into operation, in the application of kaolin poultices and in other ways. But had we violated the frontier without a permit, our chances of ever travelling through the country might easily have been ruined.

Accordingly, on October 23rd, we struck camp and trekked a long way, some twenty miles, to the foot of Jebel Harir. Our route lay all round the eastern end of Jebel Jihaf, then up the deep valleys penetrating the wall of mountains east of Dhala plateau: first over the stony scrub-covered ridges of the mountain-girt plain, and across flat-bottomed hollows where rich *dhurra* crops, tall and fat-looking, grew. In one such hollow, containing a marsh with standing water in a deep pit and thick copses of tamarisk, our Somalis bought camel-milk from herdsmen in charge of a herd kept only for milking. Farther on, round the base of the eastern end of Jihaf, the country changed to pleasant flat land where harvesting was over, and the fields of *dhurra* stubble were dotted with large shady '*ilb* trees (*Zizyphus*). The final stage, striking eastwards into the foothills and deep valleys, was mostly hidden from us by oncoming darkness.

Here was the trouble! Probably the trek should have been spread over two days, but the " locals " thought they could cover the distance in one. Despite very early rising, and the assembly of twelve camels, a pack-donkey and six or eight riding-donkeys, the loading of so much paraphernalia took a long time, and we had hardly started from Al Muriah before a camel bolted and hurled off its load. This meant the substitution of another camel, with much vociferous argument between '*askaris* and camel-men. So when, late in the day, we got deep into the eastern mountains, we and our servants were racing ahead against the darkness. The moon rose too late to help us. As to the riding-donkeys (I had changed on to one with a native saddle and no stirrups, a quicker beast than that on which I had started with my European saddle), these wonderful little animals carried us swiftly and safely over ground more and more broken, up and down the sides of steep ravines, long after we could no longer distinguish rocks and thorny bushes. They seemed like cats in the darkness. The camel-train was left far behind and, for all we knew, lost in a maze of valleys. The deep wadi resounded with the stentorian shouts of Naji (the chief '*askari*), bawling into the night "*fain el gimāl?*" the local pronunciation of *wēn al jimāl?* (where are the camels?). At length we found ourselves on top of a declivity so steep that even the donkeys could not go down it with us on their backs. But here appeared men with lights, and we were led to the solitary house of a peasant, where the little low upper rooms were given up to us, and we slept on the flat roof of the lower part of the house. Beneath us a cow bumped its back against the low ceiling of a ground-floor room. The baggage-train arrived at last, too late to pay the men off and send them home with their camels till next morning. The following night, also spent on the roof of the lone house, we had to cover our bedding with waterproof groundsheets against a chill drizzle, the first taste of rain for weeks.

The marked individuality of donkeys did not always manifest itself in behaviour as good as that of the " mounts " figuring in the episode just told. At the other end of the scale was one which I hired on an excursion from the Rest-House at Dhala to the Wadi Dareija (p. 41). I could do nothing with this animal, and Jam'a, though used to the riding and pack animals of this part of the world, had no better success. With apparent intention it took every wrong path, to one side or the other—any way *except* the track to Wadi Dareija. It would only run with its head right down between its fore feet. I thought it had some irritating insect hovering round its nose, or some ailment in the nostrils, but could find nothing. Finally the ass lay down quite deliberately across the path, on its right side, curled its legs under it, and gave us out of the left eye a look which was everything short of speech. We tried no more, but walked. Those with me pronounced this donkey " *mignoon* " (more correctly *majnūn*, " mad "), but it was far from insane !

The reason for spending two nights at the lonely house at the foot of Jebel Harir, instead of pitching our tents the morning after our arrival, was the difficulty of deciding, in this case, *where* to pitch them. We had intended to camp on the mountain-top, as on Jebel Jihaf, for Harir is nearly as high (7,790 feet as against 7,844). But the formation of Jebel Harir is very different. Instead of igneous rock, it is a huge block of sandstone with very steep and difficult sides and a steeply tilted table-top consisting largely of sheets of bare rock acres in extent. Although there is a good water-supply on the top, and the amazing ingenuity of the people, in building up the scanty soil into little groups of fields within stone walls, enables a large population to dwell there in several villages of stone houses, yet it was quite a different proposition to carry up all our camp kit and apparatus. No loaded pack-animal can climb the mountain. Men from the villages would have come down and carried up the minimum of baggage necessary. But, having regard to all we heard of the mountain-top, we decided to go up first and see it for ourselves.

Therefore, on October 24th, after sending away the men, camels and donkeys which had brought us from Al Muriah, we climbed Jebel Harir, a proceeding tiring enough after our long trek of the day before.

PHOTOGRAPHS 34 AND 35.

Camp at Al Muriah, near the Tiban river.
Striking camp at Al Muriah; Jebel Hesha in the background.

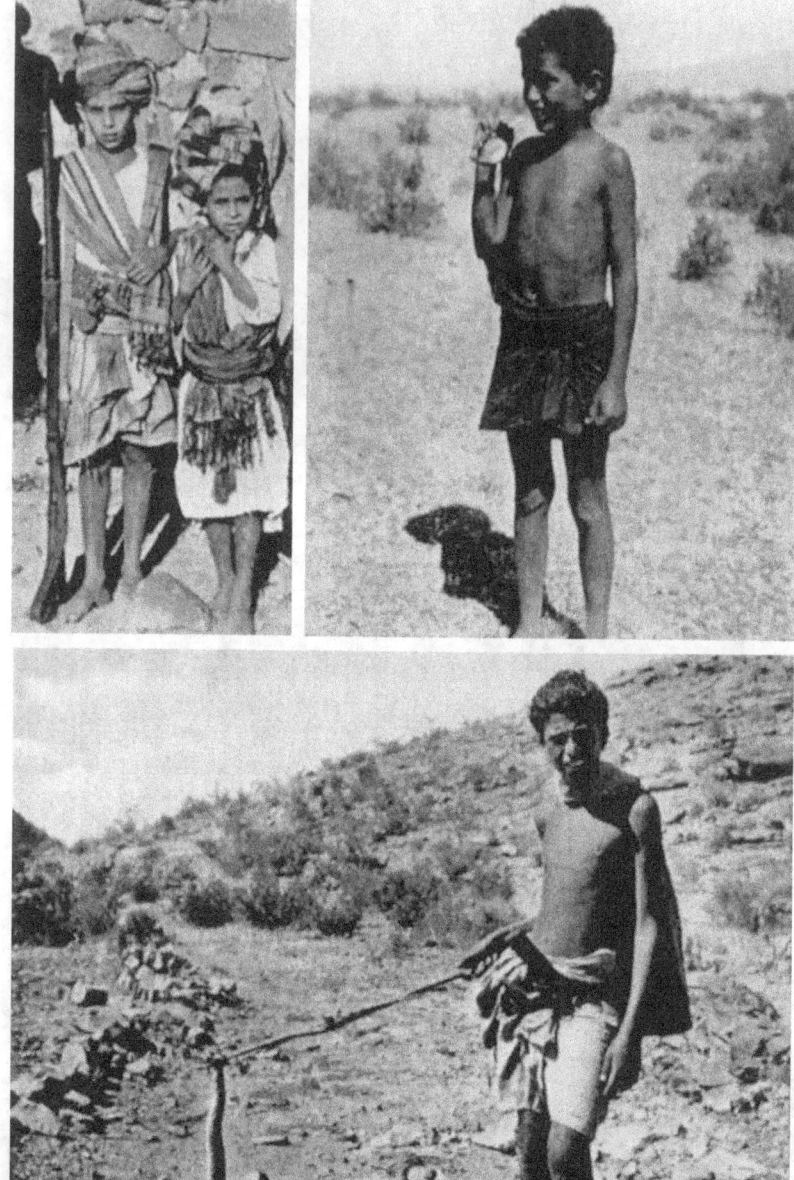

PHOTOGRAPHS 36, 37 AND 38.
The two sons of Sheikh Shaif and their servant.
A tribesman of Jebel Halmein brings a live puff-adder in a cleft stick.

It meant an exceedingly rough climb of 1,700 feet, clambering from rock to rock most of the way, from the lonely house to the western edge of the table-top. Thence a long walk upwards across a succession of sloping sheets of bare sandstone, rising some hundreds of feet more to the highest point on the far (eastern) side. Here at the summit, on the very edge of a mighty precipice, almost terrifying in its abruptness, stands the tomb-shrine of a local saint, a *weli* (Phot. 40). Hence, also, an unforgettable view (Phot. 39). As a chaos of grim, savage mountains, sharp and jagged, range beyond range, it equalled anything I have ever seen. The effect was heightened by great masses of cloud scudding across the sky on a high easterly wind, casting deep moving shadows over the many brown and tawny hues of the serrated ranges, and the faint haze of green scrub. For all the country eastward looks of a drier type than the Amiri highlands, with little cultivation in sight, only some terraced fields clinging to the sheer sides of the ranges here and there. We were gazing over disturbed districts beyond the jurisdiction of the Amirs of Dhala, the country of Jebel Halmein and part of Yafa. More will be said of them below.

Meanwhile, after eating the food we had carried up, at a point a few yards from the brink of the eastern precipice, we were constrained to partake of a second lunch in the upper room of a stone house, two or three storeys high. Our host was head-man of all the Harir district. Under his hospitable roof I had four cups of good coffee flavoured with ginger, and tried to do justice to hard-boiled eggs, chicken, chupatties and honey. A large earthenware vessel with glowing charcoal and incense was passed round, and each person made a movement of taking a handful of the smoke and putting it up to his nostrils. Here we saw one of the original uses of incense, from which is derived much of its ceremonial usage in various forms of worship, a symbol of a welcome extended to guests partaking of a common feast. Later, in the Arab quarter of San'a, an old man was to be seen carrying a smoking censer suspended from an iron arm on a long staff with a spike at the bottom. Apparently he visited tea-houses or hired himself out to parties, planting his pole and censer in the earthern floor.

At our entertainment on Jebel Harir, Naji sat puffing at a *huqqa*, with a group of men on either side of him. We were introduced to his father—for all our four *'askaris* were natives of Harir, or related to its inhabitants—a garrulous old man who claimed to be ninety, and told impossible stories of having ridden up and down equally impossible places on a donkey. His loquacity was such that we privately dubbed him an old pest.

The head-man's village, almost a small town, boasted two mosques roofed with cupolas. Indeed, the top of Jebel Harir struck me as one of the most extraordinary places I have ever seen. So many people living perched on this tilted rock-table, including many who have never been anywhere else ; no cultivation save on the little patches of built-up soil ; scarcely a domestic animal in sight, owing to the difficulty (aforesaid) of getting them up or down the mountain.

A different return path to the western edge led past what must be an important part of the water-supply of the mountain-top. This fair-sized pond, in a cleft in the rocks, fringed with clumps of willow-herb [1] and a handsome fern,[2] is a pretty place, which proved then and later a good collecting spot. The descent from the edge was made by a much less difficult track than that followed in ascending. Nevertheless, the tribal guards insisted on leading straight across huge sheets of bare rock-*glacis*, tilted at most uncomfortably steep angles. There was no real need, and at my second ascent of Jebel Harir eleven days later, knowing the land better, I prevailed on them to go round these bare and slippery spots, by paths rough and stony, but offering more foothold to one shod in European footgear.

After our first ascent we quickly decided not to haul camp kit up the mountain. So on October 25th we moved from the lone house and pitched camp a little lower down. Local people carried the numerous bales and packages left by the camel-train to the spot chosen. When the time came to pay them, a sturdy little girl was just as much to the fore as boys and men in claiming her due.

Our new camp, where we stayed nearly a fortnight, lay at an altitude of about 5,200 feet. The tents faced an expanse of level *dhurra*-stubble fields, dotted with big '*ilb* trees and hemmed in by rocky foot-spurs of Jebel Harir. One such ridge rose into a " kopje " immediately behind the tents. To one side was a graveyard, once more ! Servants and '*askaris* erected a booth made of branches and bundles of dry *dhurra*-stems, in which to cook and sleep.

Jebel Harir is some miles east of Jebel Jihaf, and dry conditions seemed to have set in longer. The little white, mauve-tinged gentianaceous flower,[3] first seen on Jihaf, was found again on the summit of Harir, but much more stunted, and only maintaining a hold in crevices of stone walls round the raised fields. Other plants were quite different from any we had seen before, doubtless partly owing to the different nature of the rock. For example, the giant bush-knapweed [4] reached a height of six to eight feet in sheltered crannies. With its great purple flower-heads, and leaves showing a silvery underside when blown by the wind, it is a noble weed. Like the bush-*Senecio* seen on Jebel Jihaf, it ranks as a giant mountain representative of a group of

---

[1] *Epilobium hirsutum*.   [2] *Pteris dentata*.   [3] *Swertia polynectaria*.
[4] *Centaurea maxima*, another of Forskål's many discoveries.

plants which in the lowlands attain only a modest size. This assumption of giant dimensions by various plants is a particular feature of the high mountains of East Africa, and the South-West Arabian forms may be regarded as outlying examples.

Much of our most profitable work was done, however, not on the top or the steep slopes of the mountain, but in deep narrow wadis radiating from its foot. Here were dense thickets of the dwarf date-palm, bushes and scrub. Here water from the rains lingered in pools. On their edges Britton made some of his most interesting discoveries by washing out small beetles from the silt, in shallow metal pans raided from the camp kitchen. Wild life in these deep ravines was diversified by the presence of tortoises in the pools, of hammerheads (see p. 65) wading in the water, and of game-birds, black-headed chikore, about the cliffs.

A low cave in sandstone rock not far behind our camp was explored for bats and for cave-haunting spiders and insects. The very steep upward slope of the smooth sandstone floor, offering no foothold, rendered this far from easy. I had to cling by one arm to a projection about twelve feet up the slope, and use the other arm to examine the further recesses with an electric torch. Even Britton and the agile bare-footed Ahmed Maḥmūd found it difficult to hold on, and the only way to come out was to sit in single file and slide down, putting on the brake by pushing our hands against the low roof—an operation which roused Ahmed's merry Somali nature to much laughter. Our efforts were rewarded by several interesting finds; among them three species of bats, all new records for the district, and one not previously found outside Africa.

For four days and nights I tried hard to rear a wild-cat kitten. A grey spotted tabby, found by a tribesman, it was still blind and very small. Even in that stage, however, the cat showed signs of a fierce and intractable nature. It was induced to suck diluted cow's milk through the perforated rubber end of a pipette, but it did not live. I would have liked to add a wild cat to a small menagerie of local beasts and birds then kept by Captain Hamilton at Dhala, where we had been fascinated by a lynx kitten and a ratel. After the death of the little wild cat, another tribesman, to console us, brought a young domestic cat. The Arabian variety is much like the Abyssinian cat, thin and small-headed, with sharply pointed nose and ears. This animal was older and quite tame, and we would gladly have kept it, had our movements made this possible.[1]

[1] Incidentally, the word by which a tame cat is addressed in this part of Arabia, *bizz* or *bizza* (perhaps short for *bazzuna*), sounds much like *puss*. Though the latter word is correlated in some dictionaries with Gælic *pus*, and Dutch *poes*, we heard the

Though our main business was always to collect insects and other very small animals, we did make some interesting additions to our small collection of vertebrates. A man who claimed special skill in snake-catching brought alive a long striped snake. This form, rare in Arabia, is greyish-brown with yellow and black markings lengthwise. Britton had been specially hoping to get a specimen, so we were glad when one appeared at last. This snake is an Arabian variety [1] of a species widely distributed in Africa, and called in South Africa the Brown House-Snake. It was probably wider spread in Arabia in former periods, when a moister climate prevailed. The cobras found on Jebel Jihaf were not seen or heard of at Jebel Harir, where, on the other hand, puff-adders are numerous. We wondered whether the different nature of the rock in the two mountains is connected with this apparent difference in the local distribution of snakes (Note A, p. 238).

We did not come on a puff-adder ourselves, but several were brought to us by tribesmen. Britton's enthusiasm led him to kill and skin these, as well as dissecting them to search for internal parasites. We had then cause to regret that the remains were not immediately burnt or buried, as we could scarcely approach our own tents for the clouds of large, loudly and angrily buzzing wasps [2] which immediately appeared, swarming to the snake-meat.

A tribesman of Jebel Halmein (Phot. 38) was much annoyed that we would not buy, for more rupees than we were prepared to give, the large living puff-adder which he brought in a cleft stick. It was not the only time that we found it difficult to convince snake-catchers that the object of our search was not venomous reptiles of well-known species! This Halmeini, however, took our refusal as a personal affront to the whole of his country and tribe.

His was one of the wild districts over which we had gazed eastwards from the summit of Jebel Harir. There, out of reach of the strong arm of the Amir of Dhala, lay, immediately to the south-east and east, the Jebel Halmein country; beyond it, in a north-easterly direction, the confines of the Yafa Sultanates. All this chaos of wild ranges, sharp and jagged, intersected by deep narrow valleys, constitutes one of the most serious problems for the Aden Government. This region has no single Arab ruler strong enough to maintain order, as in the more favoured Amiri country. Its many chieftains, despite the high-sounding titles of some of them, could not (or would not) restrain their wild tribesmen from intertribal strife, highway robbery on caravan

---

opinion that its various forms came into the West European languages, centuries ago, from the Near or Middle East. We do not recall hearing the word *dimm* used for a cat.

[1] *Boædon lineatus arabicus.*   [2] *Vespa orientalis.*

routes, and sometimes also defiance of the Government. In 1937, at any rate, the Aden Government was much too short-handed, and disposed of forces far too small, to attempt direct administration. With the subsequent increase in the number of Political Officers and the raising of the Government Guards, it is to be hoped that a new and better phase has set in. Several striking incidents related to us showed that some of these wild mountain-clans were ready enough to adopt a peaceable way of life, granted a supreme Government strong enough to prevent them " losing face " among their neighbours by giving up marauding habits practised so long as to have become traditional. If the arm of the Government is so strong that you literally *cannot* continue to live on border forays and highway robbery, neighbouring tribes cannot laugh at you for settling down as law-abiding pastoral folk!

As things were in 1937, we heard a good deal about intertribal warfare and border raids. A friendly 'Aqil,[1] head-man of a small village on the lower spurs of Jebel Harir, told stories of the Halmein cattle-stealers and their route along a valley near our camp. The trouble was evidently not all on one side, for 'Ali, our *'askari*, admitted having helped himself to someone's goats in Halmein country. The village 'Aqil further demonstrated how he would snipe at an enemy from a " hide ", a semi-circular breastwork of rough stone built up under a steeply overhanging rock. Such an ambush would be difficult enough to see, when stones and cliffs are all of the same colour. An epic was also related of a Harir man who had accounted for seven Halmeinis before being himself overpowered.

It is not surprising, therefore, that our escort were anxious about our safety. While our four original *'askaris* went on leave for a few days to their families in villages on the mountain, we had four substituted from among the local people. The chief of these, whom we called " Naji the second " (he had the same name as our original Naji, though unrelated) asked the local head-man on the mountain to supply extra guards. At his request I wrote to Dhala, whence Amir Haidara sent orders for ten extra guards to be provided each night. The only hitch occurred one night when two parties of ten arrived together, and a noisy dispute followed as to whose turn it was. However, we had pickets posted all round the camp, including one in a commanding position under an overhanging rock at the top of the hillock behind the tents. The danger may not have been as imminent as Naji II feared. After the return of our old *'askaris*, 'Ali did fire in the darkness at what he took to be a man, who refused to answer his

---

[1] 'Aqil, literally " wise man ", is used as a tribal title in this part of Arabia, principally to denote the head of an important subdivision of a tribe.

challenge. But it was doubtful if any real marauder approached, and 'Ali came in for much chaff and laughter.

Stories, not always believed by the tellers, were also told us of spirits, jinn or 'afrit. One of our *askaris* related how he had met a jinnee in the form of a woman, who had slapped his face and caused contortion of the features. But according to his fellows this jinnee was a respectable married woman who had retaliated when he tried to press his attentions too far.

With the beginning of Ramadhan during our stay at the foot of Jebel Harir, the nights in camp became noisy. The three Somalis and the *askaris* observed the fast strictly each day, but, besides breaking their fast after sunset, they awoke and had a meal before dawn, accompanied by much chatter. The fast really started on November 3rd that year, but the local people did not know this, and began one or two days late. The beginning and end of Ramadhan depend on the New Moon being actually seen in either case, a feat not always easy in a remote and confined valley, where skies, too, may be cloudy. I settled the matter, which was at last referred to me, as well as I could, by consulting the date of the New Moon in my Cambridge Pocket Diary.

Our Somalis kept the observances of Islam with exemplary devotion, not only day by day as far as possible wherever we were camped or whatever excursion we were making, but attending the Friday midday prayers whenever a mosque was within reach. So Jam'a, in particular, was rather disgruntled at finding he had begun the fast a day late, and would have to add a day's fast at the end of Ramadhan. He had already remarked on the difficulty of finding the right direction to face at the times of prayer, and had complained that the Arabs on Jebel Jihaf did not face Mecca correctly. Here again I tried to help him out with my maps and compass. But, during the opening days of Ramadhan at Jebel Harir, Somali servants and Arab *askaris* held a corporate service close to the camp each evening at sunset. They stood in one or two rows facing north-north-west to the Ka'ba, with one man in front as reader and leader, while the rest intoned responses in unison.

Occasionally we had music in a lighter vein, later in the evening, round one of the several camp-fires—and fires were wanted by the guard for warmth, apart from other reasons, in a place where, though the altitude was only 5,200 feet, the temperature fell as low as 43° Fahrenheit during one of our earlier nights (October 26th–27th). The performer of this lighter music was the genial jovial *askari*, Ahmed Hādi, whose rather high voice poured forth songs with almost countless short verses. He accompanied himself, though provided with no better instrument than a paraffin tin, by thrumming on it with his fingers in perfect rhythm, the tempo increasing sharply at a particular point in each verse.

When back at the Dhala Rest-House, for the last few days spent in clearing up before our quick and uneventful return to Aden on November 11th, we were apprised each evening of the ending of the day's fast by the firing of two old pieces, not quite simultaneously; one from the castle at Dhala itself, the other from the Yemen frontier town of Qa'taba, on the far side of Jebel Jihaf. And the booming of those two sunset guns must close my reminiscences of our two happy months in the Amiri country.

Chapter XI

THE HOT SPRINGS OF HUWEIMI. ENTRY TO THE YEMEN

BACK in Aden from the Amiri mountains, we were still uncertain if we should ever enter the Yemen. A letter had been sent during October to the Imam by Colonel Maurice C. Lake, the acting head of the Government since Sir Bernard Reilly had gone on leave to England. No answer being vouchsafed, the Aden Government telegraphed a request for a reply. This, when it arrived more than a week after our return, seemed completely to shatter our hopes. It was a polite but apparently final refusal, in which the King did not deny having originally granted permission to visit " known " places, but said that he could not allow us to explore lonely or " forsaken " places, and had never yet permitted any European to roam over the high mountains of his country. We had made the mistake of asking too explicitly for leave to visit high altitudes ! Nevertheless, some other reason, some political workings on the Imam's general dislike of European penetration, were probably hidden behind this excuse.

The disappointment was bitter, yet all hope was not extinguished. A request was telegraphed that we might at least be allowed to visit Ta'izz. A further period of suspense followed, and November had nearly run out, before a reply telegram announced that we should be welcomed at the southern capital, on condition that our movements were strictly supervised. This concession sufficed for the moment, hope soared again, and preparations for the new journey were quickly in train.

Meanwhile the weeks spent at Aden were too fully occupied for dejection. We settled into our " base " in Captain Seager's house at Khormaksar once more, and also enjoyed for some days Colonel Lake's hospitality at Government House, formerly the Residency, overlooking the sea from a cliff-top south-east of Steamer Point. Many registered parcels of precious specimens and undeveloped films were despatched to England. The kindness of Miss Margaret Hensley, Miss Vivien Jameson and Miss Nora Rasell led to our seeing more than hitherto of the old Aden in the Crater. Long hours and arduous work in the office of an important business house under French

PHOTOGRAPHS 39 AND 40.
View east over the Halmein and Yafa country, from the summit of Jebel Harir.
Tomb of a saint on the summit of Jebel Harir.

PHOTOGRAPHS 41 AND 42.

Ta'izz from the north, with Jebel Sabir in the background.
View from the roof of the 'Amil's Guest-house in Ta'izz.

proprietorship had not prevented these ladies from exploring the byways of Aden and learning much about its natural products and its history. The memories then garnered, as well as our visits to Lahej and its Sultan, and to Al Huseini, have already been told.

The New Moon of December 2nd was not visible to the Muslim watchers till the following evening, when the firing of guns announced the end of Ramadhan and the beginning of the 'Id al Fitr. Regarding strictly our work, I was glad when both fast and feast were over. Not that we would have interfered with these observances for any consideration; but (though our Somalis did their best) fasting all day and sleeping through large parts of it, and then turning night into day, do not give the best results in a task such as ours.

The most important preparation for the journey to the Yemen (as distinct from any needed before travelling in the Aden Protectorate) was the purchase of a large number of riyāls [1] or Maria-Theresa dollars. These silver coins were manufactured privately in Europe and exported to the countries in which they are still the unit of currency. In Abyssinia, years before, I had experienced how their value on the market would fluctuate from day to day, and the need of buying considerable amounts when they were cheap. In South-West Arabia the fluctuations seemed less frequent, though of considerable extent. Soon after our arrival at Aden we bought a thousand riyāls at the rate of about 1½ rupees per riyāl, but in San'a, five to six months later, they were obtainable at scarcely more than a rupee apiece. It is thus evident that these heavy silver pieces, as large as four-shilling pieces and of the nominal value of two shillings, had an actual value much less (reckoning the rupee at its standard value of 1s. 4d.).

What memories are conjured up by these Maria-Theresas, or riyāls, or Imadis (the official name in the Yemen), or simply " bir " (silver) in Amharic, as my Abyssinians used to call them! Memories of going to the bank in Addis Ababa with two men bearing rifles and a porter carrying a big sack, to draw sometimes as much as a thousand dollars; of the sacks full of thick shining discs, packed away in steel mule- or camel-trunks (and the care to keep these always locked); or of a boot-bag pressed into service as a purse, to hold enough dollars for some short trek of a few days. The riyāls bought in Aden were quite newly minted and brilliant, with the image of the Empress Maria-Theresa, dated 1780. In Abyssinia, some silver pieces were in circulation showing Menelik II wearing the triple tiara of Ethiopia, part of a coinage which the old Emperor had caused to be struck. In the

---

[1] *Riyāl* is almost certainly derived from the Spanish *real*, signifying originally a big Spanish silver piece. In the East the meaning was later extended to cover large silver coins of several countries, including the Austrian thaler (dollar).

Yemen genuine old pieces are occasionally met with, of the time of Maria-Theresa or her successors. The small currency of the Yemen is minted locally. Forty " bukhshas " (bakhsheesh) or " bogaches " are equivalent to a riyāl. There are copper half-bukhshas and bukhshas nearly the same size as halfpence and pence, and small silver pieces worth respectively two, four and ten bukhshas. The last is, of course, a quarter-dollar, but there is no piece equivalent to half a dollar. All these small pieces bear designs and calligraphic inscriptions, but no effigy of any person.

Another important preparation consisted in repairs to footballs. They were the worse for wear after matches on the parade-ground at Dhala, and kicking about in the evenings near our camp on Jebel Jihaf. Jam'a, who had visited San'a before, was anxious to play football there, if we ever reached the capital. His wish was fulfilled.

Finally, early on December 8th, a car for ourselves and the Somalis, accompanied by a very large and modern lorry packed with our gear, left Khormaksar. The owner-driver of the lorry, a short, rather stout, Aden Arab named Mas'ūd 'Awadh, of an open friendly countenance, proved indeed a good friend. The one hundred and twenty-eight miles to Ta'izz could have been covered in a day, had we not arranged to halt and investigate the hot springs at Huweimi, still within the confines of the Protectorate. Our old road was followed till some way north of Lahej, then, instead of taking the track a little east of north to Al Milah and Dhala, our route curved to the left, north-west, skirting the north (left) bank of Wadi Tiban. On the right, near the fork of the Tiban into the Wadi Kabir and Wadi as Saghir, a low rise is crowned by the fort of Al 'Anad, a lofty central pile enclosed in a large space, surrounded by a high wall with towers at the corners ; some miles farther, also on the right, stand the castle-like buildings of Nobat Dakim. After a short halt at Jol Madram, among a crowd of rather wild-looking Haushabi tribesmen (who seemed, as usual, easily roused to merriment by very small jokes), the point was reached where we must ford the Tiban, and continue nearly due west along its tributary, the Wadi 'Aqqan. So, after a midday halt on the west bank, under a very large, lofty and spreading tamarisk (unfortunately some large stumps near by showed that other trees equally big had been hacked down), we left the broad shallow river murmuring over its stony bed between low rocky hills covered with scrub. A track along the south bank of Wadi 'Aqqan, called in the upper part of its course Wadi Natīd, led at length to Kirsh. Here the officer in charge of a small military post of the Sultan of Lahej showed us a raised, open, level place above the road, on which to camp. Having communicated with Lahej by wireless, he also provided a guard of a corporal and four soldiers each night. These men of the 'Abdali Sultan's army, clad in khaki shirts and either shorts or futas, had a smart military bearing.

This camping-ground, though about three miles short of Huweimi, was chosen partly for greater security, partly for freedom from mosquitoes. But even on our bare little rocky plateau, some 2,400 feet above sea-level, we were bitten, though by what kind of mosquito could not be discovered.

Huweimi, three miles farther west, where we spent the following day, remains pictured in the mind as a very pretty spot. The hot springs lie in a broad valley, in an open space covered with close turf and surrounded by scrub. Towards the valley-head a wood of flat-topped acacias gives an African touch to the scene. Down the slope, in the opposite direction, a large pond, partly artificial, is backed by a few tall date-palms, 'ilb trees and bushes; a haunt of bush-shrikes,[1] one of which flew from bush to bush round me, chattering loudly, while I rested a few minutes under an 'ilb. Farther down, in the direction whence we had come, the valley is filled with dense thickets of the bush [2] with sticky foliage and clusters of small purple flower-heads, so attractive to butterflies and other insects, which we had previously found in the Great Wadi at Al Huseini.

The almost sylvan setting is girt by bare rocky mountains, not of great height (some 4,000 feet or thereabouts), but of fine serrated shapes. The apparently empty landscape, with no human habitation in sight, has really plenty of inhabitants. From our camp at Kirsh some cultivated fields could be seen to the North in the Wadi Natīd. At Huweimi women were grazing goats on the short turf, and Haushabi boys, wearing brimless straw hats rather like inverted flower-pots, waded in the warm pond. These people were all quiet and friendly enough, though this mountainous frontier country was not the most law-abiding part of the Protectorate, and the night-guard at our camp was probably provided by the Sultan of Lahej from other motives besides courtesy.

The hot springs bubble out of a deep hole and flow away down a steep-sided runnel scored in the earth. By dangling a thermometer in the water at the source, I recorded 152° Fahr. and saw no sign of animal life. But in a channel a hundred yards or so lower down, where the water-temperature was 120°, Ahmed Mahmūd found small water-beetles, while the edge of the pond, 94°, yielded several kinds of aquatic insects. Nor is Huweimi only a place of hot water. Cold grass-fringed pools lay on a raised part of the glade. Late in the afternoon, after returning to Kirsh, we were tempted to go back along the Wadi

[1] *Tchagra senegala percivali.*   *Pluchea indica.*

Natīd to some narrows where the river forms a deep pool between overhanging cliffs. This bottle-neck proved to be eleven miles back! Britton was just able to snatch a hurried swim in very cold water (apparently a spring rose from the river bed at this point) before dusk came on. When camp was reached after dark, the anxious Lahej officer was about to send out a search-party of soldiers.

December 10th saw us cover the remaining 61 miles to Ta'izz. In the few miles between Kirsh and the Yemen frontier, we were stopped by Hamūd, an Aden Frontier Guard distinguished by a metal badge. He begged us to voice on his behalf to the Frontier Officer his complaints of border forays and killings, and the unwillingness of the Yemenis to send *dhurra* and other supplies across the frontier. A little farther, and a fence of cut thorny branches, extending up the steep rocky slopes of the narrowing wadi, marks the line itself. Perched on the southern slope, a circular tower of rough stones forms the Yemeni post, while a barrier-pole, rather clumsily hinged to a rock, stretched across the wadi-bed. But there was no delay for us here. Beyond the barrier the track ascends and crosses arid stony ridges, sparsely covered with scrub, till a military post of some size is reached, some miles within the Yemen.

Here, at Rukheba, local differences were immediately visible. A group of soldiers in the uniform of the Yemeni army (Phot. 56), indigo-dyed shirts, white turbans or indigo turbans with fringes, and white kilts, were the first we saw of a type who were to be our constant companions for the remainder of the journey. The curved sheaths of their *jambiyas* are often decorated with plaits of green twine. By these and other signs we were plainly in another country. A crowd of country people with camels and donkeys waited to pass the post. We, expected on this date, were sent on. To the north-west Jebel Sabir rears its huge mass to 9,800 feet, the great mountain at whose northern foot lies Ta'izz. But the road does not lead thither direct, it runs northward and makes a wide sweep, till the city is approached from the east.

A level fertile cultivated plain is traversed, across which is seen the lofty tower of the great mosque of Janadīya ("Genedīya"), a landmark for miles round. Janadīya, now a small village, was in the time of Muhammad and later an important town.[1] Seen across the plain, the mosque has a body disproportionately low for its tall minaret. This is due to its being sunk in a hollow, or to the ground-level having risen round it in the course of centuries. The walls are thirty feet or more high, but the whole space on which the mosque

---

[1] Niebuhr, "Beschreibung von Arabien", p. 242. Janadīya appears also according to other writings to have been the capital of a province, Janad.

stands is about twelve feet below the general level. References to this mosque as a place of pilgrimage, and to building work there, can be found in translations of the early medieval Arab historians. But a most imaginative story is that related by my friend Dr. Petrie,[1] as told by the Arabs to explain the situation of the building. During Muhammad's lifetime, they say, Gabriel himself came to Janadīya to assist the Prophet's cause. After a most successful mission the Archangel was recalled to Heaven. Many people wished to go with him, and the very mosque rose after him as he ascended. But Gabriel pressed it back with the injunction that it must stay where it was still needed. The Archangel's action, though gentle, was so firm that the building was pushed many feet into the earth, where it has remained as a witness ever after.

On, over rolling waste lands, covered with low cactus-like euphorbias; along a stretch of dusty road shaded by large *'ilb* trees set at intervals in thorny hedges on either side, rather like an English lane; fording a flowing, tree-fringed river; a rise, and then a descent towards Jebel Sabir and the beautiful walled city at its foot. In front of us, a gate nearer the eastern end of the north wall, but there is an awkward dip and a sharp rise to the gate-house, so our drivers continue along the outside of the north wall, then turn sharply into the city through the Bab Sheikh Musa, nearer its western end. We are in the chief city of the Southern Yemen at last.

[1] " An Expedition to Ta'izz ", *Edinburgh Medical Missionary Society Quarterly Paper,* xviii, Oct.–Nov., 1932. Dr. Petrie gives a more detailed account of the building as it stands to-day.

Chapter XII

TA'IZZ, CHIEF CITY OF THE SOUTHERN YEMEN, AND ITS AMIR

TA'IZZ, the most beautiful city of the Yemen, and our headquarters for nearly three weeks, lies at 4,500 feet above sea-level, on the lowest spurs of the north slope of Jebel Sabir (sounded " Sab'r "). The ancient walls, enclosing it on three sides, run at either end up the slopes of the mountain, which forms the natural rampart of the city on the south. The city has two large gates,[1] not far apart, at either end of the eastern sector of the north wall. Both open on to the road from Mocha, which skirts that wall and continues northwards to San'a. The Bab al Kabir on the east has a busy guard-house over the archway, the steep rough slope under which leads up to a space generally alive with people coming and going, and shaded by a large spreading wild-fig tree. The Bab Sheikh Musa, to the west, is much quieter, and the rooms with plain round-headed windows on the first floor of its circular flanking towers, and over the arch, seemed little used. A precipitous detached crag of the mountain, crowned by the citadel, dominates the city on the south-east, while at the north-eastern corner the walls, with several towers and bastions, extend up a lower eminence.

Many of the houses are great blocks three or four storeys in height, with much external ornament and traceried upper windows; houses such as, with local variations, are characteristic of all the cities of the Yemen highlands.

At Ta'izz three large mosques, entirely covered with whitewash, stand out glistening against the surrounding buildings and the darker background of Jebel Sabir (Phot. 41). Some smaller mosques and tombs remain intact; ruins of a fourth mosque are shown, and others formerly existed, both within and without the walls.[2]

[1] Niebuhr (" Reisebeschreibung," Vol. i, section on Journey from Mocha to Ta'izz) writes that there were only these same two gates to the open country in his time (1763), but a gate in the western wall had then recently been built up, while yet another opened from the citadel to Jebel Sabir. Manzoni (1884, p. 314) lists yet another, built-up, making five in all. We did not see these latter.

[2] See the ground-plan and " prospect " of Ta'izz in Niebuhr's " Reisebeschreibung ", Vol. i, Plates 66, 67 (1774).

Turkish influence is plainly manifest in these mosques. Though some claim foundation by early rulers, all the principal ones, as they now appear, were built or rebuilt under the Turkish dominion in the 16th or early 17th century. Thus the Jami' Masjid or Muzaffarīya, the chief mosque, is said to have been founded late in the 13th century by the Rasulite Sultan Al Muzaffar, but rebuilt by the Turks.[1] Ash Sharifīya (Photograph 44) was founded about a century later by another Rasulite Sultan, Isma'il ibn al 'Abbās, but seems to have been likewise rebuilt. It has a single large dome and several smaller cupolas. Its two minarets, like the single minaret of the Jami' Masjid, have series of recessed round-headed alcoves one above the other. The same design reappears in the solitary tower left as a mute witness of the oldest mosque, which formerly stood in the eastern part of the city, and a variation of the same theme is presented by the minaret of the small mosque shown in Photograph 42. This architectural feature is stressed because it was not met with again, even among the mosques of the Turkish period at San'a.

While Ash Sharafīya boasts two minarets, and the Jami' Masjid but one, the third large mosque, Al Makhdabīya, has no *suma'* (tower) at all. But it possesses some ten cupolas and a wealth of crenellated parapets. Six of its dazzling white domes are grouped over the roofed portion north (Mecca-wards) of its open courtyard. It is said to have been founded by an Abyssinian slave of a 16th century Turkish pasha, Husein. The partly ruined mausoleum of the latter (Photograph 43), of reddish stone, stands in a garden amid the vivid green of fruit-trees.

The Jami' Masjid, centrally situated though in a rather low part of the city, was used for the official Friday midday services. On December 24th the garrison could be seen from the guest-house roof parading to this mosque. They marched from the barracks at Al 'Urdi, outside the walls, preceded by a band, and carrying as colours a red and green flag with an inscription in white. Arms were piled in the space outside the mosque while the soldiers entered for prayers, and squibs were fired off from a house-roof in the upper part of the town, both before and after the time of prayer. I did not discover the special occasion, but on that particular Friday we had to stay indoors. Our Somali servants, very smartly attired in bright-coloured turbans and fūtas and light short coats, attended at the mosque.

Banana, pawpaw and ornamental flowering trees, refreshingly green among the buildings (Phots. 42, 43), flourish in gardens despite the altitude and cool nights (we recorded a minimum of 54° Fahrenheit on December 14th). Streams almost without number, descending

[1] R. Manzoni, " El Yemen," 1884, p. 315 (see Note B, p. 238).

from Jebel Sabir, flow through the city or near at hand. The water is carefully conserved, led through plaster-lined channels and stored in wayside tanks, often dating from ancient times (Phot. 46).

But with all these amenities the queen of the Southern Yemen is less prosperous than in past times. Her population is estimated at only about 3,000; the *suq*, extending most of the distance between the two gates, is not large, and much ground within the walls lies waste and empty. With the old port of Mocha, to the west, now decayed, the trade of Ta'izz is chiefly with Aden. Hence cars and lorries with number-plates bearing the name of the city in both Arabic and English ply between the inland city and the British port. Unfortunately the city and district are malarious. Since our visit fell in December the risk was slight. Very few mosquitos were seen at all, and no anophelines. Nevertheless we scarcely relaxed the precaution of dosing with atebrin on alternate days. It was therefore a mischance that Britton, attacked by some unseen anopheline, contracted malaria, which developed during the journey to San'a.

Eastward of the present Ta'izz, on the lower part of the north slope of Jebel Sabir, ruined walls, some buildings and a mosque mark the site of an old Islamic city, which we might not closely approach. Our escort called it " Old Ta'izz ", but it is Thabad, once (say Arab historians) a resort of the 12th century Suleihite prince Mansūr ibn al Mufadhal of Ta'izz.

On our arriving at Ta'izz it was impressed on us in a hundred ways that we were in a new country. The landscape and the tribesmen were much the same, and we could still see eastward of us the great mountains at the opposite side of which we had gazed longingly from Jebel Jihaf. But conditions for two Europeans were very, very different. The day of our arrival being Friday, the national flag of the Yemen, the sword of 'Ali and five stars in white on a scarlet ground, flew from the house of the Amir of Ta'izz. This large white building shone out on a spur of the mountain 1,500 feet above the city, among the many round towers and rectangular tower-houses which dot the ridges of Jebel Sabir. The house, Dar en Nasr (" House of Victory "), its inmate and its flag, stood for much.

We had wondered if we should be lodged in a guest-house at Al 'Urdi, a group of buildings a mile outside the city to the east, where the Amir has a lower residence. But when our cars swung sharply round through the Bab Sheikh Musa we were taken to a great guest-house (Beit ad Dhuyūf) in the centre of the city itself, belonging to the 'Amil, and close to one of that official's large private houses. " 'Amil " seems a title peculiar to the Yemen. It means, so to say, the mayor of a town, or head of a district within a province governed by an Amir.

PHOTOGRAPHS 43 AND 44.

Qubba of Husein Pasha in Taʻizz; banana and pawpaw trees in the foreground.
Taʻizz; one of the large mosques, in the Turkish style.

PHOTOGRAPHS 45 AND 46.
A water-sprite in the recesses of Jebel Sabir.
On the road to Mocha near Ta'izz; a cistern and fountain for ablutions, near a large wild-fig tree.

The 'Amil's guest-house

Besides the 'Amil of Ta'izz city there were many other 'Amils of small towns and districts under the Amir of Ta'izz, who may be regarded as Governor-General of the Southern Yemen.

Led to the 'Amil's great new guest-house, through a garden of banana trees and under a pergola covered by a creeper, we were lodged in rooms on the top floor. Only the kitchen and servants' quarters, opening on to a flat parapeted roof, were above us. On the ground floor, in going in and out, we must always pass through a dark vestibule full of soldiers, one at least of whom accompanied us on every walk.

Our rooms, lofty and spacious, introduced us to the beautiful and elaborate interior decoration in plaster-work of large town-houses in the Yemen. That in which I slept (Phot. 73) had a lower range of windows fitted with plain glass casements, to open, and above these arched windows filled with tracery and glass, partly coloured. Some of these traceried windows were double, containing two sets of tracery of different patterns, one outside the other. This and the other rooms had also ornamented wall-niches and fretted brackets, as well as conventional designs in relief showing birds and plants, among them flowers rising from the neck of a coffee-pot. Fishes were also painted on the walls, and altogether it was clear that there is no objection to the representation of living things among some, at any rate, of the present-day Muslims of the Yemen. My bedroom had no furniture but handsome carpets. Its beauty was not marred by over-decoration, for large spaces of wall were quite plain, and all the walls and ceilings pure white. But in the other rooms the effect of the plasterwork was somewhat spoilt by inferior European tables, chairs and clocks, as well as ugly lino on the floor. The living-room was hung with modern maps of the world worded in Arabic, and some albums containing photographs of the male part of the 'Amil's family and friends were left for our amusement.

The 'Amil did not see us on arrival, but sent to visit us one 'Ali Muhammad, usually spoken of as " Sheikh 'Ali ", educated in Aden and originally a schoolmaster in the Protectorate. Sheikh 'Ali, a short, rather round-faced man wearing no beard, had been in Ta'izz several years working for the Amir. Owing to his excellent English he was naturally employed as interpreter for British visitors. During our early days he was constantly with us, conducting us on our first visits to the 'Amil and the Amir, and showing us the sights of the city. He was friendly and helpful, even if sometimes lengthy in political argument! I was glad to learn that he subsequently returned to his profession of schoolmaster in the British Protectorate.

The continual close surveillance, of which we had been forewarned, was severely felt after our freedom in the Aden Protectorate. If Sheikh

'Ali were not with us, one or other of the staff of the guest-house would be constantly coming into the room and watching us preparing and packing specimens or writing our notes. Curiosity, doubtless, partly prompted this behaviour. These people had never seen anyone packing insects or drying and pressing plants before. But they were also evidently told to keep an eye on us ! Only once did we succeed, with Jam'a, in leaving the city gates unaccompanied by a soldier. Though we went but a few hundred yards from the walls, hoping to get a photograph from the west, we were followed by a sinister-looking fellow in white. He went into a small mosque, scarcely enclosed, and affected to pray, though with one eye cocked on us the while.

Later in our stay another English-speaking Arab was several times our visitor. This gentleman, 'Ali Qāsim (Cassim) Muhammad, who wished to be known by us as " Mr. A. C. Mohammed ", had (as he put it) " spent sixteen years in the Western World ", mainly in America but also in England. Having returned to the Yemen he was then being employed as a preacher or lecturer in the mosques about the Ta'izz district. Report said he had been a Muslim missionary in America. A thin man, with long intelligent face and slight beard, his conversation was animated and interesting, while his attitude seemed open and friendly. He clearly longed for his country to progress, and to be on good terms with the British. He gave us useful hints as to how we should behave if (and when) we arrived in San'a.

For the time being, however, Sheikh 'Ali was our mentor. The morning after our arrival he took us to see the 'Amil. The latter, Seiyid Muhammad al Basha, received us in the court-house, a one-storey building with verandahs, facing a large open space and shaded by a great spreading wild-fig tree. Entering a room thronged with men between two lines of armed soldiers, we took our seats beside the 'Amil on a high divan at the far end. As we drank the coffee immediately handed to us, we noted our host's appearance. Seiyid Muhammad, then about 35, was a rather short man, whose plump clean-shaven face wore an agreeable expression. The roundness of his visage and the fullness of his clothes made him look fatter than he really was. He dressed entirely in spotless white, turban, long coat with close sleeves, and (in full dress) over it a long garment with full flowing sleeves. He wore a leather girdle decorated with the silver embroidery characteristic of the Yemen. He carried his *jambiya* on the right-hand side (instead of in the middle), the mark of a *seiyid*.[1] He received us most

---

[1] In case some readers are unfamiliar with this term, used many times : a *seiyid* (lord, master) here means one claiming descent from Muhammad through Fatima and 'Ali (the Prophet's daughter and son-in-law). The term *sharif*, meaning a noble or even a descendant of the Prophet in a less restricted sense, is scarcely used

amicably. A long talk followed, during which we showed him boxes of pinned insects, presses of dried plants, and our post card views of the Museum. But, however full our explanations, nothing could be settled as to what we might or might not do. As we had been rightly told before starting for Ta'izz, neither the 'Amil nor any minor official has real authority in such matters. All would depend on the Amir, who decided the minutest details, and even he was constantly in touch by telegraph with the Imam at San'a. The only result of our first talk with the 'Amil was that we were forbidden to take any photographs, though his manner suggested that he would have liked to give us leave. Anyhow, this restriction was soon relaxed.

In the afternoon Seiyid Muhammad paid us a return call in our rooms, bringing with him another 'Amil, from an outlying district. The latter, a tall man with close-trimmed black beard, was robed in white brocade, but wore a coloured turban and a coloured shawl over the shoulders. (The carrying of a long shawl over one or both shoulders is a part of full dress among the well-to-do and official classes; a convention which our cicerone, Sheikh 'Ali, accustomed to the greater freedom of the Aden Protectorate, thought rather troublesome!)

With the two 'Amils came a gentleman in a long green robe, and the commander of the local troops, a pleasant-looking old man dressed in a shabby khaki tunic and trousers, with a black lamb's-wool kalpak on his head. Our specimens had to be shown all over again to these courteous guests. But no further mention was made of what degree of freedom we should be allowed. Clearly much time must be given up to courtesy visits and interviews. Britton, eager to recommence collecting specimens, chafed at the enforced inaction. When his Somali, 'Omar, that evening reported a rumour that three more 'Amils were coming to call on us, Britton collapsed over the supper-table, exclaiming that we had best send for Mas'ūd and the lorry and return to Aden!

Our acquaintance with Seiyid Muhammad left pleasant impressions. At the end of our stay he received us again, with one of his sons, in a room on a lower floor of the guest-house. He then excused himself for not having seen more of us owing to pressure of work; probably a perfectly true reason, for we had often seen the crowds of pushing, shouting folk at the guest-house door, struggling to present cases and petitions to the 'Amil, who gave audience for hours at a time in the garden.

in our part of Arabia. We met many *seiyids*, but no one using the title *sharif*. (The latter word is, however, applied to a part of the Imam's palace.) In the Yemen *seiyids* do not wear green turbans as is (or was) done by them in some parts of the Arab world.

But a far greater personage than Sheikh 'Ali or Seiyid Muhammad had to be faced before we could even begin work in the environs of Ta'izz. The following morning we were suddenly summoned to the Amir's palace, Dar en Nasr. The Amir, perched 1,500 feet up the mountain, communicated with the city by telegraph. Apparently the 'Amil had only received the order late the preceding evening. Hurriedly making ready, we set off soon after 9 a.m. with Sheikh 'Ali, Jam'a and a soldier, all five of us on mules. Leaving the city by the eastern gate we rode back eastwards as far as Al 'Urdi. There, passing a great new Government guest-house in course of building, and the lower residence of the Amir, we turned southwards along the edge of a dry wadi. Our path skirted the barracks, inside which band-practice was going on, while outside soldiers were reclining under a large spreading tree, practising on bugles. A number of buglers were, indeed, sitting under this tree, all blowing different notes and calls at once, every time we passed that way. Then, across the wadi-bed and up the lower slopes of Jebel Sabir, winding in and out among spurs and ravines, along a road with about twenty hairpin bends. Higher up, the track led between terraced gardens of *qat*, grown as little trees up to ten or twelve feet high. Finally a very steep winding path, with great blocks of stone laid in rough steps, led to the gate of Dar en Nasr. The long white building, seen on its projecting spur of the mountain from the city below, is found, when the traveller reaches its doors, to dominate the country far and wide.

Through a narrow walled enclosure, up some steps, and across an ante-room, we entered a very long, large and lofty hall. The door of this audience-room was at the end. The hall had a wooden ceiling painted with designs, and was brightly lighted by large windows along one side. The whole length of the long wall facing the windows, and round the end walls, ran a low divan, divided into seats by low partitions built up of long narrow cushions. A wider and grander seat was provided for the Amir in the middle of the long wall. We saw such divans again many times, but never on so large a scale. I could have wished to see the seats filled and the Amir presiding over a gathering of personal friends or some more formal assembly of notables.

Meanwhile, seated on some European chairs placed for us in the middle of the room, we awaited the Amir. Coffee, mineral-water and cigarettes were brought by his major-domo, 'Ali Yahya, a slightly built man with close beard. At last the great man himself entered from the opposite end of the long chamber. Seiyid 'Ali ibn al Wazir, at that time Amir of Ta'izz, was a man of 53, of middle height. His expression bespoke intelligence, though the loss of an eye marred his countenance. He had a short black beard. Each time we saw him he was wearing a long, dark-coloured sleeved coat and a white or light-coloured shawl. At our first and more formal reception his appearance was made more imposing by a large spreading white head-cloth hanging to the shoulders. At the later informal interviews he wore only a closely bound white turban.

Not that the Amir needed any outward trappings to impress a visitor. His quick speech, uttered in a rather quiet voice, and the ability with which he discussed various subjects (even when his remarks could only reach the listener through an interpreter), told of a swift, clever brain. Because of these qualities, and his very courteous and friendly reception of us, we naturally liked him; while his manner, at our later interviews particularly, showed that he was friendlily disposed to us, and would have let us go about more freely, had he not been under strict orders from San'a.

When, after the usual polite personal inquiries, the conversation turned to explanation of our business in the Yemen, we tried to show the Amir the boxes of specimens and other paraphernalia which we had hauled up the mountain. But Seiyid 'Ali probably had heard enough about these from the 'Amil. After a cursory glance he rapped out " *Na'am, na'am, hasharat* " (" Yes, yes, insects ! ") and quickly turned to politics, mentioning items of news recently heard on the Rome and Paris radio. Politics, in fact, were his consuming passion, and a tendency to political intrigue may have been the cause of his subsequent removal from his high office. Unfortunately, at this first interview, he indulged in a long and controversial discussion of British policy in Palestine. His arguments need be only briefly repeated, since an account of the interview has already appeared in print; moreover, circumstances have changed immensely since December, 1937.

The attitude of the Amir of Ta'izz was not new to us. We had already learnt in the Aden Protectorate, even from friends as strongly pro-British as Amir Nasr of Dhala, how burning a question this was among the Arabs. The Amir of Ta'izz wished us to make known to " our Government " how bitterly opposed were all Arabs to any form of " partition " of Palestine. He referred repeatedly to the traditional love of the Arabs for the British, but expressed amazement at our treatment of the Arabs, who had been settled in Palestine for so many centuries. Why, he argued, could not the Arabs, Jews and Christians already in Palestine all live peaceably under a strong British administration, just as many Jews live contentedly side by side with Arabs in the Yemen ? The Jews expelled from Central Europe should be granted living room in the great, partly empty, spaces of the world, the Amir said, not encouraged to return to the Holy Land. Seiyid 'Ali did not lend an ear to the wilder rumours then current—rumours possibly set abroad by anti-British agents—such as, that the British were arming the Jews in Palestine against the Arabs. But he did warn us of the danger of turning the Muslim world against Britain by the Partition policy. It should be remembered that the officials of the Yemen were said to be suffering cuts in their salaries to support Arab activities in Palestine.

This argument lasted so long that there were only some quick references to our freedom of movement, just before we left his presence. The total prohibition on taking photographs was very largely relaxed, and we were to visit certain " appointed places ", but not, alas! the top of Jebel Sabir. Nor did we ever attain this longed-for goal.

Probably most of the comparatively few British who have passed through Ta'izz will remember the Amir's friendly major-domo, 'Ali Yahya. I recall also 'Ali Yahya's brother Nasr, with gratitude for an act of kindly consideration when I was being entertained to lunch at the Amir's lower house at Al 'Urdi. The Amir himself was absent, but our host was an amiable elderly gentleman, Qadhi Husein, 'Amil of Hujerīya, an outlying district under the Amir of Ta'izz. Dietary difficulties compelled me to refuse certain vegetables, which I tried to do without attracting remark. But the watchful eye of Nasr Yahya, who was serving, could not be escaped. Greatly concerned, he scoured the house till he produced some olives as a substitute.

All these persons have left pleasant memories. A less prepossessing member of the Amir's entourage was one Sheikh Salih ———. Like his master he had lost an eye, but unlike the Amir he had a nose resembling a hawk's beak and a thin sunken face, so that his smile took the form of a sinister leer. " Old Cyclops ", as Britton nicknamed him, wished to use his influence with the Amir to befriend us—for a consideration. He came to see us at the guest-house well after dark, to transact the necessary business.

Opinions, indeed, differed as to how far we should give presents. It seemed to me necessary, because we were not official representatives of our Government. I regarded gifts of money, fabrics or other articles only as a means of paying indirectly for the accommodation and supplies granted us by the Yemen Government. For we were theoretically their guests throughout, either in Government guest-houses or in private houses by arrangement of their Government. Our requests to be allowed to pay directly for quarters and provisions were refused, but presents offered towards the end of a stay in a guest-house were accepted.

At Ta'izz, the Government allowed a certain sum *per* day for our keep. After a time complaint was made that our household was costing too much, and the sum was fixed at seven riyāls a day. We wondered where most of this went, for after the first day or two little was provided. We had to draw on our stored provisions and anything Jam'a could buy in the city. Possibly Sheikh Salih's brother, Muhammad ———, was concerned in the daily disappearance of the seven riyāls. He was keeper of the guest-house. A less lean-visaged man than Sheikh Salih, his face usually wore an expression of cheerful rascality. Nevertheless Muhammad ———, who had travelled and spoke some queer French, was always friendly in manner, and he helped us on our way at the end.

Considerable tact was shown by our Somali servants in dealing with the men and boys of the guest-house staff. Jam'a's position was not always easy. On one of the first mornings he apologised for the lateness of breakfast, as the caretaker " had gone away and taken the key of the chicken " (chicken and kitchen were two English words which he could never distinguish). There was friction sometimes among the guest-house servants, and the Arab cook was temporarily put in irons for quarrelling.

Jam'a was also greatly distressed over the prospect of our spending a lonely Christmas. Observant of English ways he searched the *suq*, unasked by us, till he found some almonds and raisins wherewith to supplement a small tinned Christmas pudding. Though himself a Muslim so strict that he would not even smoke, much less drink alcohol, he wished us to celebrate Christmas with " all the brandy and all the whisky ". (Incidentally our supplies were one bottle of each, kept out of sight to avoid offending our Muslim hosts and friends, and regarded by us as part of our medical stores.)

Meanwhile, our work was carried on wherever we were allowed to go. At least one soldier was told off to accompany us on every walk. From now onwards we were never without these warriors, except in walking about San'a during our two months stay in the capital. On treks of several days our escort consisted of a *shawūsh* (" sha'oosh," sergeant) and one or more soldiers. Our movements were politely but firmly controlled ; there was, as a rule, no wandering more than a few yards to one side or the other of the prescribed path. " *Ma fi'sh rukhsa* " (" there is no permission ") is a phrase we should certainly have remembered, even with no other Arabic. Some sergeants remained completely impenetrable, but others became open and friendly, interpreting their orders a little less strictly. With the ordinary soldiers it was a question how long they were with us. They might seem wooden and expressionless at first, but if the same soldiers came on several excursions they soon began to show themselves as ready for a joke or a grumble, as desirous of coffee or tobacco, as our old friends the Tribal Guards of the Amiri highlands.

Immediately east of the city, towards the lowermost spurs of Jebel Sabir, a track led to a patch of green crops, rank hedges, *qat* gardens and large shady mango trees. Returning by a path over stony euphorbia-covered ridges, we passed the tomb of a Jewish saint, Weli Shebazi. The actual grave, a whitewashed oblong with a little arch on top at one end, was surrounded by a rough stone wall, with a small low one-roomed stone building opening into the enclosure. There was a narrow upright recess in the end of the tomb, near the ground, beneath the little arch. This grave with a Hebrew inscription was a place to which pious Jews resorted. Some weeping women, crouching against the grave, and a man kneeling and reading were too engrossed to notice us passing by.

The path near this Jewish shrine was the scene of a curious little discovery. A large shiny black millipede, four or five inches long, moving slowly forward, was found to be covered with tiny yellowish-red flies, riding on its back. The insects, though quite capable of flight, persistently returned to the millipede when driven off and resumed their ride after circling round in the air for a few inches— minute aircraft taking off from a slow-moving terrestrial air-craft-carrier. The flies belong to a species of Phoridae new to science. Their behaviour is either an example of " phoresy ", in which a smaller organism uses a larger merely as a means of getting carried about ; or the flies are, in their early stages, internal parasites of the millipedes. There are reasons for believing the latter to be the case. Instances of flies riding on millipedes had been observed in Africa, but not in Arabia.

Not only did we wish to see the " appointed places " named by the Amir, but it seemed politic to go. I suspected, however, that they would prove to be at as low altitudes and as far from the mountains as possible ; and such proved to be the case !

Accordingly, one day we drove some thirty miles westward along the road to Mocha, through Hidrar and Rumāda to Al Barh (" Barrah "). This entailed a descent of 2,700 feet from Ta'izz, to a point only some 1,800 feet above sea-level. Here a running stream flowed in a broad wadi among many date-palms, backed by low barren rocky mountains. Such country yielded useful material, though entirely of lowland character. The Sheikh of Al Barh entertained us in his village of low poor houses, raised a little above the wadi. He was a young man of a rather blond type ; both he and his two younger brothers had open agreeable countenances and very gentle manners. Sitting on stringed bedsteads in a low building with rough stone walls and flat thatched roof, a sort of club-room where the men meet to talk and smoke, we tried to do justice to chicken-stew, hard-boiled eggs, chupatties and cups of *kishr*. As, before the Sheikh appeared, we had already lunched off provisions brought with us, this was difficult, and much of the meal had to be turned over to the Somalis, by whom it was quickly demolished. But the hospitality of the kind folk of Al Barh was appreciated, and we wished it had been in our power to make some return.

Punctures delayed our return to Ta'izz, and, while repairs were being done, we walked ahead in the soft bright moonlight. The sloping-backed slinking form of a hyæna was seen in the road close to the city. This, with a leopard recently captured, and conies in the recesses of Jebel Sabir, completes the short list of larger wild animals seen in the neighbourhood of Ta'izz. Our not re-entering the gates till so late an hour as 8.15 p.m. gave rise to some hubbub in the city!

Usaifira, the other "appointed place", to which we went several times, was much easier of access. It is a luxuriant moist spot in a hollow a mile north of the walls. There an old tower stands beside a great rectangular masonry-walled cistern, partly shaded by spreading trees. Large handsome dragonflies sailed to and fro, while frogs,[1] lying on a bed of water-plants in the cistern, leapt several inches into the air at "flies" made of cotton-wool—the only means by which specimens could be reached. Below the cistern a stream flowed between rich irrigated fields of onions, tomatoes, a mauve-flowered mustard and other crops. Every waste place was filled with abundant flowering weeds. Beautiful butterflies of many kinds flitted among the rank vegetation which, even in the height of the dry season, teemed also with smaller insects. One of the most abundant butterflies was a wide-ranging Tropical African species related to the Small Tortoise-shell, which it resembles in shape and size; but the colouring is very different, the two wings on either side being together divided diagonally, having the inner and fore part dark brown, the outer part rich ochreous-yellow with undulating dark marginal lines. *Eurytela dryope*, as it is named, is a striking insect when in flight—perhaps an example of warning coloration.

Though the highest parts of Jebel Sabir were forbidden, we penetrated two steep winding defiles in its northern face. These valleys were not among the Amir's "appointed places", but neither were they expressly prohibited. At any rate, mules and escort for three whole-day excursions were provided, and we spoke freely to the Amir of these outings afterwards.

These two valleys presented a great contrast. Wadi Sabir, the farther from the city, was a wild and lonely cleft without visible human inhabitants. Leaving our escorting *shawūsh* with his horse and our mules at a little village where the ravine opens from the steep mountain-side, I clambered up the almost precipitous eastern slope, while

[1] The large Arabian form of the Indian *Rana cyanophlyctis*.

Britton climbed the dry boulder-filled wadi-bed round a bend into a gorge. Though I only reached about 6,500 feet, the place was different from any I had seen in the Aden Protectorate. The rock was either a granite or related, the slope covered with long grass, at this season rather dry and brown. Higher up were some grass-covered terraces, and, still higher, some very narrow fields of *dhurra*-stubble, but still no sign of those who tended the crops. Dotted in the grass were several kinds of trees, shrubs and plants not seen before, notably a juniper-tree about fifteen feet high. This was the first coniferous tree we had encountered in Arabia. (Junipers were only seen again, in dwarf scrub form, above the Naqil Isla pass south of San'a ; for we did not reach the luxuriant juniper forests which have been described as flourishing north of the northern Yemen frontier.) When the declining sun had left the deep cleft in shadow, and we were preparing to return to the city, numerous conies issued from the rocks, some to drink at a pool left from the last rains in the wadi-bed. They were the only visible inhabitants (other than insects) of Wadi Sabir.

The nearer valley, Wadi Thabad, a steep-sided cleft in the mountain behind Al 'Urdi, was, on the other hand, cultivated almost to the last square yard. *Qat* trees rise in terrace above terrace up both its steep sides ; interspersed among them are tiny terraced fields of young grain, groups of bright green banana trees, and large shade-trees, wild-figs, *'ilbs* and dark-foliaged carobs. For hundreds of feet up either side, too, are perched here and there round stone towers and rect-angular tower-houses, crowning any little eminence or dotted among the terraces. In this lovely place the wadi-bed, strewn with huge boulders, was dry indeed, but water flowed in small channels along one margin, and tumbled down little fern-fringed waterfalls (see also Phot. 45). Waste ground at the edge of the torrent-bed was filled with tangles of wild rose-bushes, tall and spreading, with a growth like our English dog-rose and woody stems thicker than one's arm. A few white roses still lingered on these thickets ; the clusters of small hips were turning red.[1]

Excepting in the sheltered and irrigated Wadi Dhahr, north-east of San'a, *qat* was not seen again on our journey flourishing to the same extent as in these recesses of Jebel Sabir. In these spots the small trees reach heights of ten feet or more. The plant, a species of the Order Celastraceæ, of which the English spindle-tree is a member, was first described as *Catha edulis* by Forskål in his posthumously published work (1775) on the plants collected during Niebuhr's great expedition. The shrub or tree, with serrate leaves and clusters of small white flowers,

---

[1] These wild roses, which carried me back in memory to the Abyssinian highlands, are probably the same species, *Rosa abyssinica*.

is a native of fairly high altitudes in East Africa. It is believed to have been introduced into Arabia from Abyssinia. The best conditions for its growth are roughly the same as those for coffee. The drug is used only in parts of Somaliland, Abyssinia and South-West Arabia. In the country last named, where it is favoured by a large number of people, the fresh leaves are chewed, but dried leaves may also be used or an infusion made and drunk like tea. Several crops are taken every year. Sprigs, six inches or more long, of the younger leaves are tied in bundles, which are wrapped in grass. Thus they will keep fresh for hours or days while being transported by camel, mule or donkey.

The addicts claim very varied properties for the drug, but all agree that it produces wakefulness and alertness of mind. To quench the thirst induced by chewing, water is drunk at intervals by solitary *qat*-chewers or during the social *qat*-parties which begin after midday and sometimes last into the small hours. Those who chew *qat* to excess sometimes behave as though drunken. One at least of the several alkaloids which have been isolated by analysis from the plant acts on the brain and spinal cord, causing varying degrees of stimulation or excitement according to the dose. When the habit is indulged in more than very little, harmful reactions follow. The poor general health of some people may well be due to this cause. The large amount of tannin and other substances swallowed can do no good to a man's physique and digestion, even apart from the specific action of the alkaloid drugs.

Altogether, it is sad to see so much of the best land, above all land which might yield first-rate coffee, devoted to this baneful little tree. But the attitude of some *qat*-chewers is shown by the following story. When a former British official in the Aden Protectorate was expostulating with an Arab for his too great indulgence, he remarked that the use of the drug would surely have been forbidden, had the Prophet ever heard of it. "No doubt," replied the Arab, "but, praise be to God, the Prophet never *did* hear of it."

After this digression on *qat*, we must return momentarily to the Wadi Thabad, the ascent to which lay by stony paths through a village, between the high stone walls of houses and gardens. Here were masses of wild clematis trailing over walls and trees, with their clusters of rich creamy blossoms now in perfection (we visited the place on Christmas Day and the day following). How like were these narrow paths between walls to many places in Southern Europe; especially, were a church and campanile substituted for the mosque and its roughly built minaret, to many a spot in Northern Italy.

From the mouth of Wadi Thabad we could gaze northward over

a landscape (Phot. 48) which we were soon to traverse; stony ridges covered with large grey-green expanses of euphorbia, backed by tawny mountains.

For, while we were engaged on our work round Ta'izz, our future plans had at last become clear. Permission had been received by the Amir from the Imam for us to continue our journey to San'a, and, what is more, by the central highland route, through the cities of Ibb and Yarim. This was far more than we had ever hoped! The King, in his apparently capricious behaviour, would grant favours which the recipient had never dared to expect, while refusing requests to visit places or travel by routes regarded as far more ordinary. Thus, we were never allowed to ascend Jebel Sabir, which several British visitors had done shortly before us, but we were to proceed to the capital over passes almost as high as that mountain, and by a route which less than a handful of living British had then covered.

In securing the permit to go on to San'a at all, the Aden Government, the Amir and the German savant, Dr. Carl Rathjens, were all active in our behalf. The last, whose learned writings on the Yemen are cited many times, was in San'a while we were in the Aden Protectorate. Letters had passed between us, beginning some time before I left England. Though Dr. Rathjens had been known in the capital for ten years he had never before visited Ta'izz. So we were astonished when he suddenly arrived there. In company with a well-known Jewish resident of San'a, he was travelling by the lowland motor route to Aden. We were invited to meet him at the Arab house occupied by Dr. Gino Cavaliere, an Italian doctor, a solitary outpost in Ta'izz of the Italian medical community in San'a.

Acquaintance with this army doctor had been made early in our stay. A note from me had resulted in an invitation to his house, and a return visit by him to ours. His manner was cordial, though our only medium of free converse was French, in which he was not fluent and which he spoke with an admixture of Arabic words. A few weeks after we had left Ta'izz a daughter was born to his wife, probably the first European child born in the interior of the Yemen. Unhappily the baby (named Franca in honour of the Spanish Nationalist leader) lived but a very short time.

Dr. Rathjens delayed his journey to Aden nearly a day in order to help us. When our difficult situation had been explained, first to him alone, then to him and his Jewish fellow-traveller together, these two went to see the Amir at his lower house. Later, they came to our house and carried us off to the Amir's presence. In our conference there Arabic, German, English and Italian were all used—the last (a tongue which I can follow while scarcely speaking it) being the only means of communication between me and the Jewish gentleman from San'a. The upshot was that both the Amir and Dr. Rathjens telegraphed separately to the Imam; the Amir writing out the message quickly, *more suo*, on a little scrap of paper held on the outspread palm of his left hand. The party then broke up, the German savant and his companion resuming their journey to Aden. We were thereafter granted somewhat more freedom of movement, till the Amir at length received a favourable reply from San'a.

So the end of December found us immersed in preparations for departure. Our tents, which it was now plain we should not be allowed to use, were sent back by lorry to Aden. All was bustle and packing at the 'Amil's guest-house, where Muhammad —— was charged with arranging means of transport for our northward trek. The first stage was to be by lorry, followed by several days on muleback, with a baggage-train of camels.

On our last day but one in Ta'izz we rode up once more to Dar en Nasr to say good-bye to the Amir, who had returned there from Al 'Urdi. We were first ushered into a little office in the upper storey, where Seiyid 'Ali sat behind a desk in a corner. The floor was crowded with men squatting or kneeling, holding small papers, and any vacant square inch was heaped with little written "chits". After greeting us with a pleasant smile the Amir sent us down to the great audience chamber. While waiting for him we were brought coffee and orange-water by Nasr Yahya. When the Amir joined us he apologised for being unable to give us more time. It was the season, he said, for receiving taxes, and he was extremely busy. Our parting interview was most amicable but not long. Since, however, it was the fourth, we had nothing whereof to complain.

Chapter XIII
THROUGH THE CENTRAL HIGHLANDS TO SAN'A

THE six days' journey from Ta'izz to the capital, December 30th, 1937, to January 4th, 1938, are among the most vividly remembered of our experiences. So much did the scene change from hour to hour, that events can only be told as they befell.

Shortly after 8 a.m. we quitted Ta'izz in a small lorry, far from full, as it contained only ourselves, the three Somalis, and such baggage as had not been sent in advance by camel, as well as an odd boy or two, and a man who got a lift part of the way. Thus we travelled as far as Saiyani, some twenty-two miles, at first going eastward by the road along which we had approached Ta'izz nearly three weeks earlier. Our farewell meeting with Seiyid Muhammad al Basha, the 'Amil, took place on this road. He was returning to his city in a car loaded with children, friends and servants ; one of the latter squatted on the dash-board, reclining against the bonnet and holding the 'Amil's water-pipe.

After a few miles our road branched northwards, passing close to the west of the tall tower of the mosque of Janadiya. There followed much switchbacking up and down, over the steep rolling foothills of the mountains which form the southern edge of the high plateau of the Central Yemen. Miles of euphorbia-covered country were traversed. We never again saw these fantastic plants growing so densely, or in such luxuriance and variety. At least one form not seen before appeared, a succulent little tree reaching quite ten feet, branching and almost without the prickly spines. Among the euphorbias rise the tall pole-stemmed aloes (first seen in Wadi Dareija near Dhala). The grey-green expanses of euphorbia and the tawny hillsides are dominated in the background to the east by the precipitous peak of Jebel Soraq. Behind it lies Jebel Hesha, and still farther to the east, beyond the frontier and the Wadi Tiban, Jebel Jihaf. But to have photographed Jebel Soraq might have excited suspicion ; it would have been a direct breach of the order not to photograph high mountains !

At Saiyani, a large mountain-village, the baggage was transferred from the lorry to a camel and some mules (our heavy kit having gone

PHOTOGRAPH 47.

Approach to Ibb over the pass, on a cold evening in December.

PHOTOGRAPHS 48 AND 49.
*Looking north from the Wadi Thabad in Jebel Sabir.
The old walls and city of Ibb, from the east.*

ahead, as stated, from Ta'izz on a train of camels). Since the unloading and loading naturally attracted a swarm of villagers, we were about to lunch under a tree away from the crowd, when the head-man of Saiyani appeared. The Qadhi, for such was his title, wore long white garments. His face was long and narrow, with moustache but no beard; his expression and manner were pleasant and friendly. The Qadhi, insisting that we must lunch in his house, led us to a small upper room, where his servants brought us *kishr* as drink to accompany our own provisions.

But however agreeable his manner, the Qadhi's suspicions were apparently roused. The door was locked on us while we lunched, and the telegraph ticked outside. As far as could be understood, our approach was being reported to the authorities at Ibb. Such incidents were probably due not only to doubt of the travellers' motives, but to lack of arrangement beforehand for forwarding them to their destination. In places where the " powers that be " should have been forewarned of our coming, we sometimes arrived to find ourselves entirely unexpected and unheard of, so that accommodation had to be hurriedly improvised.

Be this as it may, after photographing the Qadhi with his little son and daughter, we rode away on mules from Saiyani in the early afternoon. To reach Ibb meant climbing between two and three thousand feet and crossing a pass at nearly 8,000 feet. The distance, about ten miles direct, was, with the zigzags and hairpin bends, nearer fourteen.

The route leads first up the western side of Wadi Makhris, a beautiful broad terraced valley, which rapidly narrows and turns westward as one ascends. At the point where the valley bends the road crosses the stream-bed and continues in a general northerly direction. Near the crossing of the stream, if the rider turns and looks back, he sees unfolded a lovely prospect of Wadi Makhris to Saiyani and beyond, over all the country as far as Jebel Sabir, twenty-five miles to the south.

Our mule-road was broad and constructed in long steps, well paved with massive ancient stone blocks. We were told that it had been built, with the wayside watering-places, by a noble lady in ancient times, Saiyida binta Ahmed. From what is known of her this may well be true. Born near the middle of the 11th Century, the daughter of Ahmed ibn Ja'far ibn Musa as Suleihi, the Lady Saiyida was married while quite young to a ruler of San'a called Al Mukarram ibn 'Ali. She was (a 12th Century Arab historian tells) of fair complexion, " tall, well-proportioned but inclined to stoutness, perfect in beauty, of a clear-sounding voice, well read and a skilful writer, her memory stored with history, with poetry and with the chronology of past times." [1] She took over from her husband almost all care of public business, while he gave himself up to an indolent existence. She even asked to be released altogether from conjugal duties in order to devote herself to affairs of state ; but this he would not entirely grant. Queen Saiyida transferred the seat of Government from San'a to Jibla, a city which we saw a little to the west of our road as we approached Ibb. On her death she was buried in a great mosque in Jibla. Whether or not she was the builder of our excellent mountain-road, the Lady Saiyida is worthy of remembrance.

Beyond a very sharp bend an old stone bridge crosses a tributary stream. Descending to the edge of the current, under a damp cliff-face brightened by tufts of the golden-yellow primula,[2] we did some hurried but valuable collecting along the torrent-bed and among tall flowering labiate herbs. A little farther, and a small mountain village is passed surrounded by groves of an African Buddleia,[3] trained into small trees by the lopping away of the lower branches. This Buddleia, which I had seen in wild bush form in the forests of the Arussi mountains in Abyssinia, has spikes (not balls) of orange flowers and a heavy-sweet scent like heliotrope.

Still the road leads up, reaching the watershed at not far below 8,000 feet. On the left Jebel Taqar soars to 10,000 feet or more. The last part of the ascent is flanked by gullies torn by torrents, their steep red earthen sides dotted with the mauve flower-heads of homely field scabious.

The watershed is crossed by a broad saddle between mountains. On either side of the track the ground rises in terraced fields, not built up with stones, but with faces a few feet high, simply of the red earth. Here our growing collection of land-shells was increased by large shells in a sub-fossil state, dug out of the low rufous earthen cliffs. Here, too, were large brown wheat-ears as big as thrushes, a species [4] most distinctive of the Central Yemen plateau. A hoopoe, the first seen on this Arabian journey, and more of the delectable sunbirds,[5] further enlivened the ride to the top of the pass.

Just beyond the highest point we rode beside a stream flowing northwards, a rivulet fringed by a strip of greensward, with tufts of buttercups [6] and tall yellow potentilla.[7] These, fresh and tender from the perennial moisture even at the end of the year, seemed to mark

---

[1] Her full story can be read in the English translation of 'Omarah al Hakami (H. C. Kay, "Yaman, its early medieval history", 1892, pp. 38–42).
[2] *Primula verticillata.*   [3] *Buddleia polystachya.*
[4] *Œnanthe bottæ.*   [5] See page 58.
[6] *Ranunculus multifidus.*   [7] *Potentilla viscosa.*

the pass clearly as an outlier of the high table-lands. Pieces of these and other waterside plants were hurriedly put into the plant-presses. There was need for haste, for dusk was approaching and the cold increased, causing Ahmed Mahmūd to unwind his khaki turban and wrap it round his head and shoulders like a cowl.

Some distance had still to be covered, and a descent of about 1,300 feet made into a broad valley running north. The old (and erstwhile royal) town of Jibla lay below the track, a mile or two to the west. Ahead, but still far distant, the white city of Ibb gleamed on a mountain-spur, lit up by shafts of evening sunlight piercing through heavy clouds (Phot. 47).

Riding across the floor of the valley in growing darkness and cold, we were met by servants of the Amir of Ibb, carrying lanterns and anxiously setting out to search for the expected travellers. For with our halts for collecting and photography we had been nearly six hours on the road from Saiyani. Night had quite fallen when, about seven o'clock, we were taken to a house just outside and below the city walls, where the ground falls steeply away to the west.

Glasses of tea flavoured with mint were immediately served to ourselves, the three Somalis, and the Arab *shawūsh* and a soldier who had escorted us. Then followed a visit from the Amir's secretary, Sheikh Mansūr. This handsome young man, whose appearance bespoke intelligence, helped us to the utmost during our short stay. He was in poor health, and we, suspecting tuberculosis, tried tactfully to suggest a visit to the hospital at Aden. But though Sheikh Mansūr thanked us, we feared he would neglect his malady, for his replies showed the common fatalistic attitude.

Later, a substantial meal was put before us. Stews, concoctions of eggs and meat, chupatties and other delicacies were set out in two courses each of about eight dishes, on low tables a foot or less from the floor. The repast would have been more enjoyable but for the prevalence of flies and the thought of the precautions constantly needed against dysentery. We ate in a small room apart. Afterwards, the larger room was filled to crowding with visitors, including a benevolent-looking white-bearded old Qadhi. Only after their departure could our much-desired camp-beds be set up.

* * * * *

Ibb, where the whole of the next day (Friday, December 31st) and the following night were passed, is in some ways the most wonderful of all the cities of the Yemen. The impression left by it is of one of the very kernels of the East. The city stands at some 6,700 feet above sea-level, on a westward-projecting spur of Jebel Shemahé, which rises behind it to over 8,000 feet. Eastward again, Shemahé is backed by the huge mass of the far higher Jebel Badan. Ibb may not spread over a greater space than Ta'izz, but its population is far larger; excepting a central market-place thronged with people, every square yard within the walls is crowded with great lofty houses and other buildings. The streets are narrow unpaved lanes, twisting and turning, leading steeply up and down over rough and stony places.

The mosques, we were told, number about sixty. This is possible, for many, especially those more or less exclusively used by members of the Zeidi body, are small low unobtrusive buildings without towers, showing little but blank unornamented walls outside. In one narrow lane a man, agog with anxiety to show us the sights of his city, put his hand first on a rough wall on one side of the street, then on the wall opposite, exclaiming " *this* is a mosque, and *this* is a mosque "; but a stranger would hardly have recognised the buildings from outside. Only two large mosques have minarets, so that Ibb cannot vie thus with San'a of the many towers, or even with white-towered Ta'izz. One of Ibb's two towers (seen in Phots. 49 and 50) is a tall white octagonal shaft with the muezzin's gallery very near the top and shaded by a roof, a small feature not met with by us again. The other minaret, springing from the great mosque, the Jami' Masjid, close to the market-place, has a circular shaft ornamented with designs picked out in white, of a type represented by many variations in San'a.

The walls of Ibb are pierced, as far as could be seen, by only two gates. The castle-like principal gateway, flanked by tall circular stone towers, on one of which a rectangular storey has been superimposed (Phot. 52), is in the west wall. At the top of a steep stone-paved incline there is a sharp bend in the entry, to check the inrush of a hostile force. Because the ground falls away so rapidly on the west, the wonderful old city walls of stone have great curved buttresses, widening towards the base, on this side. The other gate is a comparatively small postern on the south or south-east, with a plain round arch set in a deep angle in the city wall, so that this gate is approached from outside almost through a lane between high stone walls.

Out on the plateau behind the city, to the east or south-east, a long curving ancient aqueduct brings water from the mountain. Nearer the city walls the aqueduct is ten feet or more high; over long stretches the water-channel is supported on a blank wall, but this is pierced at intervals by series of arches through which we could comfortably walk. Within the city the water is led to a tank supplying one of the large mosques. As this mosque lies at rather a low level, a very lofty wall and a pulley-apparatus is provided (Phot. 51) for raising the water

PHOTOGRAPHS 50 AND 51.

Ibb; minaret with roofed gallery.
Ibb; the crowd, and the apparatus for raising water for the mosques.

PHOTOGRAPH 52
Outside the principal gate of Ibb.

to a higher reservoir, whence it is distributed to the other mosques and the several quarters of the city.[1]

Europeans were still a rare sight. We were thronged by crowds so dense that it was difficult to walk through the streets. Our escort of soldiers had to force a way, with the customary cry " *Tariq ! Tariq !* " At intervals they charged the populace, laying about them with long reeds, which fortunately made more noise than they did any real hurt. Once I was unwise enough, outside our guest-house, to try and give small coins to some crippled beggars ; but I was rushed by a rabble with such force as to be pushed over backwards on to a pile of our camp-kit. The soldiers then slashed furiously and followed this up by bombarding the crowd with clods of earth.

In general, however, there was no deliberate rudeness, only eager curiosity to see us, to press on us and shake hands and to ask questions. In a dense multitude near the aqueduct we were suddenly addressed by one of the soldiers in French and by another man in English. The latter man, who had been a sailor, spoke of London and Cardiff. He asked for nothing and wanted merely to talk about the outer world. The only sign of hostility came from a big burly old man, whose bare chest was covered with grey hair. From the outskirts of the crowd he discharged broadsides of Arabic at us. The gist of it seemed to be : " You Aden Government people ! What do you want to take this country for ? There is nothing to eat in it ! " I tried to ask why, in that case, he was so fat, but my retort was probably lost in the throng.

Ibb was then and for some time previously the seat of an Amir, equal in rank to the Amir of Ta'izz. Both these high officers have since been removed and their offices united in the hands of one of the sons of the Imam. The then Amir of Ibb was, to give his full name and patronymics, Seiyid Yahya ibn Muhammad ibn al 'Abbās ibn al Imam,[2] a man of not very attractive appearance, with long thin face, rather sunken cheeks and henna-dyed beard. Reputed to be a very strict ruler, he was not beloved as was his predecessor, Isma'il ba

---

[1] I have tried to describe Ibb as we saw it on the last day of 1937. But so little has it changed since 1763 that the absence of more than two minarets, the many small towerless Zeidi mosques, the aqueduct, the water-raising apparatus, could all have been taken from Niebuhr's " Reisebeschreibung " (Vol. i) ! The chief difference is that Niebuhr describes the streets as paved, a refinement which I did not discover within the walls. Pavement may have worn out in 174 years, and not been replaced.

[2] The last two of these names, preceded by the definite article, are family names, not merely names of individuals, and the last presumably denotes descent from some former Imam. So also with our friends the 'Amil and Amir of Ta'izz, the names " al Basha " and " al Wazir " must signify descent from persons whose rank has become a surname for their descendants.

Salaama, whose grave outside the city was pointed out. However, during our short stay Seiyid Yahya showed us every civility in his power.

Seiyid Yahya had apparently combined with the office of Amir that of 'Amil of the city. No other person occupied the latter position, though a large house in the middle of Ibb was pointed out as formerly the 'Amil's. The Amir's own house, a great five-, or partly six-storied block, stood near the western wall, above the ancient spreading buttresses (Phot. 54). Early on the morning after our arrival Sheikh Mansūr brought word that the Amir would receive us. After the ride and the crowd of visitors the day before, we were all rather late; it was nearly nine o'clock when I hurried after Sheikh Mansūr up the dark stairs, with soldiers saluting on either hand. Hastening, so as not to keep the great man waiting, I was ushered into a long narrow room on an upper floor. On a raised seat in a corner at the far end sat the Amir; in the opposite corner, also at the far end of the room, were seated the principal Qadhi and other notables. All the space nearer the door was packed with men and boys. For some minutes I was alone in this throng, till Britton followed and later Jam'a, who had waited to find his best turban and clothes. I had opened boxes of specimens and was showing the set of photographs of the Museum, which Jam'a arrived in time to explain. The Amir and the Qadhi looked at the photographs for a long time, boys and men pressing forward eagerly to get a glimpse. The exterior views of the Museum, showing some of the surrounding parts of London, seemed to excite most interest. After conversing, and arranging to photograph the Amir, we were sent off under escort to see the city.

Seiyid Yahya's procession back from the mosque to his house was an occasion for some display. The cortège was led by four or five riflemen mounted on horses. Two drummers followed on foot, then the Amir, the Qadhi, and one or two other men on horses. They were escorted by foot soldiers, two of whom preceded the Amir, brandishing their *jambiyas* aloft and dancing as they moved forward—a ceremonial later seen on a much bigger scale at the progresses of the Imam through his capital. Pipes and bugles were played, and crowds ran beside the procession, shouting " long live the Amir ! " A large group of men locally eminent had previously assembled on either side of the door of his house, and the Amir, dismounting, took his stand in the midst, with the Qadhi behind him on his right (i.e. immediately to the left in Phot. 53). We saw few more brilliant-hued groups than this. Seiyid Yahya wore a big turban, mostly cloth of gold, a long dark coat and beneath it a long garment with full white sleeves, above his striped Arab dress ; over all the long shawl draped round his body, passing

PHOTOGRAPHS 53 AND 54.
The Amir of Ibb at his door, with the Qadhi (next to left) and chief men of the city. The Amir's house (right) at Ibb, on the ancient walls.

PHOTOGRAPHS 55 AND 56.
Makhadar in the afternoon light.
The sergeant (in middle) and soldiers of our escort from Ta'izz to San'a.

over the left shoulder and hanging down in front. Those around him were arrayed in long robes of bright blue, white, salmon-pink, and other bright colours. Soldiers made a more drab line in front. With some relief, after facing this high officer and his imposing suite, and taking the photograph, I walked up to the Amir, saluted and shook hands in farewell. Britton and Ahmed having taken their leave likewise, the Amir went into his house. That evening Sheikh Mansūr, who spent a long time with us, wrote at my request a little note of thanks, which the Amir received and returned with a few words of acknowledgment written on the paper.

After the excitements of the morning, that afternoon, sunless and chill, was gladly spent by us resting in our guest-house or on the roof. The householder had business concerns in Aden, where his son had been to school. From the son, a bright and friendly little boy named Ahmed ibn Yahya, I at last got a chance to see the various herbs grown in pots (and too often in paraffin tins) on house-roofs. I had many times gazed up at such roof-gardens from outside tall houses. Now this little Ahmed reeled off the Arabic names of rue, two kinds of basil, a sort of southernwood and other herbs. Sweet Basil [1] was met with many times later in our journey; bunches or sprigs are stuck in men's turbans at marriage-ceremonies and other festivities; little beds of the plant were seen in corners of orchards near San'a, and we were told that the fragrant herb is placed between clothes stored in chests.

* * * * *

The first day of 1938 saw us early on the road leading northwards from Ibb. The right stage would have been as far as the small town of Makhadar, about eighteen miles due north. But the number of days allowed for our journey from Ta'izz to San'a was strictly limited. In order, therefore, to get as many hours as possible for collecting on the high Sumara Pass, which lay between us and Yarim, it was decided to push on to Menzil Sumara, at the foot of the pass. This meant covering the eighteen miles—or about twenty, with the bends in the road—to Makhadar in the morning, and another seven or eight miles of stiff country after the midday halt. The whole day's ride of twenty-eight miles, though long and tiring, proved well worth the effort, for an entire day was saved and spent on the pass.

The road descends steeply from Ibb. It follows a broad valley running almost due north as far as Suq es Sabt, midway between Ibb and Makhadar. This fertile vale, the upper part of the Wadi Suhūl, is framed in grand high mountain scenery, especially on the right (east) and in front. Rocky hillocks, rising from the broad cultivated

[1] *Ocimum basilicum.*

valley-floor, are dotted with tall tree-euphorbias, all of one kind.[1] Beyond Suq es Sabt the valley begins to bend westward ; farther north it describes a complete curve round to the west, running eventually into the Wadi Zabīd, one of the main valleys leading down towards the Red Sea. Our track thus has to leave the broad valley, and, after crossing several ridges, beyond Makhadar it follows a tributary valley north-eastward up to the foot of the Sumara Pass.

Traffic on this main route was plentiful. Groups of men carrying rifles were marching up to Ibb, recruits from the eastern desert fringes of the country, called for military service. A train of camels loaded with salt had come from beyond the frontier, from Sa'udi Arabia. The men in charge, of Badawin type, and different in appearance and dress, raised their rifles aloft in a different form of salute. Going in the same direction as ourselves were many people bound for the weekly market at Suq es Sabt. For we were again lucky in our passage, and, after our Friday in Ibb, were passing " Saturday Market " (as the name denotes) on the right day. I should doubt if Suq es Sabt has many permanent residents other than, perhaps, some caretakers of stores. It is not a compact village, but a large open market-ground set in a country of sparse scrub, with stalls and groups of low shops and houses. A great concourse of people was gathered round the cattle and wares. Many of the men carried white umbrellas and a few wore rather shabby braided coats with gold epaulettes ; these garments might have been taken for an old-fashioned military uniform, but closer scrutiny suggested that they were parts of the cast-off liveries of European men-servants, which had somehow drifted to this remote corner of the world. The large open market amid scrub and bush, and the prevalence of umbrellas, recalled country-markets in Abyssinia.

A distance nearly as far as from Ibb to Suq es Sabt lay between the market and Makhadar. The track ascended and descended the sides of successive ridges. Despite the dryness at this season, and at little more than 5,000 feet, butterflies flitted, and the rather dusty and uninviting bush was brightened by clusters of orange-scarlet or golden-yellow flowers of two kinds of tall fleshy-leaved Kalanchoe. Little flocks of Golden Sparrows,[2] a bird very characteristic of parts of the Yemen, flew from bush to tree. At length a steep rise led to the small open town of Makhadar (Phot. 55), dominated by the house of its 'Amil. This tall white castle-like building had a courtyard surrounded by a high wall, the gate in which was approached by a steep flight of steps. The 'Amil being away, his deputy, a mild-looking black-bearded man of rather shy manners, received us kindly. We were sorry to decline his pressing invitation to stay the night, for he had collected

[1] Probably *Euphorbia Ammak*.   [2] *Auripasser euchlorus*.

two or three leading men of the place, one of them a doctor, to meet us; all wore voluminous white turbans and long white clothes. A large room with divans, on the ground-floor (an unusual feature in the houses we visited), was at our disposal for lunch. It was well lit, and the windows gave on to splendid prospects of the great valley and mountains, with Makhadar itself below in the foreground. After twenty miles' ride, and with another eight before us, we rested gratefully on the rather faded mattresses, carpets and cushions, while, after cups of *kishr*, many dishes were served on a monster brass tray on the floor.

By a steep and rocky descent the path winds from Makhadar down to the bed of the lateral valley running north-east. This side wadi is extremely luxuriant, with tall hedges and patches of scrub, thickets of rank herbage, and flowering trees. The fields behind these fringes on either side held crops of many kinds, among them plantations of coffee and of a citrus tree bearing large fruits with very thick peel.[1] Had our time been longer we should have stayed in this fertile and lovely place, but it was imperative to reach Menzil Sumara that night. The wadi, like so many valleys in this geological formation, is divided into an upper and a lower part by a precipitous drop. So an arduous climb of hundreds of feet had to be made to reach the upper valley, by a zigzag path between walls where the small whitish flowers of a delicate cranesbill [2] peeped here and there from between the stones. After climbing the steep upper valley we groped our way into Menzil Sumara in darkness, between seven and eight o'clock.

Menzil Sumara (" the lodging place of Sumara ") is a small poor mountain-village of rough stone houses. Two upper rooms, low, narrow, and lighted only through the door, were allotted to us in the house of the 'Aqil. In spite of night-minimums of 49° and 52° Fahr. on the two nights of our stay, we slept outside our room on the roofs of some lower buildings. The house was built against sharply rising ground, so that on one side of our beds a flight of stone stairs led steeply down into the narrow village street, while on the other side a step across an irrigation channel took us into a little ploughed field. Our mules and the camels with the heavy baggage (which we had overtaken) were lodged in the dark interior of a khan, the roof of which rested on rough stone arches.

The 'Aqil, a big black-whiskered man of middle age, wore the sleeveless sheepskin coat of the mountain-folk, with the leather turned outwards. Our dealings were, however, more with his mother, a very ugly witch-like old woman named Jemila (" the beautiful one "). Very fond of money and of cigarettes, she repeatedly asked for packets

[1] A kind of shaddock ?   [2] Apparently a true Geranium.

of the latter, till we could give away no more. Jemila's avidity may perhaps be excused, considering the hard conditions of her life. Moreover, an artistic tendency had caused her to decorate the whitewashed walls of our windowless rooms with extraordinary designs smeared in some ochreous substance. A psychologist might have divined the meaning of these patterns, if they represented anything at all.

Above Menzil Sumara the road zigzags very steeply up for some 1,200 feet to a col between two mountains. The ascending traveller, approaching this saddle, expects the track to drop on the far side, but instead of this it winds away north-eastward, still climbing, round the shoulders of Jebel Sumara. This mountain, to the east of the col, just exceeds 10,000 feet; on the west a lower peak is crowned by a guard-house, with a small village, Sumara proper, clinging to the slope beneath. The central keep, a tall massive tower-house, stands in an enclosure surrounded by outer walls with towers. Needless to say, we did not ask to go near this fort; nor would our escort allow any approach to the summit of Jebel Sumara.

The day gained by our forced march from Ibb was spent in walking up, with Ahmed Mahmūd, 'Omar, and the soldiers (Phot. 56) to the col, and collecting specimens beside the path, from which the soldiers politely but firmly kept us from wandering more than a few yards. But small pieces of ground beside the track fully occupied our energies, even in the bracing mountain air and bright, hot sunshine. Many of our most interesting finds were made here, particularly beetles of northern type hiding under stones and at the roots of tufted plants. Here several old friends among the high mountain flowers reappeared.[1] Other flowers were seen for the first time. Mingled rejoicing and grief arose in me, joy at seeing so grand a stretch of country, grievous disappointment because the long delay in getting permission to come had postponed the journey till the dry, cold, largely dormant winter. For, after more than three months' dry weather, the tussocky vegetation at this altitude, over 9,000 feet, was desiccated, often brown and frost-seared. The low papery everlasting flowers,[2] speckling the upper slopes of Jebel Sumara with yellow, were brittle and dead.

The suspicions entertained in high quarters, which forced our *shawūsh* and soldiers to watch us so closely, were not shared by the country-folk. These were, as usual, very friendly. An old indigo-turbaned man passing by on the track beside which I was working remarked to his companions "that is a *hakīm*". He may have thought I was collecting insects and plants for the concoction of medicines. I had heard this comment from Galla peasants in Abyssinia years before.

[1] Notably the edible campanula (*Campanula edulis*).
[2] A species of *Helichrysum*.

PHOTOGRAPH 57.
View from the Sumara pass; village of Menzil Sumara in the foreground.

PHOTOGRAPHS 58 AND 59.
*On the highest point of the Sumara pass, before our descent to the plain of Yarim.
In the city of Yarim, after sunset.*

In spare moments we could gaze northward from this col over a series of wild craggy ridges and deep valleys ; or south-westward to Menzil Sumara at our feet, and over the valley up which we had ridden the day before (Phot. 57). Many of the terraces on the sides of the gracefully winding upper valley were bright green with young corn. The steep mountain-sides were painted in various shades of brown, with a haze of duller green from the wild herbage. Fainter in the background rose, pale tawny and buff, the great mountains beyond the Wadi Suhūl.

As we explored the upper valley after descending in the afternoon to Menzil Sumara, I came, on the rough steep ground a little behind the village, on large patches of the wild iris [1] of the Yemen, not in full flower but displaying some dozen pure white blossoms, fairly large and sweet-scented, on short stalks amid short leaves. The people had also planted the iris on the graves in the little cemetery hard by. It is thought that the wide range of this iris, from Southern Spain and Barbary along the Mediterranean and down to South-West Arabia, may be partly due to the Arab custom of planting it on graves. A few small tubers brought home have flowered freely in several successive early summers in England. But from some cause, real or imagined, the blooms have never again seemed quite so fragrant as in the approaching cold and dusk of that January evening at Menzil Sumara.

On January 3rd we rode from Menzil Sumara to Yarim, about sixteen miles. Awakened at four o'clock by the din of preparations, while the stars were still brilliant and the Great Bear lay low in the heavens just over the mountain, I heard the camels of our baggage-train move off. After the clamour of loading, how musical the tinkle of the double brass bells hanging from the harness, one on the right shoulder of each camel ! These were great shaggy, rather dark camels of the mountain-breed. The contrast was noticeable when, later in the day, another caravan loaded with salt was met. The camels composing it were small sand-coloured beasts, under the charge of foreign-looking Arabs from the eastern desert towards Marib.

How beautiful that early hour, with the stars fading ; later, mist rising from the valley condensed into light clouds which left the lower air clear but very cold. At 6.30, soon after daybreak, we rode off. Beyond the col, on the road winding eastward and still upward along the north side of Jebel Sumara, the sun's rays at length struck over the huge mass of the mountain. They were welcome, for the air, though exhilarating, was very sharp. Will there always be (I thought) some places left where people can ride and hear the tinkle of bells on the old mountain roads ? Or must mechanical transport

[1] *Iris albicans* : there is a rare blue form of this iris which we did not see.

invade every corner of the world? May the old method of travel survive! For, whatever the delays and irritations, due to grazing animals straying when they should be loaded, or the occasional bolting of beasts and casting of loads, how great are the compensations of the leisurely pace and the wayside halts. He who travels in this way can really take in the country.

Near the highest point of the road we took our last toll of specimens on the mountains of Sumara, beetles and shells, at the roots of little low woody bushes, tough and wiry, with white daisy-like flower-heads.[1] From the highest point, about 9,700 feet, an abrupt descent of some hundreds of feet leads down to the plateau of Yarim. For the top of the Sumara Pass, Naqil Sumara,[2] lies not between mountain peaks but on the lip or upturned edge of the great central plateau. The highest point between mountains is the col some distance back and several hundred feet lower. From sea-level the upturned plateau-edge is reached by an ascent of thousands of feet, over a succession of immense shelves or steps facing sea-ward.

Later in the year the plateau of Yarim, 9,000 feet or more in altitude, must be a waving sea of cereal crops. What we saw (Phot. 58) on that January day was a treeless dun-coloured patchwork of ploughed fields, across which stretches a line of little stone cairns, whence rise the rough poles of the telegraph line to Yarim. From now on, for many a mile, the great beauty of the "verdant Yemen" (as the country has been called by one who knew and loved it well) was left behind. Not till we reached the fertile parts of the district round the capital, rich in fruit-orchards and fields, and the deep tropical valleys running westward to the Red Sea Tihama, did we see anything comparable in fertility and beauty with the country traversed between Ta'izz and the Sumara Pass.

Not that the plateau of Yarim (more correctly Qa' al Hagle [3]) was without variety and interest. Rocky eminences rise here and there from the general level. A mile or two north, as the traveller descends from Naqil Sumara, is Jebel Zafar, commemorating by its name ancient Zafar or Sapphar,[4] royal city of the Himyarites; but even had we realised our nearness, we could not have approached the site. Besides occasional traffic on our road, there was bird-life in the fields; kestrels, large falcons and hawks, white wagtails, more of the large wheat-ears [5] and other chats, and a flock of curved-billed, dark-

---

[1] A species of *Phagnalon*.

[2] Naqil Sumara, "the Sumara Road". The word appears again below in Naqil Isla, the name of another mountain pass. Apparently it can also be used in another sense, to denote a stream.

[3] Qa', a flat expanse of land.   [4] See Chap. xix, p. 209.   [5] *Œnanthe bottæ*.

plumaged ibis [1] on the ploughed land. A flower quite new to us, a spreading fleshy-leaved plant with purple thistle-like heads,[2] hanging from crevices in rocks, proved to be characteristic of the high plateaux as far north as we reached. A mile south-west of Yarim, a wayside tank, fed by a spring, overflowed into runnels fringed with long green grass, brightened by buttercups, a creeping cranesbill and other flowers.

At Yarim a very military reception was accorded us in the courtyard of the Hakūma, the great Government House. Dismounting, we walked to the door between two lines of soldiers, with an officer and a colour-bearer holding the national flag—the smartest military array we had yet seen. Led up the dark stairs to the office of the 'Amil of Yarim, we took our seats beside that official against the long wall facing the windows. The telegraph operator, a Turk, sat in the corner by his instruments. The 'Amil, a stern-faced old man, made little attempt to be agreeable. Our interview lasted only a few minutes, while Jam'a answered some questions which the 'Amil put in a severe tone of voice : why had we been so long on the road ? the ride from Menzil Sumara should occupy only five hours, and we had taken nearly nine. We made the usual explanations about halts to look for specimens. We were then conducted to two rooms on a still higher floor, one for us and one for our servants. A soldier was posted on guard outside our door. However, our wants were looked after and, though we had lunched beside the road, a late second lunch was served in the Arab style. Britton, developing malaria, could not partake ; after doing my best I hurried out with our *shawūsh* to see what I could of the town. For we were to be sent on early next morning by car to San'a.

Not beautiful as Ta'izz nor imposing as Ibb, Yarim is still interesting. A largish unwalled town on the plain, it is backed by rather low rocky mountains, the nearer of which, as the traveller approaches from Sumara, presents roughly the shape of a broad-based pyramid. A castle or fort, apparently ruined, is raised above the town on a detached rock. The great houses are built in the style of those at San'a, the lower parts of stone, the upper of brick (apparently baked only by the sun). In a street near the castle lay an antique object, one of the great monolithic stone mortars, several feet long, used

---

[1] These undoubted ibis, seen with field-glasses at fairly close quarters, certainly appeared to be the Glossy Ibis (*Plegadis falcinellus*) ; the late Mr. G. L. Bates, however, thought the place and season unlikely, and suggested that we might have seen the " strange rare Hermit Ibis, once obtained in Arabia " and more recently in Syria. The question cannot be settled without specimens.

[2] *Notonia obesa*, related to groundsel and ragwort.

formerly for the grinding of grain. I had, however, to end my sight-seeing and escape from an excited (though not hostile) crowd by climbing up a broken wall on to a low house-roof, and scrambling thence to an adjoining higher roof. There I took several photographs (Phot. 59), though it was now near sunset. (Niebuhr and his party, 1763, first lodged in a public inn, but were so thronged by the curious that they later rented private quarters. He drew a view of the town from his window.[1] Its general appearance has changed little.)

Though the 'Amil did not see us again, we had plenty of company in our room that evening. One Seiyid Muhammad, a dirty old man blind in one eye, was deputed to look after us. Our visitors included also a younger official and the Turkish telegraphist, besides a young secretary. The last, of kindly and refined appearance, made up by the extreme gentleness of his manners for the laconic sternness of the 'Amil. The secretary spoke a little Italian and also spelt out a few English words in a newspaper. Commenting intelligently on affairs in the outside world, he remarked that people of education find life in the Yemen very depressing. We asked whether any tradition lingered of the death and burial in Yarim of Dr. Forskål, the botanist of Niebuhr's party. But our visitors had never heard his name. If a man lived a good life there he might hope to reach eighty years, we were told: but events of more than 150 years ago were forgotten. That my travelling companion should have been ill with the first stages of fever in the very same place is a coincidence strange enough. That the results were far less serious is due to modern tropical medicine.

The remaining stages, nearly eighty miles, to San'a were covered by motor on the following day (January 4th) in a Government car sent from the capital. It was obviously impossible for this vehicle to carry more than a fraction of our baggage, so instructions were asked by telegraph. The reply from San'a, that we were to come at once, leaving our heavy kit to follow on the camels under the charge of the *shawūsh*, necessitated some hasty re-packing. In fact most of our personal luggage, apparatus and stores did not arrive in San'a till three or four days later (Phot. 61). Meanwhile we squashed ourselves, the three Somalis, one mule-trunk and all the small luggage and apparatus into (or on to the back of) the old "box-body" car, and set off soon after 9 a.m. Some of the military array which had welcomed us the preceding evening in the courtyard of the Hakūma would have been welcome, but no soldiers appeared; so our departure took place after a difficult escape from an excited crowd who mobbed the car.

This venerable "box-body" had half the glass of its windscreen

[1] "Reisebeschreibung", Vol. i, Plate 68.

missing and a bullet-hole in the lower part of the bonnet. The latter damage had been caused (truth compels the telling) by one of the Imam's many sons lying in wait for and shooting at another; for which the assailant was then in prison. Our chauffeur, Muhammad, a merry and effusively friendly soul, wore a European waistcoat and shirt, combined with a white turban and kilt. This skilful driver negotiated the "road" to San'a wonderfully well through the long day. In places he must stop, get out and remove huge stones from the track; elsewhere patches of sand had to be dodged. For long distances the road was crossed slantwise at regular intervals by worn-down irrigation ditches and banks; at each of these the car must be turned obliquely, to charge the obstacle head on. It was often well to hold on to the seat with one hand and to press the other against the roof, to save one's head from crashing against the top.

Only one of the historic cities of the Yemen, Dhamar, lies on the road between Yarim and San'a. For the rest, few places are directly on the route, and those but villages or little more. In the twenty-three miles from Yarim to Dhamar, the track leads over a rocky pass down to a bare level plain between 9,000 and 8,000 feet. Here cultivators, wearing the sleeveless sheepskin coats with leather outwards (and we also found it none too warm in our car, even in the middle of the day), were guiding their ploughs behind yokes of oxen or camels; the harness of the oxen furnished with double bells, one within the other, like the camel- and mule-bells. Great cisterns,[1] deep and wide, with plastered walls and sometimes with steps down to the water, are passed at long intervals. At these reservoirs many country people with donkeys were gathered. The cistern shown (Phot. 60) is at a point where the track almost marks the boundary between dun-coloured ploughed fields on the west and yellow sandy desert on the east. Halting here, we were approached by some rather Badawin-looking tribes-people, unlike the ploughing cultivators in appearance or dress. Bare-headed men and boys wore little but a waistcloth, girdle and *jambiya*. The girls were fully clothed in indigo-dyed garments, cowl-like hoods (but faces unveiled), close-sleeved knee-length garments girded in at the waist, and trousers tied in above the ankle. Some of both sexes were handsome. The girls pretended fear of the camera, running away and coming back several times over, amid much merriment.

Closer to Dhamar the road enters a monotonous expanse of black volcanic country of the type called *harra*. The impression left by the forbidding-looking landscape is of black rocky crags and mountains rising from the dun-coloured level, of shimmering mirage (though the

[1] See Chap. xx, p. 220.

heat was not great), and tall slender whirling " dust-devils " moving across the plain ; nearer the city, a plateau of rough blackish lava. In this *harra*, one of the areas of volcanic activity so recent as to be not yet quite dead, Jebel Hammam al Issi (or Alesi) raises its head to over 10,000 feet some eight miles east of the town, whilst about four miles to the west the old crater of Jebel Gheriat Jaffa reaches nearly 9,000 feet. In the crater of Hammam al Issi sulphurous vapour is said to be emitted from fissures,[1] while farther from the city, about eighteen miles east-north-east, another high crater (Jebel Haidar al Issi) boasts one of the numerous hot springs and baths of the Yemen. We could only see these grim old volcanoes from a distance, and must wait till our journey took us north of San'a to scramble on extinct craters and ash-heaps in the Harra of Arhab.

Dhamar, a large spreading city of tall houses, mosques with minarets, and square tomb-mosques with cupolas but no towers, is unwalled. Its buildings are mainly of bricks composed of mud and straw, plastered over. Doubtless it owes its origin partly to the fruitfulness of the volcanic soil in the level plain between the two craters. At close quarters, as one comes from the south, the city is seen to consist of two parts, separated by a broad stretch of market-gardens. These are mainly given up to irrigated beds of onions (including a broad-leaved kind, perhaps a sort of chive, of which only the leaves are eaten). In gardens, too, a few sombre cypress trees stand out against the brown or whitewashed buildings and the light green of young crops. These, the first cypresses we had seen in the Yemen, are (like those at San'a) a legacy of Turkish rule. North or northwest of the ancient city, near the route leading northwards, lies the vast cemetery.

Dhamar was formerly famous for horse-breeding, and also as the seat of a University of the Zeidi body (in Niebuhr's time there were some 500 pupils). More recent writers do not mention these activities, and no chance was given us, in a brief hour's halt, to find out whether they still continue.

We were taken to a house by which several lorries and cars were drawn up. A police-officer, in old khaki uniform and black kalpak, who spoke some English, said our arrival at Dhamar would be telegraphed to San'a. A Mongol, possibly a Muslim pilgrim or trader from Central Asia or China, among the crowd of loitering Arabs seemed to strike almost as foreign a note as we did.

After the morning's jolting in the car we were thankful to eat our own provisions alone in a little upper room, far from luxurious, and

---

[1] Niebuhr speaks of the exploitation of sulphur in a mountain east of Dhamar, called Issi or Jebel Kibūd ("Reisebeschreibung", p. 324).

PHOTOGRAPHS 60 AND 61.
An ancient cemented cistern, south of Dhamar.
Arrival of our heavy baggage in San'a.

PHOTOGRAPH 62.
Qadhi Mohammed Raghib, the Imam's foreign secretary.

filled with smoke from the adjacent kitchen, above which it was raised by a short flight of steps. The window looked over the dividing belt of onion beds to the farther quarter of the city (Phot. 78, p. 133).

About two o'clock we were rattling northwards again, with still nearly sixty miles to run. Nearly twenty miles north of Dhamar, after another hour and a half of jarring, Ma'bar was reached. This poor village street of mud-built houses is yet a place of some importance as the junction of the motor-route from Hodeida, through Madinat al Abid, with the route running through the central highlands. Consequently a great tall guest-house with a courtyard stands on the west of the road. We were to know this better on our final journey of exit from the Yemen.

Leaving Ma'bar and continuing northwards, the traveller sees before him a mighty range of barren mountains lying athwart his track. The route crosses the Naqil Isla pass at well over 9,000 feet, between the domes and peaks of Jebel Jalal on the west and Jebel al Meriat on the east, both exceeding 10,000 feet. The old caravan-road ascends sharply, with hairpin twists, to the pass. The new motor-road, though describing much wider curves, is yet very steep and rough. Our old car, often stopping on the more abrupt inclines, had to be hurriedly propped with large stones behind its wheels. Finally nearly all of us climbed a good stretch on foot. It was between five and six o'clock, about sunset, and very cold. Only one plant could be hastily snatched from among the tough and wiry herbs and shrubs sparsely dotted over the barren rocky slopes—a kind of lavender,[1] with a scent more like that of citronella oil.

In the growing dusk and cold there was no halting at the top of the pass. But on our " exit journey ", over two months later, we spent several hours there in hot midday sunshine ; scrambling up the steep slopes of Jebel Jalal almost to 10,000 feet, and shaking insects from the branches of dwarf juniper-bushes (the only junipers met with besides the solitary tree in the Wadi Sabir near Ta'izz). Then, too, we had leisure to gaze southward over the noble prospect from Naqil Isla (Phot. 112), framed on the right by spurs of the great range, and with the village of Kheriat en Naqil grandly set on cliffs to the left.

After Naqil Isla darkness fell quickly. Little could be seen of the descent to San'a plain and nothing of the twenty-eight miles traversed between the mountains and the capital. When at last San'a was reached about eight o'clock, after nearly eleven hours on the road, the city gates were shut. Our car stood long outside the Bab al Khusemeh, which the guard at first refused to open. The shouts of Muhammad,

[1] *Lavandula pubescens.*

the driver, of "Nasara (Christians), Britton wa i-Scott!" were unavailing. But a note written in Arabic by Ahmed Mahmūd, handed through a chink in the heavy wooden gate and carried to a high personage, caused the gates to be swung back. The journey of 160 miles, 58 of them by mule, was over. We had reached the capital of the Yemen.

Chapter XIV
MANY-TOWERED SAN'A

AFTER unfavourable first impressions of San'a, it is pleasant to recall with what affection we came to regard the capital and with how much regret we left after more than two months. When, on that cold January evening, the gates were at length opened, we were driven in darkness across an open space. On the right a lofty pile of buildings loomed up, with traceried windows brilliantly illuminated, which we later knew well as the Imam's Palace. Through an inner archway we were taken into the walled western division of the city, to a guest-house in a street of the quarter called Bir al 'Azab. After the splendour of our rooms in the 'Amil's guest-house at Ta'izz, our lodgings had progressively declined. This first abode in San'a was a low unornamented Turkish house with plain windows. The rooms, medium-sized, bare and whitewashed, were carpeted but none too clean. Flies swarmed so badly that windows had to be kept shut all day. Later, apologies were received from the Imam's ministers that this was the only guest-house available. We could hardly have expected the Government to house us in the great stone building with an arcaded courtyard and fountain, in the spacious upper rooms of which the visiting official missions representing foreign Governments are lodged.

Conditions were the more dismal in that we were closely confined to the house. Foreign new-comers cannot go about freely on first arrival in the capital. Neither should they expect official visitors, nor to be summoned to an audience, for some days at least. In our case, the Imam being indisposed and not receiving Europeans, it fell out that we did not see His Majesty for more than five weeks. Even so, respects must be paid to his Prime Minister and others in high positions before we could move about freely. As a necessary preliminary to these visits we provided ourselves with kalpaks, the black lamb-skin caps worn by non-orientals in San'a. The maker of kalpaks arrived with a sack of lamb-skins over his shoulder, took our head-measurements, and in a day or so provided us with neatly-made kalpaks lined with orange-coloured silk; a comfortable form of head-gear, but lacking any brim to shade the eyes or back of the neck.

While preparation of the specimens collected since leaving Menzil Sumara fully occupied my time, Britton's illness would have kept him indoors in any event. Happily, even before we realised the serious stage it had reached, help was on the way. Jam'a, knowing the city well since a previous visit with Captain Seager, sought out the only permanent British residents. These were three members of the Keith-Falconer (Church of Scotland) Mission at Sheikh 'Othman (Aden), namely, Dr. Patrick W. R. Petrie and his wife, both medical doctors, and Miss L. J. Cowie, a nursing member of the Mission. Arrived in San'a (with the Petries' small son, Jimmy) nearly a year before, they were working in the Imam's hospital, by arrangement reached between the Aden Government and the King. Dr. Petrie, visiting us on our third evening, suspected malaria, took blood-films for further diagnosis and immediately set about getting permission for us to establish ourselves at his large house in Bir al 'Azab.

The next day being Friday, the day for official visits, he set out with me early on a round of introductions. I was first taken to the tall house of the Prime Minister, Qadhi 'Abdullah al 'Amri, in the old Arab city. Leaving our boots outside the reception-room on an upper floor (a procedure which had not hitherto been always demanded), we entered, wearing our kalpaks. I had heard much of the personality and ability of Qadhi 'Abdullah. I found him a man over sixty, of a fine presence and capable of exerting considerable charm. His complexion is dark (he is not of the noble race of *seiyids*); he wore a black beard close trimmed. He is known to be reserved, one who does not easily manifest his inner thoughts, loyal to his king and country from an old-fashioned Oriental standpoint, and (like his master, the Imam) extremely industrious. So it was a great concession on his part that he devoted a whole hour to this first interview. To make a good impression on him was most important; therefore the friendliness of the reception accorded to us and to Ahmed, who was with us, was gratifying.

Boxes of specimens and the pictures of the Museum were shown once more. Of course the question asked was, what practical use or material reward we hoped to extract from our work. The same " query " was put by nearly every person of high station who received us, and not the least of my indebtedness to Dr. Petrie is for his able attempts to explain. After this the Qadhi brought out much curious local lore. He seemed very learned in the history of his country, and spoke of a scheme for a complete written record. For my benefit he narrated curious sayings about insects, though whether believing them himself or not I cannot tell. On scientific matters his statements certainly sounded odd to western ears. One strange tale was that there is poison in one wing of a fly but not in the other, so that, if a fly falls into any beverage, the drinker should be careful to immerse both its wings, thereby imbibing the antidote as well as the poison.

We got, by the way, a scrap of humorous folk-lore relating to insects from our Somalis. When a large hawk-moth emerged from its pupa, Jam'a and Ahmed both said that, as boys in Somaliland, they used to call the chrysalids of butterflies and moths " angels ". Neither " devils " nor " jinn ", they assured me, but *angels*; and this was not because a winged insect emerged from the chrysalis, for they did not know that this happened. The boys would hold the chrysalis in the hand and ask it " which is the north, or west ? " or whatever direction they wanted. Whatever way the chrysalis bent its hinder segments was supposed to give the answer. (Compare with this an American boy, Tom Sawyer by name, who, searching for hidden treasure far away on the banks of the Missouri, put his mouth close to the little funnel-shaped pit made by an insect, presumably an ant-lion, and repeated " Doodle-bug, doodle-bug, tell me what I want to know ! ") [1]

To return to our round of visits : taking leave of Qadhi 'Abdullah, on whom I was destined to call again before both our longer treks in San'a district, Dr. Petrie and I rode on mules sent from the Beit al Mal (the Treasury) to the house of the 'Amil of San'a, Seiyid Husein 'Abdul Qādir. This stout and genial elderly official, the Lord Mayor of San'a (he might almost be called), received us in a pavilion or *mifraj* in the garden of his house in Bir al 'Azab. Sitting beside him on the cushioned floor, where he was most anxious that I should be quite comfortable and " at home ", I had leisure to take in some of the pleasantest surroundings yet seen. Outside, tall jets of water were playing in an oblong tank surrounded by a plastered balustrade and a paved walk ; beyond was a garden of fruit trees, still bare. The middle of the room was occupied by a noble array of brightly polished metal objects on a huge brass tray, censers, the brass frameworks of water-pipes and other brazen utensils (compare Phot. 72). We were each given an elegant brass stand as high as a candlestick, on which a coffee-cup was rather precariously balanced. I drank the excellent coffee rather quickly, fearing to knock the cup over ! Seiyid Husein jokingly played on the name of the garden quarter of San'a. He remarked that Bir al 'Azab, the " well of the unmarried ", was a misnomer, since its inhabitants are nearly all married people. It is tempting to consider the view that the name is a corruption of Bir al Azal. Azal, said to be an old name of San'a, is traditionally

[1] Mark Twain, " The Adventures of Tom Sawyer ", Chap. viii.

identified with the Uzal mentioned in *Genesis* as a son of Joktan or Qahtān descendant of Shem.[1]

Seated on the floor in an upper room of his house near by, Seiyid 'Ali ibn Ahmed Ibrahim (?), the War Minister, was receiving courtesy visits from officers. Elderly men with black beards or side whiskers, they knelt, put their hands in his, and bowed their heads almost to the mild-mannered old gentleman's lap. Despite their dark complexions some of these officers were probably Turks. The Turkish officers who have stayed in the Yemen in the Imam's service after the departure of the Turkish rulers doubtless represented a conservative element in the army, which was under reorganisation by two Syrian Pashas. Weeks later, at the Great 'Īd, much younger officers, trained under Syrian influence, led detachments in the procession.

Last of these introductory visits was a call on the Minister of whom I had heard most, and who (with the Prime Minister) was most important to us: namely, the Foreign Secretary, Qadhi Mohammed Raghib Bey (Phot. 62). This charming Turkish gentleman of sixty or more was receiving a crowd of visitors in a ground-floor room of his house, again in Bir al 'Azab. Some of us sat on a high cushioned bench against the wall, the rest on upright chairs. Little was possible then but polite inquiries and answers.

During our stay, however, we saw Qadhi Raghib many times and on ever more friendly terms. Having been a member of the old Turkish Diplomatic Service he was fluent in French. He narrated many anecdotes of his diplomatic career in St. Petersburg (as he still called it) and other European capitals before 1914. A fine *raconteur*, he sometimes launched into reminiscences; how, when holding a post at Cetinje (Montenegro), he heard of his appointment to a position at the Turkish Embassy in St. Petersburg; how he returned to Constantinople and did everything to avoid being sent to Russia, but he was sent, and was thankful ever afterwards. For he enjoyed his three years (1900–3) in St. Petersburg to the utmost. The Dowager Empress specially befriended him, having first noticed the young Raghib at some public function, through a likeness to an uncle of his, an earlier sojourner in St. Petersburg. Besides these diplomatic posts under the Turks, Raghib Bey had held office under them in the Yemen before or during the war of 1914–18. Stranded in San'a at the end of that war, he had been retained in the Imam's service, and had been unable to leave the Yemen for twenty years. After such a career his readiness to converse with foreign visitors is understandable. He now found himself obliged to adopt the long robes and conform to the strict old-fashioned Muslim standards of San'a. But he used to visit us inform-

[1] See Chap. xix, p. 209.

ally in the evenings at Dr. Petrie's house, and, towards the end of our stay, he entertained us alone in his own house, in an upstairs *salon* well furnished with chairs and small tables, in which the bare white walls set off some pretty bright-coloured hangings. We even saw once, but only for a moment, his wife. The Qadhi wished to be photographed with Britton and myself in his garden; as no other member of the household was available, a grey-haired lady ran out unveiled (tell it not in San'a) and released the trigger. Mrs. Petrie spoke also of the cleverness and wit of his two daughters.

Qadhi Raghib, witty and clever in argument, professed himself always a lover of Great Britain, but he lamented her (then) policy with regard to the Jewish question and Palestine. It would surely, he said, antagonise the Muslim world. As to our natural history work in the Yemen, he of course believed in the innocence of our motives. But he could never fully convince his royal master, and he failed to get us permission to visit certain places among our most longed-for objectives. His endeavours and kindness were, however, constant. Many letters in French passed between us. The Qadhi's French was full of the most courteous expressions. His letters were addressed "Au très Honorable", or "Au très Respectable Monsieur Dr. Scott". In writing or speaking he himself was addressed as "Votre Excellence".

After the Friday morning visit Dr. Petrie saw Qadhi Raghib again on our behalf, and also the Minister of Health, Seif al Islam Qasim, one of the Imam's younger sons. This prince, on whom I later called at the Ministry of Health (one of the former Turkish Government buildings), was a pleasant-mannered spectacled man with close black beard. He was rather stout and bullet-headed, like his father and his eldest half-brother (the Crown Prince Ahmed). Dr. Petrie's efforts resulted in permission being at last extracted from the Imam to move not only Britton, the sick man, but our whole establishment, from the unsavoury guest-house to Dr. Petrie's house. Our luck turned and impressions of San'a rapidly brightened.

Our new home was a roomy three-storied building, broad and not deep, with a little pinnacled *mifraj* (or belvedere) rising from the roof. It stood in a spacious walled garden cultivated by a market-gardener who dwelt elsewhere; apparently the usual arrangement with the large houses in the garden-quarter of San'a. Another *mifraj*, or garden-pavilion, stood in the garden some way from the house; this formed a little rectangular enclosure, with low buildings round two sides of a tank (then dry), while the other two sides were balustraded. Near the entrance from the street to the large compound stood an outbuilding, the Beit ad Dawa ("house of medicine"), used as a dispensary.

Our Somalis, with Britton (after he had been tended and cured in the doctor's own room), established themselves in the garden *mifraj*. I settled into the *mifraj* on the roof. This small self-contained one-roomed flat had large windows on three sides, little traceried windows with stained glass above, and a high shelf round the walls, most useful for cameras and apparatus. The climb of forty-four stone stairs, well constructed of massive blocks but of unequal height, was worth the effort many times over. For from the top of the staircase I could not only enter the *mifraj*, but walk out on to the flat balustraded house-roof, thence to gaze in every direction over town and country, but especially eastwards to the old Arab city and its mountain background (Phot. 63).

* * * * *

It is time now to say something of the capital itself. San'a, the largest city in South Arabia, with a population estimated at between 40,000 and 50,000 stands on a plain between mountains, at rather less than 8,000 feet above sea-level.[1] Extending some two and a half miles in a direction a little north of east to south of west, the city has in plan

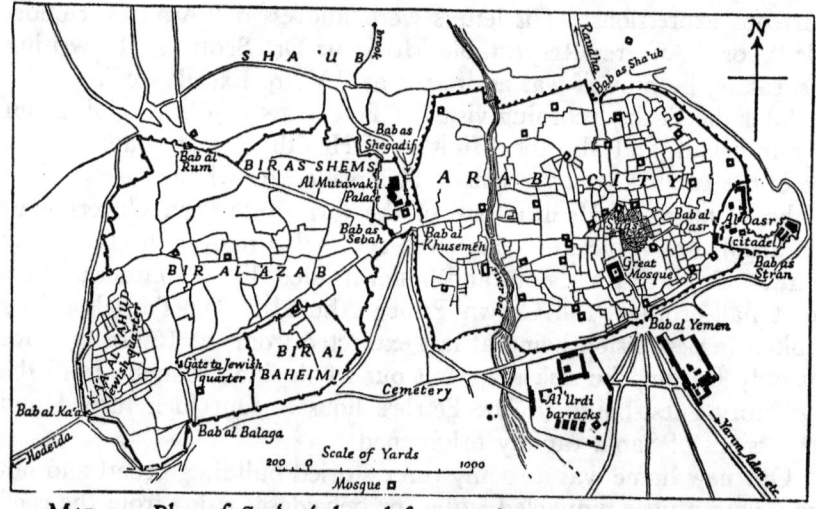

MAP 3. *Plan of San'a (adapted from Rathjens and von Wissmann).*

the form of an irregular figure-of-eight (Map 3). On the east the old Arab city, San'a proper, stands within its ancient walls of sun-dried brick. Its northern gate, Bab ash Sha'ūb, and the southern gate, Bab al Yemen, lead directly to the open country. At its eastern end another gate leads into the citadel, Al Qasr, which is raised above the city on a foot-spur of Jebel Nuqūm. The pre-Islamic stronghold of Ghumdan lay

---

[1] The altitude is mentioned again in the following chapter.

PHOTOGRAPH 63.
San'a : the Arab city in the afternoon light, from the housetop in Bir al 'Azab.

PHOTOGRAPHS 64 AND 65.
*San'a : soldiers drilling on the parade-ground outside the palace, the main building of which is on the left.
Outside the palace precincts, the main building in the background.*

in the south-eastern part, between the present citadel and the Great Mosque. From the citadel a further gate, Bab as Stran, leads also to the country. The remaining gate of old San'a, the Bab as Sebah on the west, has been demolished, and the name is applied to a more modern gateway a few yards farther west, communicating with the western division of the city. The old walls rise to heights between twenty and thirty feet. Their effect as seen from outside (Phot. 113) is very impressive, from the numbers of semicircular bastions, which, with the round towers flanking the gates, amount to one hundred and twenty-eight. Near its western end old San'a is traversed from north to south by a broad *seil*, a water-course, dry and dusty during most of the year, spanned by a stone bridge only used in times of flood.

The figure-of-eight shape of the whole city arose through the building on the west of suburbs, later walled in. In Niebuhr's plan (1763) these suburbs are shown unwalled,[1] and the walls since constructed have their bastions set at much wider intervals than in old San'a. This western division, which may cover an area even larger than the old city, is subdivided. Its greater part is occupied by the garden quarter, Bir al 'Azab, but smaller quarters called Bir ash Shems and Bir al Baheimi lie on the north and south, the latter being bounded by walls of its own. These three quarters take their names from wells, and indeed the seemingly numberless deep wells hereabouts supply the whole of San'a with water. But most distinctive of the quarters of the western division is Qa' al Yahūd, the Jewish quarter, shut off from Bir al 'Azab by a wall, pierced by a gate flanked by a large round tower with a guard-room. This dividing wall is no cypher; for, though the Jews go freely about their business in city and country by day, certain activities are only permitted within their own quarter.

The western division has three gates leading to the open country, north, south-west and south. The northern gate, Bab ar Rūm, takes its name from the route leading eventually to " Rome " (Constantinople). Two more gates yet, in the north and south walls of the narrow waist joining the western division to old San'a, complete the sum: seven gates through which the city can be entered by day, or eight if that through the citadel be counted.

The narrow waist holds the most important enclosure of all, Al Mutawakil. These precincts, in which stand the Imam's massive seven-storey palace and adjoining buildings, have their own high walls, towers and bastions (Phot. 65). A great gate-way opens eastwards into a narrow space between the precincts and the walls of the old city. The name in full, Bustan al Mutawakil Allah (" the garden of him who relies on God "), refers to one of the titles of the Imam, explained

[1] " Reisebeschreibung ", Vol. i, Plate 70.

in a later chapter. Here the monarch now dwells, midway between the older and newer halves of his capital. Not long since he lived in a smaller house on the open Sherara place in Bir al 'Azab.

The walls of the old city and the western division do not at present enclose every house. Conspicuous among the groups of buildings scattered without are the barracks and other large 19th Century Turkish buildings south of the old city, near the Bab al Yemen (Phot. 102). The present gate of that name is also Turkish, parts of the Arab walls having been demolished for its insertion.

Such is the plan of the capital. If one bent on seeing the life of the city start from Bir al 'Azab on a walk through old San'a, he must first cross the Burjet Sherara, the broad open space used as a parade-ground, where as like as not soldiers are drilling (Phot. 64); he must go through the Bab as Sebah and pass the small domed mosque just outside the palace, where the Imam daily performs his private devotions. Straight in front is a broad street of shops, the Haret en Nahsein, running east from the entry through the old walls as far as the dry flood-bed. If a less crowded thoroughfare is preferred, turn off on the south side along a narrow street, which curves round to touch the dry watercourse at a point farther south. This quieter way and the streets opening off it on either hand lie between tall houses, the style of which we can begin to note (Phot. 66). Apart from the houses bordering these streets there is much ground occupied by walled-in gardens, even within the old city walls, on this side of the *seil*. Our curving street opens out on to the latter, the dry watercourse, by the large mosque of Mahdi 'Abbas (Phot. 67). This building, one of the two larger mosques built by the Turks in the 16th or early 17th Century, has a large cupola surmounted by the crescent. But its minaret shows something of the San'a Arab style, designs picked out in white against the warm dark brown brick, and a fluted cap. Under its shadow the cutters and polishers of agates, cornelians and other semi-precious stones have a row of little shops.

Cross the wide dry water-channel, scramble up the piles of dust, stones and rubbish on the far side, and enter the larger eastern part of the old city. Here there is little open space, saving a few high-walled gardens near the *seil*. Otherwise nearly all the ground is covered with lofty houses and other buildings. The narrow lanes, unpaved and uneven, are a maze with sharp turns, often at right angles, and frequent blind alleys. Here and there the explorer emerges into little irregular-shaped " places " or " squares " (Phot. 71). Nearly all the forty-four mosques of the capital are in the old city, and most stand in the crowded quarters east of the watercourse. More than twenty minarets rear their heads towards the sky. Charming glimpses of

Mosques and lofty houses

them appear in most cramped and unexpected places (see for instance, Phot. 70).

The two main groups into which the mosques fall—excepting the Great Mosque, which is in a class apart—are not difficult to distinguish. Those built by the Turks or showing Turkish influence have a large dome surmounted by the crescent, and perhaps smaller cupolas as well, though their minarets display ornament in the Arab style. Such are Mahdi 'Abbas, which we have passed, and the great Bakiliye Mosque right against the eastern wall of the city. Al Bakiliye, built during the earlier Turkish dominion and restored when the Turks reoccupied the city in 1872, forms with its adjacent buildings a group roofed by a large dome and ten smaller cupolas. Most of the mosques, however, are smaller and older buildings in the Yemeni Arab style, having flat roofs and minarets most intricately designed. To a lover of buildings the diversity of their beautiful patterns is a constant source of delight. Look, for instance, at the small mosque (Phot. 69) of Al Madressa ("the school"), near the north-eastern part of the city wall. Above the quadrangular base of its tower, decorated with calligraphy, is an octagonal stage, topped by a coronet of arrow-shaped ornaments, possibly survivals of a pre-Islamic symbol; above this, a tall cylindrical stage, with patterns in relief picked out in whitewash; above the gallery again, a slender polygonal shaft, capped by a graceful fluted cupola, surmounted by a metal dove. This symbol is emblematic of an incident in the Hejira, when the Prophet, in flight, hid in a cave; whence his pursuers departed without search, thinking that no one could have entered for a long time past, because a pair of doves were nesting on the rocky walls.

But a good part of the city has been skipped to reach these mosques by the eastern wall. Return to the "square" (Phot. 71) close to the tall whitewashed minaret of Al Abhar, and see the wealth and variety of ornament, constructed in relief and whitewashed, in the house-fronts; the windows filled with thin sheets of alabaster quarried locally, or the double series of windows in the well-lighted upper floors, the lower row unglazed but furnished with wooden shutters, the upper row of arched windows filled with tracery made in hard plaster. Jewish craftsmen may be seen carrying these traceried window-heads, as yet unglazed, all in one piece; for these medieval-looking forms of ornament are not a dead but a living craft. The double rows of windows may, from outside, make the number of storeys seem greater than they really are. The tall houses are of three, four or more storeys, with the common feature of the *mifraj* or belvedere occupying part of the roof-space. Massive stone blocks make up the walls of the ground-storey; above this, the walls are of dark brown bricks, first sun-dried then baked in kilns (Phot. 80) outside the city.

Queer little observation-places project from the upper floors (several are seen on the left in Phot. 71), whence the inmates may peer down and see who is knocking at the great iron-studded door; for every massive front-door has an iron knocker, usually a thick, somewhat shovel-shaped, plate, on which a hinged clapper strikes. Sometimes, particularly when a walled garden lies between the street door and the house, the door can be opened from the upper floors by a cord.

Against the spaciousness, the beauty, and the variety of intricate designs must be set the very primitive sanitation. From the bathrooms and privies in the upper floors, holes open through the walls and wide cemented channels lead perpendicularly down to little walled-in drainage-spaces at the foot of the house. You may meet the men of the town sanitary service driving donkeys carrying away garbage of all kinds in panniers. Much refuse is thrown outside the north-eastern walls of the city, where dogs tear at carcases, and kites and vultures [1] congregate.

The ornament inside the living-rooms in the better houses, fretted plaster-work supporting brackets, conventional designs in relief forming string-courses or surrounding wall-niches, is not unlike the decoration of the 'Amil's guest-house at Ta'izz (Phot. 73)—though in some small details this differed from the San'a style. Beautiful indeed are such rooms when the pure white walls and ceilings contrast with rich carpets, bright cushion-covers, and stained glass in the traceried windows.

A little east of Al Abhar and the "square", a double right-angled turn opens into a space in front of the Great Mosque (Phot. 68). In this great building the Imam is wont to lead the garrison, as spiritual head of his people, at the Friday prayers. But, though the vast oblong measures about 197 feet from south-west to north-east and nearly 214 from south-east to north-west, it has little to show outside but blank walls. On the south-west and south-east sides it is separated from tall houses only by narrow lanes. On the north-east, towards the site of pre-Islamic Ghumdan and the present citadel, there is a wider street. But only on the north-west, where is the broad oblong space called Waqf, can the famous sanctuary be viewed at all satisfactorily. For, though the Jami' al Kabir is in many parts of its structure rough and plain, lacking the more delicate finish and elaborate ornament of the smaller mosques, it is one of the oldest and most venerable buildings in the Muhammadan world. It preserves the primitive form of an open courtyard surrounded by covered spaces, the roofs of which are borne

[1] Probably all the Egyptian Vulture, *Neophron hercnopterus.*

PHOTOGRAPH 66.

San'a : in the Arab city.

PHOTOGRAPHS 67 AND 68.
San'a: mosque of Mahdi' Abbas, 16th Century Turkish style; shops of lapidaries on left.
San'a: courtyard of Great Mosque, showing small rectangular local ka'ba in the open court.

by rows of columns and arches. There are three rows apiece on three sides of the building, and five rows of columns in the broader covered space on the north-west side, in which is the Mihrab, giving the direction of Mecca. The pillars number about 177 in all. Happy is a non-Muslim if he catch a passing glimpse of these columned halls

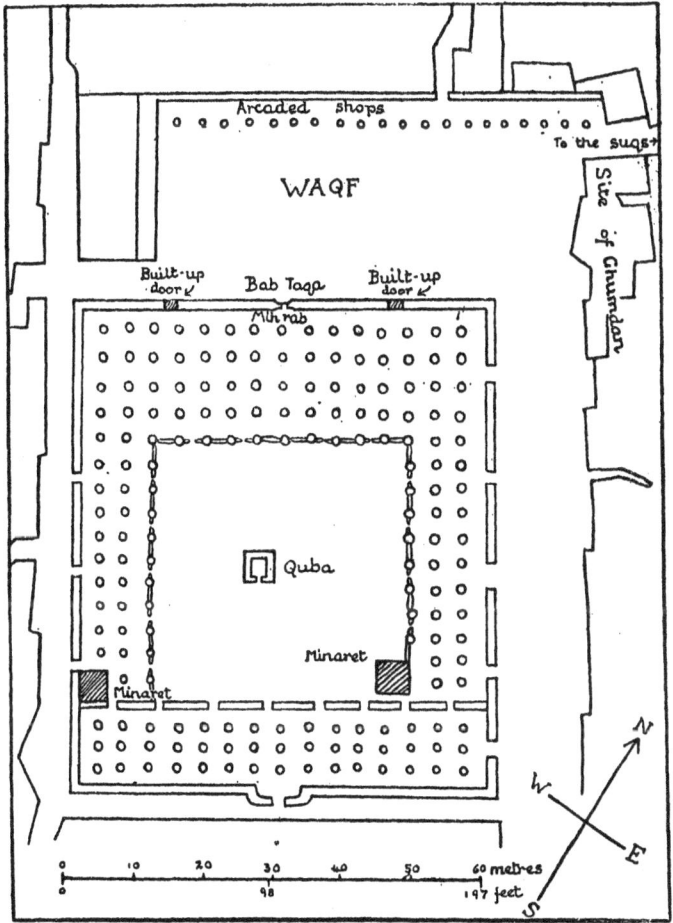

FIG. 1. Plan of the Jami' al Kabir (The Great Mosque) at San'a (adapted from Rathjens and von Wissmann).

through one or other of the nine open doors in the side and back walls of the mosque (the tenth door in use, in the middle of the front or north-west wall, is said to be only opened for the Imam). The twin minarets, roughly finished and whitewashed, stand shining when viewed from outside the city (Phot. 113) but are difficult to see near at hand. They are placed far towards the back (south-east) of the building, unsymmetrically, one rising from the outer wall on the south-west side, the other from the eastern corner of the courtyard.

In the open courtyard, a little west of the middle, a small rectangular domed building represents the Ka'ba at Mecca; indeed, it is—or was—the local Ka'ba of San'a.[1]

One chronicler at least has recorded that this famous mosque was first built in the time of the Prophet, and that it early assumed the dimensions of the present courtyard. Extensions of the original mosque are recorded as early as the 8th, and at various dates till the 12th, Century A.D. The two minarets were first erected, it is said, in 878, and brought to their present form in 1261. Remains of pre-Islamic buildings are certainly incorporated in the mosque, but to determine exactly to what extent or whence they came would need close archæological examination. Many of the great blocks of

FIG. 2. *Much-weathered sculptures built into the outer wall of the Great Mosque, San'a (from photograph by the writer).*

masonry were taken, according to the same early chronicler, from the pre-Islamic castle of Ghumdan, immediately to the north-east of the present mosque. The weathered sculptures of birds and conventional rosettes (Fig. 2) at the sides of two built-up doors in the north-west wall could have been part of Abraha's (the 6th Century Abyssinian Viceroy's) great church.[2] In the rows of ornaments surmounting the walls of the Ka'ba, and along the top of the arcades of the great courtyard (Phot. 68 again), various pre-Islamic emblems may be represented. Are some of those in the foreground degenerate survivals of Christian crosses? Built into the outside of the north-east wall, too, are stones different from the surrounding masonry, inscribed with early Islamic texts.

By this time the hot and dusty sightseer, skirting a crowd round a

---

[1] I have alluded to the local Ka'bas of San'a and Nejran instituted to rival that at Mecca on pp. 212–3.
[2] See Chap. xx, p. 212.

PHOTOGRAPH 69.
Mosque of Al Madressa, San'a, built in the Yemeni Arab style, with flat roof and richly ornamented minaret surmounted by a metal dove.

PHOTOGRAPHS 70 AND 71.

A street in San'a leading to the mosque of Al Abhār.
A "square" close to the same mosque.

professional story-teller in a little space near the entrance to the *suqs*, may be glad to turn aside to Haj' Ahmed's tea-shop. It is cool and dark, lighted only through the big doorway of the deep, narrow room, which can be closed at night by heavy and much-patched wooden doors. Haj' Ahmed's beard and moustache are turning grey. His face is deeply lined. He wears an indigo turban, and a shabby old sleeveless garment of nondescript dark colour over a white shirt, kilt and girdle. He serves glasses of tea flavoured with mint or cups of coffee, leaving the amount of the payment to his customer. You may be joined by the old Anatolian Turk who keeps a general store hard by. Hajji Mu'tassar, (such is his name), sometimes styled "Effendi", has a close-trimmed white beard and moustache. His head is covered by a black kalpak and beneath it, because he suffers from neuralgia, a plaid shawl hanging below the waist on either side; he wears a long black overcoat of European cut, over long white garments. His speech is soft and slow, his manners very gentle. If you sit with him in his store he is glad to talk, but never presses you to buy his wares. He may walk some way with you, to point out, through a gap in the crowded buildings, the minaret of the ancient Salah ad Dīn mosque (Phot. 74), surmounted by its metal dove. Or it may chance that the tea-shop is patronised by some 'Amil of an outlying district, visiting the capital to report to the Imam. One such, a youngish man, brought out of his capacious garments handfuls of fresh limes which he handed to all sitting round. The least amiable frequenter of the café is a Turkish beggar, a well-known character. Wearing nothing but a shabby tarbūsh, cocked at an angle, and a worn khaki military overcoat several sizes too large and reaching the ground, he plants himself in front of a newcomer. He is mad, when it suits him to be, loudly announces that he is "king of the Yemen", and holds out his hand to receive tribute. For all his tales have but one end, to demand money. Captain Seager, on his visits to San'a, would give him no money; but he used to buy several dollars' worth of food and send it under strict guard to the beggar's wife. For the rascal was reputed to keep all his "earnings" to himself, while he starved his unfortunate spouse!

About a quarter of a mile farther east is a wide open space fronting the Bab al Qasr, the great gateway flanked by towers leading into the citadel. A broad way runs northward past the Bakiliye mosque till it touches the city walls where they bend to the north-west, and so follows the line of the walls round to the northern gate, Bab ash Sha'ūb. But we can turn back into the heart of the city and find our way through a maze of narrow lanes, with many sharp turns, to the *suqs* (Phot. 75). These, a little south-east of the centre, are a network of narrow streets and some small irregular spaces, lined by one-storey shops with untidy projecting awnings. Owing to the lowness of the buildings there are good view-points among the *suqs*, whence may be seen the minarets of several mosques in their richness and diversity of ornament. At one such point four are visible, in a curving line. The *suqs* themselves have probably much in common with those of other oriental cities. There are the surging crowds, the pushing through of heavily laden donkeys and camels, perchance of riding mules and horses; the chatter, the shouting, the flies. Yet many of the wares are distinctive of the Yemen, and even of San'a. Such, for instance, are the embroidery in gold and silver thread, largely made up into caps and belts for men and into parts of women's dress; and the *jambiyas* with ornamented handles and sheaths of silver filigree-work.

In these jostling crowds, and perhaps still more in the quieter lanes and streets, peculiarities of dress strike the beholder. Caps (*kuffīze*), richly embroidered with gold and silver thread and shaped rather like inverted circular baskets, and the embroidered leather belts seen on sale in the *suqs*, are much in evidence. Little grandsons of the Imam himself or young sons of great *seiyids*, walking attended by servants, have their heads covered only by these caps, not binding a turban round the cap till they are older; and this may be said of all small boys in better circumstances. Then there is also the largely idle class of *seiyids*, young or middle-aged men, strolling in twos and threes, holding hands; they sport the embroidered cap and turban, the gorgeously sheathed *jambiya* in the embroidered belt, girt round the ordinary long striped garment of the townsman, with the long shawl draped over one or both shoulders. Soldiers off duty also stroll in pairs, holding hands, a strange sight to western eyes.

Perhaps the most curious sight is the dress of the San'a women, a thing quite distinctive of the capital and the smaller towns within its orbit. We had, for instance, seen nothing like it till we reached Yarim. Not the dress of the poorest townswomen, but of those in better circumstances—though the highest-placed probably do not walk about the city at all, or only visit the ladies of other harems towards evening, when they walk carefully attended by serving-women. But, during the day, the strangest-looking figures move about the streets. Not only is the whole body enveloped in a long brightly coloured, printed or embroidered shawl, covering the head, held in by the hands, and hanging to the ankles; but, beneath this, the whole head and face is shrouded in a long silken veil, leaving no part uncovered. This veil is dark blue, variegated with large diamond-shaped rectangles about six inches long, spaced at regular intervals and each having a black outer and a white inner border surrounding a red space. The veil is arranged so that two of these large patterns lie over the wearer's

PHOTOGRAPHS 72 AND 73.

An interior in the suburbs of San'a. The great brass tray bears water-pipes, candlesticks, censer, tobacco-box and basket of bread.

Plaster-work and double traceried windows in an upper room.

PHOTOGRAPH 74.
Minaret of the mosque of Salah ad Dīn at San'a.

eyes, giving her a most eerie look. When I first met ladies thus attired towards dusk in Yarim, I started back as from an apparition ! Women go shod in red or black shoes or slippers, not sandals as are worn by men. Women of higher station naturally did not pose for the camera, but some of these strange shrouded figures can be seen in the background in Photographs 66 and 71.

As to the " largely idle class of *seiyids* " some of these nobles are busy men, holding responsible posts, for instance those of the Imam's sons who are ministers, and the Amirs of provinces whom we had met. But noble birth is not a necessary qualification for high office, as we have seen in the case of the prime minister, and many of the blue-blooded are unemployed. Such men have little or no occupation save to stroll about the streets or gather together in the *mifrajes* or reception-rooms of friends, where for hours at a time they converse, blow smoke through the water-pipes, and chew *qat*.

Behind the strictly closed doors of the harems there appear also to be plenty of social diversions, and the inmates may be well aware of much that is happening in the world. Such things we could only learn at second-hand, largely from Mrs. Petrie and Miss Cowie, who had access to the women's apartments in households of all classes in the course of their medical work, and who were also invited to social functions in great houses from the Palace downwards. Various amusements, music, dancing and the like, permitted in the time of the Turks, have now to be indulged in secretly, since they are frowned on or forbidden by the Imam. Yet even he could not resist innovations for ever, and during our stay he not only withdrew his opposition to the use of wireless sets, but even listened to one of his sons, Seif al Islam Husein, speaking in Arabic from London, soon after the British Arabic programme was inaugurated. It was noted with amusement in European circles that, the royal permission once given, the existence of many wireless sets belonging to Arab residents suddenly became known in San'a, far more swiftly than the sets could possibly have been transported thither ! Had certain of the Imam's subjects been covertly listening for some time past ?

We sometimes discussed among ourselves to what century the life of San'a, so largely medieval, chiefly belonged. But in fact it pertains to no one century. Against the medieval background stand out curious survivals of the 19th Century, such as the Imam's great horse-carriage and the large barracks and other buildings dating from the second Turkish dominion (1872–1918). Then there impinge on this medley quite modern inventions such as bicycles, motor-cars, wireless and aeroplanes—for San'a had been visited by aircraft, and a level stretch of the plain south of the city is known as the aerodrome.

Meanwhile we are walking back towards the Bab as Sebah and the western division of the capital. Passing the great gate of the Palace precincts again, we can stop to look at the waiting crowds and the professional scribes who sit to write out petitions for the illiterate. If the Imam is prevented by his health from dealing with such matters, the Crown Prince, Seif al Islam Ahmed, may be sitting outside to receive these prayers. Some petitioners go the length of setting their turbans afire to attract attention. We may go through the gate into the courtyard of Al Mutawakil, to a little building used as a post office, with a caged leopard and hyæna near its door. There can be bought sets, more or less complete, of the modern Yemen postage stamps. But if you over-stamp a letter, so that some philatelist at home may get cancelled stamps of many values, it is likely to be found on its arrival in England that the excess stamps have been taken off again, probably before the letter was ever despatched!

The postage stamps are mainly for letters going outside the country. Within the Yemen, and especially in the capital, written messages are frequently sent by the hand of servants. These notes, rolled up like cigarettes and without envelopes, are often stuck in the bearer's turban. Even the local postmen of San'a carry such notes stuck in their kalpaks, the crowns of which are embroidered in yellow. The postman, delivering the weekly mail from Aden via Hodeida, comes upstairs and sits on the floor beside you while he sorts and gives you your letters.

As we leave the space outside the Palace precincts and return through the Bab as Sebah to the western half of the city, the Imam may be returning from a drive in his great carriage ornamented with carving, with outriders, and his personal bodyguard of foot-soldiers dancing and singing in perfect time as they move along in front. Behind the carriage follow sometimes an empty motor-car and a led riding-horse, in case the monarch should wish to change to either of these modes of progression. But there will be more to tell of his cortèges later.

This is a composite account based on many walks about old San'a. It would certainly be enough for one day, especially in the hotter hours! Best to climb up again to the house-roof in Bir al 'Azab, and gaze once more eastward over the Palace, the Arab city, and the great mass of Jebel Nuqūm (or "N'goom", as one is more likely to hear it pronounced) in the background. For no catalogue of details conveys an impression of the whole. From the house-roof the more squalid sights are invisible; but clouds of snowy apricot blossom, at the end of January, or later, masses of green foliage, may be seen above dun-coloured walls of sun-dried brick. It is now afternoon and, if there

PHOTOGRAPHS 75 AND 76.
One-storied shops in the suqs of San'a.
Children in the lucerne-fields outside the city walls.

PHOTOGRAPHS 77 AND 78.
*Raising water in Bir al Azab; dung drying for fuel on the right.
View in Dhamar.*

is cloud and a little haze, the intensely hard, sharp outlines are softened, making the whole scene one of great and rare beauty.

Bir al 'Azab, the large garden-quarter, and its smaller sister-quarters of Bir as Shems and Bir al Baheimi, consist mainly of large houses in the Arab or Turkish style, set wide apart in spacious walled gardens, often cultivated by market-gardeners or laid out as orchards. There are, too, some enclosed gardens without houses, some little *suqs* or groups of shops, and a few mosques. But the most remembered feature of these quarters is the many great wells and the water-raising apparatus (Phot. 77). It matters not whether " Bir al 'Azab " really means " the well of the unmarried " (according to the 'Amil's play on the words), or is a corruption of " the well of Azal (Uzal) " or of " Bir al Adhab " (the well of sweet water), nor why Bir ash Shems (the well of the sun) is so called. In any event, the wells sunk in the loess-deposits supply almost the whole capital with water.[1] From these great shafts, some fifteen feet in diameter and sixty or more feet deep, water is almost ceaselessly drawn by animals descending inclined planes. These slopes are usually excavated deep into the earth, but sometimes height is gained by banking them up above the well's mouth. The beasts are often mixed teams of two or three, camels, oxen and donkeys. Descending side by side, they draw up several water-sacks simultaneously by ropes passing over wooden pulleys. By an ingenious arrangement of trip-ropes the sacks are emptied into a reservoir beside the well-mouth, whence the water flows away along channels. The toil, beginning at earliest dawn, continues till dark, or, on moonlight nights, even through the night. The only pauses are for changing of teams, or short halts when the boys driving the animals feed their patient charges with green fodder or carrots. The creaking of the wooden pulleys (well likened by Dr. Petrie to the cries of seagulls) and the shrill song of the camel-boys [2] form a continual accompaniment to life in Bir al 'Azab. When we left San'a it was hard to realise that we should hear no more these homely, pleasing sounds.

In Bir al 'Azab, too, are seen pairs of ibex horns fixed to the corners of houses, outside and above the ground-storey. These are tokens of good luck, as horseshoes in England. But are the ibex-horns also survivals of the moon-god's emblem? [3]

A further walk must be taken before our survey of San'a is complete : a walk to the quite separate Jewish quarter, Qa' al Yahūd, at

---

[1] A perennial stream, flowing through the city from south to north, on the west side of the dry *seil*, is covered in throughout its course within the walls, except in the palace precincts.
[2] This recalled somewhat the opening bars of " Here's a health unto His Majesty ".
[3] See Chap. xx, p. 217.

the extreme western end of the western division. Pass through the gate, with its single large and rather squat round tower, leading from Bir al 'Azab into the Jewish quarter. First there is a wide open space, the Solbi. North and south of it (its greater length runs in this direction) there is again much garden-ground within the city walls. But west of the Solbi lies the crowded Qa' al Yahūd proper, a mass of buildings penetrated only by a network of narrow lanes. Here the houses are lower, for the Jews may not build more than two storeys high. The dwellings are far plainer outside, the windows being simple rectangular or round-headed openings with little or no tracery, and filled with thin alabaster sheets. The shops have narrow projecting awnings, from which hang widths of sacking like ragged valances (Phot. 79).

The Jews have complete freedom of worship within their own quarter, but no large or imposing building, which would vie with the mosques, may be built. Hence there are many small synagogues, little one-storeyed buildings distinguished by their uniform coat of whitewash. That to which we were taken had a door leading into a forecourt, open to the sky and divided by a transverse wall with an arch. The inner part of this court had little lockers in its wall, for the shoes of worshippers. The synagogue itself was a single-roomed edifice, small but fairly lofty, very plain within and without. All round it, against the walls, were small mats and low wooden desks for adult worshippers. Very narrow plaster shelves projected from the walls, high above the floor. On these (we were told) boys sit through the services, with legs dangling. If this is so, I wondered, do the poor little boys ever get sleepy or restless, if the prayers and readings are long and the day is hot? If they do, they risk a much worse tumble than a monk, propped against his misericord seat, turning drowsy during the recitation of the nocturnal choir-offices. However, a lot of little Jewish boys in a school near by, reading with their teacher, looked happy enough.

The caretaker of the synagogue opened one of two large cupboards, disclosing several upright objects two and a half to three feet high, covered in bright silken wrappings. One of these cases containing the scrolls of the scriptures, which they took down and unwrapped, was a long box, polygonal in section and covered in bright red. Opened lengthwise, it revealed a great parchment scroll (Phot. 82) with a rod at either end, the ornate silver tops of the rods projecting beyond the box. This roll, which (they said) contained all the books of " Meysha " (Moses), was beautifully written in Hebrew manuscript. Such an arrangement of scrolls and boxes is probably general in synagogues, but many of the copies of the scriptures in San'a are very old.

PHOTOGRAPHS 79 AND 80.

A street in the Jewish quarter of San'a.
A brickfield and kiln, San'a; two wooden brick-moulds are seen just to the right of the labourer.

PHOTOGRAPHS 81 AND 82.

Meysha al Abyadh, the leading Jewish silversmith of Sania, and his son. Scrolls of the Jewish scriptures in a synagogue.

Jews of San'a and their crafts

The San'a Jews are light-complexioned. The long curling side locks of men and boys, their shaven crowns and little black skull-caps are much as we had seen in the Aden Protectorate. The men carry no *jambiya* or other weapons, hence their dress is ungirded. But the costume of the women and girls is distinctive. A cowl or hood, rising to a peak at the back of the head, and bordered in front with silver embroidery, is drawn in under the chin. A long narrow-sleeved blouse, usually of dark colour or striped, reaches half-way from the knees to the feet. Below this appear rather close-fitting trousers, ornamented with embroidery above the ankles. Out-of-doors, the women are not enveloped from head to foot as are their Arab sisters. But they wrap themselves in a large flowing shawl, dark blue or black, with a broad patterned border and round or oval patches in which red predominates. This shawl, worn over the head above the hood, hangs below the waist. Though not veiled, Jewesses pull the shawl across the face quickly on the approach of strangers. Little Jewish girls, some of them very pretty, were shy of the camera, fleeing apparently half in earnest and half in play.

Silver-work! that is the craft specially associated with the Jews in San'a. The leading silversmith, Meysha al Abyadh or "Moses the White" (Phot. 81), executed silver and silver-gilt filigree work of the finest degree. The same principal *motif*, rosettes, often with curving petals, can be traced in many of his designs. They can be seen in the little silver-gilt cosmetic-holder (left in Phot. 83), made either to stand or to be strung on a man's belt. In the silver-gilt necklace made by him (Phot. 84) heart-shaped pieces and conventionalised birds appear in alternate rows, while tiny stars and crescents are superimposed on delicate coils. The other cosmetic-holder (right in Phot. 83) is not his work; it is plainer, older, and without any stand. These little vessels hold the black antimony powder (*kohl*) into which soldiers and others dip the thick silver pin attached by a chain, to darken their eyelids withal. The object in the middle (Phot. 83), a cylindrical holder for Koranic texts, to be hung as an amulet on a horse's harness or a man's belt, is of more ordinary form, not special to the Yemen.

Meysha toiled at his craft, seated on the floor of a little workshop in a yard at the back of his house in the Jewish quarter. But he often came to our house for instructions, either for copying one of his own pieces or for making something to special order. He would then hold the pattern very close to his eyes—small wonder that he is extremely short-sighted—and memorise the design.

Though so much fine craftsmanship, particularly metal-work, is in the hands of the Jews, the Arabs do not restrict themselves only to the rougher kinds of construction, such as carpentering and building;

witness the Arab spinning sheep's wool with a simple hand spindle (Phot. 86), and the weavers of mats in black or brown, with white patterns, at work under a great wild-fig tree (Phot. 85).

Meysha, the silversmith, lived in a good-sized house. He received us one Saturday morning in a large bare first-floor room, but would not even talk of his craft that day; for the Sabbath is very strictly kept. This and other Jewish houses in San'a showed a high degree of cleanliness. The staircases and the great stone blocks paving the entrance halls had been recently scrubbed. The same cannot be said of Jewish houses in outlying places!

The Jews may make both red and white wine in their own quarter, but are forbidden to bring it into the Arab quarters. Smuggling of wine by night to the more lax Muslims is, however, not infrequent. Red wine given to me in his house by a well-known Jewish merchant, Sa'id Subeiri (whose better-known brother, Israel, was away on a mission to Europe), was pleasant to the taste, but somewhat heavy and potent; not the best drink for ten o'clock on a hot bright Saturday morning.

Outside the gate at the extreme south-west of the city, Bab al Qa', lies the Jewish cemetery, quite separate from the great Arab burial-ground. The latter extends far south of the narrow waist uniting the two halves of San'a.

* * * * *

Meanwhile we had settled down to our daily life and work in the Petrie household. Our Somalis, who helped in the house when not out with us, added to the Somali element in this international establishment. The staff comprised a Turkish head house-servant, an Arab male cook, an Abyssinian maid-servant, and Jimmy Petrie's Somali nurse. After the departure of the Turk an old San'a Jewess partly filled the gap. Two Yemeni soldiers, Hassan and Yahya, were told off to act as guards at the gate. Hassan, a rather short, slightly built tribesman, with pleasant lean countenance, a little black moustache and curling black locks showing beneath his white turban on either side, became a close friend. Accompanying us on our outings, he ran nimbly about the roughest ground, and developed a wonderful eye for plants. He nearly always returned from a search on a mountain-side with his arms full of some bush or herb new to us. Hassan was grateful for a small monthly present of five dollars, which doubled his army pay. An old Arab *sais*, Muhsin, also often attended, for Dr. Petrie had a horse, and the ladies had mules, put at their disposal by the Government. Last but not least of the household was a gazelle, who not only roamed the garden and entered Britton's *mifraj* to greet

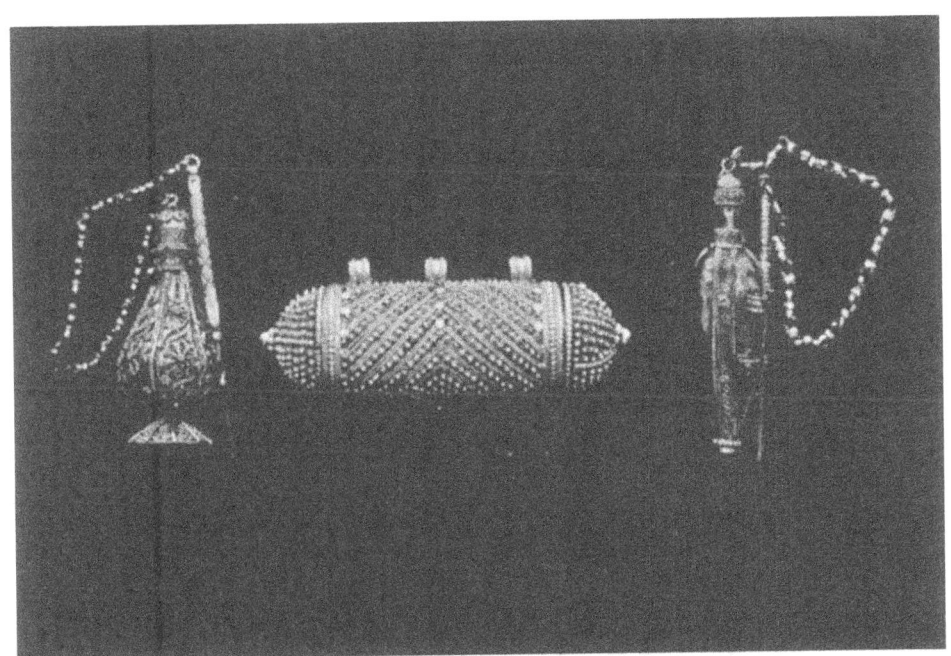

PHOTOGRAPHS 83 AND 84.
Silverwork: two vessels for antimony powder (cosmetic) and a cylinder for religious texts used as a charm; nearly half actual size.
A silver-gilt necklace made by the silversmith in Phot. 81; about one-third actual size.

PHOTOGRAPHS 85 AND 86.

Weaving at Beit Baus.

him each morning, but whose desire for society often led him upstairs in the house itself. Alas, poor *dhabi*, his love of green crops led to repeated complaints from the market-gardener. It was impossible to keep the gazelle within bounds, and at length, reluctantly, orders were given for his despatch.

Other foreign households occupied large houses in Bir al 'Azab. Close by, four or five young Syrian medical men were presided over by one of the two Syrian Pashas engaged in reorganising the army. Short, stocky, and bald, clad in a black kalpak and a khaki uniform, this jovial officer had behind him a chequered career. For anti-French activities he was proscribed under the severest penalty from returning to his native land. He spoke both German and French, the former more readily, as he had been trained in the old Turkish army under German instructors. Dr. Petrie's household and the Syrians frequently visited one another in the evening. At a special feast of a dozen persons in the Syrian house, dishes of very tender roast turkey were served, ready carved, accompanied by a dish of rice flavoured with almonds and raisins, and bowls of yoghourt. The Petrie house gave back as good as it received, if in a slightly different style.

Another large house was occupied by a Russian medical lady, the last of a delegation formerly maintained by the U.S.S.R. A few months after our departure, the "Hakīma" also left and representation of Russia in the Yemen ceased. This lady's major-domo was a smiling elderly Sudanese, dressed in a white suit and scarlet fez. Her flower-garden was the best seen in San'a. Even in dry cold early January, verbenas, petunias, antirrhinums, marigolds, sweet williams, and other English garden plants were in bloom. The strange butterfly-like red and yellow blossoms of a sub-tropical leguminous bush (Cæsalpinia?) showed up amidst rose-bushes (not then blooming). In the fertile soil of San'a, with proper attention to irrigation and the seasons, beautiful gardens can be made.

A Polish engineer and two German business-men lived in other houses near by. Nor must Hajji 'Abbās 'Abdullah Effendi be forgotten, a British subject from Aden, newly arrived to act for the Yemen Government as interpreter with English-speaking people. This gentleman was most helpful in writing letters in Arabic for us.

But far the largest foreign establishment was the Italian. They numbered about ten or eleven, mostly representing branches of medicine, though all were known to be strong Fascists, so that the delegation had a medico-political complexion. They occupied a larger and a smaller house within a big walled garden in Bir al 'Azab, close to the open Sherara. The senior member, Dr. Emilio Dubbiosi, the Imam's personal physician, after twelve years' service in San'a obtained a longed-for release and returned finally to Italy in 1938. Before our arrival little social intercourse had taken place between the British and Italian establishments. Political relations between the two countries had been strained, and linguistic difficulties existed to some extent. Dr. Dubbiosi, however, a few weeks after our arrival, invited us with Dr. Petrie to his house. Henceforth we met occasionally. Dr. Dubbiosi spoke French and German, the former by preference. We were indebted to him for several personal kindnesses, notably in the shape of specimens collected for us. His colleagues, too, were friendly, though intercourse was less easy, because several spoke only Italian. But even the slightest reference to political matters affecting Britain, Italy and the Yemen was always studiously avoided.

Excepting on Fridays, Dr. and Mrs. Petrie, with Miss Cowie, rode early each morning to the Imam's new hospital, a one-storey building, situated near the gate (the Bab al Balaga) on the south side of the western division of the city. There a long hard morning's work lay before them. After their return to the midday meal followed a needed rest. Later in the afternoon they would set out on visits to houses (the ladies to the women's apartments), while towards sunset they saw patients at the dispensary within their own compound. I would emphasise the immense value of their work from every point of view, for the direct alleviation of suffering, for the betterment of understanding between the nations represented on either side, and on the highest spiritual grounds.

Patients from many parts of the country come to the Imam's hospital at San'a. Even in the highlands, despite the healthy climate, there is disease enough to combat. Much of this arises from lack of proper sanitation and the ignorance of the people. In the case of other diseases the greater number of sufferers come from distant districts, especially the foothills and middle altitudes, the most fertile and least healthy part of the whole country. Probably the most common malady of all is trachoma, the eye-disease so widespread in Arabia. This dirt-disease is spread largely by flies. In San'a about 80 per cent. of the Jews and 90 per cent. of the Arabs are infected. The Jews are less prone to trachoma than the Arabs, because their houses and markets are cleaner and less fly-infested; while the habit of darkening the eyelashes with powdered antimony, sometimes taken from a common vessel and applied with a metal instrument provided for common use, may also render the Arabs more subject to this scourge. Fortunately Dr. Petrie had specialised in ophthalmology, and was thus able to effect the surgical operations necessary to cure the results of trachoma, such as the curling inwards of the eyelashes and eyelids. Bilharziasis, due to infection with the parasitic worm *Bilharzia*, which passes part of its life-cycle in certain water-snails, is common. Most of the patients come from districts of the foothills and middle altitudes, or have visited these places, where the disease may be spread partly by the practice of bathing in the hot springs without necessary precautions. The majority of cases of malaria also hail from the foothills and middle heights. The same can be said largely of Yemen ulcer, a malady not fully understood, possibly due in part to malnutrition. The ulcers usually appear on the lower part of the leg, and sometimes resort must be had to amputation. Leprosy also occurs in particular districts. Smallpox, happily, has apparently ceased to be a scourge, though pock-marked people may be seen. But vaccination has become widely popular, introduced, it is said, by the Italian doctors. Many other maladies could be mentioned.[1] I have, however, written enough to emphasise the need of doctors and nurses, and to reinforce the hope that British medical representation in the Yemen may be maintained and, if possible, increased.

In short, almost any and every medical task came within the scope of the doctors in their daily work. They were even asked to remove a tumour from the eye of the Crown Prince's favourite horse, an operation which we saw carried out, in the open, with the aid of local anæsthetics.

The casual, fatalistic attitude of even well-to-do people towards easily preventable accidents and diseases constitutes a grave handicap to medical work. So did the Imam's very severe ideas of discipline. Credit must indeed be given him for the high degree of law and order maintained over most of the country. But when such conceptions are applied to the running of a hospital, serious difficulties ensue for the medical staff. Thus, hospital discipline was mainly the affair of the sergeant and the officer of the guard; so, when a ward-full of boys, mostly suffering from eye-trouble but otherwise well, became a bit rowdy, three of the boys were found next morning to be in chains. Each had a heavy iron hoop round either ankle, the two hoops being joined by two heavy links each six inches long. A patient thus hampered may be more difficult to treat, but only after much argument would the hospital superintendent allow the doctors responsibility for discipline in their own wards.

Various degrees of chaining are the commonest type of punishment in the country. A hoop round one ankle and two links dragging along the ground; or the two legs chained together; or, for really serious offences, double chains of such weight that the victim can hardly move about at all.

The Imam had, by arrangement with the Aden Government,

[1] Further information is given in an article by Dr. Petrie cited in the Bibliography.

secured the services of the Petrie team. He wished his subjects to have up-to-date medical services, and did not desire these to be only in Italian hands. But he would allow no evangelistic work. Dr. Petrie, besides being a general medical practitioner and an eye-specialist, is a Minister of the Church of Scotland, specially ordained for missionary work overseas. The Church of Scotland services which he conducted privately on Sunday evenings for his family, in which we gladly joined, were the only corporate Christian worship taking place in the Yemen.

Our Somalis, besides ourselves, collected mementos of the journey. On our departure from Dhala for Aden in November a donkey-load of enormous dry gourds had been added to our baggage, since one of the Somalis declared he could sell them for drinking vessels at a small profit in Somaliland. In San'a, Omar procured the skin of a leopard killed locally (the ground-colour of which seemed very pale). The first use which they made of this was for practical joking, to startle members of Dr. Petrie's domestic staff, by crouching behind doors and pushing the leopard skin out suddenly as some unsuspecting person entered. Jama's preoccupations were more serious. Though he already had a wife in Somaliland, he was very susceptible. At several points on our journey he had expressed the wish to take rustic maidens to wife, and desired to begin negotiations with their parents. " Go away, you black Somali ", was the rejoinder of an Arab matron on Jebel Jihaf. Not desiring the addition of a young bride to our caravan, we did not encourage these projects. In San'a, he scraped acquaintance with the youthful daughter of a *seiyid*. This was against all the conventions and without her parents' knowledge, but for a while he seemed in earnest. He wished to approach the Imam for permission to marry the girl. This, if granted, might have meant his leaving our service and remaining in San'a. I was, therefore, relieved when he returned one morning from an errand in the city with a bright new bicycle, said he had given up the marriage idea as too difficult, and added ; " *W'allah*, sir, I hire this bicycle for four bukhshas an hour ". I remarked that he really must decide for himself between an extra wife and a bicycle, but that I thought the latter would cost far less.

So the weeks passed, with still no hint of our being received by the Imam, or of opportunity to ask his permission to visit outlying districts. After several postponements an interview was arranged for us with the Crown Prince, Seif al Islam Ahmed. Soon after nine o'clock one morning Dr. Petrie, Britton and I, with Jam'a and Ahmed Mahmūd, all in our best clothes and kalpaks, called at the Prince's house. Passing through a small outer enclosure inhabited by several tame gazelles,

We are received by the Crown Prince

we entered his *mifraj* on the ground-floor. Having left our shoes outside, we seated ourselves on the cushions on the floor along either side. I was placed immediately on the left of the Prince's seat, with Britton and Petrie below me ; Jam'a and Ahmed Mahmūd facing us, on the opposite side of the room. At length Seif Ahmed appeared, a stout and genial man, fatter than his younger half-brother Qasim. Both he and Seif Qasim throw their bodies about somewhat when talking, and the Crown Prince's beard is much longer on one side, due apparently to his pulling at it while conversing. There seems to be a degree of " nerves " in the family, and Seif Ahmed has to cope with several of his sisters, rather excitable ladies, who live in his house. He was said to be not very popular except with the army. But his manner to us was very friendly. He looked at the specimens and apparatus shown to him, asked the usual question " what good does all this work do ? " and laughed heartily when told that Ahmed Mahmūd had caught a moth in the room before he entered. He spoke very affably to the two Somalis, asking each in turn a few questions. The foreign mail arriving during our visit, a great pile of letters and parcels was cast on the floor before the prince. Opening a big parcel full of tins of ovaltine and glucose, he asked Dr. Petrie about their use and wrote down the doctor's directions. Whether these things were for himself or his neurasthenic sisters, I cannot say. I caught the glance of the two Somalis across the room, and our gravity nearly broke down. After we had left, I said as sternly as I could manage, " Jam'a, you must *not* look at me across the room during these interviews ". Gurgling with suppressed mirth he answered, " *W'allah*, sir, I could not help it ; the Seif is such a *funny* man." Nevertheless we were grateful to the prince for his kind reception.

Chapter XV

TREKS IN SAN'A DISTRICT: OUR FARTHEST NORTH

THE long deferment of our reception by the Imam made it impossible directly to ask his consent to visit the places we had at heart. But we were, meanwhile, fully occupied. We were free to wander, attended only by one of the Somalis and possibly Hassan, the soldier, and collect specimens in the gardens and open ground within, and immediately outside, the city walls. Nor was special permission necessary for whole-day excursions to recognised " beauty-spots ". These outgoings took place in company with the Petrie family, and sometimes other Europeans, on the official weekly holiday, Friday. Moreover the King, even before our audience, prescribed two more remote districts to which we might go. Each of these, Bilad Hamdan and Bilad Senhan, involved an absence from San'a of several days.

Though the sharpest of the winter, with several degrees of frost, was over before our arrival on January 4th, the nights were still cold. On the roof of the house in Bir al 'Azab the lowest minimum temperature which I recorded was just over 33° Fahrenheit on the night of January 12th–13th. The clear dry winter days, becoming hotter, were broken by occasional afternoon rainstorms, as on January 19th, when a dull morning was followed by a rainy afternoon, the first real rain we had seen since a smart afternoon shower at Ta'izz on December 15th. A sharp thunderstorm broke during the late afternoon, March 3rd. Our departure on March 8th was too early for the spring rains, but there were signs of their slow gathering.

For in San'a, typical of the Yemen highlands, there are usually two wet seasons. The spring rains, spread over about three months, may amount to some six inches, the late summer or autumn rains (of which we had experienced the fag end in September, in the Amiri highlands) are generally heavier, so that the total yearly average would be about fourteen or fifteen inches. Contrast with this the annual average in Aden, two and a half inches, most irregularly distributed. Again, the division into spring and autumn rains in the highlands corresponds to the " little rains " and " great rains " in the Ethiopian highlands, though the total rainfall in Abyssinia is far more.

Further, the mean temperature at San'a in June is 68° Fahrenheit;

in November, the coldest month, 59° Fahrenheit. The maximum in the whole year is about 80°–82°, the lowest night-minimum 17° Fahrenheit. Though we missed the coldest nights of the early part of the winter, we also had hotter days than would have been experienced during the summer rains. The wide gap between the extremes in San'a may again be compared with Aden, where shade-temperatures below 70° Fahrenheit are rare and 97° in the shade is reached in the hottest months.

These climatic features of San'a are bound up with the question of its altitude, mentioned in the foregoing chapter as nearly 8,000 feet. Repeated aneroid readings (less adequately confirmed by observation of the boiling-point) invariably pointed to about 7,900 feet. A longer set of observations recorded by Dr. Carl Rathjens resulted in a slightly lower figure, nearer 7,700 feet.[1] The discrepancy may be due to the time of day (we always read at about 7 a.m., before going out), for the daily range of humidity is very wide; in January, early in the morning, the humidity may be 60 per cent., but by early afternoon this will have fallen to 20 per cent. At Aden there is little variation in the twenty-four hours, and humidity is between 60 and 80 per cent. throughout the whole year. In plain words, the air at San'a is on the whole far drier despite its much greater rainfall, while at Aden the air is often " sticky ".

Such are the conditions under which we saw the phases of spring follow swiftly one on the other. In the orchards apricot trees, bare when we arrived, were in full bloom at the end of January and in full leaf, with green fruit, a month later. Fig trees, in open orchards, put out their young leaves early in February. Quinces and pomegranates were in bloom, walnut trees still almost leafless, early in March. In the vineyards at Ḥuqqa and Raudha no life seemed stirring in the vines when we saw them in late January and the first days of February.

Before our departure the number of Little Green Bea-eaters had increased, and a pair of hoopoes appeared in the garden at Bir al 'Azab on March 6th; signs of the upward and northward movement of migrant birds.

In the area called Sha'ūb, immediately north of the city walls, a brook bordered by pollard willows winds through watered fields, in which green wheat was already in ear in late February. (For some cheerful inhabitants of Sha'ūb, see Phot. 76). Except in such irrigated

[1] Observations prior to mine or Dr. Rathjens' placed San'a at little over 7,500 feet. The nature of the vegetation and other considerations, however, incline me to think that " nearly 8,000 " will prove not wide of the mark. The facts about its climate are clearly summarised by Dr. Petrie in an article cited in the Bibliography.

spots, the open fields of San'a plain were bare and dry. They were still covered with last season's stubbles, or were undergoing winter ploughing in preparation for the sowing of wheat, barley, *dhurra* or pulses. Here, close to the city, were ploughmen with their yokes of oxen, sometimes followed by the team of three men wielding the heavy shovel already described (Phot. 25, p. 50). Twelve miles or more to the north men, standing knee-deep in trenches, were breaking and turning the soil with long-bladed mattocks.

In Bir al 'Azab itself there were small insects in plenty to be swept from the green crops, and butterflies flitting over the lucerne fields. In the garden of the Hospital Mudir's private house, a pile of dead apricot boughs on a rubbish-heap yielded, when shaken, quantities of bark-beetles (Scolytidæ), ready to fly away and infect healthy branches or trees (this was on January 26th). I tried, later, tactfully to instil in high places the idea that it would be better to burn this dead wood from the orchards, and so get rid of the pests. At various times we were also brought larvæ or adults of Longicorn beetles, which bore deep into timber; these were mostly found in acacia-wood (locally *tulh*) carried in from the country as fuel for kitchen fires.

To Dr. Dubbiosi we owed the knowledge that a certain cypress tree had previously been the roosting-place of a colony of large fruit-eating bats.[1] Though these " flying-foxes " had deserted the tree, probably for apricot orchards in the neighbourhood, the doctor kindly gave us specimens which he had preserved.

In the south-western corner of Bir al 'Azab great excavations, several acres in extent, mark the former removal of material for brick-making. Report had it that the walls of San'a had been built of these bricks. The flat floors of the hollows were given up to little cultivated fields. The surrounding hummocks and earthen cliffs were dotted with clumps of the imported prickly pear (*Opuntia*) and thickets of tamarisk. Some traps were set for foxes at the bottom of these cliffs, in principle like an ordinary mouse-trap. A spike planted in the earth at the back is baited with meat, the sides and roof are rough slabs of stone. When the fox pulls at the meat, a cord along the top is released and a stone slab drops, imprisoning the animal alive.

As to places outside the walls, we had been forewarned never to mention Jebel Nuqūm to those in authority. Not that any sanctity attaches to it, as far as I am aware. But either it, or places overlooked by it, are fortified or used for storage of ammunition or treasure. We did no more than climb the rising ground at its base, to see from the

---

[1] The species was *Eidolon sabæum*, a South-West Arabian variant of the African *E. helvum*.

PHOTOGRAPHS 87 AND 88.
San'a plain from the hills above Hada.
Bare walnut-trees in the orchards at Hada, in January.

PHOTOGRAPHS 89 AND 90.
*Beit Baus: the walled town on its slab of volcanic rock (trap).
Houses at the foot of a cliff of trap, Beit Baus.*

east the city outspread at our feet (Phot. 113). The curious triangular fort on top of the mountain is, therefore, known to me only at second hand.[1]

Hada, some miles south-west of San'a, was visited on January 14th. Britton, still only convalescent from the malaria, and other members of the party reached it by car, by a track circumventing a mountain-ridge. The rest of us, on horses or mules, struck directly across the plain, between bare ploughed fields and over stony tracts. A low pass between barren mountains led us into a slightly higher piece of country. Here a wide stretch of cultivation (at that season, young green corn, lucerne, beans in flower) and orchards, dotted with several villages, extends along the foot and into the folds of the bare, tawny, rocky range of Jebel Hada. Leaving the larger village of Hada proper to one side, a path led steeply upwards towards the source of a stream. Part of this stony way is overhung by walnut trees, the leafless boughs of which formed a pattern of brightly sunlit surfaces and deep shadows (Phot. 88). Our resting-place was a terraced orchard shaded by wild-fig trees and large, still bare, apricots. In more sunny spots the apricots were already thick with white blossom and peach-trees with pale pink flowers. Some of the fruit trees stood among young evergreen bushes of *qat*, only a foot or two high. A few yards farther up the path, and a wide prospect could be had over San'a plain, south-westward (Phot. 87). As to insects and flowers, the whole setting was reminiscent of places on the Mediterranean in very early spring: bright sunshine after a cold night, trees still mostly bare, some wild flowers in bloom, some insects on the wing. The last were mainly certain flies and butterflies; clouded yellows and bath whites flitting over the lucerne fields; elsewhere battered painted ladies, overwintered from the preceding year, and wild-flying large brown and grey butterflies related to the English greyling.

At Beit Baus, some miles south of the capital, interest centres in the little walled town (Phot. 89) perched on a huge detached slab of trap rock. It lies at the edge of a vast horizontal blanket of the volcanic trap, which was poured out in a thick layer over the sandstones of the Cretaceous. From the main formation this slab has become separated, through erosion, by a valley between sheer cliffs. Without scaling the rock, the only entrance is by a rough inclined plane and through an arched gateway (Phot. 91, and seen on the extreme right in Phot. 89), flanked by rough stone towers. Within the town each street and lane, each little open space, is paved simply with the living rock. Every inch of the surface of the great crag is

---

[1] Described by the explorer Glaser and since photographed from the air: Rathjens and von Wissmann, " Südarabien-Reise ", Vol. ii, pp. 183-4.

occupied. The walls of the outer buildings rise from the very edge of the cliffs. The place seems almost to have grown upwards as an excrescence of the rock on which it stands. Its mosques are inconspicuous, no minarets rise above the roofs. Former inhabitants used smooth expanses of the cliff at the nearer end to carve records thereon in Himyaritic characters. As if the main township were not strange enough, an outlying group of houses (Phot. 90) is cramped against the foot of the cliffs on the opposite side of the valley. The weavers of mats (Phot. 85), already spoken of, were at work outside the town under a spreading wild-fig tree. Above the town the valley, deepening and narrowing, winds between grim, barren, brown cliffs and hills. But the wadi itself was full of blossoming apricots, and there was occupation for naturalists along channels still moist from recent irrigation.

Al 'Asr is closest to the capital of all the green and fertile spots where springs break from the bare, stony, brown mountains bounding San'a plain on the west. Lying only between two and three miles due west [1] of the capital, it consists of a lower and an upper village (some of the villagers are shown in Phot. 101). The lower, crowning an eminence among orchards and cultures where the valley opens out on to the plain, is enclosed by walls and towers. The upper village stands considerably higher, on a crag projecting from the hills at a point where the valley begins to close in. Above it a path leads up a narrow wadi. Terraced orchards cover the ground falling away from this track to the stream. Here the silver-grey boughs of large walnut-trees, still leafless, contrasted with the brilliant green young foliage of giant apricots, grand, twisted old trees, the largest seen. These were already weighted with green fruit in mid-February, while the white blossoms of quinces and the fluffy scarlet flowers of pomegranates were coming to their full, and the branches of fig-trees were just tipped with young translucent leaves, in the bright sunlight like little green flames. Looking eastward from beyond the orchards, the distant city, its plain, and Jebel Nuqūm lay outspread ; the foreground was formed by this verdant Wadi 'Asr and the upper village on its rock, framed by arid hills (Phot. 93).

Above the orchards the valley is a barren defile. At its head two streams well out at the foot of bare brown cliffs. Both above and below the point where they unite to form the winding Gheil Wakra, the water is led through roofed-ih channels pierced at intervals by circular shafts, surrounded by low walls of rough stones. Local folk, anxious to guide us to the springs, put these ancient conduits down as " Himyaritic ", a period to which they assign anything of forgotten

[1] If Al 'Asr is really the same word as that for " the afternoon " the name of the village may be derived from its direction.

Photographs 91 and 92.

Beit Baus : looking in through the town gate.
Beit Baus : woman feeding a camel.

PHOTOGRAPH 93.

East from Wadi 'Asr: upper village of Al 'Asr on right, lower village on left; San'a and

origin. But, as said elsewhere,¹ this construction of water-tunnels may have been due to Persian influence ; while in the hilly parts of the Sultanate of 'Oman, at any rate, subterranean water-channels (*felej*) are in use. Lower down the *gheil* flows in an open channel, narrow and about six feet deep. Out of its stone-walled sides spring flowering weeds. Lower still, in the orchards, it runs through a broader, shallow bed, fringed with water-mint.

The orchards and wadi of Al 'Asr, to which I took a great liking, were the scene of several excursions. Among many finds made there was a large, handsome, very dark brown butterfly, with a yellowish band (broken up into patches in front) across both wings ; each hind wing has blue marks near its margin and two slender tails. The underside is wonderfully marked with white, black, reddish-brown, dark brown, and blue. This insect eluded us until the nimble 'Omar Isma'il succeeded in netting a single one in its strong swift flight. Having been familiar with a large black yellow-flecked swallow-tail butterfly,² flying in numbers round bare stony knolls on Jebel Jihaf and elsewhere, we supposed that we had added another species of this family to our collection. But the resemblance was only superficial, and our new capture proved to be more interesting. It is a representative of a quite different group, related to the European purple emperor. It serves as an illustration of the small facts which, pieced together, throw light on the questions that prompted us to undertake our journey. This handsome butterfly (*Charaxes hansali*) was known only from the Eastern part of Africa (where it appears to be quite rare). But in 1930 Bertram Thomas discovered a new form of the species in South Arabia. His discovery was made in the Qara mountains, in Dhufar, hundreds of miles east of the Yemen. We rediscovered this Arabian sub-species at Al 'Asr. Here is one of many little pieces of evidence pointing to the close connection between South Arabia and Eastern Africa, but also indicating that the separation of the two land-masses has lasted long enough for divergence of the species into distinct forms on opposite sides of the sea—a divergence of which there are many instances, and which has proceeded further in some cases than in others.³

The Al 'Asr outings are associated, too, in memory with various steeds (or the lack of them). For our longer treks horses or mules were provided by the Government, but for short excursions these were not

[1] Chap. xx, p. 221. [2] *Papilio demodocus*.
[3] I cannot say what is the food-plant of this butterfly in South Arabia. The caterpillar may feed on *Salvadora persica*, a bush which we found at much lower altitudes than San'a, or on *Osyris abyssinica*, also known from the Yemen, though at lower elevations. The butterfly has been bred from both these plants in Uganda. The *Charaxes*-butterflies are, however, wide in their tastes. An Indian species feeds on tamarind, and the only European species feeds on the strawberry-tree (*Arbutus*).

always available. We then relied on what could be hired from one Sheikh Hamād in Bir al 'Azab. Once, when I had started rather late from San'a and searched long on the wet clayey sides of a stagnant pool in a dry wadi, where all the small beetles of the place seemed to have concentrated round the last remaining moisture, I had to hurry Sheikh Hamād's old horse to reach the city again before dark. The horse was a tall chestnut, rather slow and lumbering. Not only the western gate, leading from the open country into the Jewish quarter, but the second gate, separating Qa' al Yahūd from Bir al 'Azab, were shut when we reached them; fortunately the good-natured soldiers of the guard made no difficulty about opening the heavy doors. Another day, a nice little white horse provided by the Beit al Mal (the Treasury) was taken from me in the afternoon, for use elsewhere, by a man with a written order from the Imam himself! Our last excursion to Al 'Asr began with a series of accidents which looked at one point like developing into an ugly "incident". There were mounts enough for all, and I was again fortunate, getting a dark horse, which went well. Ahmed Mahmūd, however, was given a fresh little animal with neither bit nor bridle, but only a halter. Though used to camels from boyhood, he had never ridden horses before his visit to San'a.[1] Unwisely, thermos-flasks and packages of provisions were tied to the saddle. These things clanked, and the frightened horse ran away at the very start, dashing through the gate into the Jewish quarter. Ahmed kept his seat till he could dismount and struggle to quiet the animal. But it broke loose, the saddle came off, the flasks were broken and all the day's provisions spoiled. Our little cavalcade went on, trusting to get some food at the village. But fresh troubles were in store. Crossing the fields to the lower village, we turned aside to enjoy a few gallops over *dhurra* stubbles, where no harm could possibly be done. Returning to the path, to our dismay we found ourselves followed on foot from the city by a *sais*, an unpleasant-looking young man, with a wild expression in his eyes as though he were slightly mad or intoxicated with *qat*. He was furious, apparently because we had dared to ride at more than a walking pace. Seizing Ahmed's horse by the halter he threatened to take it back to San'a. A quarrel arose between the two. Ahmed said the fellow threatened him with stones and with his *jambiya*. I tried to quiet my Somali friend, who was hurt at not being allowed to fight for me! But I begged him to remember where we were, and not to get us involved in a brawl. Though his devotion was gratifying, I feared the consequences should he act on such sentiments as: "I am your servant, and when this man makes

[1] Though, as already said, he afterwards became a mounted N.C.O. in the Aden Government Guards.

A country house of the Imam

trouble for you, he makes trouble for me also," and " *W'allah*, sir, I know, if you let me, I smash him ! " The squabble kept breaking out afresh. The angry *sais* had to be forcibly restrained by Ahmed and 'Omar from riding back to San'a on one horse, leading another. Despite the intervention of a friendly *'aqil* of the village, calm was not restored till our good friend Hassan, the soldier, returned from Suq al 'Asr, a small group of shops. Thence he had procured green fodder for the horses and *kishr*, chupatties and hard-boiled eggs for all of us. Finally a peaceful afternoon was spent collecting specimens in the orchards. These incidents, if small in themselves, exemplify the difficulties with which naturalists may have to contend.

Wadi Dhahr, some miles north-west of the capital, differs entirely from any of the foregoing places. It is a winding valley, the lower part of which forms a wide V between precipitous cliffs of sandstone. Coming over the high ground from the city, you reach a great sandstone bluff on the right side of the V, near the angle. Hence a wonderful prospect (Phot. 114) meets the gaze. To the left, up the left-hand limb of the V, the valley narrows, its floor rises, and the cliffs become gradually lower. Immediately south, Jebel Fiddi, a " neck " of volcanic rock, rises starkly like a great pinnacle above the sandstone. To the north-east, the right-hand limb of the V opens out widely into cultivated plains. The many reddish tones of the cliffs contrast with the green flat floor of the valley, crammed with walled gardens of *qat* trees, sweet limes and other fruit. Some of the earliest fruit of the season is brought to San'a from the sheltered gardens of Wadi Dhahr. Scattered groups of buildings become concentrated about the angle of the V into the village of Suq al Wadi, dominated by the amazing new house of the Imam (Phot. 94). This country retreat consists of three storeys and a roof-terrace, perched on a detached rock. It was scarcely finished at the time of our visit. In the photograph a workman can be seen on the rock, supported by ropes from the lower windows. But the construction may be partly old, for a traveller of just 50 years earlier saw to the east of the village, on an isolated cubical rock, the magnificent chateau, deserted and closed, which had formerly served as summer residence for the Imam.[1] This was during the second Turkish dominion, when the Imam of that day was much under a cloud.

The descent, some hundreds of feet, from the bluff to the valley, is by a rocky path, partly laid artificially in rough steps. At the bottom a wide open road runs between the high mud walls of orchards. A stream flows along one side, margined with short turf and the fluffy purple flower-heads of water-mint. Small patches of waste ground

---

[1] Deflers, " Voyage au Yemen ", p. 63.

occupied us, as did the enclosed orchard of a house then shut up, to which we were admitted by the caretaker. Later we worked in a much broader and more open part of the valley to the north-east, where are many thickets of tamarisk-trees, some shut in by mud walls. Britton and Dr. Petrie scaled the cliff-face of a low hill to the entrance of a pre-Islamic tomb (Phot. 95), which they found empty. Collecting grasshoppers on stony ground among the tamarisks, we became a centre of attraction to a number of small boys. After first giggling and whispering " Nasrani, Nasrani " (" A Christian, a Christian ") among themselves, they joined in the chase, and then showed us with awe and delight a large scorpion beneath a stone.

All these places, Wadi Dhahr, Al 'Asr, Hada, and Beit Baus lie in a curved line, respectively north-west, west, south-west and south of San'a (Map 4, p. 142). There are other such oases in that wide arc, marking the zone where the western mountain-ranges bound San'a plain. For they are indeed oases, not in deserts of sand, but among almost bare, stony hills. Their fertility is due to the streams welling forth in sheltered valleys near the foot of the mountains, many of which unite to form the Wadi Kharid. This great wadi runs north-eastward towards the system draining Al Jauf. Its waters, now probably lost in the interior, are inhabited by a species of barbel.[1] These fishes are brought into San'a from some twenty miles away and sold in the market. They grow to a good size; a specimen sent to us by Dr. Petrie is about 14 inches long.

Out on the open exposed plain the country was usually less interesting. Nevertheless, on our final outing for collecting, early in March, beside the Alaf brook on the flat plain only about a mile south of the city, we found the close turf bordering the brook brightened by green cushions of chicory, starred with brilliant blue flower-heads. For this familiar plant here grows, not tall and erect, but as a close, tight, tuft, in which the stalkless flower-heads are flattened down. It is evidently the dwarf chicory discovered over a century ago by Botta in the mountains of Tāif (east of Mecca) but never described till it was rediscovered a half-century later in the Yemen by Deflers,[2] who named it *Cichorium bottæ* after its first finder. Its dwarf tufted form may afford some protection against the ceaseless browsing of sheep and goats.

A few miles north of the capital lie two small towns, Al Jiraf and Raudha, also on the open plain. The latter (and farther) of these did not prove very attractive in late January. Many of its houses were

[1] Described in 1941 as *Barbus arabicus*; more closely related to forms from the Jordan and from India than to African species (see Note C, p. 238).

[2] " Voyage au Yemen ", pp. 54, 159.

PHOTOGRAPH 94.
The Imam's new country-house in Wadi Dhahr.

PHOTOGRAPHS 95 AND 96.
A cliff at Wadi Dhahr, with the entrance to a pre-Islamic tomb.
The cactus-like spurge, Euphorbia officinalis, *growing at 9,000 feet, near Haz.*

Trekking north

ruinous. Other large country-houses were in good order. But the great feature of Raudha, its vineyards, showed no sign of life. We had accompanied the Petrie household, who were summoned to see a child of about seven, an ailing son of Prince Qasim. The prince himself was not at his country house. After coffee in his *mifraj* we occupied ourselves by " beetling " along a damp ditch running across an open green, while Mrs. Petrie and Miss Cowie visited the women's apartments. Apparently the ladies of Prince Qasim's household found our doings more interesting than we found Raudha. We were told that, from the upper windows, they eagerly watched us supposedly grubbing for worms !

*   *   *   *   *

Our trek to the northern district prescribed by the Imam, the Bilad Hamdan, lasted six days (January 31st to February 5th). The northernmost point reached was not more than about fifteen to seventeen miles north of San'a. The distances travelled on mule-back, including détours to reach points of special interest, totalled about sixty-one miles (with a further eight by car at the end of the last day). The longest distance ridden in a day was some fifteen miles. Yet the caravan amounted to fifteen persons, six mules and six donkeys. Besides ourselves and Dr. Petrie (who, by now an enthusiastic naturalist, had got leave of absence from his medical work), it included our three Somalis, a young Arab servant, a *shawūsh* and two soldiers, three muleteers, a guide and a boy. The military escort, one muleteer and four mules were provided by the Government. The other muleteers, the guides, and the remaining mules and donkeys were hired privately. The *shawūsh* was, unfortunately, the most suspicious with whom we had to deal. He interpreted the written *rukhsa* with extreme strictness, and not even Dr. Petrie's fluency in Arabic and knowledge of the people could make any impression on the man's wooden exterior. It was lucky, indeed, that one of the two soldiers was our friend Hassan.

The whole trek was arduous, owing largely to the roughness of the volcanic country and the lack of shade. We were all fairly tired at the end, especially the soldiers, muleteers and guides, who were on foot. Even Hassan, despite his good-natured wish to help and his keenness to find new plants, showed symptoms of fatigue. For those of us who had mules, however, riding over such country on such an errand as ours was far more suitable than jolting over it in cars.

On the first day we rode some fourteen miles to Huqqa, nearly due north of San'a. The first eight miles or so, as far as Al 'Azraqein, our course lay a little to the north-west, over bare monotonous country. A short distance from San'a, at a wayside *khan*, were three Arabs whose different dress and physiognomy proclaimed them strangers to San'a district. In fact they were not Yemenis at all, but hailed from Sa'udi Arabia. One of the three wore a cord round his neck, at the ends of which were plugs for stopping the nostrils in dust-storms; this was the solitary occasion on which we saw such an appliance, for which there would normally be no need in the settled parts of the high Yemen. Al 'Azraqein was found to consist only of a wayside khan, a great rectangular cemented cistern, in which the water was now low, and some orchards of fig-trees just breaking into leaf. But when, after a long midday halt there, we set out north-eastwards towards Huqqa, a rather sudden change was noticeable. The southern fringe of the Harra of Arhab is entered, a region of black volcanic rocks and lava-flows which, though forbidding and awe-inspiring, is new and interesting. Our track led us close to the east of Kaulat al Hauri, a very perfect extinct volcanic crater. It is a truncated cone of loose ash, dotted with small plants, rising perhaps 300 feet above the plain. Inside the crater (which we had no chance to ascend) the raised flat floor has a cistern excavated in its surface, which seems formerly to have been cultivated, though it is now covered again at the sides with stones and rubble.

Beyond this crater, near the villages of Beit al Hauri and Huqqa, wherever the ground is not covered by geologically recent lava-flows or otherwise impossible of cultivation, lie fertile vineyards. These are enclosed in dry stone walls of black lava, as much as eight to ten feet high, making a black fretwork when seen against the sky-line, owing to the spaces between the jagged stones.

At Huqqa, a very dirty village, the high houses are built mainly of the black volcanic rock. Many are in a ruinous state. This was said to be the result of " fighting against the Turks ", which, if true, may have referred to the rebellion in 1911. Britton, Petrie and myself were lodged in the long, narrow, second-floor room of a house. The ground floor (occupied by the usual cow) and the twisting staircase seemed exceptionally dark. Our room, lighted by small unglazed rectangular openings low down in the walls and a row of smaller openings above, had half its floor raised about a foot above the other half. We made the higher part our living apartment, the lower our bedroom. The sanitary arrangements described in San'a are modernity itself compared with those in the country villages. Our house in Huqqa had no such accommodation except part of the roof, surrounded by a low wall which gave little privacy from the village. Our servants slept on a higher part of the roof, while the soldiers curled themselves up in corners of the staircase from the second floor upwards.

Huqqa was in 1928 the scene of excavation of a great temple devoted to the pre-Islamic astral worship, which is discussed more fully in Chapter XX. A pillar, inscribed stones and other fragments of nearly white fine-grained limestone, built into the walls of the houses of the modern village, stand out sharply against the surrounding blocks of dark stone. At the site of the temple, just south of the village, comparatively little was to be seen. The more valuable objects had been removed to San'a, where they are housed in a ground-floor room of the large Turkish building used for accommodation of visiting diplomatic missions ; this nucleus of a museum was duly visited by us, provided with the necessary *rukhsa* ! At Huqqa, however, some lower courses of the ancient masonry remain *in situ*. Besides these huge dressed blocks of black stone we were also shown, through openings in its roof, the vast subterranean cistern, now dry, underlying part of the temple. The village stands almost touching the southern edge of a tongue projecting from a great stream of scarcely weathered lava. The eruption which caused this outpouring may, it is supposed, have caused the destruction of the temple, possibly as late as the third century of the Christian era.

The next day (February 1st) was spent in an excursion from Huqqa to Jebel al Kohl, five miles or more to the north-west. This extinct crater, never (as far as I know) before trodden by Europeans, was the northernmost point of our whole journey. Its name (as we understood) is the same as the *kohl* or fine powder of antimony used as a cosmetic ; hence it would be identical with the word *alcohol*, derived therefrom, since the Arabic word came to signify " essence " or " spirits ". Riding past the village of Al Hamra we ascended some thousand feet to about 9,000, and then walked up the cone to about 9,500 feet above sea-level. Approaching the great red cinder-heap from the south-east, our party got separated through my staying behind with Jam'a to take photographs. The rest, excepting the *shawūsh*, rode quickly ahead, dismounted, and started to walk up the crater. The *shawūsh*, distracted with trying to look after two rather widely separated groups of people, displayed some agitation. Apparently the crater was " out of bounds ", and had not our advance guard swiftly reached the summit and presented him with a *fait accompli*, we should never have climbed it at all. As it was, the unfortunate officer went rushing up the steep slope of the hill after the forward party, his rifle in one hand and a silver-handled black umbrella in the other !

Though from the south-east Jebel al Kohl appears as shown (Phot. 97), it is not a perfect crater. On the west the wall is broken, so that the hill forms a gigantic horseshoe with a narrow ridge-top sloping down steeply at either end. The crater is in itself more lofty than the perfectly formed Kaulat al Hauri, and, moreover, it rises from a point a thousand feet higher. This and its isolated position render Jebel al Kohl a wonderful view-point. Immense prospects lie spread out in every direction; north and north-east over the volcanic country changing farther east to yellow sandstone; southwards over the dun-coloured San'a plain, its cultivation and villages, to Jebel Nuqūm and the eastward brown and yellowish mountains. But the strangest view is that to the north (Phot. 98), over the volcanic *harra*. It can be summed up as red cones and mounds of cinders, and black lava-flows. Without difficulty it could be imagined as part of some dead planet.

Since Jebel al Kohl is not, however, without animal and plant life, the several hours spent on top of this giant ash-heap resulted in interesting finds. The plants rooted in the loose ash, though wide apart and separated by bare spaces, were a varied association. Several were low and compact, such as a species [1] with tiny white flowers. Shining black weevils and a few other beetles were hiding at the woody roots of these tufts. Other rather taller plants comprised a wild mignonette [2] and a thyme with pale lilac flowers.[3] But the floral prize was a tall herb with greyish foliage and hanging clusters of yellow flowers, growing on the inner face of the crater wall. To assign it to its right place in the classification not only baffled ourselves (who are not primarily botanists) but at first puzzled our botanical colleagues, after our return to England. Had we crushed and smelt the stems and leaves, we might have got a clue from a faint smell of lavender, of which the plant is a rare species,[4] though its blossoms lack the normal lavender colour. Originally found on mountains in the high Yemen, it is apparently unknown outside that country.

Butterflies of at least five species were flying about the top of the narrow ridge. Their presence may have been partly due to the strange attraction which high places exert on some butterflies, and on certain other flying insects as well. They included painted ladies, a " blue ", a fritillary,[5] and brown Satyrines so strong of flight that none could be taken.

Though we scarcely regained our " hotel " at Huqqa before dark, we must be soon on the road again next morning. For the written *rukhsa* (permit) allowed no dawdling. So from nine o'clock till shortly before dusk we rode in stages, with halts for rest and for collecting specimens, some fourteen or fifteen miles westward, to Haz. First the track led south-west, to a very large water-hole or cistern called Birka Qa' Raqqa, not far from the village of Beit al Hauri. In traversing these few miles in particular, men were seen at work in the

[1] *Minuartia filifolia*, related to *Arenaria*. [2] A species of *Caylusea*.
[3] *Micromeria biflora*. [4] *Lavandula atriplicifolia*.
[5] Resembling the European *Melitæa didyma*.

fields, digging deep with the great long-bladed mattocks. They stood waist-deep in the trenches, hewing away enormous clods from the earth in front of them, and hurling these on to the turned-up soil behind. Heavy toil indeed !

The vast pre-Islamic cistern of Birka Qa' Raqqa is of simple type, fed only by surface drainage; circular, with sides not " stepped ", but falling in a single nearly vertical drop to the water. Its sides now consist of large blocks of rough masonry, for most of the ancient plaster or cement lining has gone. Four rough inclines, which may once have been flights of steps, lead down through the walls to the water. They serve, we were told, as many villages. Descending to a narrow shore of mud, exposed by the shrinking of the water at this season, we searched for aquatic insects. The most striking was a species of " water-boatman" (*Notonecta*) of giant proportions. Meanwhile our riding and pack animals were watered.

The large plastered circular cistern by which we had halted south of Dhamar, the rectangular cistern at Al 'Azraqein, the wide circle of Birka Qa' Raqqa, and (later to be mentioned) the deep rectangular Mījāl al As'ad, with others, large and small, are all examples of the water-storage works so essential to the ancient civilisation of the land. I have remarked in a later chapter (p. 220) that the famous Tanks at Aden are spoken of sometimes as unique. They are indeed wonderful in their number, and as a series with outflow channels from each to the next below. But those who travel in the interior find that single cisterns and reservoirs of several types are scattered along the travel routes throughout the country.

A few miles beyond Birka Qa' Raqqa, we were ascending to the Al Kabar pass. This, like so many " passes " in the country, is not an ascent of a range with a corresponding drop on the far side, but a gigantic step up a precipitous escarpment from one plain to another. There is a difference of about 1,300 feet between Huqqa and the highest point of Al Kabar, which stands (according to our reckoning) at about 9,300 feet. A little short of the top we halted for lunch and rest in a small cave with an uncomfortably steep-sloping floor, the only shady spot within sight.

From the top of the winding track a ride of eight or nine miles due west led to Haz. There was little change in level. I reckoned a slight descent of 100 feet or so, but my figures do not entirely agree with previous calculations. At the highest point we halted to resume our search. Scorpions, beetles and ants were found under stones, but the soil is quite different from that of the volcanic *harra* behind us, so that less was obtainable by this method. A few insects were taken from between the bases of the fleshy leaves of aloes, a manner of collecting which, applied to palms and other plants in moist luxuriant tropical forests, has yielded an extraordinarily rich and interesting booty.

Hassan's enthusiasm for plant-collecting now got him into trouble. We had reached an altitude above the tree-limit, beyond which the succulent cactus-like euphorbias do not extend their range upwards. Here, however, at somewhat above 9,000 feet, the last of them (*Euphorbia officinalis*) (Phot. 96) [1] are found scattered over the barren, stony ground; a species not assuming the form of a branching candelabra-tree, but of a compact cushion a foot high or less. In fact the plant might be called a pin-cushion, since it is armed with spines up to three-quarters of an inch long. But these protective weapons were not the cause of Hassan's hurt. He dug up and tore off a part of one of the cushions, not knowing how strongly irritant is the milky latex of this plant. The juice dried on his hands. Later, when saying his prayers, he performed the customary ablutions and the juice spread to his face and legs. The pain set up was so severe that Dr. Petrie was obliged to administer morphine that evening. This euphorbia is confined to certain districts, even at high altitudes, and it may not have grown in places familiar to Hassan. Otherwise it seems strange that a native of the country should not have known of the burning properties of the milky juice. Forskål, who discovered and described the species, named it "*officinalis*" on account of the medicinal properties of the latex, from which, he wrote, a drastic purgative was made. We heard nothing of the plant being used thus. But we ought perhaps to have been on our guard, for the latex of many kinds of euphorbia is pungent and corrosive. So much so that those who formerly collected the juice, which dried as an acrid gum called " euphorbium ", from several species in Arabia, North Africa and the Canary Islands were obliged to protect their mouths and nostrils with a cloth, or a violent irritation and sneezing would be induced. So vehement, indeed, is the action of these gums that their use in medicine, whether as purgatives or emetics, or as irritants for external application, is almost obsolete. It might console Hassan to know that the piece of this strange plant which he got for us is flourishing in a pot! Besides this euphorbia, the only other succulent at these high altitudes is a species of *Stapelia*, of the Asclepiad family, a grotesque plant with fleshy finger-like stems a few inches high.

Leaving Jebel Reiyani soaring to (probably) well over 10,000 feet

---

[1] " Flora Aegyptiaco-Arabica," 1775, p. 94. Forskål gave the Arabic name as *Schörur*, and wrote that the latex mixed with flour was made into pills, or was taken in milk, especially during the late summer rains. The latex of this euphorbia was even more potent than that of others similarly used.

PHOTOGRAPHS 97 AND 98.
*Approaching the extinct crater of Jebel al Kohl, in the Harra of Arhab.
Red cinder-cones and black lava-flows seen from Jebel al Kohl.*

PHOTOGRAPH 99.
Sheikh Husein of Gheiman.

on the right, the path lay between fields, the furrows of which were bright green with young cereals. This welcome verdure on the western side of the lip of the Al Kabar escarpment came as a great relief after the utter brownness and dryness of even the cultivated land, at that season, below this plateau to the east. These grain-fields were not irrigated, and the young growth was presumably due to late autumn or winter sowing on the higher plateau.

At Haz, a small walled town, we were lodged in the Jewish quarter, immediately outside the walls to the south. In a substantial house, where the sanitary arrangements were a trifle less primitive than at Huqqa, we were given a large room on the first floor. It was, however, somewhat verminous. Strange to say, we had hitherto suffered very little from vermin, but here bed-bugs were unpleasantly numerous. We probably escaped largely by sleeping, as usual, on our camp-beds, which raise the sleeper well above the floor, and can be placed some way from the walls. They are, moreover, too often moved from place to place, sunned and aired, to become infested with these pests. Far more abundant on the walls of our room were grain-weevils (*Calandra*). But these little long narrow beetles did not annoy us. Their presence was due to some agricultural produce having been previously stored there, and hurriedly cleared out.

More persistent in their attentions than bugs or beetles were the Jews themselves. We had already found in small country places how their excessive curiosity leads them to stand and stare at Europeans. At Haz this defect in manners went beyond anything we had experienced. So large and dense a crowd of Jews, of both sexes and all ages, gathered in the lane below, staring fixedly up through the low-set windows of our room, that we had to close the wooden shutters. They steadily watched our every movement. Even the closing of shutters did not give us privacy. In the back wall of the room some unglazed openings gave on to the staircase. A crowd of Jewish women collected on the stairs, pushed their faces into these holes and would, no doubt, have eagerly watched us going to bed. But we stuffed our rolled-up mosquito-nets (unwanted at this altitude and season) into the apertures. After this we were left in peace.

Two days and three nights were passed at Haz. Its ruined Qasr, or citadel, at the north end of the town, is partly of pre-Islamic construction. The lower courses of masonry consist of huge squared blocks of dark stone, far larger than any used in more recent building. Into this castle, and into the walls of houses, are also built many of the white Himyaritic stones. In fact, the whole district is full of pre-Islamic remains. Within a mile north lie several large ponds, made in ancient times by the damming of a valley. These reservoirs of simple type have walls of masonry in parts, while elsewhere their edges are natural, consisting of large rocks and boulders interspersed with patches of close green turf. The margins of the ponds, especially of one called Birkat al Bu'r, were for us highly productive. Small carnivorous ground-beetles were captured on the wet mud. Large stones and boulders sunk several inches deep in the soil and surrounded by turf were uprooted and rolled over, disclosing ground-beetles [1] of other types, as well as ant-like beetles of another family. Martins of some kind, resembling our sand-martin, flew to and fro, while redshanks among the rocks near the muddy edges gave a homely touch to the scene.

Just north of Birkat al Bu'r stands another pre-Islamic site, a hill called Al Errein. On its top, among tough and wiry herbage, flowering-weeds and loose blocks of black volcanic stone, lay part of a white eight-sided Himyaritic column about four feet long, with other white stones from vanished buildings of the Himyarites. Some of the plants were Composites, either displaying yellow flower-heads, or low woody bushes with mauve flower-heads like Michaelmas daisies.[2] Level patches of ground hereabouts are cleared of the loose volcanic stones, which are piled up into heaps, while the underlying windborne soil is cultivated as small fields. In one such little field, just below the summit of Al Errein, the stubbles of last season's crop were dotted with a yellow-flowered aromatic Composite. Here specimens of the familiar small copper butterfly were captured, while shiny black weevils were found under stones on the hill-top. These finds have a certain importance in relation to the geographical distribution and northern affinities of the insects.

On our second day, while Britton remained faithful to Birkat al Bu'r, Dr. Petrie and I rode a few miles farther north of Haz, in the direction of Beit al Ghofr. The latter village, impressive in situation, crowns a steep crag, geologically a volcanic " neck ". Much of the surrounding land is exceedingly barren, particularly where the loose volcanic blocks have not been gathered into mounds. In photographing the place from a distance I chose a point whence a solitary small apricot tree was a prominent feature in the foreground. This afterwards evoked ironic comments from Britton, as though forsooth I had tried to make a Dead Sea Plain look like a Garden of Eden !

Since white Himyaritic stones could be seen from afar, gleaming in the dark walls of its houses and round towers, Dr. Petrie and I would

---

[1] The small ground-beetles were Carabidæ of the Bembidiine group, the others represented various sections of this immense family. The " ant-like beetles " were Anthicidæ.

[2] *Felicia abyssinica.*

have ridden up to Beit al Ghofr, but our mistrustful *shawūsh* would not allow this. Hurrying ahead, he spoke to villagers descending from the hill, so that, when questioned, they one and all averred that their village contained no object of interest whatever. So we turned aside and lunched at the edge of a lucerne field where many butterflies, clouded yellows, bath whites, blues and skippers, were flying. Later we rode still farther, to the base of a hill east of Beit al Ghofr, called Kaulat al 'Asakeir (" the hill of the soldiers "). One of the escort would have prevented us approaching even this, but a good-natured muleteer insisted. The other man (who was trying to carry out the *shawūsh's* orders strictly) shrugged his shoulders and gave way. Happy for us that he did so, for Kaulat al 'Asakeir presented a very strange natural feature. Facing us was a bare slope of huge, almost smooth, black volcanic rocks. It was surrounded along the top and down the sides by rough stone walling, presumably to prevent straying goats and sheep from slipping and falling on the crags. But the resulting effect was as though titans had made a gigantic black rockery. What could one hope to find in so forbidding and lifeless-looking a spot? There were many tufts of a campion (*Silene*), with foliage like the leaves of a pink and (in the only one still blooming) long narrow flowers of creamy-white. Better still, the crevices between the great rocks were brightened by the pale lilac flower-heads of a rock-plant growing in large patches. This, which puzzled me as much as did the yellow lavender on Jebel al Kohl, proved to be a creeping scabious.[1]

A pleasant prospect lay before us, as we rode back to Haz in the clear evening sunshine. The high plateau country, all divided up into fields, though treeless, was now becoming verdant with young corn; a herd of six gazelles, appreciative of this, went bounding over the nearby plough-land. Far to the south the long ridge of Jebel Hadhur Nebi Shu'aib was canopied high above by a few fleecy clouds hanging in the limpid blue sky. That great mountain-massif, much the highest in any part of the Yemen that we touched, had been our most cherished goal before leaving England. But, seeing the mood of the " powers that be ", we had long since given up any thought of travelling thither. After the way the Imam has suffered at the hands of foreign adventurers, small blame to him if he be suspicious of intruders. But it is regrettable that mistrust thus sown prevented our investigation of places several thousand feet higher than any altitude we attained.

The last day's journey, about twenty-two miles from Haz back to San'a, involved a ride of some nine not very interesting miles over the cultivated plateau to Beit an N'am. Here the irrigated fields of a shallow wadi stood out, bright green with young crops, against the surrounding

[1] Belonging to the section *Pterocephalus* of *Scabiosa*.

stony and dry land. After halting for the midday meal in an unfinished khan, the only available patch of shade, we rode another six miles; first, north-eastwards along a rocky valley, the western side of which is crowned by black basalt cliffs of vertical columnar formation. These are the result of a vast outpouring of molten material in very remote times over the sandstones of the Cretaceous epoch. But we reached this interesting geological structure in the hottest part of the afternoon, when I, for one, was so sleepy after five hours' slow riding over stony ground that I could scarcely avoid sliding off my mule! At length this valley opened into the upper part of Wadi Dhahr, down which we rode past the striking walled village of Taiba and the towering isolated crag of Jebel Fiddi to Suq al Wadi. Hence another seven or eight miles had to be covered, to complete the circuit of our northern trek. Some of us accomplished this by a car sent from the city. For one member of the party this last day was most trying. 'Omar Isma'il had fallen badly sick with fever and cough. After two days in bed at Haz, he managed to ride the fifteen miles to Wadi Dhahr. Thence he was hurried back to San'a in the car, where he passed several more days in sickness and convalescence.

* * * * *

Last of our wanderings in San'a district was that to the Senhan country (February 16th–18th). Our centre, the small hill-town of Gheiman, is about thirteen miles by road south-east of the capital. Gheiman is perched on steep crags several hundred feet high, rising from a narrow plain. But the eminence on which the town stands is so dwarfed by giant mountains that it was a surprise to find, on arriving by motor-lorry at dusk, a steep climb on foot necessary to reach the town, while a camel and three porters carried up our kit. The old head-man of the place, Sheikh Husein (Phot. 99), had not been forewarned. He read the letter from Qadhi 'Abdullah, brought by our *shawūsh*, by the light of a lamp set on the rough path. He then led us to a house at the top of the crag. There we were lodged in a rather small dark upper room with tiny windows. But the people of Gheiman did their best. They were a friendly and, to outward appearance at any rate, a healthy community (Phot. 100). Incidentally they were almost all Arabs, the number of Jews being very small. We were left in peace; no crowds thronged us like those at Haz.

Marriage festivities were being celebrated in Gheiman. In a small open space men, sometimes followed by boys, danced to the rhythmic beating of a drum. Their indigo turbans were newly starched. Some wore green bunches of sweet basil in the turban-folds. Their white knee-length skirts and the white sheeting wrapped round their bodies swayed with the movement. *Jambiyas* were flourished aloft. In parts of the dance boys and men went round in a circle, after a " follow-my-leader " fashion. At other times several men advanced abreast. Nearly all the while they revolved with a slow, rather waltz-like action. The bridegroom stood apart, looking on.

The plain at the foot of the town is some hundreds of feet higher than San'a, and the top of the crag must be little below 8,800 feet. The two nights passed there were very cold. A fine and varied landscape met our gaze from the house-roof at dawn on the morning after our arrival. Fertile flat-bottomed valleys, plantations of tamarisk and terraced lower slopes are hemmed in by barren yellowish-brown mountains. The dominating feature is the giant Jebel Girwan. While this lifts its huge bulk to the north, away south of the valleys lies a confusion of bare brown ridges and flat-topped mountain-masses, backed by another giant, the more distant (and probably even loftier) Jebel She'ani.

Jebel Girwan is a fine example of step-formation. Alternation of harder and softer layers of rock (apparently of the ancient series of traps) has given rise to an outline of alternate steep inclines and precipitous cliffs, rising to a horizontal table-top at 10,000 feet or more. In our search for insects and plants we reached a height of some 9,200 feet on its stony slopes. Pity that, owing to the shortness of the time we were allowed to stay, we could not try to reach the top ; for the *shawūsh* in charge of us was as open in countenance and ways, as our conductor on the northern trek had been dour and suspicious.

Gheiman is associated with a famous monarch, or Tubba, of the Himyarites, named As'ad Kamil. According to local Jewish tradition he was the first Tubba to embrace the Jewish faith, an act assigned to a date late in the 4th Century A.D. The Arabs contest this tradition, asserting that not he, but one of his successors, was converted to Judaism ; possibly the last of the Tubbas, Dhu Nowas, who fell before the second Abyssinian invasion in A.D. 525.[1] However this be, Tubba As'ad Kamil apparently resided at Gheiman, or at least he was buried there. In 1931 his grave was excavated under supervision of the Crown Prince. We saw nothing of the tomb, but Seif al Islam Ahmed had also caused to be cleared out and repaired an enormous rectangular ancient cistern. This reservoir, Mījāl [2] al As'ad, a mile or so north of the town, is reached by a path along the bottom of a valley. Its sides, walled with large squared and dressed stones, fall

---

[1] These historical matters are discussed more fully in Chap. xix.

[2] Mījāl (literally, it seems, a place of storage) was sounded " *Migyal* ". Birka (or *Birkat*) and *Mījāl* are the two words we heard for large ponds or cisterns in the highlands. We did not hear *Mājil* used for a cistern, as recorded by some travellers.

in a single drop (not "stepped") sloping slightly inwards from top to floor. The only access to the bottom is by flights of separate projecting stones, not joined into stairways. By these we descended to the wet mud and the rank growth of grass, rushes and water-dock, some ten or twelve feet below the edge. For the water at this season was very low, and only a trickle was entering from the spring which feeds the cistern. Bright green tree-frogs [1] lurked in the wet grass. The pond-vegetation swarmed with flies of many kinds, but the sweeping of it gained us few other insects. There was, however, no lack of these along the stony banks and strips of waste ground bordering fields of young cereals close at hand. Turning over stones close to the cistern in our hunt for beetles, we came on several small sculptured fragments of the ancient work. With this gathering of material for modern scientific research among the remains of a long vanished culture, the tale of our journeyings round San'a may be brought to a close.

[1] A form of the European tree-frog, *Hyla arborea*. We found specimens only at Mījāl al As'ad and at another great cistern south of San'a. This form of the tree-frog has been recorded from the Southern Hejaz.

PHOTOGRAPHS 100 AND 101.

Boys of Gheiman want a place in the picture.
Mother and children at Al ʿAsr.

PHOTOGRAPHS 102 AND 103.
San'a : outside the Bab al Yemen.
San'a : crowd outside the Meshhed during prayers at the 'Id al Kabir.

Chapter XVI

THE GREAT FESTIVAL : WE MEET THE IMAM AT LAST

SOON after our return from the northern trek related in the foregoing chapter, San'a became all astir with preparations for the greatest festival of the Muhammadan year. The 'Id al Kabir or " Great 'Id " (also called Id al Kourban or " Festival of Sacrifice "), lasts nearly a week. It is held simultaneously with the sacrifices performed during the pilgrimage at Mecca in commemoration of the offering of Isaac by Abraham. In 1938 these celebrations fell in the second week of February. What we saw early in December at Aden and Lahej of the " Little 'Id " or 'Id al Fitr, marking the end of the Ramadhan fast, has been told. As the Muslim calendar does not synchronise with ours, and these festivals are consequently held at different times in succeeding years, it was fortunate that our seven months in Arabia happened to embrace them both.[1]

The receptions held by the Imam at the festival, first for his own subjects and then for Europeans, marked his reappearance in public after his long indisposition. Thereafter the granting of private audiences was also resumed. Since, therefore, our meeting him at long last came about through the Great 'Id, it is fitting to tell of the festival first, and so lead up to the throne and the monarch.

The culminating day of the festival was February 10th (a Thursday), when cattle and sheep were sacrificed. On that day the Imam drove in state to lead the prayers at a mosque specially reserved for this annual occasion outside the city walls. Afterwards he viewed a march-past of schoolboys and troops. But for a day or two beforehand a holiday mood, an air of expectancy, was observable. People were getting ready bright new garments in which to appear on the great day. Within our circle in Bir al 'Azab presents were given to servants and to others attendant on the household. On the Wednesday fat sheep, particularly a breed with long and fat tails, were to be seen on sale near the Great Mosque, in readiness for sacrifice the following day. Later on the Wednesday the firing of cannon from a fort on

[1] The Little and Great 'Ids are probably better known by their non-Arabic names, Bairam and Kourban Bairam.

Jebel Nuqūm, and from the Qasr at its foot, announced the opening of the 'Īd.

The mosque in which the Imam led the prayers next morning, Al Meshhed Shaʻūb,[1] lies to the north-east, in the area called Shaʻūb immediately outside the walls of the Arab city, from which it is separated by a few hundred yards. We could never approach the Meshhed closely, but from a distance it appears as a vast quadrangular enclosure (Phot. 103) almost entirely bare and open to the sky within. The walls are battlemented, there is a single low quadrangular tower and several gates. Tower and battlements are whitewashed, contrasting with the dark brown walls.

The Imam's procession emerged from the city through the Bab ash Shegadif, in the northern wall of the narrow waist uniting the palace precincts to the Arab city. The cortège wended its way along outside the walls to the Meshhed, which the Imam entered by a door in the middle of its north wall. After the prayers the procession continued round the outside of the city to the east and south, in the direction of the citadel. By what gate it re-entered the city I cannot say; possibly by the Bab as Stran, through the citadel, or the Bab al Yemen (Phot. 102), so that the monarch would make a progress through the most populous quarters of his capital before returning to his palace.

The Petrie family, ourselves and the Russian medical lady had, by previous arrangement, taken our places early on the roof of an isolated house in Shaʻūb, some hundreds of yards north of the Meshhed (an interior and the owner of the house are shown in Phot. 72). Thence we had a good, though somewhat distant, view. This point was the nearest we were allowed to approach; cameras were not prohibited, as long as we avoided photographing the forbidden and sacred central figure, the Imam. Even so, an over-zealous mounted officer dashed across the intervening ground and threatened to " report " Hassan, who was escorting us, because we had been seen taking photographs without a special permit. But no more was heard of this threat.

Troops lined either side of the road from the Bab as Shegadif to the Meshhed. Bands played lively airs, apparently more Turkish than Arab. A mounted escort led the procession. The Imam's carriage was immediately preceded by his personal body-guard of footsoldiers, some of whom held aloft their *jambiyas* and danced. But, as said in an earlier chapter, the dancers maintain their ranks perfectly, and keep time with the moving procession, while performing their steps and gyrations. The national songs sung in unison by the soldiers in these progresses are uttered in the highest possible tones, rising on the

---

[1] *Meshhed* (or *mashhad*), a place of witness or martyrdom. I have not discovered how this particular Meshhed came to be so named.

closing notes to shrill screams and shrieks. These songs, it has been justly remarked, are scarcely to be represented by our notation.[1] It is difficult for a newcomer, hearing the distant singers for the first time as they draw near, to believe that the shrill, high voices are those of grown men.

The Imam rode in his great state-carriage, an old four-wheeled, hooded vehicle with ornamental carved woodwork at the back, drawn by two pairs of horses with postilions in dark green liveries. Two of his sons, Qasim and 'Abdullah, rode with the king. A saddled riding-horse was led behind, and an empty motor-car followed as usual, in case either should be required. Special to the festal occasion was an attendant who walked beside the carriage, holding over it an enormous umbrella about eight feet across, bright orange with a green fringe, which the bearer meanwhile twirled round and bounced up and down.

A strange pageant indeed! An odd mixture! The movements of the revolving, dagger-brandishing dancers must have their origin far back in tribal history. The curved gold-scabbarded sword carried by the Imam as an emblem of sovereignty, and the whirling umbrella, seemed to express the quintessence of an ancient oriental autocracy; while the lumbering carriage and outriders recalled European pomps of yesterday.

Men of all ranks and conditions were admitted to the Meshhed for the prayers. Two of our Somalis, Jam'a and Ahmed Mahmūd, took part in the worship. The third, 'Omar Isma'il, was only prevented by being still convalescent after the journey north. The fact that they did not belong to the peculiar Zeidi body of Muslims was no deterrent. After they had prayed standing behind the spiritual head of all Zeidis, the Imam himself, they only remarked on the postures of prayer being slightly different from those to which they were accustomed in the Sunni mosques of Aden and Somaliland. Jam'a and Ahmed had left the house in Bir al 'Azab early, clad in bright new turbans and futas and the smartest of short coats. Jam'a, in fact, now sometimes adopted the local custom of carrying a bright-coloured shawl over the shoulder.

After the prayers, while the Imam's cortège went on its way eastward and southward round the outside of the city walls, we went back to the city from the house whence we had viewed the procession. Re-entering by the Bab ash Shegadif, we ascended to a little room built on the outer wall of the palace courtyard, overlooking the narrow space between the precincts and the wall of the Arab city. The Imam (whose procession we saw from the windows as it returned from the circuit of the

[1] An attempt has been made to record the musical score of some of these songs: Rathjens and von Wissmann, "Südarabien-Reise", Vol. iii, p. 148.

city) took his station farther south (out of our view). Many men of high position were assembled about the great gateway of the palace. In the room on the wall with us was a slightly built young *seiyid*, pleasant and intelligent-looking, the son of our old friend the Amir of Ta'izz. He expressed the opinion that the ceremonies of the Great 'Id had their foundations far back in pre-Islamic times. Our cameras, this time, were left at the back of the room, for we were not to photograph the military march-past, immediately below the windows.

First came groups of boys from the schools, each detachment headed by the national flag, the white sword of 'Ali and the five white stars on a scarlet ground. These boys were headed by large numbers of yellow-coated orphan lads educated and maintained at a special school by the Government, for military service. The later detachments, from the ordinary schools, consisted of boys whose long striped garments, embroidered caps and belts were very bright and new.

After the schoolboys, several thousand soldiers marched by. These made a less bright colour-picture; most wore light yellow turbans, khaki coats, and white knee-length skirts. But the young mounted officers, Syrians and others, were brilliant enough, in black kalpaks and uniforms of modern cut; each officer seemed to have chosen whatever colour pleased him, blue, green, or purple, without reference to the detachment he led!

The troops in this march-past numbered, we were told, some six thousand. They were in two divisions, commanded by the two Syrian pashas engaged in training the army. These high officers did not take part in the march, but were among the notables surrounding the King. The function was conducted with military precision, and many of the arms were of modern type (though second-hand). Each detachment of infantry comprised, besides riflemen, a man carrying an easily portable machine-gun in a waterproof case. Batteries of mule-guns and some pieces of field-artillery completed the review.

One strange emblem, far from modern (Fig. 3), was carried by a soldier in the procession. It is a combined standard and musical instrument, with star, crescents, bells and long whisks of horse-hair. As the troops dispersed after the march-past the bearer was found and photographed by Britton (the figure has been traced from a print). We were at a loss to explain this object, but have since learned that it is a "Jingling Johnny", almost exactly like a famous one that belonged to the Connaught Rangers. There seems to be no doubt of the eastern origin of the instrument, which found its way into the armies of several European states in the 18th Century. The example belonging to the Connaught Rangers, so nearly the double of the one seen in San'a, had a remarkable history. The Spaniards captured it

A "*Jingling Johnny*"   167

from the Moors, the French took it from a Spanish regiment during the Peninsular War, and the Connaught Rangers captured it from the French at Salamanca in 1812.[1]

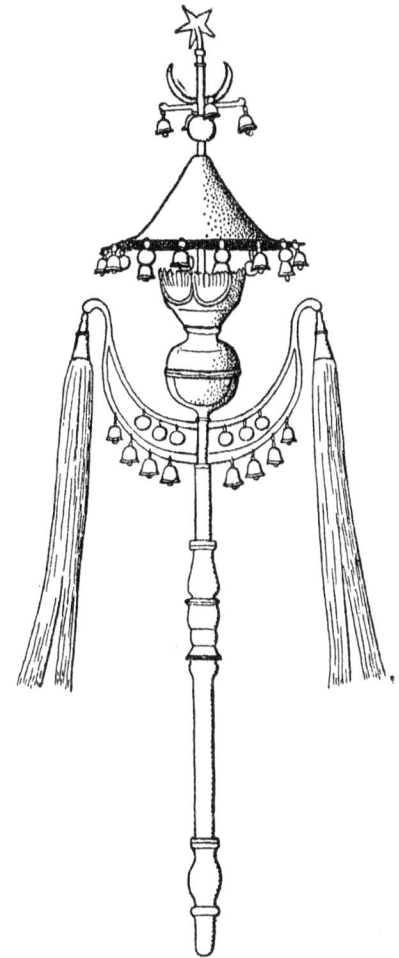

FIG. 3. *Jingling Johnny carried by a soldier in the procession at the 'Īd al Kabir (from photograph by E. B. Britton).*

Neither schoolboys nor soldiers, but the onlookers, made the brightest picture at the 'Īd procession. What an array of colours!

[1] In certain regiments of the British Army, which had black bandsmen, Jingling Johnnies were in use as late as 1840. In some German regiments, and in the French Spahi cavalry, something of the kind is—or was till quite recently—used either as a band-instrument or a standard. My sources of information are acknowledged in the Preface.

New striped garments, embroidered belts, long robes, shawls and turbans of every imaginable hue! Such were to be seen among the group of distinguished persons, mounted and on foot, gathered about the palace gates, and in the throng of men and boys in better circumstances lining the roads.

After the march-past the Imam held a reception for his subjects inside the palace. As we descended from the room on the wall, a concourse of men, among whom various high officials could be picked out, was streaming up a wide curving stone staircase leading to the presence-chamber. Two days later we were to ascend these same stairs. But now, as the crowd dispersed, we walked through the Bab as Sebah and across the open Sherara on our way home. On the Sherara tripods made of poles were still standing and pools of blood lay soaking into the dust. These signs marked the spot where a number of beasts had been sacrificed according to the rites of the festival. Here the poorer folk, a crowd of indigo-turbaned men and boys, were scrambling for fragments of the slaughtered animals. While mounted officers tried to see fair play, members of the populace straggled off with gory and unappetising-looking booty. One boy carried the whole head of an ox or a cow slung over his shoulder. A youth turned and shook a stick at us as we photographed. But this little gesture, and the behaviour of the angry young *sais* at Al 'Asr recounted in the last chapter, were the only demonstrations of hostility that we ever experienced from the people of San'a during our long stay.

Two days later, February 12th, the Imam held a reception at 9 a.m. for the few male Europeans in San'a. Then at length we saw him face to face. With Dr. Petrie we walked through the great gates of the palace precints, crossed the courtyard, ascended the wide curving stone stairs and went through a long passage. At the end was an audience-hall, not very large, but lofty, well-proportioned and somewhat elaborately decorated, especially in the plaster tracery supporting brackets in the corners. In the doorway, at the end of one of the long sides of the room, stood Qadhi Raghib in white turban, long dark blue coat, and with a long white scarf over the shoulders. Greeting us in French, he begged us to " saluer Son Excellence le Grand Qadhi ", that is, to pay our respects to the prime minister, Qadhi 'Abdullah, who was standing just behind. When all had entered, the prime minister, attired in a white turban and long green gold-embroidered robe, took his seat on a throne-like chair in the middle of the lower end of the hall, close to the door. At the upper end a large carved and polished seat, apparently of Japanese work, stood ready for the Imam. The Europeans were given chairs along the two long walls on either side. Some sixteen or seventeen of us were present. Apart from Dr.

Petrie and ourselves, the two German business men and the Polish mining engineer, all the rest were accounted for by the Italian community. Levée dress consisted of a black kalpak and the tidiest lounge suit which the wearer had with him, except in the case of the Polish engineer ; he, besides being directly in the Imam's service, held the rank of colonel in the Yemen army, and possibly for those reasons appeared in a black morning coat.

After a long pause, the Imam was heard to emerge from a room opening into the corridor outside the audience-chamber. As he came towards the door of the hall, he cried loudly the opening clauses of the Fatha (the first chapter of the Koran) : *Bismillah, ar Rahman, ar Rahim* (" In the name of God, the Compassionate, the Merciful ", followed by " Praise to God, Lord of the worlds "). Then he entered the audience-hall, walking quickly. According to prescribed etiquette, the two lines of guests pressed forward to the middle of the room, leaving a narrow alley along which the King walked, smiling, saying quickly *marhāba* (" welcome ") to each of us, as he shook hands.

After taking his seat, with Qadhi Raghib standing at his right hand, the Imam conversed genially with the company. As a rule Qadhi Raghib translated his remarks into French ; but the King spoke directly in Arabic to Dr. Petrie. We were seated near the lower end of the hall on the left. Raghib, anxious that special notice should be taken of us, twice mentioned my name ; but the Imam was not to be hurried. Later, of his own accord, he suddenly asked that I and Britton should come up and sit in the chairs immediately on his left. He then put some questions, asking our impressions of San'a, in a most friendly manner. As this was a public audience, conversation could only be more or less formal. The Imam spoke of the 'Id, remarking that while Muslims hold only two such festivals in the year, Christians appear to be always holding festivals ! He fingered the beads of a rosary throughout the audience. On this public occasion the same peculiarity was noticeable in him as in the two of his sons whom I had met, that of throwing the whole body in this direction or that while speaking, in an oratorical manner. He displayed no such habit at the private audiences when we later saw him at work. Soon after his remarks to us the Imam politely took leave of his guests, saying that he was going on one of his progresses through the city. We were left in the audience-hall, to regale ourselves with tarmarind syrup, coffee and sweets, handed round by servants.

What kind of man is the Imam, and what impression did his appearance and personality make ? In answering these questions, it is well to remember who and what he is. The spiritual head of the peculiar Zeidi body of Muslims, whose stronghold is San'a and the surrounding highlands, he is the successor of a long line of Imams dating from the beginning of the 10th Century A.D. He is the representative of the dynasty of Imams of San'a, tracing its succession back to an earlier series of Imams residing at the northern city of Sa'da, and claiming descent from the Prophet through 'Ali and Fatima (Muhammad's son-in-law and daughter). The dynasty is spoken of as "Rassite", from 'Ali Qasim ar Rassi, descendant in the sixth generation from Fatima and 'Ali. The grandson of this 'Ali Qasim, by name Al Hādi Yahya, was the first Imam of Sa'da. Moreover the dynasty of the Imams claims succession to the pre-Islamic Himyaritic princes of the land, from the last representatives of whom descent can probably be traced.

The Zeidis, of whom the Imam is thus the spiritual head, form a link between the Shi'ah body of Muslims (centred in Iran) and the great Sunni body. With the rest of the Shi'ahs, they regard it as essential that a true and fully qualified Khalif (successor) of Muhammad must be an actual descendant of the Prophet. While therefore they may, like the Sunnis, accept the first three Khalifs as having been *de facto* heads of the whole body of Islam at that time, they do not (as the Sunnis do) attach to those first three successors the same sanctity with which 'Ali and his descendants are invested. The basis of the veneration in which the Imam is held by the Zeidis lies in the personal sanctity attributed to him, an infallibility (it may almost be said) regarded as inherited by his descent from the Prophet. The view has even been held that the Zeidis possess an instinct for incarnationism, which demands that their spiritual leader should possess these inborn supernatural qualities.

These ideas have resulted in the Imam leading the life of a sacred being, to some extent secluded and apart from his people—though he is, as King, accessible to the humblest of his subjects. The office of Imam is not necessarily directly hereditary. Within certain limits it is elective, and the candidate must possess many peculiar qualifications, such as freedom from any physical blemish. In practice, a member of the original (Rassite) dynasty is invariably chosen, and usually a son of the last Imam, but not always the eldest son. At present the Qasim family of Shahārah is in power. With the strengthening of the temporal kingship, the tendency is probably for the Imamate to become more directly hereditary.

Such is the claim to succession in spiritual leadership. As regards temporal power, the Imams have been a dominant force over much of the country in past centuries, except during the periods of Turkish dominion (about 1538–1630, and 1872–1918). But only since the withdrawal of the Turks in 1918 has the present Imam gradually consolidated his power as King of the modern realm of the Yemen.¹

Besides Imam and Malek (King), denoting spiritual and temporal sovereignty respectively, the holder of this ancient office is Amir al Muminin (Commander of the Faithful) and possessor of many other styles and titles. Among them is Al Mutawakil Allah ("he who waits, or relies, on God"), a title assumed by many former Imams since the early centuries of their dynasty, and borne by the great Isma'il ibn Qasim in the 17th Century. How the palace precincts in San'a have come to be known by this name has been told in Chapter XIV.

Ilal Hadhurat al Jalalat Maulāna al Imam Yahya ("to his Excellent Majesty our Lord the Imam John" is a slightly free translation) is the way in which I was instructed to address a letter to the monarch. If, like Shakespeare, some are tempted to exclaim

> Here is a silly stately style indeed!
> The Turk, that two and fifty kingdoms hath,
> Writes not so tedious a style as this— ²

it should be remembered that the present Imam's titles imply no empty boast. He is as absolute a monarch as any left in the world. No ruler can in greater measure attend personally to every detail of his administration—as we had opportunity to see with our own eyes. He has consolidated his kingdom over highlands and lowlands. He has reduced the tribesmen to submission and maintains among his several millions of subjects a high degree of law and order, excepting some lawless mountainous border districts. If anyone on earth can say "I am the State", it is the Imam of the Yemen.

YAHYA IBN MUHAMMAD AL MANSŪR IBN YAHYA HAMĪD AD DĪN was born in (or about) 1869. He succeeded to the Imamate, the spiritual leadership of the Zeidis as distinct from the temporal kingdom, in 1904. From then till 1912, securely throned in the mountainous northern part of the country, he was nearly always a rebel against the Turkish masters of the Yemen. In 1905 he appears to have succeeded in expelling the Turks from San'a for a short time, while early in 1911 he headed a formidable rebellion, besieging the Turkish Governor in his capital for three months. Though this rising was quelled by an army sent from Turkey, the Turks soon afterwards came to an agreement with the Imam. Under this arrangement his status was recognised; he resided undisturbed, largely at the northern stronghold of Shahārah, till the final withdrawal of the Turks at the end of 1918.

¹ This much is inserted in my narrative. More about the Zeidis, their Imams and later history of the Yemen, will be found in Chapter xxi.
² *King Henry VI*, Part I, Act 4, Scene 7.

Since then he has gradually consolidated his temporal power, not only over the Zeidi highlands but over the coastal lowlands and the southern districts where Sunni Muslims of the Shafeʻi school prevail. This process has been fairly rapid, and bears witness to the Imam's determination. Though he may never have visited the coastlands of his own country or beheld the sea, he probably has a shrewd appreciation of events in the outer world. His policy of keeping the Yemen closed is deliberate, arising not only from conservatism in religious matters, but from his great jealousy of his country's independence. Who shall blame him?

Notwithstanding his nearly seventy years, the Imam seemed at the time of our visit most vigorous and energetic. And indeed, though his health is the subject of extreme care, the European doctors appeared to consider him, despite rheumatism and minor ailments, thoroughly sound.

At the public audience the Imam was dressed in white brocaded robes, with a small tightly folded white turban, the end of which hung down at the side. He carried, as well as the rosary, the gold-scabbarded sword denoting his sovereignty. Some disillusionment was, perhaps, felt at his personal appearance. He is not very tall, rather bullet-headed, he has become rather stout, and his face, though showing intelligence, would not be taken to show aristocratic breeding. He wears a short beard, now white. But no matter what the Imam's exterior; his forceful personality makes itself felt, and we later had evidence of his unremitting industry.

Comparatively few Yemenis have more than one wife, though, with the easy divorce allowed by Muslim law, men frequently divorce their wives and remarry. The rareness of polygamy is probably in large measure due to economic conditions, which make it difficult for a man to support more than one woman at a time. Yet the King lived in patriarchal style, usually with his full complement of four wives. At the time of our visit he had recently married a new bride, but had sent her back to her family in a few weeks. He attributed a return of his rheumatism to a spell of bad luck which she had cast upon him! Soon after, he took yet another youthful bride, younger than some of his grandchildren. The European medical ladies, who had access to the palace, bore witness to the high character and charm of the senior, or presiding Queen.

The King had fourteen sons living (out of fifteen), of whom the youngest was then but three months old. His family also included many daughters. Early in our stay Qadhi Raghib dictated to me a list of the princes, all of whom have the title Seif al Islam. He described them as " un bataillon " and listed them in six " divisions " under

Seals used by the Imam

their respective mothers. Three of the princes were then under restraint, having incurred the royal displeasure. One was confined in a room at the top of a tower in the wall of the palace precincts (shown in Phot. 65), the other two were in the citadel. The conditions of their imprisonment were sufficiently comfortable—though one at least had previously been chained—but, according to their doctor, they suffered much from lack of occupation. As related in Chapter XIV, I met only two of these princes, the Crown Prince Ahmed and Prince Qasim. Among the younger princes were some whom I was sorry not to meet, since they were, judging from hearsay, men of ability and character.

We had seen the holder of this centuries-old office at a public reception. Now we were to see the Imam at work. That same evening we received our summons to a private audience on the following day, February 13th. We were to present ourselves at " ten o'clock ",

FIG. 4. *Impression of triangular seal stamped in red pigment on the envelope containing our summons to a private audience with the Imam (the date 1331 A.H. on the lower margin corresponds to 1912 or 1913).*

that is at four o'clock in the afternoon (the Arab time-reckoning, starting at 6 a.m., being used in all such arrangements). The command consisted of three lines of Arabic script written on a sheet of plain foolscap in ordinary ink; but the handwriting had then been smeared with red ochre, a sign made by the Imam with his own fingers, as important as his seal. The envelope was stamped in red, both in the top right-hand corner and on the middle of the back, with a seal shaped like a right-angled triangle and showing calligraphic devices (Fig. 4). Triangular and circular seals, and black as well as red colouring matter, are used on different kinds of documents. Several explanations have been suggested for the use of the red ochre; one is that it symbolizes the Imam's succession to the throne of the Himyaritic princes, whose flag was red. Red, it will be recalled, is also the ground-colour of the modern flag of the Yemen.

At the appointed time we climbed the curving stone steps at the palace once more, and were ushered into a small room opening out of a short passage branching from the long corridor leading to the big audience hall. Shoes were left outside, our kalpaks remained on our heads. This little room or office, the Maqam Sharif,[1] was lofty, long, narrow and rather dark. At the far end a throne stood untenanted, while a carved and gilded rod was leaning against the wall near by. The Imam was seated on cushions on the floor in the middle of the left-hand side. Qadhi 'Abdullah al 'Amri sat immediately on his right, leaning on a pile of cushions. To the right again Qadhi Raghib took his seat, to act as interpreter. We squatted against the wall on the other side of the room, immediately opposite to the King. On our left, nearer the door, sat Jam'a and 'Omar, bearing (at Qadhi Raghib's advice) boxes of pinned insects, a net, collecting boxes and other apparatus, and a bundle of dried plants in papers, to be shown to the King.

The Imam was wearing the same tight-folded turban that he had worn at the public reception, but his brocaded garments were exchanged for the ordinary long, striped, sleeved robe of an Arab townsman. The curved gold-scabbarded sword which he had carried at the festival hung on the wall. He looked at a first glance a very ordinary old man. But to regard him as such would be an error of judgment. The Imam Yahya is far from ordinary.

On his left stood some well-worn pieces of furniture with drawers full of papers. All round the Imam, on the floor, lay piles of papers of every shape and size. He was dealing with these swiftly, signing or writing a word or two on some; throwing them when dealt with rapidly aside to one or two clerks or servants sitting on the floor in the middle of the room. These men treated the papers in various ways, stamping some with one or other of the several seals, either in black or red; for tins of the black and red colouring matter stood close at hand. At one point a servant entered carrying a number of silver dollars in a wooden tray; after this had been shown to the King, the coins were shot into a pile on the floor. It must be remembered that there is no vestige of a banking system, and all the national revenue and treasure is collected and kept in coin.

The minuteness with which the King supervises details can be further illustrated by the following incidents. A European visitor, fluent in Arabic, had at a recent audience seen a written petition brought to the King from one of the latter's own sons, requesting the use of a motor-car for a day; this paper had to be passed before the prince could have the use of a vehicle. Another time, I was told, a paper was brought announcing the death of a sick soldier in hospital;

---

[1] "The noble place of standing" is the nearest translation.

the Imam marked or signed the document with a formula tantamount to giving the already deceased warrior permission to die.

Notwithstanding his almost ceaseless industry we were, at this first private audience, highly favoured. After some time the King put his papers aside and asked us a series of questions. For a while he looked at our specimens and apparatus. But he paid little attention to the postcard-views of the Museum, which he turned over hurriedly. There was the usual difficulty in explaining the purpose of our work, though both we and Qadhi Raghib tried to make some of its practical uses intelligible. This led to inquiries on the Imam's part about a wonderful stone which, if it can be found, will cure snake-bite by its touch. (Perhaps he meant the half-precious stones, *fusūs*, used for medical and other purposes, with which certain people claim to heal snake-bite.) I could only reply that I had heard or read of such a thing, but could not suggest where it might be found. The King's attention was, however, by now wandering back to his work. For some moments he held a dried plant up in front of him, but appeared not to be looking at it, as though his thoughts were elsewhere. Qadhi Raghib, speaking aside in French, advised me to hasten if I had any request to make. I therefore quickly asked him to thank the Imam for his permission to visit the northern Bilad Hamdan (which we had already done). I mentioned also the Bilad Senhan, whither we had still to go. The Imam said that permission to go thither was already granted, and there was nothing further to discuss. I asked Qadhi Raghib if I should beg the King's permission to travel by the old Manakha mule-road to Hodeida, when our time came finally to leave the country; but the Qadhi begged me not to, saying that we should speak of that matter when we came for our parting interview with the King, after visiting Bilad Senhan. So naturally we said no more, but we little knew the disappointment in store for us. In taking our leave, I stepped back, at a hint from Raghib, and kissed the Imam's hand; which, the Qadhi said aside in French, His Majesty liked, though Europeans did not usually show respect to him thus. Jam'a and 'Omar in turn crouched right down on the floor and put their heads in his lap. They had been silent till now, but the Imam spoke to each in turn. He asked 'Omar " of what nation are you ? " " I am a Somali ", was the reply; " No, you are a San'ani now ", replied the Imam kindly (and perhaps playing on the slight similarity of the words). The manner in which our servants were received throughout the journey by people in high positions was pleasing, and characteristic of Arab ways.

Hitherto we had made no direct request to the Imam by word of mouth. Consequently we had seen him in good humour. We had yet to learn how he can treat those who ask favours which he is not disposed to grant. After our journey to Bilad Senhan, when we stayed at Gheiman (as has been told), we were summoned once more to the Maqam Sharif for our parting interview before leaving the country. This, again at " ten o'clock " (4 p.m.), was on Saturday, February 26th. For an hour or more we sat in complete silence facing the King, while sheaves of papers were carried into the room in seemingly endless procession, swiftly dealt with and taken out again. Once or twice the Imam looked up from his work, and I seized the opportunity to thank him (through Qadhi Raghib) for having allowed us to visit Gheiman. Then he asked, very agreeably, my opinion why the old Himyaritic princes had chosen that place to dwell in ? But he sank deep into his work again, only occasionally stopping to drink water from the mouth of a bottle wrapped (for coolness) in damp cloth. At each draught he cried aloud *w'al hamdu lillah* (" and praise be to God "). At length Qadhi Raghib (who addressed his royal master simply as " Sidi ") ventured to say, with great deference, that the time for our departure had come, and that we wished to ask His Majesty's permission to travel by the Manakha route to Hodeida.

There was nothing unusual in this request. The permission had been granted to a number of foreign visitors. Since we had been given the rare privilege of journeying to San'a from Ta'izz through the central highlands (for we were then among the half-dozen or so of living British people who had travelled this route), everyone to whom we had spoken, even Arab acquaintances, had regarded it as certain that we should be allowed to make our exit by the old Manakha road. We were most anxious to do so on account of the magnificent scenery and the high altitudes traversed.

Judge then of our astonishment and dismay when the King replied verbally to Qadhi Raghib that we were to go to Hodeida by the new motor-route, by way of Madinat al Abīd. A little later in the interview Raghib tried again. This time he wrote our request on a slip of paper, which he handed to the Imam. The latter wrote on the slip the same refusal which he had uttered verbally, and gave the paper back to Raghib. Qadhi Raghib, looking extremely chagrined, tore the paper slowly into small pieces, which he dropped on the cushions ; this, I gathered, was according to the etiquette prescribed in cases when a request is refused.

I was so dumbfounded at the turn our affairs had taken, that I did not at first realise the greatness of the disappointment. Little remained of our final interview. Soon after his second refusal of our petition, the Imam seemed to get angry. He spoke loudly to members of his household who were in the room, and tossed some of his papers about. Whether our request or some other business had annoyed

Last glimpse of the Imam

him, I cannot say. He quieted down and resumed work for a short time. Then suddenly he rose, looking straight in front of him. He loudly exclaimed a religious expression (I think it was: " In the name of God, the Compassionate ", again) and strode from the room. We had no chance to pay any parting respects, but were left standing in the Maqam with Qadhi Raghib. The latter seemed nearly as disconcerted as ourselves. The King may, indeed, have meant to show us unmistakably that our presence was no longer welcome. From certain signs, however, it is just as likely, perhaps even more likely, that he had entirely forgotten our existence. Whatever the explanation we saw the Imam of San'a and King of the Yemen no more.

Chapter XVII

LAST DAYS IN SAN'A AND EXIT *VIA* HODEIDA

AFTER the sudden reverse in our fortunes just recounted, we still remained in San'a over a week. Since no orders had been given for our departure, I refused at first to take the Imam's decision about our route as final. On the day after our farewell audience with the King, Qadhi Raghib called on us and tried to smooth the matter over. He was, as usual, most courteous and charming. He had, he declared, tried for three weeks to get the King's consent to our travelling by the old Manakha road. I verily believe that Qadhi Raghib had done his best for us. He could not or would not, however, explain the King's refusal to grant this favour. He drew a comparison between an absolute and a constitutional monarch. Such men as the Imam, he justly said, are " des souverains ", absolute autocrats, obeying no laws ; and Raghib cited in contrast an instance in which a famous British prime minister of the 19th Century had felt obliged to remind the monarch that she too was bound by the constitution. Yet Raghib agreed that we should make " dernières démarches " to the Imam. When asked if he advised our doing so, he remarked, after a moment's reflection, " vous n'avez rien à perdre ". " Nothing to lose, Excellency ! " I replied, " but suppose the King closes *both* routes against us and keeps us here ? " At this sally our old friend roared with laughter, saying, " Ah ! Non, non, mon cher ami, le Roi ne va pas faire cela ". He insisted, however, that extreme politeness should be maintained in any steps we took : " On ne perd rien par la politesse, et quelquefois on y gagne quelquechose ", was the sage counsel of the old diplomat. Qadhi Raghib also told a little parable to emphasise that, whatever our disappointments, in a closed country such as the Yemen we had been allowed to see a fair amount. The story was of a man who travelled right across Asia Minor with a donkey, to carry out his lifelong ambition of visiting Istanbul. Arrived at the Asiatic shore of the Bosporus, he fell into a dispute with a boatman over the price asked for ferrying himself and his donkey across. The sum involved was only a few " bogaches " (*bukhshas*), but the traveller in anger turned back home without ever setting foot in the city. We must be contented, Raghib argued, with what we *had* been permitted to see and do.

Acting on Qadhi Raghib's advice to make a "last attempt", I sought the help of an influential San'ani. He in turn visited the Qadhi 'Abdullah, who wrote out the draft of a letter for me to sign and send to the King. Whether Qadhi 'Abdullah was personally opposed to our project, I do not know. At any rate he sent a farewell message of regret that it had been impossible for permission to be granted. The letter to the King was not answered, nor was a second one sent through a different channel. Both these letters were couched in the most deferential and correct style. The substance of them was mainly that we were ready to pay all expenses of the mule journey ourselves. We thanked the King anew for all that had been done for us, and expressed the wish not to impose further burdens on the Treasury. I had thought that the greater expense of the mule caravan needed for travelling by Manakha was possibly the cause of the refusal. But still no answer came. At length, after a week had elapsed, I had to tell Qadhi Raghib that we simply must leave San'a by one route or the other, as it was already impossible to reach England without overstaying our leave of absence. That evening he called to tell us the King's pleasure. The Manakha route was finally refused, no reason was given and the question of expense was brushed aside. His Majesty had decreed (*ordonné*) that we were to leave on the morning of March 8th in a lorry and a car, and to travel by way of Madinat al Abīd to Hodeida, and thence to Ta'izz, where we could send for cars to take us back to Aden. In the event, however, not all of this could be carried out. We left Hodeida by sea.

Meanwhile our last week in San'a was fully occupied. Several days had to be devoted to clearing up and packing kit and specimens. A few of the latter, such as larvæ of wood-boring beetles, were living insects in their early phases of development. Some of these, brought home with a supply of their food in tins or bottles, reached the adult stage during the voyage or after our return.

Farewell visits were interchanged with the Italian and Syrian households. Indeed it was impossible not to feel increasingly pangs of regret at our approaching severance from many who had shown us kindness, and from the ancient city which had been our home and base for many weeks. Last walks were taken through the old Arab quarter.

Late in February an unpleasant form of laryngitis swept through San'a. Neither we nor the members of Dr. Petrie's household escaped; most or all fell to it in turn. As a lifelong victim of catarrhal ailments, my experience is that they are not necessarily avoided during an expedition such as this. It seems much easier, however, to throw off their after-effects in so dry, sunny and bracing a climate.

The excellent Jam'a had his wish to play football in San'a fulfilled. Captain Seager having arrived from Aden on an official mission, an improvised match was held on the aerodrome. The teams numbered five apiece; goal-posts and other such refinements were absent. Yet he and his servants represented Aden, while Britton, our Somalis, and an Eritrean dispenser from the Italian medical community managed to represent San'a. I have forgotten the result! Perhaps because, after photographing the teams on a rather chilly, dull and rainy afternoon, I did not wait to see the end.

Our journey to Hodeida was to be made in company with a Swiss gentleman, who had arrived in San'a some weeks before. He had contracted a severe attack of malaria on the journey up from Hodeida by Madinat al Abīd, and had been tended back to health by Dr. Petrie in the same room where Britton had earlier convalesced. Since then he had been, like ourselves, a member of Dr. Petrie's family circle. As he had lived for many years in Abyssinia, and only left through the troubles following the Italian occupation of Addis Ababa, he and I had much to talk of in common.

So the morning of our departure came. I finally vacated the *mifraj* on the roof, and heard for the last time the creaking of the wooden pulleys over which the water was ceaselessly being dragged up from the great wells of Bir al 'Azab. Good-byes were said to our kind friends the Petries, Miss Cowie, and the members of the household. We, our Swiss fellow-traveller and our three Somalis were away in the laden lorry and car soon after 8 a.m. At the great stone building facing the Sherara Place, where Captain Seager was staying, we picked up an 'Audhali tribesman from the Aden Protectorate. This man had come up with the British Frontier Officer, and wished to " work his passage " back to Aden. He was introduced simply as 'Abdurrahman, but as some kind of surname proved necessary on the journey we told him to call himself 'Abdurrahman al 'Audhali, and to stick to this designation.

To mitigate our disappointment about the Manakha road, it was arranged by those in authority that we should spend some time over the journey to Hodeida. The drivers of the lorry and the car were friendlily disposed, and for escort we had only a *shawūsh*, of the most amiable. We might have gone anywhere or done anything as far as these three men were concerned. And indeed the country traversed by the motor-route, while not rivalling in magnificence the old mule-road, is so varied and in parts so grand, that we were in large measure consoled. The journey of roughly 160 miles, which can be covered in three or even in two days, was spun out to four. This proved a source of trouble at Hodeida !

Departure from San'a was so timed that the top of Naqil Isla pass was reached about 11 a.m. During a halt we scrambled up the slopes of Jebel Jalal to just on 10,000 feet. In fact the summit (which Britton reached, while I remained about fifty feet below) may exceed that altitude. Here, for a few short hours, we did the kind of work and found specimens of the sort which had been my main object on this expedition. But, as has been shown, such chances had to be snatched here and there. On these slopes a rich haul was made among white jasmine and other flowering bushes, nice little woody-stemmed Composites with white flower-heads,[1] and dwarf junipers (about two to six feet high). Weevils of northern appearance were found under stones, tiny ladybird-beetles [2] were beaten in great numbers from the juniper-bushes; from a juniper, too, a beautiful green Geometrid moth was shaken by a chance sweep of the net. Our party lunched by the roadside (overlooking the scene shown in Phot. 112). Then, sending the vehicles on to the bottom of the pass, we walked down the southern side. What a difference in warmth and light from the cold, darkening early January evening when Britton and I had walked up in the reverse direction, on our way to San'a! On this day (March 8th) we drove on from the foot of the mountains to the great guest-house at Ma'bar, into which we settled ourselves just in time to avoid a sudden heavy rainstorm.

The following day, our last opportunity for collecting specimens in the highlands, we drove to the crest of Jebel Masnah. Only the small car was used, for we returned to Ma'bar that night. The scene of our activities lay at somewhat over 8,000 feet, on the very edge of the high plateau. From the brink of a chasm we looked over a grand stretch of country (Phot. 104). The Wadi Masnah wound away below, while on the right towered the giant Jebel Doran, and the soaring pinnacle (Sub' Doran?) seen in the middle of the view. Aloft on Jebel Doran, though we could not see the building, is the tomb of one of the noblest Imams of the Yemen. He was Isma'il ibn Qasim, who acceded towards the middle of the 17th Century and reigned gloriously some thirty years. He was one of the many Imams who assumed the title Al Mutawakil Allah (" he who relies on God ").[3] Other great men, too, have elected that their mortal remains should rest on the high places of the earth.

Our day on Jebel Masnah was spent working in the hot sunshine on the rough stony surface of a dry hill-crest dotted with scattered bushes. Painted lady butterflies and the large brown-and-grey butterflies like greylings flew wildly about the top of a bare rocky knoll. This was also the only occasion on which we captured black and red

---

[1] *Antithrixia abyssinica.*   [2] Probably one or more species of *Scymnus.*
[3] See p. 171.

burnet-moths (Zygænidæ) ; they too flew hither and thither so swiftly and wildly that all the nimbleness of Britton and 'Omar was taxed to secure specimens. It might further almost be called a day of " big game " ; several gazelles watched us passing by from some fields on the plateau, a mountain-hare leapt from its form at my feet, large grey partridge-like chikore [1] flew among the rocks at the foot of the cliffs, and grey shrikes [2] perched on the tops of thorny bushes. But the collapse of a very personal part of my kit indicated that it was time we wended homewards ; for the last pair of boots which had withstood the sharp-edged stones of the highlands gave out, and a flapping sole had to be bound to its " upper " with string.

Next day (March 10th) saw us cover a long distance, to a point some way short of Behih, in the foothills. It was planned to avoid spending the night at Madinat al 'Abīd, on account of the evil reputation of that place for malaria. Our Swiss friend in particular, having for many years successfully evaded the disease in passing up and down between Jibouti and Addis Ababa, had fallen a victim to it soon after landing in Arabia ; he had (as has been told) contracted the illness on his way up to San'a, and was therefore particularly anxious not to linger in the same malarious spot on the downward journey. So we rose in the dark at 4 a.m., but did not eventually leave Ma'bar till six o'clock ; the lorry driver had omitted to fill his tanks with petrol overnight, and then both drivers departed to their morning prayers. But even after the two hours' delay it was still very cold, and the plateau was blanketed in thick mist as we drove again to the crest of Jebel Masnah. Thence, walking part of the way, we descended a steep zigzagging road into Wadi Masnah, along which the journey continued through wild and rugged scenery into the Wadi Hammam 'Ali. At Hammam 'Ali, one of the important thermal establishments of the Yemen, the lower part of the valley slope behind the hot springs is crowded with small rough stone huts of one storey (Phot. 105). These serve as temporary dwellings for those who come to take the baths. A large concourse of people was gathered here because several of the royal princes had been on a visit for a course of treatment. Cars were waiting to take them back to San'a.

After a short halt we continued our journey to a spot rather lower down the valley. Here, at nine o'clock, we stayed an hour to rest and breakfast. We had descended about 2,800 feet from the crest of Jebel Masnah, and were now some 5,600 feet above sea-level. What a change in three short hours from the chill and foggy early morning on the plateau to tropical luxuriance and heat ! The exhilarating

---

[1] The Black-headed Chikore, *Alectoris melanocephala*.
[2] *Lanius excubitor arabicus*.

PHOTOGRAPH 104.
On the edge of the Yemen highlands; looking west down Wadi Masnah.

PHOTOGRAPHS 105 AND 106.
*The rough dwellings used by visitors to the hot springs at Hammam 'Ali.
The last of the mountains, in the Wadi Siham.*

climate of the highlands was left behind. Our resting place was under a great wild-fig tree. Close by, a stream murmured between fringes of bright green grass, rank and tall. Beyond lay fields of green *dhurra*. Brilliant tropical butterflies, mainly African, flitted to and fro. The exuberant vegetation included several flowering bushes and trees new to us, notably a small tree with yellow flowers and little spherical green fruits. One of our Somalis recognised this as a product of his native country, yielding (he said) edible fruit.

Three hours more of long winding descents, to about 4,000 feet, brought us to Madinat al 'Abīd (" the city of slaves "). Here the valley is broad, open and very fertile, though girt about with jagged, barren, rocky ranges. The streams have become a small river. Fields of cereals (wheat was already ripening) are dotted with large dark green trees. Indeed small patches of tall trees, very large wild-figs and acacias, formed the nearest approach to real forest that we saw in Arabia. Some of these trees seemed to have been left as shade to plantations of coffee.

The village or town itself was left to one side of our route. It appeared only a small cluster of low buildings. The valley in which it lies descends south of west into the great Wadi Rima, which runs between the cities of Zabīd and Beit al Faqih towards the coast. Our route, however, left this valley-system and took us in a general northwesterly direction, through wild and grand mountain glens, across a watershed into the valley-system of the Wadi Siham. Another halt was made about 3 p.m. in Wadi Jaira (a tributary of Wadi Siham), where we lunched under a giant tamarisk. We had now come down to 3,000 feet, and had pushed on thus far in the hope of collecting specimens by running water. Though the bed of Wadi Jaira was dry, an irrigation channel along the side was full and flowing. The rank herbage in a little field beside the runnel yielded many insects to the sweeping-net. On again at four o'clock, and some time later we found that our afternoon halt had been made too soon. For we came to a most tempting valley with a broad shallow stream flowing over stones. So much did Britton, in particular, wish to " hunt " here, that I consented not to try and reach Behih, but to camp in the open. Our Swiss friend mildly urged the danger of fever, but I promised to insist on a camping ground far from water. So, at a spot where the road descended close to the river, we two and the three Somalis " bottled " specimens till we could see no longer for the oncoming dusk. Our haul consisted entirely of beetles [1] which hide under stones at the water's edge.

[1] Various species of ground-beetles (*Carabidæ*), of *Staphylinidæ*, and a click-beetle (*Elateridæ*).

The next thing to search for was a place in which to camp for the night. We pressed on once more. The road ran roughly parallel with the Wadi Siham, across a wide plain with mountains far distant on either side and the wadi forming a shallow canyon across the level. Just as dark fell our drivers turned off the road on the side further from the wadi. They drove some distance through open spaces among thin leafless thorn-scrub. A half-laager was made by placing the lorry and the car at right angles. Our beds and mosquito-nets were set up in the angle thus formed. We hoped no mosquitoes would trouble us; I think that a few did, but fortunately no one was the worse! The place was called Ghailima, its altitude about 2,200 feet, 6,000 feet lower than our starting-point that morning at Ma'bar. Our men made a great fire of dry wood. The three Somalis (as if the day had not been long enough) performed dances of their country, singing and clapping their hands in rhythmic unison, in the firelight. This last bivouac might for all the world have been in the thorn-scrub of Eastern Africa.

March 11th saw the end of the journey to Hodeida. Leaving Ghailima at 8 a.m., we were stopping an hour later in a wadi of the same name; a pretty place with a running stream bordered by short green grass, dense thickets of tamarisk and clumps of dwarf date-palms.[1] Here we had an hour's hard work collecting water-insects, grasshoppers and butterflies. Here too, people first appeared in the dress of the Tihama lowlands; men with brimless straw-hats like inverted flower-pots, and women with tall wide-brimmed straw-hats. These latter hats, very characteristic of the Yemen Tihama, recall by their shape those worn by Welsh women in bygone days, except that the Welsh hats were of black silk while these are of undyed straw.

Two hours more of driving over stony ridges sparsely covered with dry scrub, and we stopped again from eleven o'clock till midday at the ford where the road crosses to the north side of the main Wadi Siham (Phot. 106). This is some way south-east of 'Obal, at about 2,000 feet. At that season the river was shrunken but still flowing. Its broad pebbly bed, mainly dry, is dotted with tamarisk-covered islets. Other thickets of tamarisk line the banks, with a growth of low broom-like *Indigofera*-bushes and a huge clump of screw-pine, a tree not seen since our stay at Al Huseini, north of Lahej. (The species appears to be *Pandanus odoratissimus*, imported from India; its fragrant heads of flowers, with their enfolding spathes, are (or were) sold in the Tihama under the name 'Aūd adh Dhib to be added to the bunches of sweet basil placed in the folds of men's turbans on festal occasions.[2])

[1] *Phœnix reclinata*.   [2] Deflers, "Voyage au Yemen", p. 214.

The Wadi Siham here is a luxuriant spot, where another valuable haul of insects, aquatic and terrestrial, was made. The thickets were, moreover, enlivened by some of the most gorgeous birds found in the Yemen, the Abyssinian Roller,[1] of a beautiful vivid blue and red-brown plumage, with long tail-spines.

At 'Obal, on the north side of the Wadi Siham, the (to us) forbidden Manakha road and its accompanying telegraph-line join the road from Madinat al Abīd. Away to the east the great mountains—our last view at close quarters—presented a lovely scene. The presence of much cloud and haze hid the barrenness of their seaward slopes, softening their outlines and imparting to them the colouring of mountains in parts of Europe.

After a sharp rainshower we were halting again at Behih, in an enclosure of brushwood built round huts of the same material. These were circular structures (Phot. 107) with conical roofs of grass-thatch. They were of a characteristically African type, unlike the rectangular brushwood booths in the foothills north of Aden. The appearance of the people also testified to their African racial affinities. In short, though Behih lies surrounded by spurs of the mountains, it is near the inner fringe of the coastal lowlands.

A Punjabi Muslim dressed in a long peach-pink shirt here hailed us, asking for a lift for his companion, an old Punjabi man, to Hodeida. It seemed that these two had tried to make the Pilgrimage to Mecca. Somehow they were too late, as the Pilgrimage was a month past. The younger Punjabi wanted to continue to San'a, whence he would go to Mecca with the next year's pilgrims. The old man, who had injured his leg, was returning. Needless to say we gladly conveyed him to Hodeida. Ahmed Mahmūd spontaneously gave the younger pilgrim several riyāls out of his wages; we gave the pilgrim several more. The pink-shirted man was left calling down many blessings on our heads and professing delight at learning that we were " Angrez " (English). The working knowledge of Hindustani possessed by Jam'a and 'Omar had proved useful.

Soon after quitting Behih the last projecting spurs of the foothills were receding on either side and the track led out on to the Tihama. A pause at the lowland town of Bājil was long enough for the purchase of some earthenware vessels of a kind there exposed for sale and also used in the local coffee-houses. This ware was said to be made at Hais, a town south-east of Zabīd, on the lowland route from Hodeida to Ta'izz. The pottery manufacture of Hais has been of local note for several centuries. Samples which I brought home are small basins or handleless cups from about three and a half to seven inches in

[1] *Coracias abyssinicus.*

diameter and standing from two to nearly four inches high. They are of rough reddish earthenware rather like flower-pots, but the inside is coloured and glazed, either in sage-green, or more commonly in buff-yellow with a sage-green rim and sometimes green cross-stripes. One is also ornamented with rough dark brown streaks, but we saw none showing other than these three colours. The Hais ware, though crude, is attractive and seems to be characteristic of the place of its origin. No such articles were seen in San'a, where the pottery utensils seen were different in shape and of a smoother, plain red ware.

From Bājil a final run of about thirty miles, occupying two hours, brought us to Hodeida. This last stretch lay across the coastal plain of the Tihama in a south-westerly direction. At first there were scanty dwarf bushes, then large stretches of sand dotted more or less uniformly with clumps of *bokar*-grass,[1] rarely less than a yard apart, each growing out of a little mound of blown sand accumulated among its own stems. Here and there long-legged bustards[2] scurried away from our cars across the plain. Vegetation seemed to be sparser and sparser, till it became thicker again on assuming a maritime, coastal type. For the " zone " of *bokar*-grass lies just inland of the maritime zone of *Suaeda* and other coastal sand-dune plants. Then the Red Sea came in sight ; the track turned more to the southward along the coast, and led at length to Hodeida.

*   *   *   *   *

At Hodeida, the chief sea-port of the Yemen, we stayed four nights. The obstructions which arose here were such as to make us think that the Yemen was a country more difficult to quit than to enter ! Unfortunately we were without the help of the only permanently resident British diplomatic representative in the Yemen. This gentleman, Mr. Salih Ja'far, M.B.E., a member of the important Aden family of Ja'far of Iranian origin, held the status of British Political Clerk. He was usually stationed at Hodeida but had been summoned to San'a by Captain Seager, and had passed us on the road, travelling in the opposite direction. We had heard much of Mr. Ja'far, whom we would gladly have met. The few British in San'a were dependent on him for various services connected with the passing in and out, through Hodeida, of passengers and goods. In his absence, his nephew 'Abduljabbar Ja'far helped us as far as possible.

Darkness fell just after our arrival in the town. No word had been received by the authorities of our coming, and we still sat in our car outside the great Government Guest-House facing the sea, while the

---

[1] *Panicum turgidum.*
[2] Probably *Chlamydotis undulatus macqueeni*, in Arabic *hūbara*.

custodian and key were sent for. Meanwhile our Swiss friend was carried off to the house of a Greek business acquaintance. (Incidentally the latter was the only Greek whom we met in the Yemen. It had seemed strange to me, after my experience in Abyssinia years before, to find in this part of the world a city the size of San'a without Greeks or Armenians.) When the guest-house was at last unlocked, we climbed fifty-three stairs to the spacious top floor, where piles of carpets were brought out and rooms hurriedly prepared. The ground-floor of this guest-house is a lofty warehouse, across which we passed to the stairs between bales and cases. The upper floors have not the elegant ornamentation of corresponding buildings in the highlands, but are light and airy. Our top floor was composed of one large room with smaller rooms partitioned off in the front. A row of fifteen big windows faced the little harbour and the sea. The staff were friendly and anxious to please, the fare supplied was excellent. Our troubles at Hodeida were not in that direction ! So far as cuisine went, we might almost have been in an hotel. Our beds were set up on the flat roof, for in mid-March the nights in Hodeida were already very warm.

The day following our arrival was occupied with packing and preparing all the plants and insects collected since we left Ma'bar. We had intended to rest in Hodeida that day in any case, but had hoped to continue our journey by road to Ta'izz on the day following. There was, however, to be no more travelling by land. I had been guardedly warned, before leaving San'a, that the Amir of Hodeida might mistrust us, and we gradually found how deeply his suspicions were aroused.

We were taken to see the Amir at the Government Offices, the Hakūma, by young Mr. Ja'far on March 13th. The Amir drove down to the Hakūma from his house at the back of the town in a closed car with an escort of six or seven soldiers on fast-trotting camels. Amir Seiyid 'Abdullah ibn al Wazir (a cousin of our old friend the Amir of Ta'izz) is a handsome man, in outward presence the noblest of the high personages whom we encountered. But his distrust was unconquerable. Though he looked attentively at the specimens and apparatus shown to him, he plainly did not believe that our motive for entering the country was to collect insects. In fairness it should be said that his attitude might have been different, had any warning or explanation of our coming been sent him in advance. As it was, he questioned us closely about where we had been and what we had done since entering the Yemen three months before. To our answers he usually responded " ajeeb ! " an exclamation of approval, but he did not believe they were true. This appeared not only in our interview with him, but in his questioning of Jamʻa and our Swiss friend privately about our movements. We also, by the way, had from the Amir a long and forcible allocution about British policy with regard to the Jews and Palestine.

The upshot was that the Amir could not or would not allow us to continue by road to Taʻizz. Before our interview he had sent a message that this was impossible, as the engines of our motor vehicles needed repair. This was not so; our drivers said the engines were in order, and they were only too willing to drive us on to Taʻizz. The next reason given was that the rain had damaged the road; this, which the Amir said was "from God, not from him", was merely a polite excuse.

Had we been allowed to proceed by land we should have passed through Beit al Faqīh, through the ancient city of Zabīd, still an important centre for the local Sunni Muslims of the Shafeʻi school, and through Hais, noted for its long-standing manufacture of pottery. But this fresh disappointment had to be swallowed.[1]

When arrangements to leave by sea were put in train, fresh obstacles arose. Small British steamships of the Cowasjee-Dinshaw house are the normal means of sea-communication between Aden and Hodeida. But none was expected till an uncertain date, which might mean a delay of many days in Hodeida. An Italian (Lloyd-Triestino) steamer was to leave for Aden on March 15th. Owing to the rapidly approaching expiry of our leave of absence, we were anxious to travel by this vessel. But trouble arose with the local Italian manager of the line over the question of passports. Departure in an Italian ship had not been foreseen. Our three Somalis and ʻAbdurrahman the ʻAudhali possessed no such documents, and our own British passports, not required in the Yemen, had been left for safety in Aden. The Amir ʻAbdullah, when told of this, talked no more of broken motor-engines or damaged roads. He simply said he had no authority from Sanʻa to send us on by land, and if the Italian steamer wouldn't take us, well, we must wait for a British one. In desperation I telegraphed to Captain Seager in Sanʻa. A favourable reply came at length. So far as the passport difficulty went, it was smoothed out by the kind intervention of Dr. Dubbiosi, acting through an amiable young Italian doctor resident in Hodeida. No further question was raised by the local manager of the steamship line.

Meanwhile, though we lived most comfortably in the guest-house, our every movement out-of-doors was intently watched. Our Swiss

[1] Early in 1892 the late W. B. Harris underwent exactly the same disappointment. The (then) Turkish Governor of Hodeida refused to allow him to travel by this same route ("A Journey through the Yemen", 1893, p. 365).

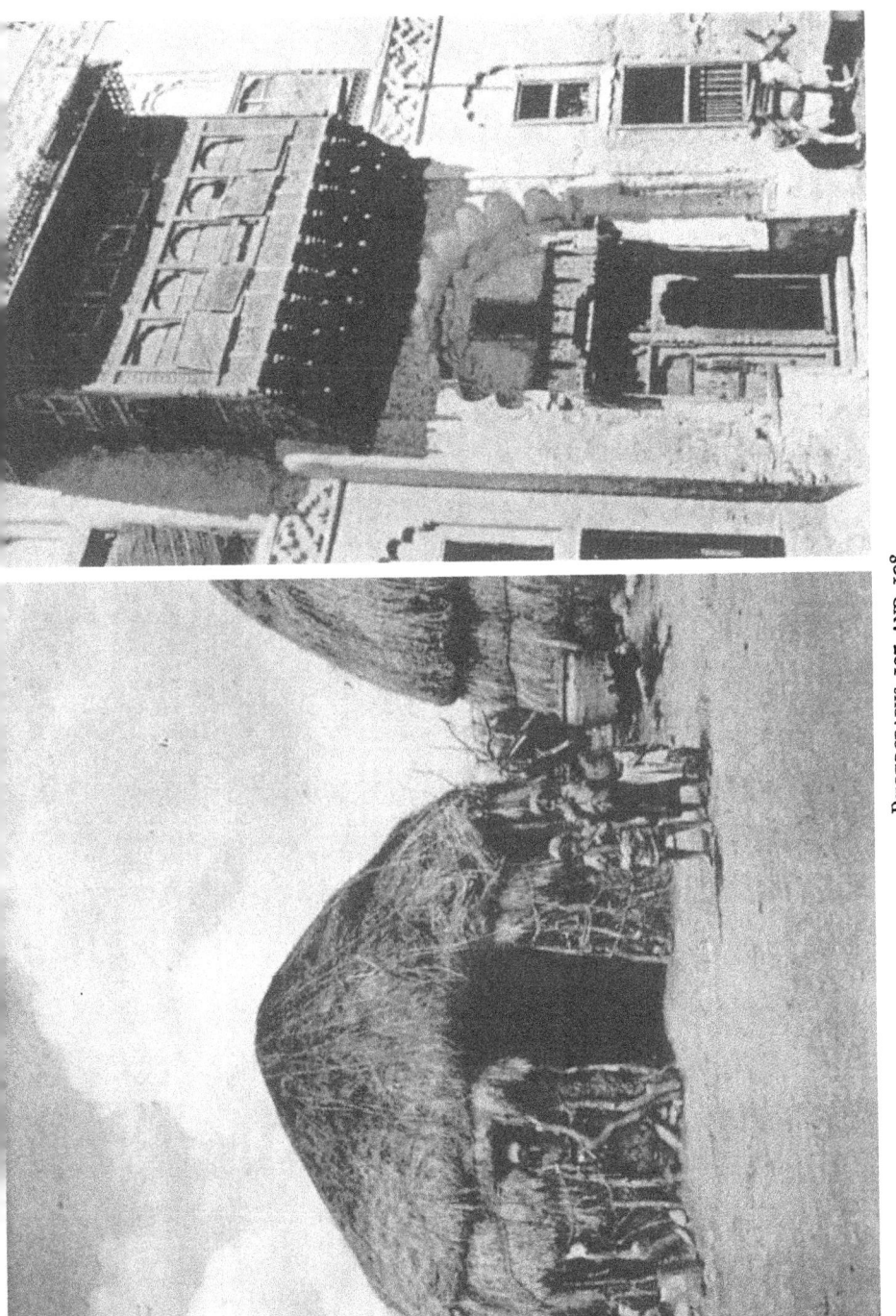

PHOTOGRAPHS 107 AND 108.

Grass-thatched huts in the Tihama; a large earthenware vessel for storing food on right. A doorway at Hodeida.

PHOTOGRAPHS 109 AND 110.
Hodeida: houses, mat-walled huts, bundles of hides.
Our embarkation in the sambuq at Hodeida (the steamer lies on the horizon above the fore part of the boat).

friend walked freely about Hodeida, albeit he was followed by a considerable crowd of the curious. We, however, could not even cross the few yards of open space between the guest-house and the sea-front without being closely shadowed by a soldier. All the same, we explored the suqs, visited the boat-building quarter to the south, and collected maritime insects on the sea-beach and the sand-dunes thickly covered with a sage-green growth of coastal plants north of the town. Evening brought the diversion of bathing in the warm shallow water close inshore—safe from sharks through its shallowness. Even in this pastime the soldiers never left us, but came right down to the water's edge while we bathed. When we asked with slight irony if they feared we should escape by swimming acrosss the Red Sea to Africa, the question was answered only by broad grins.

Hodeida consists of a walled inner town and scattered outer suburbs. Within the city walls the houses are large rectangular stone-built structures; the suqs and many other of the narrow sharply turning lanes are roofed over. In the outer town great rectangular stone houses stand cheek by jowl with straw huts. The latter are rectangular, with high-pitched roofs of thatch; they have yards enclosed in tall fences of a kind of wicker-work. Often a large stone house and several of these humbler buildings form a single unit, the huts being linked to the stone building by straw or wicker fences; the whole then rather resembles a country-house and its outbuildings. On the landward side the town wall has a gateway between twin towers.

The ornament of the stone houses is often very rich, but differs in material, and usually in pattern, from that of the great houses in the highlands. Here are none of the alabaster and the elaborate reliefs in brickwork which delight the eye at San'a. Instead there is rich decoration in plaster-work. Some of the designs are mainly geometrical, displaying many straight lines, as in the highlands; such are more native of the soil. But other noteworthy examples show complicated interlacings of tendril-like patterns, producing an extraordinarily rich effect. This work, seen particularly in doorways (Phot. 108), is believed to owe its origin to countries farther east, especially to India. So also does the richly-carved woodwork of the doors themselves and (in the photograph) the projecting screened balcony above. Partitions of painted wooden fretwork of Indian design are also met with inside some houses, such as the Hakūma where we saw the Amir.

The view shown in Photograph 109 is highly characteristic of Hodeida. Huts and shanties walled and roofed with fibre-mats stand in an open space among large stone houses of several storeys. Bales of skins lie in the open, awaiting shipment. There might well have been bags of coffee for export, or sacks of imported rice. What the photograph cannot show is a troop of pretty little girls, perhaps ten or twelve years old, with dresses and fluttering head-veils of many brilliant colours. They ran up to us at this spot salaaming and crying " peace on you ! " only to run away laughing at their own boldness.

Though they gave the greeting in Arabic, some of these children were Indian. Many Indians live in Hodeida, as well as people of numerous other races and nations. Even the genuine natives are made up of several distinct racial elements ; the townsfolk, the boatmen and sailors, black-skinned negroid lightermen, or members of black negroid tribes from the Tihama. All these are of different physical types which cannot be discussed in detail. We were leaving the Yemen by the door at which most travellers enter. The composite nature of the people of Hodeida must impress itself strongly on foreign visitors at their arrival.

The news that the obstacles to our leaving were surmounted only reached us late in the evening of March 14th. The permit from the Amir for our departure was read aloud to us by a subordinate officer who called during our evening meal. So the following morning, three months and five days after we had entered the Yemen, packing was hurriedly completed. With our Swiss friend, our three Somalis and 'Abdurrahman the 'Audhali we embarked from a stone jetty in a *sambuq* (Phot. 110). Our packages numbered forty-seven, besides the Swiss gentleman's luggage. The steamship *Adua* lay anchored over two miles out. To reach her, the *sambuq* sailed for two hours. First she sailed a long way north of the town, coming almost in to the beach, then tacked about several times.

Other than Somalis, Eritreans and Arabs holding deck-passages, we were almost the only passengers. The *Adua* weighed anchor late that afternoon. The low flat Yemen coast faded from view. Early next morning the ship was off the dark volcanic African coast at Assab, where she lay nearly two days. No disembarkation was allowed by the Italian authorities except for those leaving the ship for good. Early the following morning the *Adua* reached Jibouti. Here the Swiss gentleman bade us farewell. The day was spent ashore at this port, which I had first seen thirty years before. It has fallen out that I should in that period several times have to spend hours or days waiting for trains or ships at Jibouti.

Our journey was fast nearing its close. Once back at Aden, there would remain only a very few days for the final clearing up and leave-taking. Expeditions such as this, worked for long in advance, are of absorbing interest at the time and for long afterwards. But at the end a phase of sadness must inevitably be passed through, due to severance from scenes one has come to love, and from newly made European and Eastern friends. Shall we (one asks) ever see these people or places again? However, since our second departure from Khormaksar in December we had made a full circuit. Early on March 19th, from the deck of the *Adua*, we saw once more the busy water-front at Steamer Point and the crags of Aden.

PART III
HISTORICAL—AND THE FUTURE

Chapter XVIII

THE PEOPLES OF SOUTH-WEST ARABIA, AND BEGINNINGS OF THEIR HISTORY

THE most recent of the geological changes recounted in Chapter II (to which this and the following chapters are linked in historical sequence) occurred well within historic times. For example, as has been told in the narrative, the pre-Islamic temple at Huqqa, north of San'a, was probably overwhelmed by a volcanic eruption as late as the 3rd Century A.D.[1] Man had appeared on the scene millenniums before this. Little can be said here about his prehistoric beginnings in the south-western corner of the peninsula; for, though a fine opening to this study has been made in South Arabia as a whole,[2] its scene has lain largely in the Hadhramaut, several hundred miles to the east.

Agreement as to relative dates and the centres from which the earliest cultures radiated has not yet been reached. But it appears that the oldest stone implements found, though belonging to a recognised phase of palæolithic culture, are on the whole crude when compared with examples of the same types from North Arabia, Palestine, and Africa. Several causes have been suggested for this, such as the bad quality of the available stone, generally poor conditions of life, and absence of contact between the inhabitants and more progressive peoples. This last suggestion not only presupposes a separation of South-West Arabia from East Africa at a very early date (early in the Pleistocene, perhaps a million years ago, or even before), but also presupposes that East Africa was a centre of cultural diffusion during part, at least, of palæolithic times. The theory of early separation of the two continents is supported by the apparent absence from South-West Arabia of examples of one of the three main culture groups into which palæolithic industries are classified, the " hand-axe industries ", which

---

[1] It has been suggested by Mr. Philby (*Geographical Journal*, 92, pp. 127-8, Aug. 1938) that other human works, including the temples of Shabwa itself, may have been destroyed by volcanic activity.

[2] By Mr. and Mrs. Ingrams in 1934, Miss Freya Stark in 1935, Dr. S. A. Huzayyin in 1936, and Miss Stark, Miss Caton-Thompson and Miss Gardner on the Lord Wakefield Expedition in the winter of 1937-8.

are distributed all over East Africa from north to south.[1] The Egyptian archæologist, Dr. Huzayyin, is less favourable to the idea of East Africa as a centre of cultural diffusion. He is, moreover, very definite in his views on the age of objects made of volcanic glass or obsidian, found in the Hadhramaut. These objects, belonging to the cultural group known as " blade industries ", were found associated with ruins as late as the centuries immediately before and after the opening of the Christian era. Dr. Huzayyin does not regard this culture in South-West Arabia as a survival of one which had existed earlier in East Africa ; he would look rather for South-West Arabia to be in advance, having regard to the progressive nature of its civilization.[2]

However wide the gap between these remote beginnings of human culture and the earliest historic times, we must pass to what little is known of the latter. This brief outline will be more intelligible if a short space is first devoted to the outward appearance and physical characteristics of the peoples of South-West Arabia at the present day. The question of their anthropological classification is thorny enough.

The Arabian peninsula, roughly 1,500 miles long and 1,000 miles wide, supports only about 6,000,000 inhabitants, of whom at least half are estimated to live in the south-western corner, and mainly in the fertile highlands of the Yemen.[3]

As the Yemenis appear to the ordinary traveller, the tall, bearded, aquiline Arab type is rather lost among the mountain tribesmen. The latter vary much among themselves, but are generally dark-skinned, rather short and slightly built, with short straight noses ; they are nearly beardless, but have thick black hair, usually wavy, sometimes hanging in long wide open curls, but not negroid. One need not be a trained anthropologist to notice the difference in type of Arabs from the centre and north, such as some traders from Sa'udi Arabia whom we met riding up to the city of Ibb on their camels. Many of the photographs and allusions in the narrative have shown the distinctive appearance of the mountain tribesmen, and still more the difference of their dress, from that of the northern Arabs.

Probably the fullest measurements and records ever taken in any part of Arabia are based on inhabitants of the Yemen plateau. Here 1,500 men were examined according to anthropological methods, in 1933–4, by Carleton S. Coon, who has incorporated the results in his

---

[1] See Miss Caton-Thompson in " Climate, Irrigation and Early Man in the Hadhramaut ", *Geographical Journal*, 93, pp. 18–19 and 29–35, Jan. 1939.
[2] *Nature*, Vol. cxi, pp. 513–14, 1937.
[3] Carleton S. Coon, " The Races of Europe ", p. 401 (Macmillan, New York, 1939). A popular account of Coon's journey is contained in his " Measuring Ethiopia and Flight into Arabia " (London, 1936).

book, " The Races of Europe ". Some rather more technical details may be added from his summary (pp. 404 sqq.), viz. that these slightly built plateau-dwellers are relatively long-legged ; their heads of moderate size, and intermediate in form between those of the extremely long- or narrow-headed peoples and the short- or round-headed ones ; there is a considerable protrusion of the back of the head, this feature being, indeed, in many cases as marked as in the Nordic races. If we use the technical terms *dolichocephalic*, or narrow-headed, to denote peoples in whom the width of the head is never more than 80 per cent. of the length and often less, and *brachycephalic*, or short-headed, for peoples in whom the width is over 80 per cent. of the length, then highlanders of the Yemen are mainly near the upper limit of dolichocephaly, an intermediate condition called *mesocephalic*. On the whole the shape of their heads is very like that of Nordic races, though the actual measurements are considerably smaller. Furthermore, though their head-hair is nearly always black, the beard, when present at all—and then with bare patches between moustache and chin—is of various shades of brown or red in about a quarter of the men examined. About half these men had dark brown eyes, black or light brown eyes were in a minority, but green-brown was a colour frequently found. The eyebrows are medium to very thick, but the brow-ridges slight. The high-bridged narrow nose, convex or straight in profile, varies little. The lips are moderately thick ; prognathism, or protrusion of the lower jaw, is rare ; the chin is moderately prominent, while in development of teeth and jaws the Yemenis possess the characteristics of Mesopotamian skulls dating from as early as Sumerian times. In all these characters, especially the moderate degree of development of features and absence of excessive prominence of such parts as the eyebrow ridges, Coon sees the marks of a branch of the pure " Mediterranean " race. I shall revert to this term below.

In the population of the Yemen plateau several " sub-types " can be distinguished. The cities teem with men of shorter stature, with narrower and lower-crowned heads, narrower faces and a lighter complexion, representing the " quintessence of the Mediterranean race ", while the country-folk are generally larger built, broader-shouldered, and have more wavy or curly hair. Tribal and village sheikhs are usually tall, very long-headed and long-faced (Phot. 99). Civil officers and religious leaders are often drawn from a social stratum including quite Nordic-looking people. The *seiyids* (acknowledged descendants of the Prophet through Fatima and 'Ali) show more blond characteristics than the rest, a suggested explanation being that a Nordic strain was associated with some of the holy families which entered the Yemen from the Hejaz in early Islamic times.

198 *The peoples of South-West Arabia, and beginnings of their history*

So far we are dealing only with the inhabitants of the high plateau, and mainly with those of the district surrounding the capital—the smaller strain of the Mediterranean race in its purest form. But in the southern part of the mountains, about Ibb and Ta'izz, an admixture is seen of the Veddoid type characteristic of the Hadhramaut. The term "Veddoid" must also be left for further explanation below.

Next, there are the coastal lowlands. Here the Somalis, Negroes and Indians who throng the larger sea-ports are recent immigrants or descendants of such. But there exist much older foreign-looking communities. Along the western Tihama of the Yemen negroid farmers, originally brought in as serfs, occupy much of the country. In the Tihama, and in parts of Southern Yemen at intermediate altitudes, a very old community of negroids called *Hujeris* is established, dating possibly from the importation of serfs under the Abyssinian dominion in the 6th Century. Again, in the larger towns and villages of the coastal plain are found people of an entirely different physical type, short in stature, small and short-headed, with broad, short faces, broad noses and dark skin; these have some resemblance to Malays, and are traditionally supposed to have absorbed Malay blood in some families—just as, farther east, in the Hadhramaut Malay wives are brought back by Arab traders returning home at the present day. All these foreign elements have, however, exerted scarcely any influence on the people of the high plateau, who penetrate the unhealthy lowlands very little.

The Yemen Jews, a very ancient and interesting community, are the last racial element to be mentioned. Jews were numerous in Central and Southern Arabia in the centuries before Islam, but it is uncertain when they arrived, or by what route. As pointed out below, the South Arabian Jewish colonies may have originated in the commercial and naval enterprises of Solomon and his ally Hiram, King of Tyre, early in the 10th Century B.C. These colonies dwelt in the cities of the Hejaz and the Yemen, but during Muhammad's life-time they were expelled from the Hejaz. To-day they are met with in the Yemen and the western part of the Aden Protectorate, in the cities and many of the villages on the high plateau and at middle altitudes, but not, apparently, near the coast (excepting the large ports).[1] Living apart from the Arab inhabitants, either in walled ghettoes as at San'a, or in separate clusters of houses outside the smaller Arab towns, they form isolated racial enclaves. While the country Jews are darker and often more heavily built, the city Jews (Phot. 81) are short slender people of light complexion, but with black hair and dark brown eyes;

---

[1] A map of the places with Jewish quarters in Central Yemen is given by Rathjens and von Wissmann, "Südarabien-Reise", Vol. iii, Fig. 64.

the greater number have short, straight noses and thick convergent eyebrows, while some of the men have bushy beards. But among the town Jews of the wealthier families are seen people of a less common type, more slender, with small hands and feet, and very narrow heads projecting at the back; in such persons the forehead, seen in profile, has a sweeping curve, the face is very long and narrow, the nose very long and the lips thin.

In stature and in dimensions of the head and face, the city Jews of San'a greatly resemble the Palestinian Jews (though the latter include a short-headed element not detected in the Yemen). If we accept the classification of all Jews into three main categories—the Ashkenazim of Central and Eastern Europe, the Sephardim of the countries fringing the Mediterranean, and Oriental Jews—the South Arabian communities belong to the third. Moreover, while the aristocratic city families look more typically Jewish to a European traveller, the less refined short-nosed individuals are really equally typical of the race, and both types look equally Jewish to the Arabs among whom they live.[1]

Another channel of recent anthropological information, not taken into account in any of the works on which I have drawn, consists of records of "blood-groups". I have learnt from Dr. Morant that some such records exist,[2] relating to 1,000 Yemen Jews and to small numbers of non-Jewish people from the Yemen and the Hadhramaut. But this subject must be left almost entirely, until further data are made known. Examination of drops of blood (on what is called the A.B.O. system, whereby every individual person can be assigned to one of four groups) would make it appear that Jewish and non-Jewish South Arabians correspond closely in this respect, and are clearly distinguished from all other groups in Western Asia for which more or less adequate blood-group records are available. Moreover, it seems established that the South Arabian Jews are clearly separated in this respect from all other Asiatic, African or European Jewish populations. It is hard to reconcile this evidence, as far as it goes, with the suggestions about racial relationships based on other sources of information.

Leaving aside the Jews as an isolated element, we may consider briefly the suggestions put forward to explain the racial composition of the population, more particularly the Arab tribes. Here it is

---

[1] These remarks on the Jews are based on Coon's "Races of Europe" (pp. 437-41); that author having drawn partly on data published by Weissenberg in 1909.

[2] See "Blood Groups", by William C. Boyd, *Tabulæ Biologicæ*, Vol. xvii (The Hague, 1939).

difficult to discuss the Yemen apart from all Southern Arabia or, perhaps, the peninsula as a whole. Among earlier students and explorers, Burton regarded the inhabitants of the south-eastern part of the peninsula as being the aborigines. Maitland formed a very similar opinion, stressing the relationship between the Southern Arabs and the Abyssinians, and concluding that the Egypto-African race are the original Arabs, while " the stately Semites of the north are Arabs by adoption and residence rather than by descent ". Professor C. G. Seligman, who collected the little evidence available in 1917, was impressed by the high degree of round-headedness among the Southern Arabs, which was surprising, as the North Arabians, and also the peoples of Africa, are predominantly long-headed. Indeed, there was a tendency to regard South Arabia as " an oasis of brachycephaly in a wide desert of dolichocephaly " (to quote the words of Sir Arthur Keith and Dr. W. M. Krogman).[1] This is, however, contradicted in some cases, such as the burial sites at Wadi 'Amd in the Hadhramaut excavated by the Lord Wakefield Expedition, where the few skulls found were all long-headed.[2] Dr. G. M. Morant, who examined these remains, was impressed with the extreme shortness of the skull in proportion to its width, a feature in which these skulls differed from those of any living people in South-West Arabia who have been examined. Since these skulls were assigned to the beginning of the Christian era, a definite change seems to have taken place in Christian times in the racial constitution of the people of at any rate part of the Hadhramaut.

The brachycephaly of the round-headed Southern Arabs is further seen, on detailed analysis, to have come about in two quite different ways. In the extreme south-eastern corner of Arabia, in 'Oman, are found people with the back of the head much flattened (so that the distance from ear to occiput is greatly reduced), and with lofty foreheads, long faces and aquiline noses; the presence of these " Armenoids ", as they are termed, may be accounted for by a very early trade migration, perhaps millenniums before the Christian era, from Armenia and Mesopotamia along the Persian Gulf to India. Secondly, not so far to the east in South Arabia, there are tribes in which round-headedness is due simply to lessening of the head-length, not to any change in the width, nor to any flattening of the back of the head.

Sir Arthur Keith and Dr. Krogman concluded that the Southern Arabs represent the residue of a Hamitic population which once spread

[1] Appendix, entitled " The racial characters of the Southern Arabs ", to Bertram Thomas's " Arabia Felix ", 1932, pp. 301-33.
[2] See Miss G. Caton-Thompson and Miss E. W. Gardner, the *Geographical Journal*, 93, p. 33 (bottom, and footnote 3), Jan. 1939.

over all Arabia. To account for the round-headed tribes of the second type, and for certain " Caucasian " features, they postulated that round-headed peoples from the north broke through the Hamitic belt to South Arabia and that interbreeding with the aborigines followed. This " break through " would have occurred in Pleistocene times, when fertility and pleasant climates were spread over all Arabia, not confined to the south-western highlands, or the coastal belt of Dhufar, as at the present day.

Meanwhile, the fact remains that the tribesmen of our south-western corner are in head-dimensions intermediate or " meso-cephalic ". Carleton Coon, on whose work I have drawn so largely in describing their physical characteristics, regards the whole problem from a somewhat different angle. In considering " The Races of Europe " he has found himself compelled to include peoples as far south as Southern Arabia, as far east as Persia and Afghanistan. The races of north and central Europe, he concludes, are derived from a blend of *food-producing* peoples, i.e. agricultural and pastoral, from Asia and Africa, of basically " Mediterranean " form, with descendants of the *food-gathering* peoples (i.e. hunters) of interglacial and glacial times. While the " Mediterranean " Sub-group is of purely *Homo sapiens* ancestry, the descendants of the food-gatherers may be supposed to have their ancestry complicated by " re-emergences " of elements derived from other species of men now extinct, possible Neanderthal man, or at any rate anthropoids resembling him. With this latter category we are not concerned when discussing the peoples of South-West Arabia.

Further, the Mediterranean race may be regarded as the entire family of narrow-headed or intermediate (dolichocephalic or meso-cephalic) whites, including both blond and brunette varieties. Its chief differences from the family of races with an element of Neander-thaloid ancestry consist in moderate size of body, smaller size of brain, and lack of excessive development of particular parts of the body, such as the eyebrow ridges.

The Mediterranean racial zone extends unbroken from Spain to India, but a branch of it reaches far southward along both sides of the Red Sea to Southern Arabia, the highlands of Ethiopia, and the Somali-land " horn " of Africa. The pre-dynastic Egyptians represented the central and most highly evolved of its several sub-races, but to-day the largest single area in which the moderate-sized, mesocephalic Mediter-ranean race exists in greatest purity is the Arabian peninsula.

Such is the general sense in which Coon uses the term " Mediter-ranean ", and our highlanders of Central Yemen apparently form the purest nucleus of the brunette form of the Mediterranean race yet studied in Arabia.¹ They are indeed Arabs in a geographical sense, in language and institutions, but far removed from the bearded aquiline type of some of the northern Arab countries. Moreover Coon, from his examination of so many living men, is much less exclusively dependent than previous students on skull-measurements.

Migration, amalgamation of races, selection through various causes, and other factors are not excluded. Thus, with the drying up of so much of Arabia after the end of the glacial epochs—when the great areas now desert gradually ceased to be the fertile plateaux which they were during the moist, cool pluvial periods of the Pleistocene—great numbers of inhabitants which Arabia could no longer support may well have migrated within the peninsula, or emigrated altogether. This continued in historic times, as instanced by the early wanderings of the Jews, the probable settlement of the Ethiopian highlands by colonists from the Hadhramaut, and the great expansion of the Arabs in the early centuries of Islam. Thus the southward extension of Semitic conquerors, and the invasion by them of vanished states in South-West Arabia to which I refer in later chapters, is not precluded by this modern view of the racial composition of the people. But the term Hamite is scarcely used in a racial sense.

An outline of the racial composition of the Yemenis is not, however, completed by assigning the bulk of the tribesmen of the highlands to the Mediterranean race, nor by listing the negroid communities of the lowlands and the isolated enclaves of Jews. Dwelling as a minority in parts of the Western Aden Protectorate and in the Southern Yemen there are people with an admixture of "Veddoid" affinities. These are related to that racial group to which the *Vedda* of Ceylon, the *Shom Pen* of the Nicobar Islands, and the *Toala* of Celebes belong. The Veddoid race has many other eastward extensions existing as a substratum through the islands from Sumatra to New Guinea, with an obvious relationship to the aborigines of Australia and less marked affinity with the negritos of the Philippines. It is believed to be one of the major divisions of mankind, and like all major divisions it includes both long-headed and round-headed sub-races.

In Southern Arabia the Veddoids only become numerically important farther east than the Yemen, in the Hadhramaut. Still farther east, they are the principal factor among the tribes of Mahra in the extreme south-eastern corner of the Aden Protectorate, and of Qara and Shahara in the adjacent Sultanate of 'Oman. These all

¹ The purest Mediterranean group in the northern part of the peninsula is the *Solubba* (*Sleyb*), the almost outcast people who wander in small family groups from camp to camp, possessing neither camels nor horses, but acting as tinkers and leather-workers to the Badawin.

speak pre-Arabic Semitic languages. To discuss these Veddoid people fully would necessitate a detailed account of the peoples of the Hadhramaut and other parts of Southern Arabia farther east than the Yemen. But it can be said that these Veddoids exist, as a submerged racial element, along the shores of the Indian Ocean from Bab el Mandeb to the western part of the Sultanate of 'Oman, again in the coastal regions of Persian Makran and Baluchistan, and still farther east ; and that they are related to the whole South Asiatic racial group, which includes, as a section very backward in evolutionary development, the Australian aborigines. Whether the Veddoid substratum in Southern Arabia is as old as the Mediterranean racial element, or is a fairly recent prehistoric arrival from farther east, cannot yet be decided.

* * * * *

On the cultural side, the results of the Egyptian University Expedition should throw much light. Its leader, Dr. Huzayyin, has already indicated the existence of interesting links with parts of Persia and the West Deccan as well as with Eastern Africa, links which should tally with the findings, based on the physical characteristics of the people, of Mr. Carleton Coon. The cattle-culture of South Arabia is closely related with that of India and East Africa. The vexed questions of the date of introduction of the little humped cattle (Phot. 26) into South-West Arabia and the country whence they came may be closely bound up with the origin of the South Arabian Veddoid people and their connection with South-East Asia. (Humped cattle are found on the mainland in South Arabia and in Eastern Africa, but not in the island of Socotra, the primitive inhabitants of which own a straight-backed breed). The camel-herding and horse-breeding cultures of the Badawin farther north are believed to have been derived, in their turn, from the cattle-culture of the southern part of the peninsula. As desiccation advanced and the early kingdoms of South Arabia collapsed, not every tribe may have clung to the narrowing belt of fertile land. Possibly some tribes or families moved northwards, ceasing to possess cattle but becoming owners of camels and horses, with all the changes in social and economic organisation which this involved.

Lastly, I hope that the personal narrative will have shown something of the purely human side of the people as the traveller finds them, lovable whatever their faults, usually friendly and courteous, with a lively sense of humour ; displaying in their monarchic form of rule, combined with an intensely democratic outlook, a passionate love of freedom.

Chapter XIX
HISTORY BEFORE THE COMING OF ISLAM

THE name Al Yemen has usually been taken at its literal meaning, "the right hand". Among the several reasons suggested are, that the country lies to the right of the Ka'ba at Mecca as one stands facing east, or that Qaḥtān son of Abir (Joktan son of Eber) [1] and his companions turned to the right when they separated from the other Arabs. Others believe that the name originated from an Arabic word meaning "happiness" or "prosperity" (derived from the same root as that for "the right hand"), and that the Greeks and Romans translated this word "happy", whence the Roman term *Arabia Felix*. The Roman conception of "Happy Arabia", however, comprised all Arabia south of Arabia Deserta, extending as far east as the toe of the Arabian boot formed by the peninsula of 'Oman. The old Arab geographers gave much narrower limits to Al Yemen, and the modern state is even more restricted.

Whatever be their racial composition, the people of this part of Arabia have an age-long history and an ancient culture dating from centuries before Islam or Christianity, and far anterior to the times when their country was included in the classical Arabia Felix. But when it is attempted to give a historical outline of the earlier centuries, the evidence is still extremely defective. Assertions based on the slenderest original evidence have been repeated till they have assumed almost the complexion of established facts. There is the further difficulty of sifting what is historically true from what is purely legendary in the ancient traditions of the country itself. It has been remarked that modern exploration, especially the deciphering of inscriptions, has abundantly confirmed the few Biblical texts bearing on South Arabian history, and the Greek and Latin authors, but has seriously challenged the truth of Arab traditions.[2]

A wonderful field of study was, indeed, opened up for archæologists by the deciphering of South Arabian inscriptions, the first copies of

---

[1] See below, p. 209.

[2] See the outline of the history of an adjacent part of South Arabia, the Hadhramaut, in W. H. Ingrams's, "A report on the social, economic and political condition of the Hadhramaut" (Colonial Office, 1936), p. 14.

which reached Europe over a century ago. These were not, however, deciphered till much later, and the discovery of additional ones continues. Several thousand of these inscribed texts, in the ancient South Arabian alphabet, related to Phœnician,[1] are now known, chiefly from the Yemen. Mainly votive and commemorative, they apparently fall into two principal dialectic groups, Minæan and Sabæan. But though they tell the names of many rulers of these vanished states, the chronology before the Christian era remains vague.

It is impossible to outline the history of South-Western Arabia without mentioning some events belonging to that of the peninsula as a whole. The pre-Islamic kingdoms with which we are specially concerned are, however, those of the Minæans, Sabæans, Katabanians, and lastly, the Himyarites. These must not be regarded as a lineal succession, for there was considerable overlapping, and periods elapsed when two or more of these states may have existed at the same time. The Hadhramaut, too, was for long periods an independent country, but it lies to the east of the area under review, and is scarcely touched on here.

In trying to delineate the first shadowy traces of Yemen history, the writer is confronted with at least two sets of ideas. According to the former, the Minæan State, the Kingdom of Ma'in, existed roughly from 2000 to 700 B.C.; it may, indeed, have existed much earlier, though the evidence in support of this conjecture appears very slight.[2]

A second set of ideas, which are at least very suggestive, is put forward by the explorers Rathjens and von Wissmann.[3] These writers do not carry the Minæan State back earlier than the 8th or 9th Century B.C. Though, according to recent views, the term " Hamite " may no longer be used in a strictly racial sense, Dr. Rathjens inclines to the belief that a Hamitic people possessed the land until about

[1] The language is a link between North Arabic and Ethiopic : See Miss Caton-Thompson, " The Hadhramaut and its Past ", *Journal of the Royal Central Asian Society*, xxvi, p. 83, Jan. 1939.
[2] According to the article " Arabia ", Section c (by F. Hommel) in the *Encyclopædia of Islam* (Vol. i, 1, pp. 377–80), it is conjectured that the Minæan kingdom may have embraced the whole of South Arabia, and included, or at least been contemporaneous with, a more remote northern territory identical with the Old Testament Amalek. The latter was denounced by the prophet Balaam as " the first of the nations, but his latter end shall come to destruction " (*Numbers*, Chap. xxiv, v. 20). Allusions to the Amalekites appear also in the history of the Hadhramaut, as told by the people of that country (see the Report by Mr. Ingrams cited above, pp. 19, 20).
[3] Concluding remarks to Vol. ii (" Vorislamische Altertümer ") of their " Süd-arabien-Reise ".

the end of the second millennium before the Christian era. These
" Hamites ", according to him, originated from peoples who wandered from Southern Asia over Arabia to Africa, mingling in Arabia
with Semitic, in Africa with negro, races. From about the beginning of the first millennium B.C. Semitic conquerors pushed their
way southwards along the route skirting the inner border of the
Yemen highlands. These conquering Semites, with more or less
mingling of the older blood, prepared the ground for the later
kingdoms of the Minæans, Sabæans, and Himyarites. This southward movement would also account for the successive removals
southwards of the centres of rule in these ancient kingdoms. The
German savants draw a distinction between the remains of pre-Islamic buildings with rectangular ground-plan and those with oval
or circular ground-plan; they conjecture that the latter pertained
to the very ancient Hamitic culture, the former to the Semitic
civilisation.

Furthermore, Rathjens and von Wissman would identify the
ancient inhabitants with that famous " Land of Punt " which, according to Egyptian inscriptions, handled the commercial traffic between
Southern Asia and Egypt from the third millennium B.C. onwards.
This opinion is based on several grounds—topographical, biogeographical, climatic. To name only few instances, the wonderful
terraced cultivation, so striking in the Yemen to this day, was characteristic of Punt, and also the occurrence of some animals. The
lion possibly lived till fairly recently, the giraffe is reputed to have
existed in historic times, in North-Eastern Yemen.[1] The prosperity of Punt, based on the traffic between Asia and Egypt, prepared the way for the later prosperity of the Minæans, the Semitic
conquerors from the north. The people of Punt can hardly be
pictured without a written language, but, if they possessed any such,
either no remains of it are known or it has not been distinguished as
pre-Minæan. From the people of Punt are thought to have originated
the Phœnicians, with whose help King Solomon about 1000 B.C.
organised the first Jewish voyages to Southern Arabia—to Punt and
Ophir. These commercial enterprises may in turn have been the
forerunners of Jewish settlement in South Arabia, resulting in the
existence to-day of communities numbering up to 60,000 souls.

[1] Amir Haidara of Dhala told us of an extraordinary animal with a very long
neck, which lived in the Yemen. The name, as near as we could get it, was
" dufaira " or " dhufaira ". We failed to establish its identity; could the Amir
have meant the giraffe? Rathjens was told that lion, giraffe and rhinoceros live
still in the Yemen Jauf; an unlikely story. The term Punt may, however, have
signified the country on both sides of the southern part of the Red Sea (above,
pp. 13, 14).

The ruins of Ma'in lie in the district of Jauf [1] (roughly 70 to 100 miles north-east of San'a). Near it are remains of temples and other sites; farther east, vast series of circular tombs of finely dressed masonry. The whole is some way north of Marib, the Sabæan capital afterwards famous for its wonderful system of irrigation.

In the latter part of the Minæan dominion, the Sabæans appear as a horde of nomads roaming over the country north of Yemen and raiding the Minæan caravans to North Arabia. If part of the present Yemen was (as is believed by some writers) the " Land of Uz ", and if the Old Testament figure of Job represents a Minæan (a view which has also been put forward),[2] a passage in the tale of disasters which Job suffered becomes vividly intelligible; " the Sabæans fell upon them (Job's sons) and took them away; yea, they have slain the servants with the edge of the sword " (*Job*, Chap. i, verse 15).

Whatever overlapping there may have been, the Minæans were eventually followed by a succession of priest-kings of Saba. Owing to the uncertain chronology, dates must be given with reserve, but 700–500 B.C. has been assigned to this phase. Then, possibly from about 500 to 115 B.C., the title " King of Saba " was borne by princes ruling in Marib. During part, at any rate, of this later Sabæan phase, there were still independent kingdoms of Qataban (Kataban) and of the Hadhramaut.

The briefest reference only can be made to the northern colony, in the land of Midian, which the Minæan kings had held for the protection of their incense-trade with the countries to the north. The incense-producing country and the trade-route lay in the main to the east and north-east of our area, and the reason for mentioning them is that the Sabæan kings may have been heirs of the Minæan colony in the north, just as they were of the Minæan state in the south. If this were so, the origin of the numerous Old Testament references to " incense coming from Sheba " is explained.[3]

Marib, the Sabæan capital, lay over seventy miles from San'a, a little north of east. The remains of the great system of irrigation-works for which it was famous have been investigated by several modern travellers. Such works were not confined, however, to Marib, for the ruins of a like system were examined by Mr. Philby [4]

[1] Distinct from an oasis of the same name in Northern Nejd.
[2] See, for instance, the Preface by the late Major-General P. J. Maitland (formerly Political Resident at Aden) to G. Wyman Bury, " The Land of Uz " (1911).
[3] For instance, " frankincense from Sheba " (*Jeremiah*, Chap. vi, v. 20) and " the dromedaries of Midian and Ephah; they all shall come from Sheba: they shall bring gold and frankincense " (*Isaiah*, Chap. LX, v. 6), texts probably written respectively about the 7th and 5th Centuries B.C.
[4] The *Geographical Journal*, 92, p. 120, Aug. 1938.

also in the Wadi Markha, far to the south-east; and this explorer believes that similar methods may also have been in use at Shabwa [1] itself. The system was, as he remarks, a controlled and directed flooding. It consisted of the impounding of water in a valley by a dam, through sluices in which water was admitted to strips of cultivable land, ever broadening downstream and separated by walls radiating fan-wise.

The destruction of the works at Marib, traditionally ascribed to the bursting of the dam, forms a tragic landmark in Arabian history. Different writers have, however, assigned to it the most divergent dates, ranging from early in the 2nd Century A.D. till after the Abyssinian conquest in the 6th Century. Possibly leaks were followed by repairs, till the final collapse occurred. Whatever may have been the cause of the destruction of this and similar irrigation-systems, whether or not it was a combination of volcanic activity with other factors, the vanishing of the irrigated areas may well have assisted the process of desiccation, and the gradual encroachment of desert conditions from the interior. The two processes, disappearance of irrigation and increase of aridity, possibly worked in a vicious circle. Owing to this change, which may have hastened the decline of the traffic along the incense trade-route, the ancient civilisation seems to have moved outwards like an expanding girdle, though not as far as the hot malarious valleys of the foothills and the coastal lowlands.

With little imagination it may be asked whether such irrigation-works could ever be restored in modern form at Marib or elsewhere? Were the task possible, not on the abrupt outer, seaward, edge of the highlands, the valleys in which are too deep, narrow and confined, but in the wadis draining towards the interior on the inner slope of the high table-lands, great areas might be reclaimed from desert and arid steppe, and some of its ancient prosperity restored to the Land of Sheba.

* * * * *

As to the Katabanians there is evidence, both in South Arabian inscriptions and in Greek and Roman literature, of the existence of a kingdom of Qataban from about 500 B.C. till it was absorbed in the Himyarite State early in the Christian era. Their capital, Tamna, identified with the present Timna‘, lay in the land of Harib, that is (very roughly) more than 50 miles south-east of Marib and over 100 miles east (bearing a little south) of San‘a; in other words, they lay

---

[1] Shabwa, the ancient city of temples, is not written of here. It lay even farther outside the area of our journey than Marib, being over 100 miles east-south-east of the latter.

mainly to the right of the top right-hand corner of Map 2 on p. 20. Their expansion into a kingdom took place probably south-westward. To the north and east they were surrounded by the Sabæans, with whom, to preserve their independence, they had long wars.

* * * * *

The Himyarites, latest of the pre-Islamic states and dynasties, are those of whom the traveller in the modern Yemen hears by far the most. This is admittedly due in part to the habit of ascribing almost every vestige of pre-Islamic culture to the people of Himyar, descendant in the third or fourth generation of Qahtān (Kahtan) who is traditionally identified with Joktan, mentioned in the tenth chapter of *Genesis* as a great-great-grandson of Shem. The present ruling house of the Yemen claims to have succeeded to the throne of the Himyarite princes. One explanation of the continued use of red ochre for stamping letters and documents with the Imam's seal, and also for smearing the handwriting of letters from the monarch, is that the Himyaritic princes used a red flag.

Though it is difficult to sift the purely legendary from the historical, the Himyarites, appearing on the scene about 115 B.C., probably first mastered Qataban and then the Sabæan capital of Marib. After this, their princes assumed the title " King of Saba ", and also " Dhu Raidan " (" lord of Raidan ").[1]

Some time in the 4th Century A.D. perhaps about a century after the Katabanian kingdom was absorbed, the Hadhramaut [2] also seems to have lost its independence, and the Himyaritic rulers then and later added several other titles to denote lordship not only over Saba and Raidan, but also over the Hadhramaut, and the mountains and coastal lowlands of the Yemen.

The old Sabæan capital at Marib was superseded by Zafar, or Safar, now a group of ruins about ten miles south-west of Yarim. Latin and Greek writers refer to this as " Sapphar " : thus Pliny, " regia Sapphar ". It has been told how near to and yet how far

---

[1] Raidan is referred to as identical with Zafar, near Yarim, and also as the name of a mountain near the old Katabanian capital, Tamna.

[2] According to Hadhramaut history, Yarub, son of Qahtān, made himself ruler of all the Yemen as then understood, which included the present Hejaz, Hadhramaut and 'Oman. Yarub appointed his brothers governors of provinces, and Hadhramaut governed that which bears his name. After Yarub's time the provinces became independent, but were reunited into a kingdom by his grandson, 'Abd esh Shems. The real name of Hadhramaut was 'Amr, but he was surnamed " Hadhramaut " (" Death is present ") ; see Ingrams's *Report*, p. 20. In *Genesis* (Chap. x, v. 26) the form " Hazarmaveth " (" village of death ") is used ; he is given with Uzal, Sheba, Ophir and others in the list of the sons of Joktan (= Qahtān).

from this ancient royal site we were when we were hurried through Yarim, resting only for the night and under guard, on our northward journey to San'a.

The Himyarite kingdom in the south was, for a while, contemporary with the Nabatæan kingdom in Northern Arabia. The latter kingdom, having its capital at Petra, was, however, ended by the Romans early in the 2nd Century, whereas that of the Himyarites continued till it was conquered by the Abyssinians in the 6th Century. The Himyarites maintained fairly close intercourse with the Mediterranean world, a fact which profoundly affected their later architecture and art (see below, p. 219).

A short space must here be accorded to an event affecting a larger part of the western side of Arabia than the Yemen. This was the expedition under Ælius Gallus sent out from Egypt by Augustus in 24 B.C. One of its aims was to open up the riches of Sabæa to Roman trade, making that part of Arabia a dependency of the Roman dominion in Egypt. The expedition landed on the Red Sea coast of Arabia at Leukē Kōmē some distance north of the latitude of the present Al Madina. The force marched thence south-eastwards, along routes some distance in the interior for about 900 miles, skirting the eastern confines of the present state of the Yemen, till it reached Mariaba (Marib) and places even farther south. Had these aims been fully realised, the Himyarite dominions in the south-west would have been incorporated in the Roman Empire, as were the Nabatæans in the north-west.[1]

After a short Ethiopian invasion or occupation in the 4th Century A.D., the Himyarite kings with their long titles ruled in unbroken succession till their final overthrow by the Axumites, or Northern Abyssinians, in 525. Much discrimination is required as to what events in the chronicles of these Himyaritic kings, or "Tubbas", are truly historical. For instance, the 4th Century Tubba As'ad Kamil, mentioned in the following paragraph, is credited with having constructed part at any rate of the road leading northwards through Nejran towards Mecca—the road along which the Abyssinians advanced nearly two centuries later in their attempt to capture Mecca, an attempt which was defeated at the "Battle of the Elephant".

One or more of these Tubbas, however, adopted Judaism. Local Jewish tradition assigns this act, before the end of the 4th Century A.D., to Tubba As'ad Kamil, who was buried at Gheiman, south-east of San'a. But this is contested by the Arabs, who hold that not this

---

[1] For a fuller account, see Kiernan, "The Unveiling of Arabia" (1937, Chap. i) and elsewhere.

Tubba was converted, but one of his successors, possibly the last, Dhu Nowas, who fell before the final Abyssinian invasion. The ancient Jewish communities in South Arabia may owe their origin to the commercial enterprises of the old Jewish kingdom and the Phœnicians, centuries before the Christian era (p. 198). Judaism was at all events established in the country before the very early centuries of that era had ended.

The date of the introduction of Christianity seems very uncertain. A probable explanation of apparently conflicting traditions is that there were successive waves of penetration by Christian missionaries. In the Eastern churches, particularly, missionary work in Arabia Felix has been traditionally ascribed to the Apostles Thomas and Bartholomew, the former of whom is believed to have visited the country on his way to India. About the close of the 2nd Century, Pantænus, a theologian of Alexandria, is said to have undertaken missionary journeys, but whether to Arabia Felix or to India, or to both, is not clear; for the term "India" may have been loosely used to cover several Eastern lands. It is further claimed that in the 4th Century St. Frumentius, native of Tyre and apostle of Ethiopia, also visited South Arabia. Though the evidence is slight, this last supposition is quite possible, from the nearness of the two countries and the fact that the first Abyssinian occupation of South-West Arabia was in progress about that time. At any rate Christianity was apparently established by the 4th Century, if not earlier. A 5th-Century writer, Philostorgius, tells of the conversion of the Himyarites about 354-5, in the time of Constantius II, under whom one Theophilus, later consecrated bishop, got permission from the ruler of Zafar to erect churches there and elsewhere. This lord of Zafar, friendly to Christianity, may have been either a prince of the old Himyaritic line, or a governor appointed by the Abyssinians during their first short occupation.

The last Himyaritic Tubba, Dhu Nowas ("Lord of the forelock" or "of flowing locks"), having then embraced the Jewish faith—whether the first of his line to do so or no—became a great persecutor of the Christians in the Yemen. After a general massacre ordered by him, the country was invaded by the Abyssinians under a Christian ruler. In this invasion, which took place in 525, Dhu Nowas was defeated and slain. During the Abyssinian occupation which followed, and the succeeding period of Persian rule (570 to 628), Christianity evidently spread rapidly. This was assisted by forcible measures used by the Abyssinians. Churches were built in more than one centre. Nejran, a wadi and district in the far north-east of the Yemen, was a stronghold of Christianity with a bishop. After the conquest of San'a (or its predecessor, the ancient stronghold of Ghumdan) by a later Abyssinian viceroy, Abraha, a famous church, still referred to as the "Kalis" (*ecclesia*), was built there. Some remains of it may be incorporated in the present Great Mosque (see above, p. 128).

Much legendary literature, but probably also some that is historical, has accumulated round the name of Saint Gregentius, bishop of Zafar in the mid-6th Century. He is believed to have persuaded Abraha to adopt a more lenient policy towards the inhabitants.

At length Abraha's great church at San'a was defiled by persons from Mecca. These may have been fanatics. But a more probable explanation is that they were agents of the Qureish, the tribe who then controlled Mecca, and who saw the ancient pagan shrine of that place, the Ka'ba, losing its attraction, as pilgrims were drawn away by the counter-attraction of the church at San'a. Abraha then resolved to capture Mecca and destroy the Ka'ba. According to the commonly accepted account his army, accompanied by elephants, advanced northwards, but from one cause or another it was defeated and dispersed, while Abraha himself died shortly after. This "Battle of the Elephant" is believed to have occurred shortly before, or in the actual year of the birth of the Prophet Muhammad (? A.D. 570). But modern students have thrown some doubt on the story of the expedition against Mecca, and particularly on its date, as not leaving time for the remainder of Abraha's rule and that of his sons.[1]

After Abraha's death the Abyssinian rule weakened, and about that time the Persians under Chosroes I conquered the Yemen and installed Wahriz as Governor.

Under Persian rule the ancient astral worship and Judaism were apparently tolerated, while Christianity maintained its ground, especially in Nejran, the far north-eastern district already mentioned. Here there is said to have been a bishop named Kos.[2] Indeed, Nejran would appear to have been an important religious centre from the days of the ancient astral worship, during Christian times, and in the early days of Islam. In the first phases of Islamic history it had a

---

[1] Abraha (Ethiopic form of Abraham) is recorded by the historian Procopius to have been the slave of a Roman in Adulis (on the Eritrean coast a little south of the present Massowa). He is said to have revolted against the King of Ethiopia and taken prisoner the Abyssinian Governor of the Yemen, but to have later submitted to the King's successor and been recognised as Viceroy of the Yemen. Procopius, who incidentally was contemporary with these events, also records that Abraha was persuaded by the Byzantine Emperor to make an attack on the Persians, who were already penetrating Arabia. Could this attack, which appears to have been abortive, have been identical with the Mecca campaign of the Arabian historians?

[2] W. B. Harris, "A Journey through the Yemen" (1893), pp. 45, 46.

Persian viceroys

local Ka'ba, instituted like that at San'a to counteract the growing importance of Mecca as a centre for pilgrimage.[1]

However, though Persian viceroys succeeded one another for nearly sixty years, the last of them, Badhan by name, after the death of Chosroes II accepted Islam in A.D. 628.

Thus the long period of native pre-Islamic dynasties, Minæan and possibly pre-Minæan, Sabæan and Himyaritic, ended early in the 6th Century, after well over one thousand years. It was followed by about a century of foreign rule, first Abyssinian then Persian. After this the history of the Yemen becomes part of the history of Arabia under Islam.

[1] Mr. Philby has identified a great block of basalt rock, at a place called Taslal, as the forgotten and disused Ka'ba of Nejran (*Geographical Journal*, 92, pp. 14, 15, July 1938).

Chapter XX

REMAINS OF THE PRE-ISLAMIC CIVILISATION

THE ruined cities and temples of Ma'in and Sheba, the ranges of circular blockhouse-like tombs in the vast desert necropolises, lay far east of our route. These notes must be limited to the country which we saw. Here most pre-Islamic objects are assigned to the later phases, Himyaritic or even more recent.

The old Arabian states were monarchial, but not necessarily hereditary monarchies. It has, however, been well said that the importance of Arab influence in the ancient world lay far more in the spheres of civilisation and religion than in their political history. In religious ideas, particularly, they strongly influenced their nearer and remoter neighbours, especially the Hebrews and Greeks.

In the astral worship of Southern Arabia (or indeed of all Arabia, for in the north the same ideas prevailed, though not always under the same names) the cult of the moon-god takes complete precedence over that of the sun. In the lists of gods there is a dominant triad composed of Ishtar (Venus), god of the heavens, regarded as male; the moon-god, Sin, also masculine, who is the real chief god; and Shems, the sun-goddess, a female deity. There were various lesser astral deities, for example personifications of particular phases of the heavenly bodies, such as the waxing and waning moon or Venus as the morning and evening star.

Temples: Naturally the interest of archæologists is focused on the remains of places of worship of these astral deities. Allusion has already been made (p. 206) to remains of buildings with oval or circular ground-plan, which the German explorers believe to have been constructed by an older people before the advent of Semitic conquerors from the north. They instance the temple of Bilkis at Marib as typical of such buildings, and draw attention to the resemblance between this temple and that at Zimbabwe in Southern Rhodesia.

The temples, Semitic in style, raised by the people of the later kingdoms were rectangular in ground-plan. In the famous example at Huqqa, north of San'a, and in the remains of other pre-Islamic buildings near it, the ornamentation consisted almost exclusively of rectilinear geometric forms, traceable to a few simple elements (see, for instance, the column shown in Fig. 5). This tendency to geometric forms of ornament is visible in the architecture of the Yemen highlands to this day.

The temple at Huqqa, excavated by Rathjens and von Wissmann in 1928, is assigned by them to the 3rd Century B.C. and believed to have been overwhelmed by an eruption of the volcanoes of Arhab, the district on the southern fringe of which the temple stands, not

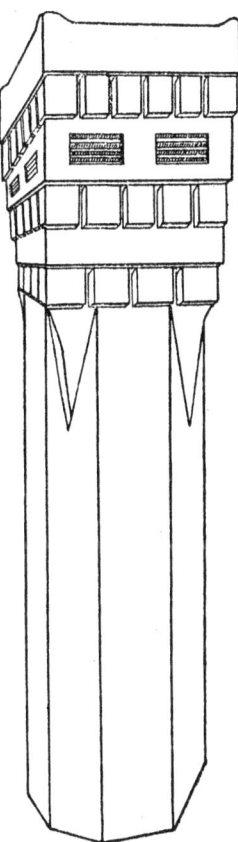

FIG. 5. *Column from the temple at Huqqa (from Rathjens and von Wissmann).*

earlier than the 3rd Century A.D. In their conjectured reconstruction it appears as a complex system of buildings, including a rectangular court with pillared loggias on the east, north and south sides, the main entrance in the east façade and the west side occupied by a raised building. Early in 1938 little was to be seen but some lower courses of squared masonry. The great blocks of black igneous rock, some three feet long, were much larger than the stones of which the modern villages are built. The more valuable objects could be inspected at San'a in a government building, where they formed the nucleus of a museum. But in the present village of Huqqa and other places in the district, in the walls of houses and enclosures, many sculptured and inscribed stones, finely worked in a fine-grained white limestone brought from a distance, contrast with the rough cubes and blocks of dark volcanic rock. Among such built-in remains is the part of a column shown in Fig. 5, one of several types of eight-sided monolithic pillars. Their height, reckoned from fragments in most cases, was ten to eleven feet, while the one figured was about eleven inches thick in the shaft.

Little can be seen but these fragments, and the shafts opening into a vast subterranean cistern, now dry, beneath part of the temple site. But it is easy to appreciate the high order of workmanship, the great size of the blocks of masonry,[1] and the closeness of the stream of scarcely weathered lava which probably destroyed the temple. There is, indeed, no proof of this destruction of the temple by an eruption. No record of such a tragedy is known in documents or inscriptions. But the discovery of many charred wooden objects indicates that the temple was burnt at some time, while the present inhabitants of Huqqa relate how the ancient Himyaritic people were overwhelmed by darkness and fire from Heaven, because of their evil life.

The temple dedicated to the moon-god at Wadi 'Amd in the Hadhramaut, 300 miles to the east, and excavated early in 1938, was more primitive. Possibly because it was older, or belonged to a provincial community far from the centre of the ancient civilisation. This temple had a raised platform of rubble blocks, a superstructure of partition walls separating courts and passages, and a pavement of finely dressed sandstone slabs. The columns supporting the roofs have perished, but may have been of wood on bases of masonry.[2]

It is easy to speculate how from these temples may have been derived the ground-plan of some of the earliest and most famous mosques of Islam—those in which a vast courtyard surrounded by pillared loggias is the dominant feature. Among such is the Great Mosque at San'a itself, which has been compared with the most ancient mosques of Cairo, with that at Kairouan in Tunisia, and with the tomb-mosque of the Prophet at Al Madina.

Judging from inscriptions the temple at Huqqa was probably

[1] Compare part of the town walls at Haz, north-west of San'a, where the lower courses are of pre-Islamic masonry consisting of great squared blocks over thirty-one inches long and nearly sixteen inches high, about twice the size of those in the more recent courses above.

[2] Miss Caton-Thompson, "The Hadhramaut and its Past", *Journal of the Royal Central Asian Society*, Vol. xxvi, p. 88, 1939.

dedicated to the sun-goddess.[1] If so, the moon-god was apparently also honoured there, for many of his emblems were found, in the shape of bull-headed stone waterspouts (Fig. 6) such as were also discovered in his temple at Wadi 'Amd in the Hadhramaut. The bull's head, an object always before the eyes of pastoral people, was chosen as the moon-god's emblem owing, it is believed, to the likeness of the horns to those of the crescent moon. The visual resemblance between the two was, however, forgotten at an early date. The bull's head and the crescent had become separate symbols probably about 400 B.C. Possibly the fixing of ibex-horns, to this day, to the outsides

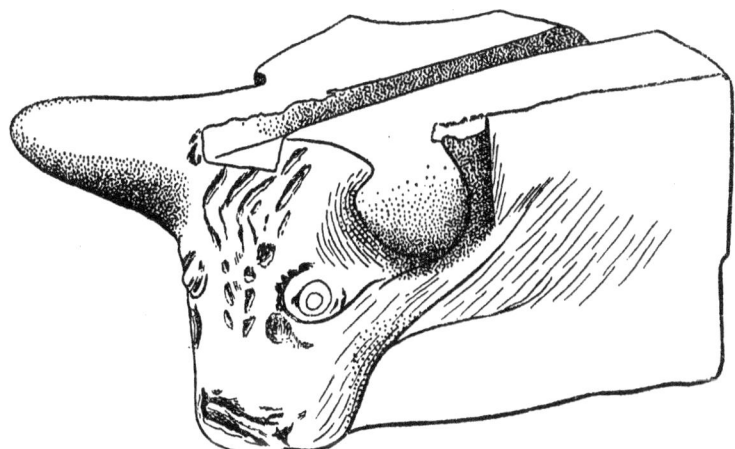

FIG. 6. *Bull-headed waterspout from the temple at Huqqa (from Rathjens and von Wissmann).*

of houses at the corners, to bring good luck, is also derived from this symbol of the ancient religion. I have heard the same suggestion made (but cannot trace it in the literature) regarding the curious horn-like projections which appear in many forms at the base of processional crosses (Fig. 7) used in churches in Abyssinia, where in pre-Christian days the ancient astral worship prevailed as in Southern Arabia.

Rock Sepulchres: A number of rectangular openings to burial chambers are to be seen in sandstone cliffs and hills north of San'a. Situated usually in nearly vertical rock-walls, they are so high above the ground as to be inaccessible without the use of ropes. Britton, however, having succeeded in climbing to the one shown in Photograph 95, found that the walls of the opening have a thick flange of rock left projecting at the outer edge, as though a door were to be

[1] Called here Dhāt Ba'dān; Rathjens and von Wissmann, "Südarabien-Reise", ii, p. 32.

shut against the flange from within. The same form of doorway prevails in other examples, but no hinge-sockets or other traces of a door have been found. Moreover, if the assumption that the chambers were burial-chambers is correct, the door could hardly have been closed from inside. Some of these excavations, of uncertain date, have niches in the vertical walls of the chamber. As no definite traces of

FIG. 7. *Abyssinian processional cross with horn-like projections from the base.*

sockets for scaffolding have been found, it is supposed that the excavators were lowered from the cliff-tops with ropes, and that the body was finally lowered to its resting place in the same way, after which the entrance was walled up. Even so, the present emptiness of these graves proves that difficulty of access did not preserve them from spoliation at a later period.

Sculptures and Bronzes: Many statuettes up to about one foot high have been discovered. Some of these have found their way to Museums outside the Yemen. They represent seated human figures, with arms bent at the elbow and hands projecting forward. Usually they are crudely wrought, showing no separation between the figure and the seat on which it rests. These little statues are said to have been found in the rock-tombs just described, and are supposed to be figures of ancestors which formerly stood in the niches in the walls of the sepulchres. Many faked examples are extant. Though a tourist traffic can hardly be said to exist yet in the Yemen, beware of objects sculptured in alabaster and other soft materials, rather than in the hard fine-grained limestone of the genuine examples!

Other sculptures of a much later date, such as graceful designs in relief of trailing vines, plainly show Hellenistic influence, and may in some cases have formed part of Christian churches. To this class belong the much-weathered reliefs of birds and conventional rosettes shown in Fig. 2, p. 128. These latter, now built into the north-west wall of the Great Mosque at San'a, may possibly have been taken from Abraha's great church on or near the same site.

To the early centuries of the Christian era may also be assigned certain bronze objects, a human head and a whole human figure, and heads or busts of lions. There seems little doubt that the original inspiration for the manufacture of these came from the Mediterranean world, but oriental characteristics are in some instances mixed with classical. This is the case with a bronze lion's head, probably of the 1st Century, from Nejran.[1]

The existence of great *Castles* is also recorded. Such was the famous stronghold of Ghumdan, formerly situated where the south-eastern part of the Arab city of San'a now stands. The old Arab writers tell us that it was built on a rock, that the lower courses of its many storeys were of freestone and the upper part of polished marble, which would have shone in the brilliant sunshine. It is said that four bronze lions stood on its marble roof, and that the wind blowing through them made a roaring sound. Deprived of its former splendour and ruined at the time of the Abyssinian invasion, the great castle was rebuilt under the Persian viceroys later in the 6th Century. It was finally overthrown at the Mohammedan conquest, though as late as the beginning of the 10th Century it still stood as a gigantic

---

[1] For these bronze objects, see articles by Roger P. Hinks and Sidney Smith in *The British Museum Quarterly*, vol. xi, No. 4, pp. 153-4, plates 40, 41, 1937; also Rathjens and von Wissmann, "Südarabien-Reise", vol. ii, p. 89. The whole human figure referred to is in the Museum at San'a, and as far as I am aware it has not been illustrated.

ruin close to the Great Mosque. This we learn from Al Hamdani, a man erudite in many kinds of knowledge. He was a native of San'a, where he died A.D. 945–6.

Cisterns and other works for conservation and storage of water are among the most impressive ancient structures to be seen. On them has depended the whole life of the country for unnumbered centuries. I do not now refer to the ruins of the extensive irrigation-systems at Marib and elsewhere (*ante*, pp. 207–8), but to the great masonry cisterns, very difficult to date, existing in many parts of the Yemen highlands.

Travellers landing at Aden and visiting the famous Tanks are perhaps prone to imagine that these are the only works of the kind in South-West Arabia. They are, in fact, a noble example and remarkable in forming a descending chain, leading from a narrow gulley in the crater walls down towards the centre of the old town. Constructed partly by excavation in the solid rock, partly by masonry walls built across the valley, every feature of the adjacent crags being made use of to increase their capacity, the tanks are a complete series in which the overflow of each is conducted into the next one below. According to the evidence of early travellers there were formerly many more great cisterns in the Aden peninsula, which have gradually decayed, become choked with rubbish, or been demolished for building material. The preservation of the great series which remains is due to British enterprise. Apparently the only suggested date for the Aden Tanks is the period of Persian rule, roughly A.D. 570–628.[1] But may they not be even centuries older?

In the Yemen highlands many great cisterns are seen, as a rule singly. The simplest are those made by damming small valleys and by the addition of masonry to the natural rock where necessary, as in Birkat al Bu'r and other large ponds near Haz, north-west of San'a. A very widespread type consists of cisterns sunk below the surface on flat land, and fed only by surface drainage, as in the example shown in Photograph 60. These may be quadrangular or round; the walls of some fall inwards in a single nearly vertical slope, in other cases they are "stepped" in a succession of projecting stages. The cisterns vary in diameter from about twenty to one hundred and thirty feet, and in depth from about thirteen to twenty-six feet. Some are provided with flights of stairs; in the very large, simple, circular reservoir called Birka Qa' Raqqa, between Huqqa and Haz, there remain four rough inclines, serving as many villages, leading down to the water. Other reservoirs have no stairs, and in such cases it is easy to visualise the biblical story of Joseph being lowered into a dry

[1] Playfair, "History of Yemen", p. 7.

cistern whence he could not escape. Some of these reservoirs are subterranean, with only small openings from the surface, as in the vast cistern below the temple at Huqqa.

In the better preserved cisterns, or those recently repaired, the walls are coated with a cement or stucco, often with clay in its composition. In others the coating has broken away and the walls are much patched with later masonry. Cisterns with darker-coloured mortar and with projecting edging stones are thought to be the older, but precise dating is very difficult.[1]

Among many other contrivances for storage and distribution of water, some are probably pre-Islamic, others of more recent date. Springs breaking forth on hillsides are guided through cemented channels or over aqueducts, and the water is stored in large masonry tanks, as in the one by the road from Ta'izz to Mocha shown in Photograph 46; in such cases a small place near by is marked off for prayers and ablutions, perhaps by no more than a line of stones in the ground. Above Al 'Asr, a few miles west of San'a, streams, welling out at the foot of barren cliffs at the valley-head, are led down to the cultivated ground through deep roofed-in channels. The roofs are pierced at intervals by circular shafts surrounded by low walls of rough stones. The whole construction is said locally to be " Himyaritic ", but like structures are found in parts of 'Oman and Iran.

[1] Rathjens and von Wissmann, " Südarabien-Reise ", vol. ii, p. 145.

Chapter XXI
SINCE THE COMING OF ISLAM

IN resuming the historical sequence, only the more important landmarks can be outlined. Minor events, comparatively well known,[1] are too numerous and too complicated to be dealt with in a brief space.

Badhan, the last Persian viceroy, having accepted Islam, was confirmed by the Prophet in his governorship. For a few years the Christian chiefs and ecclesiastics of the Yemen made treaties with Muhammad, under which they were free to practise their religion. But the outbreak of disturbances led to the despatch of the prophet's son-in-law, 'Ali, with a band of followers, and under pressure of argument and force the tribes rapidly adhered to Islam. Under the earliest Khalifs, all territory that is now called Yemen, and much beyond, was divided into three provinces, San'a, Al Janad and Hadhramaut, under Governors. (The period during which the Hadhramaut was subject to Yemen domination, lasting about 450 years, from shortly after the Hejira till 1087, can be read of in the outline of Hadhramaut history already cited.)[2]

During the disturbances which marred the Khalifate of 'Ali, the Yemen was invaded about 660, despite efforts to defend it made by 'Ali's Governor, 'Abdullah ibn 'Abbas. The invaders are said to have massacred many of 'Ali's adherents, especially in San'a. Subsequently, after the death of 'Ali, the country was in general subject to the Omeiyad Khalifs, and after them to the Abbasides, till early in the 10th Century.

At this period of Islamic history, after the early phases of swift conquest, the immense Khalifate was breaking up into independent sovereign states. The Yemen seems to have been among the first to separate itself. Its new ruler claimed descent from 'Ali, and as that Khalif had been styled " Seif Allah " (" the Sword of God "), the new prince of the Yemen is said to have adopted the title " Seif al Khulifah " (" Sword of the Khalifs ") and to have chosen as his

---

[1] Detailed accounts : Playfair, "History of Yemen", 1859, and Harris, "A Journey through the Yemen", 1893.
[2] W. H. Ingrams, "Report on the Hadhramaut", 1936, pp. 25-7.

Rise of the Zeidis

badge the two-edged sword of 'Ali. This emblem still appears on the flag of the Yemen, in white on a red ground (as mentioned previously, red is the colour said to have been used by the Himyaritic Tubbas). To this day also the sons of the ruling house have the title of " Seif al Islam ".

According to the Arab historians, the Karmathians encamped in or near Ghumdan (on the site of the present San'a) about A.D. 908. This politico-religious sect was then raising serious disturbances in the Khalifate; indeed, their activities at Mecca caused suspension of the annual pilgrimage for over twenty years. They had risen to great

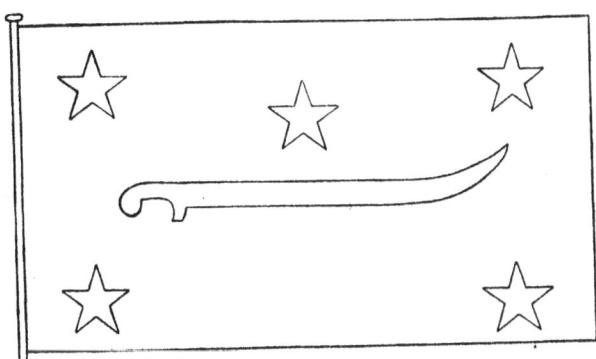

FIG. 8. *Flag of the modern state of the Yemen. The sword of 'Ali and five stars in white on a scarlet ground (this is as flown on Government buildings, but on small sailing craft, etc., the flag is sometimes flown the other way up, with the two stars uppermost, and the sword-point curving down; the sword-handle is always towards the staff).*

power in the Yemen under certain leaders, notably 'Ali ibn Fadhl. This man, a hermit who was later regarded by his followers as a prophet, marched northwards from the Southern Yemen. His army captured Dhamar and San'a. Their strange tenets and barbarous excesses cannot be detailed here.[1] It is problematic whether any traces of their encampments could now be discovered (Note D, p. 238).

At the beginning of the 10th Century occurred the most distinctive event in the history of the Yemen since the coming of Islam, and one which has profoundly influenced its social structure, its thought, art and architecture, to the present day. This was the rise of the ZEIDI

---

[1] Account translated by H. C. Kay in " Yaman, its early medieval history ", 1892; résumé by W. B. Harris, " A Journey to the Yemen ", pp. 87-8.

Sect and the dynasty of Zeidi Imams. This sect took its name from Zeid, a great-grandson of 'Ali. The theological subtleties here involved are beyond my scope. But it can be said that the adherents of the Khalif 'Ali—the Shi'ah body of Muhammadans—comprise many subdivisions, all of whom recognise 'Ali himself and his sons Hassan and Husein; but the Zeidis, a peculiar body, differ from the rest on the question of recognition of his descendant, Zeid, and also in their ideas as to the grounds on which 'Ali himself secured the office of Khalif. They maintain that he was appointed in virtue of his peculiar merits. Further, the Zeidis are said to venerate only the earlier of the twelve great Imams, having diverged from the main line under Imams of their own. This alludes to the veneration accorded by the majority of Shi'ahs to a succession of twelve great Imams, of whom the last disappeared but is to reappear as the Mahdi; whence this majority are sometimes called Dodekites or "Twelvers". Another of the smaller Shi'ah bodies, the Isma'ilis, split off in the 8th Century after the death of the sixth Imam, following his son Isma'il; one of their widely separated foci is Nejran, north-east of the Yemen highlands, while there also are (or recently were) small groups of Isma'ilis in the high Yemen mountains.

Zeid ibn 'Ali Zein al 'Abidin, whose name the Zeidis bear, did not live in the Yemen. He was killed about the year 740 in early middle life by the troops of the reigning Omeiyad Khalif, against whom he had been induced to rebel. He met his death at Kufa in 'Iraq, the very city where his great-grandfather 'Ali had been slain. He became revered as a political and religious martyr, though his followers did not at first show any cohesion. Later, two definite bodies of Zeidis formed themselves. The first, near the southern shores of the Caspian Sea, existed under a line of Imams till the 12th Century, when they became merged in a different sect. The second body of Zeidis was established in the Yemen at the end of the 9th or beginning of the 10th Century. These latter, under the line of Imams founded by Al Hādi ilal Hakk Yahya (his full designation means "the guide to the Truth, John"), have survived all religious changes and political storms.

This first Imam of the Yemeni Zeidis, Al Hādi Yahya (to give him the shorter name by which he is generally known), was the grandson of 'Ali Qasim ar Rassi, descendant in the sixth generation of Fatima and 'Ali, daughter and son-in-law of Muhammad. Thus the descent of the Yemen Imams from the Prophet is established, and their house is called the Rassite Dynasty. In strict truth the succession of Imams in the early centuries passed for a time away from the descendants of Ar Rassi. But it reverted to the Rassite house (it is said, about 1170) so that the line has been for generations, and is now, Rassite.¹

Al Hādi Yahya ruled, died and was buried in the northern city of Sa'da, which long remained the seat of the Imams. But as far back as the early part of the 15th Century a ruler who assumed the title of Imam is said to have taken up his residence in San'a, while, from the time of the Imam Mansūr al Qasim, early in the 17th Century, Imams of one branch or another of the Rassite house have succeeded one another at that city. The inheritance has not, however, always passed directly from father to son. A candidate for the Imamate must conform to several peculiar requirements, among them freedom from any physical blemish. But the succession has been kept within the Rassite family, so that the Imam to-day claims lineal descent from the first Imam and eventually from the Prophet.

It has been shown that the Zeidis have developed their own style of architecture. They do not erect domes over their mosques or small cupolas on the tombs of saints. The mosques and tombs built at Ta'izz and San'a during the periods of Turkish dominion contrast strongly with the Zeidi buildings in this and other ways.

The Imams and their followers have never converted the whole Yemen to their Zeidi views, nor have they usually, until recently, been undisputed rulers of the whole country. As well as the smaller bodies of Isma'ilis, there have been and still are numerous orthodox Sunni Muslims of the Shafe'i school, particularly in the Tihama lowlands and in the district of Ta'izz, chief city of the south. There were also periods in the Middle Ages and later, when the Sunni Tihama with its capital at Zabīd was independent of the Zeidi highlands and their capital, San'a. Even in modern times Zabīd, though but a provincial town, has kept some prestige as a spiritual centre for the Shafe'i Sunnis.

If we anticipate, this divided state of the country can be seen again at a much later date. Niebuhr, describing conditions in 1763, used the term "The Yemen" in two distinct senses. Broadly it included most of the country comprised by the modern kingdom, though not extending so far east, and it also included Aden, Lahej, and their immediate hinterland. (The Hadhramaut was excluded.) But in a narrower sense Niebuhr treated "the Yemen proper" as one of fourteen independent districts. Regarded thus, it was a much

¹ According to the pedigree of 'Alid Imams given by Kay (opposite p. 302 in the book cited in the preceding footnote), Zeid was descended from 'Ali through the latter's son Husein; but Ar Rassi and his descendants, the Rassite Imams of the Yemen, belong to the other branch of 'Ali's posterity, being descended from his son Hassan. I do not know if this has been modified by later research.

smaller part of the modern kingdom, embracing indeed most of the present coastline and parts of the highlands. From the latter, however, many independent chieftaincies were cut off on the north and north-east, as well as enclaves in the centre ; while on the south the " Bilad Aden " was excluded, for the 'Abdali chief had already set up as independent Sultan of Lahej, and other chieftains had thrown off (if they ever owned) allegiance to San'a.

During the periods of Turkish dominion the Imams of San'a were reduced to the position of spiritual heads of the Zeidi highlanders. Only since the end of the Great War in 1918 has the Imam combined spiritual leadership of the Zeidis with absolute temporal kingship (formally recognised by Britain in 1934) of the whole country ; a state over 300 miles in length, with an area estimated at about 74,000 square miles, and a heterogeneous population computed at from under three to over four millions. The office (as related in Chapter XVI) carries with it many other titles besides those of Imam and *Malek* (king), among them " Commander of the Faithful ". For some centuries at least each Imam has, on his accession, assumed a special surname [1] denoting some attribute. Such is the name *Al Mutawakil Allah* (he who relies on God), used many times since as far back (it is said) as 1152.[2]

In the Middle Ages dynasties rose and fell. Several old cities have been capitals of small states. In the 9th Century Ibn Ziād founded Zabīd, reigned over the Tihama and for a time over San'a, where he subjugated the Banu Ya'fur, descendants of the Himyaritic Tubbas. The Ziādites and their successors ruled, at Zabīd at least, till the mid-12th Century. In the 11th Century arose the Suleihites, continuing long with varying fortunes in highlands and lowlands. In the south the Zurei'ite princes of Aden arose in the 12th Century. After Salah ad Dīn's conquest the Eyyubite governors, and their successors and freedmen the Rasulite Sultans, made Ta'izz their seat. Meanwhile, from 901 onwards, the Zeidi Imams of Sa'da maintained themselves in the mountainous north.

The names of several rulers, not always in the line of the Imams, nor always arising within the Yemen, deserve to be recalled. About 1173, Salah ad Dīn subdued the country by sending from Egypt an army under his brother Turan Shah, who made first Zabīd, later Ta'izz, his capital. In the middle and latter part of the 13th Century the whole country, down to and including Aden, was for a while united under the Rasulite Sultan Al Muzaffar, commissioned by the Khalif to subdue disorders. Again, in the late 15th or early 16th Century, 'Abdul Wahab ibn Tahir, entitled Malek al Mansūr, immensely

---

[1] Recalling the like procedure in the Papacy and some other institutions.
[2] Playfair, " History of Yemen ", p. 87.

benefited the land, distracted as it was by constant rebellions and the rise and fall of minor dynasties. He built colleges at San'a, Zabīd and Ta'izz, and constructed many cisterns and conduits ; to him is attributed the aqueduct, now in ruins, along which water flowed from Bir Hamīd to Aden.

The first Turkish occupation began soon after 1538. The Sultans of Turkey were ambitious to control the Red Sea route to India, and to extend their conquests eastward. Therefore in the reign of Suleiman the Magnificent the Ottoman fleet captured Aden (1538), and shortly afterwards a Pasha was installed at San'a as Governor of the Yemen. Turkish rule lasted nearly a century. It left its mark specially in the building or reconstruction of several large mosques at Ta'izz and San'a. In these edifices the Turkish style finds expression in the domed roofs (see Phots. 44 and 67) and minarets surmounted by crescents, an emblem not used in purely Arab mosques. By 1630, however, the Turks had evacuated the country, partly as the result of risings of the Arabs, perhaps also partly on account of the Red Sea trade-route having declined in importance as the Cape route to the East became more frequented.

The Yemen was then left principally to the dynasty of Zeidi Imams, which continues to this day. The progenitor and first of the Rassite House of San'a was a descendant of the old House of Sa'da, Imam Mansūr Al Qasim, called " The Great ". The second of this line, Isma'il ibn Qasim, styled Al Mutawakil Allah (see p. 181) stands out as a ruler of great capacity and piety. During a reign of some thirty years, ending with his death about 1668, he lived chiefly at Doran, south of San'a. As told in Chapter XVII his tomb is on Jebel Doran, the mountain probably exceeding 11,000 feet on the right in Photograph 104. Whether or not this monarch of high ideals yearned for the mountain-tops, his burial-place was chosen in accordance with general custom ; for the tomb of a *weli* (saint) crowns many a summit in the wild mountains of South-West Arabia (see Phot. 40).

For at least a century and a half before this the Yemen had no longer remained entirely unknown to the nations of Western Europe. The romantic exploits of the Portuguese in Abyssinia and elsewhere in the East, in the latter part of the 15th Century and later, threw light on the sea-ports of South Arabia. In 1503 the Bolognese Ludovico di Varthema, in the course of his strange Arabian adventures, visited many parts of the interior—partly perforce, for he was at first carried northwards as a captive from Aden to the Yemen highlands. His accounts [1] of San'a, Zabīd and other places, often mistrusted, have been repeatedly confirmed by later travellers. Just over a century

[1] See note at beginning of Bibliography, p. 239.

later, when the British first visited the Red Sea in 1609, the Yemen was penetrated for the first time by an Englishman, the intrepid John Jourdain of Lyme Regis. His trade journey northwards from Aden lay via Ta'izz and Yarim to San'a (the route we were destined to follow in 1937-8), where the Turkish Pasha was then supreme. He returned by way of Ta'izz to Mocha. The details can be read in his own Journal.[1]

The Dutch East India Company had sent a fleet to the Red Sea in 1614, so that when the French first appeared on the scene at the beginning of 1709, they found a Dutch "factory" at the then flourishing port of Mocha. The Governor of the port, on behalf of the Imam (the Yemen having become again independent of the Turks since 1630), made a treaty with the French, but nevertheless Mocha was bombarded and temporarily occupied by the latter in 1738, owing to a dispute over debts to the French traders.

In 1728 the chief of the 'Abdali tribe, whose capital is the town and oasis of Lahej, declared his independence of the Imam. He took the title of "Sultan", which has been kept by his successors. Thus it fell out that the agents of the Bombay Government, seeking (under orders of the East India Company) a coaling station in 1829, made contact with the Sultan of Lahej as overlord of Aden. The capture of Aden by the British ten years later, on January 11th, 1839, after incidents leading to a skirmish with the Sultan's forces, marked the beginning of the British Settlement of Aden and the subsequent development of the Protectorate. Lahej has since become a protected state and its Sultan is now one of the leading rulers in the Aden Protectorate.

After the opening of the Suez Canal in 1869, the Turks undertook to subjugate anew the Yemen, and 'Asir, the wild mountainous province immediately to the north. Mohammed 'Ali of Egypt had occupied the coast towns in 1819, but the Egyptians withdrew in 1840. However, in 1849 a Turkish Expeditionary Force occupied Hodeida and parts of the Tihama, and even advanced into the highlands, though no permanent hold was gained in these or in San'a. Nevertheless the Turks maintained their foothold on the coast, till in 1872 they again placed a Pasha as Governor-General in San'a. Thenceforward, during their second dominion, they restored the great Bakiliye mosque, a noble building, which they had erected during their earlier occupation in the 16th Century, close to the eastern wall of the old city at San'a. They also remodelled parts of the city, built a number of houses in the garden quarter which forms the western division, and large barracks outside the walls. Their development of Hodeida as chief port of the country completed the decay of Mocha, which still

[1] See under Foster in Bibliography, p. 240.

gives its name to the coffee grown at altitudes between 4,000 and 7,000 feet in the interior.

This second Turkish occupation lasted until the Armistice in 1918, but was chequered by rebellions of the Arabs. A very serious rising against the extortions and misrule of the Turkish officials broke out in 1891. Conducted in the name of Yahya Hamīd ad Dīn (grandfather of the present Imam) who, however, appears to have taken little active part, it was only put down after a severe campaign and much bloodshed. Ahmed Feizi Pasha landed at Hodeida with a Turkish army, fought his way over the mountains *via* Manakha, and relieved San'a from the besieging Arabs.[1] Ahmed Feizi had to return to the Yemen and repeat the whole process in the general rising which began in 1904, on the accession of the present Imam after the death of his father, the Imam Muhammad al Mansūr. In spite of a peace negotiated after that rebellion, San'a was beleaguered once more in 1911 by the insurgent tribes. The present Imam, with perhaps 150,000 men and about seventy guns (an odd assortment, but quite serviceable) tried to drive out the Turks. He advanced with his main army from his northern stronghold and besieged the Turkish Governor-General in San'a from early January till early April. The city was then relieved a third time by an army from Turkey (on this occasion under Izzet Pasha) landing at Hodeida and marching over the mountains by way of Manakha. This siege has been graphically described by the only Englishman in the beleaguered city.[2]

After this Izzet Pasha, as military governor, adopted a conciliatory policy towards the Imam. Finally Izzet induced the Turkish Government to grant the Imam a " mediatized " status, formally proclaimed in September, 1913. Thenceforth the Imam, now subsidised by the Turks and allowed to administer the old Islamic code of laws through his nominees, lived quietly, mainly at his northern residence, Shahāra, till the final withdrawal of the Turks after the Armistice in 1918.

Viewing the policy of the modern Ottoman Republic, it seems strange that the old Turkish Empire should have gone to such lengths to hold so distant and turbulent a country as the Yemen. It has been thought that its efforts were prompted by fear that, if the Yemen were lost, disaffection might spread to the Hejaz and the Holy Cities, on the control of which the prestige of the Sultan of Turkey as Khalif greatly depended.

The eventful story of the last forty or fifty years largely concerns

---

[1] This rebellion is dealt with at length by W. B. Harris, " A Journey through the Yemen ", 1893, Chap. v.

[2] A. J. B. Wavell, " A Modern Pilgrim in Mecca and a Siege in Sanaa ", 1912, Chaps. xiii and xiv.

the development of the Aden Protectorate, and dealings between the British and the Authorities in the Yemen, that is, first the Turks, and latterly the Imam. But it is not my province to relate the political development of the Protectorate. Had it not been for the world war, an official account marking the centenary of Aden as a British possession would by now have appeared; it may be hoped that this publication, though postponed, will still see the light. Very shortly, the following phases may be mentioned : our first entry in 1902 into the mountain principality of Dhala, north of the Sultanate of Lahej, the successive Amirs of which had previously held their territories as viceroys of the Imams of San'a, but had complained of Turkish inroads since 1872 ; the fixing of the frontier between the western part of the Protectorate and the Yemen, by arrangement with the Turks, 1902–5 ; then the invasion of the Protectorate by Turkish forces during the Great War; the fall of Lahej on July 5th, 1915, when the Turkish artillery overcame the brave resistance of the Sultan's force north of the town, and the Sultan himself (predecessor of the present ruler) lost his life from a wound accidentally inflicted in the darkness by men on his own side ; and the retention of Lahej by the Turks till their final departure from the Yemen after the Armistice. Events still more recent have been as follows : the development of the Imamate, while maintaining its spiritual headship of the Zeidis, into an absolute temporal monarchy under its present holder ; a treaty between Sa'udi Arabia and the Yemen, following the short campaign which in 1934 embodied a disputed part of 'Asir in the Sa'udi dominions, and reinforced in 1937 by a pact of friendship and brotherhood ; questions of frontier demarcation with the Aden Protectorate, and the Treaty of San'a (1934) between Great Britain and the Imam (by which the British Government officially recognised the latter as King) ; successive treaties between the Imam and the Italian Government (the most recent in 1937) ; increased penetration of the Yemen by Italian medical officers and other Government agents ; and the undertaking of Great Britain and Italy mutually to maintain the independence of the Yemen, as part of the Anglo-Italian Agreement of April 1938 (torn up by Italy becoming our enemy). Many further steps have been taken to organise and develop the vast Aden Protectorate, since Aden itself became a Colony on its final transference from Indian to Colonial Office supervision early in 1937.

In this bare enumeration of recent happenings, one matter may be elaborated, namely, the Italian penetration, and recent relations between Italy and the Yemen generally. It is hard to say just when penetration first became a set policy. But it is of some interest that two Italian business-men had established themselves in San'a in the late eighties of last century. These, the brothers Luigi and Giuseppe Caprotti (representing the firm of Mazzucchelli e Perera), figure in several travel-books. They welcomed the botanist Deflers on his arrival in San'a in May, 1887.[1] Luigi Caprotti died early in 1889, but Giuseppe remained there many years, despite the efforts of the Turkish officials then governing the country to eject him. He was still in San'a in 1911, when he and the English traveller A. J. B. Wavell were the only Western Europeans in the city during its three months' siege by the present Imam.

In 1912, again, during the Italian-Turkish war, the Italians blockaded the Yemen coast, using Massowa as a base. This harmed the Turks little. They merely withdrew their forces inland whenever bombardment threatened. Their only coastal defences were at Sheikh Sa'id (opposite Perim Island), and here the Turks more than held their own. The trade of British subjects, however, suffered, and the whole country was indirectly affected, because the Italians backed the turbulent Idrisi chieftain in 'Asir, whose activities were a constant menace from the north.[2]

Since the rise to power of Mussolini, at any rate, the Italians had plainly wanted control of the Yemen for some years, and they also desired to spread their influence into the Hadhramaut. So far as the Yemen goes, they received a severe setback in 1934 through the counter-influence of Sa'udi Arabia. The Sa'udis, having established by force of arms their dominion over the disputed frontier territory, having also (in the process) occupied Hodeida but subsequently relinquished it to the Yemen, insisted on a halt being called to the growth of Italian influence. Later that influence grew again, mainly through the establishment of medical men (at the same time active Fascists) in groups or as solitary outposts. Italian prestige was fostered by the impressive political mission sent from Rome to San'a in the summer of 1937, accompanied by much expenditure, at the time of the new Italian-Yemen Treaty. Thereafter Italian influence was paramount for some time (including the period of our stay), so far as any external influence counts in the Yemen. The British Treaty of San'a (1934) and other steps taken by Britain (through the Aden Government) acted in some measure as a counter-weight. But I have no information as to how affairs stand during the present phase of the world conflict. It has been said, no doubt correctly, that the limitation to the growth of Italian control in the Yemen, combined with inflexible British opposition to Italian interference in the

[1] Deflers, " Voyage au Yemen ", 1889, pp. 56, 76.
[2] Wyman Bury, " Arabia Infelix ", 1915, p. 17.

Hadhramaut, caused the fading of Italian visions of the Arabian half of their dreamed-of Empire, intended to embrace the lands on both sides of the Southern Red Sea. This led the Fascist Government in 1935–6 to throw all its energies into the conquest of the African half, Ethiopia—since liberated.

In the office of an Italian agent in Hodeida, early in 1938, there hung a calendar illustrated with Oriental scenes having the general heading " Visioni Coloniali ". While the ultimate settlement after the present world-war cannot be foreseen, these visions of a great Italian colonial empire in the Middle East seem at present to have been unsubstantial indeed.

Chapter XXII
PRODUCTS AND POSSIBILITIES

UNDER present world conditions it is almost useless to speculate on the political future of the countries under review. All the more is this the case since, though constituting geographically a unit, they are politically two very distinct entities.

In our wanderings within the Aden Protectorate we saw only a part, but an important part, of the Western Division of a very extensive territory. The whole Protectorate, Western and Eastern, extends about 600 miles along the coast in a north-easterly direction from a point opposite Perim Island to Ras Dhurbat 'Ali. It embraces an area of more than 100,000 square miles and supports about 600,000 inhabitants. In all dealings between the British administration and the native rulers, great and small, it is a fundamental policy that the Arab character of the country shall be preserved and development must take place on lines suited to this policy.

So far as the Yemen is concerned, it is well to stress the importance of maintaining friendly relations with the Imam and his people. Consideration must be given to the situation of his country just north of the narrowest part of the Red Sea, and abutting on the Aden Protectorate.

The political relationships between the Yemen and neighbouring states have been outlined in the preceding chapter.[1] So far as treaties and agreements go, the integrity of the Imam's state, of which he is extremely jealous, is guaranteed. Italy's action in the world war, however, has nullified the Anglo-Italian Agreement of April 1938. It is easy to understand the Imam's mistrust of his powerful neighbours and his extreme dislike of foreign penetration. He may be excused if, viewing the present state of Europe, he believes that the social and political system of his country and the life of his people will not benefit by European exploitation. In matters such as medical science, on the other hand, he has shown himself ready to accept help from without.

One who could speak with authority has said that Britain has in

[1] See also *Journal of the Royal Central Asian Society*, vol. xxvii, pp. 21-44 (especially p. 32), Jan. 1940.

past decades "spurned endless opportunities", fought shy of the friendly advances of the Arabs, and rejected actual invitations to establish herself as the guiding influence in the Yemen.[1] Happily a very different policy is pursued now. But in the meantime Italy had penetrated the country and made herself paramount before the world war—so far as the Imam will permit any outside influence at all.

Whatever the future holds politically, there is no doubt of the fertility and agricultural possibilities of much of the "verdant Yemen" and of the Western Aden Protectorate. The following remarks on agricultural products apply to the area as a whole. The preceding narrative and the photographs testify to the large areas of plateau and intricately terraced mountain-sides under cultivation of cereals, and to the market-gardens and orchards in and round San'a. I can write less at first-hand of the coffee-growing districts, situated mostly on the steep mountain-sides of the torn western escarpment of the highlands, at altitudes between 4,000 and 7,000 feet. Nor can I do more than refer again to the possibility (if it *is* possible) of reclaiming by irrigation-works, from desert or arid steppe, districts on the inner slope of the highlands, which were fertile in ancient times.

While we noted the principal cultivated plants in the places visited, with the altitudes at which they were growing, Rathjens and von Wissman have shown diagrammatically the zones of cultivated (and wild) vegetation from sea-level up to over 9,600 feet.[2] These authors deal mainly with the old route from Hodeida to San'a by way of Manakha, which (for reasons stated) was not traversed by us. But the vegetational zones are, broadly speaking, the same as those through which we travelled. Putting our observations together with theirs, it is possible to give the following list of cultivated plants, with the approximate altitudes at which they flourish. Needless to say, the successful cultivation of these crops does not depend solely on altitude. Many other factors are concerned, soil, moisture, and general topography of the country. Some places are exceptionally favoured. But the following list, though far from complete, will be found in the main correct:

DUKHN or "BULRUSH MILLET" (*Pennisetum*), near sea-level to 2,000 feet.
DHURRA or "WHITE MILLET" (*Sorghum*), near sea-level to over 9,000 feet (but characteristically a highland plant).
MAIZE, 1,300 to 3,500 feet (Rathjens): I only noted this in irrigated fields near Ta'izz, 4,500 feet.
WHEAT, 2,200 to over 9,000 feet.
BARLEY, 5,000 to over 9,000 feet.

---
[1] (the late) Col. Harold F. Jacob, "Kings of Arabia", Chap. viii, 1923.
[2] "Südarabien-Reise", vol. iii, Figs. 21, 56.

Crops, fruit-trees and stock

LUCERNE, 7,000 to over 9,000 feet.
CHICK-PEAS, about 7,100 feet (Jebel Jihaf).
FIELD-BEANS, about 8,000 feet (near San'a).
ONIONS (and CHIVES?) in irrigated fields, 7,000 to about 8,000 feet.
COFFEE, 4,000 to about 6,500 feet.
QAT (*Catha edulis*), 4,500 to about 8,000 feet.
DŪM-PALM (*Hyphæne*), sea-level to 600 feet.
DATE-PALM, sea-level to about 2,200 feet.
MANGO, TAMARIND, 400 feet (Lahej) to over 6,000 feet.
BANANA, CITRUS-FRUITS, 400 feet (Lahej) to about 7,500 feet (sweet-limes at Wadi Dhahr, near San'a, somewhat higher).
PAWPAW (*Carica papaya*) seen at Lahej, 400 feet, and Ta'izz, 4,500 feet.
PANDANUS, seen at Lahej, 400 feet, and Wadi Siham, about 2,000 feet (see p. 184).
TOBACCO, small crops seen in the Amiri highlands, 4,800 and 5,600 feet.
TOMATOES, MUSTARD (KHARDAL, mauve-flowered), seen in irrigated fields near Ta'izz, 4,500 feet (tomatoes are cheap and plentiful in San'a district, where other vegetables, not mentioned here, grow easily).
'ILB-TREES (*Zizyphus spina-christi*), about 300 to over 7,000 feet.
PEACH, APRICOT, PLUM, PEAR, POMEGRANATE, WALNUT, from 6,500 to about 8,000 feet (a few small apricot trees as high as 9,000 feet).
QUINCE, FIGS and GRAPES near San'a, at about 8,000 feet and a little under.

I cannot write of SESAME or COTTON from personal experience; nor of INDIGO, except the wild *Indigofera* on river banks at altitudes from about 2,000 to 4,500 feet.

Honey and bee-keeping are once mentioned in the narrative, Chapter IX.

Mention has been made of the humped cattle, of sheep, goats and donkeys; of the absence of mules in the Amiri highlands of the Aden Protectorate, and their abundance in the Yemen; of horses, and the horse-breeding industry carried on, formerly at any rate, near Dhamar; lastly of camels, both the large dark mountain-breed, and smaller sandy-coloured desert race. Enough has been said to indicate that there is no lack of stock, nor of the means for its maintenance.

*   *   *   *   *

The Imam's desire to furnish his people with up-to-date medical services has been spoken of more than once. In Chapter XIV, I have very briefly indicated some of the diseases with which the European doctors in the Yemen have to cope. The subject cannot be fully discussed here. A valuable article by Dr. Petrie is listed in the Bibliography. Further, so far as the Aden Protectorate is concerned, he has since the end of 1939 been employed by the British

Government on a Medical Survey of great importance. But his report is not available at the time of writing.

* * * * *

There seems no doubt of the generally friendly disposition of the country people, especially those of the settled agricultural parts of the highlands. The strict supervision under which we were kept was due to the Imam's mistrust of our motives, not to any unfriendliness on the part of the tribesmen. But in the wild mountainous border districts on either side of the frontier between the Aden Protectorate and the Yemen, there are admittedly some very unruly elements, as both Governments know to their cost. These lawless folk, however, direct their activities largely against one another or against travellers on the trade-routes, rather than against the Government.

Little can be said here about the country's wealth in minerals, and nothing of the chances of finding oil. So far as the Yemen goes, even had we wished (or been competent) to investigate, we should certainly have been given no opportunity, for the Imam, his ministers and provincial governors, jealously keep these matters secret. The tragi-comic experiences of a European mining expert who was employed by the Imam during and after the time of our visit would form remarkable reading, could they be told in full. He was at times almost a prisoner. On one occasion, when called on to examine oil-boring possibilities in a certain district, he was driven there by night, lest he should know where he was and learn the way to the place!

In San'a we could get plenty of metal-work in iron, silver, and silver-gilt, new and old, the handicraft of Jewish smiths (Phots. 83, 84). Brass-work, mostly old, was also to be had. But I have no idea where or by what processes the metals are obtained.

A friend who had long experience of the country in recent years has given his opinion that the highlands offer the prospect of a little gold where outcrops have been cleaned off in early historic times, but no indication of any rich deposits. On the other hand Niebuhr was convinced that there was no gold in the country. He wrote that, shortly before his visit (1763), the Imam of that day had caused imported gold coins to be melted down to provide material for a local coinage. Yet gold-workings in 'Asir were apparently mentioned in medieval writings. I have also seen a brief statement that the San'ani Jewish guide who accompanied the explorer Halévy in 1870 left in his account of their journey (posthumously published in 1941) a note on gold and lead mines examined by him in the Yemen. I cannot say whether these mines were disused or not, but doubt whether the metals would be present in large quantity.

Minerals and precious stones

Niebuhr also wrote that iron mines were being worked in the district of Sa'da, north of San'a, and that he suspected their existence in other parts of the country. Further, he mentioned the exploitation of sulphur in a mountain east of Dhamar, probably the volcano which still emits vapour from fissures.

There is a well-known deposit of rock-salt at Salīf, on the Red Sea coast, about forty miles north of Hodeida and immediately opposite the British-occupied island of Kamarān. I am told that this deposit is very rich. Others exist at Luheiya and elsewhere on the coast of the Yemen.

The semi-precious stones locally found, and cut and polished by lapidaries in San'a (see Phot. 67) were, as far as we saw, all of the agate or chalcedony group. Our selection includes moss-agates, carnelians and blue chalcedonies—the last sometimes called "moonstones"; which (I am told) is inaccurate, since true moonstones belong to a group of different chemical composition. To this same group of stones, doubtless, belonged the onyx mentioned by Al Hamdani early in the 10th Century, as found at ancient royal Zafar; and the fine dark red "cornaline" found near Dhamar, of which Niebuhr wrote nine hundred years later.

NOTES

Note A (p. 72). ARABIC NAMES OF SNAKES: in the Amiri highlands both our local tribal guards and our Somali collectors called the puff-adder *hayya*, while the word *hanash* was applied to snakes of longer and more slender form. With these men *hanash* did not include *hayya*. In particular, 'Omar Isma'il (the Somali who worked for Britton) differentiated sharply between the puff-adder (*hayya*) and other snakes; he appeared to regard the former as a legless lizard. As in other parts of Arabia both words seem applicable to snakes in general, this distinction may have been only local or individual, but it is worthy of note.

Note B (p. 83). The principal MOSQUES OF TA'IZZ: unfortunately their names were not noted on the spot. But I have followed Niebuhr and Manzoni, and have no doubt of their identity. Niebuhr ("Reisebeschreibung", Vol. i, plates 66, 67) called the Jami' Masjid (or Muzaffarīya) "Ismail Mülk", as noted by Manzoni. It may perhaps have borne two names, possibly at different times. Manzoni's descriptions ("El Yemen", pp. 314-6) are clear. Some confusion exists in later books. Thus in Mittwoch's "Aus dem Jemen" (1926, Plate 19) the name Muzaffarīya is applied to Ash Sharifīya, but the photograph was not published till years after the traveller who took it, Burchardt, was murdered in 1909.

Note C (p. 150). FISH-POISON: We did not go to Wadi Kharid, but understood that the fish caught there were netted. According to Hayyim Habshush, Jewish guide to Halévy in 1870 (see Note in Bibliography under Halévy) the fish were first narcotised with the black seed of a wild plant called *dhafar*. This is evidently a low-growing Leguminose plant of the genus *Tephrosia*, several species of which yield fish-poisons in Africa and Tropical America. Some species of *Tephrosia* are found in Arabia. In the British Museum Herbarium Miss D. Hillcoat has shown me specimens of *Tephrosia Apollinea* found by Mr. Philby at Raiyan in 1936 and labelled *dhafar* (Raiyan is roughly 150 miles northeast of San'a, near the southern edge of the Rub' al Khali). No note of the plant being used to poison fish accompanies these specimens, but considering the identical Arabic name and the widespread use of *Tephrosia* for this purpose, there can be little doubt that the *dhafar* used in Wadi Kharid is a plant of the same genus. It seems that in Africa the leaves (rather than the seeds) are used; they are bruised or torn and thrown on to the water.

Note D (p. 223). KARMATHIANS: Habshush, the San'ani Jew cited above, recorded that the name "Karmat" was used in 1870, though its meaning was forgotten. In cemeteries a little north of San'a (at Al Jiraf and elsewhere) graves unlike ordinary Arab tombs were attributed to Karmats. The editor of Habshush's story (S. D. Goitein, 1941) considers that the term Karmat was equivalent to Isma'ili.

BIBLIOGRAPHY

THE following is a very short list of books and articles of a general nature on the parts of South-West Arabia under review. Works dealing more widely with Southern Arabia and only concerned to a lesser degree with our area are excluded, though some of them are cited in footnotes to the text. Some recent books on Shabwa itself (or attempts to reach it) by travellers who approached the old sacred city without touching the country we traversed are also omitted. So also are purely technical books and articles on the natural history of the country; these works will be taken into account in the scientific publications of the British Museum (Natural History) Expedition.

The works of PLAYFAIR, DEFLERS and SCHMIDT, listed below, all contain bibliographies of this part of Arabia far fuller than I have attempted here.[1] In SCHMIDT's compilation, published in 1913, more than 180 books and articles and a number of maps are enumerated.

On the historical side, nothing is listed below further back than the account of the first penetration of the interior of the Yemen by an Englishman in 1609 (see under FOSTER). But it may be recalled that, besides the accounts given by classical writers, those of medieval Arab historians are available. Some of these latter were natives of the Yemen.[2] Moreover, a description of San'a and other cities about 1330 may be read in " The travels of IBN BATTUTA, 1325–54 ", by H. A. R. GIBB (London, 1929). The first account of the Yemen by a European, the Bolognese LUDOVICO DI VARTHEMA, as he saw it in 1503, is included in his " Travels " (HAKLUYT SOCIETY edition by J. W. JONES and G. P. BADGER, London, 1863). Episodes in the dealings of the Portuguese with South-West Arabia are also on record, e.g. the attacks of AFONSO D'ALBOQUERQUE on Aden in 1513, in his " Commentaries ", translated by W. DE GRAY BIRCH (London, 1877).

For general information on the natural history, products and human history of the country, the works of NIEBUHR, PLAYFAIR, MANZONI, DEFLERS, HARRIS, WYMAN BURY, JACOB, and RATHJENS and VON WISSMANN have proved the most useful.

---

[1] Lists of works on Arabia as a whole will be found elsewhere. For instance, R. H. Kiernan, " The Unveiling of Arabia " (London, 1937), has a short bibliography on pp. 341–3, besides mentioning other writings in the text.

[2] Translations of several early chroniclers will be found in " Yaman, its early Medieval History ", by Henry Cassels Kay (London, 1892).

BOOKS AND LONGER ARTICLES

1905. FOSTER (SIR) WILLIAM. "The Journal of John Jourdain, 1608–17", describing his experiences in Arabia, India and the Malay Archipelago (Cambridge, Hakluyt Society, 2nd series, No. 16. Though not published till 1905, this is given first place as containing the account of the first Englishman to penetrate the interior of the Yemen and reach San'a in 1609).

1772. NIEBUHR, CARSTEN. "Beschreibung von Arabien" (Copenhagen).

1774. NIEBUHR, CARSTEN. "Reisebeschreibung nach Arabien und andern umliegenden Ländern", Vols. i–ii (Copenhagen : the Yemen is dealt with in the later part of Vol. i).

(Later editions of Niebuhr's works in German and French, and translations into other languages, are not listed here.)

1841. BOTTA, PAUL ÉMILE. "Relation d'un voyage dans l'Jémen" (Paris).

1845. ARNAUD, T. J. and MOHL, J. "Relation d'un voyage à Mareb (Saba) entrepris en 1843" (Paris, *Journal Asiatique*, ser. 4, Vol. 5, pp. 208–45, 309–45; Vol. 6, pp. 169–237).

1859. PLAYFAIR, R. L. "A history of Arabia Felix or Yemen from the commencement of the Christian era to the present time, including an account of the British Settlement of Aden" (Selections from the Records of the Bombay Government, No. 49, new series. Bombay; contains a bibliography).

1872–7. HALÉVY, JOSEPH. "Rapport sur une mission archéologique dans le Yemen" (Paris, *Journal Asiatique*, ser. 6, Vol. 19, pp. 5–98, 129–266, 489–547, 1872); "Voyage au Nedjran" (Paris, *Bulletin de la Société de Géographie*, ser. 6, Vol. 6, pp. 5–31, 249–73, 581–606; Vol. 13, pp. 466–79).

(*Note* : The Hebrew University, Jerusalem, has just published (1941) "Travels in Yemen : an account of Joseph Halévy's Journey to Najran in the year 1870, written in San'ani Arabic by his guide, with detailed summary in English and glossary of vernacular words".)

1885–99. GLASER, E. Some twelve works, articles in journals or separate books, on his journeys from Hodeida to San'a and in the country north of San'a, and on archæological and historical matters connected with the Yemen. These are listed in the bibliography contained in Schmidt's Dissertation cited below.

1884. MANZONI, RENZO. "El Yemen : tre Anni nell' Arabia Felice" (Rome).

1889. DEFLERS, A. "Voyage au Yemen" (Paris ; general narrative of a botanical journey, with a long systematic list of plants, tables of observations of altitude, and a bibliography).

1893. HARRIS, WALTER B. "A journey through the Yemen" (Edinburgh and London. Besides the lively personal narrative, there is a first part consisting of general information, especially a valuable historical summary).

1911. WYMAN BURY, G. "The Land of Uz" (London).
1915. WYMAN BURY, G. "Arabia Infelix, or the Turks in Yamen" (London).
(Both the above are of great general interest, and include chapters on natural history and agricultural products.)
1912. WAVELL, A. J. B. "A modern pilgrim in Mecca and a siege in Sanaa" (London).
1913. SCHMIDT, WALTHER. "Das südwestliche Arabien" (An Inaugural Dissertation published at Halle ; a compilation of geographical information, including a long bibliography and a chronological list of travellers and their routes).
1923. JACOB, HAROLD F. "Kings of Arabia" (London. Much valuable information on ancient and recent history, the people, etc.).
1926. MITTWOCH, E. "Aus dem Jemen : Hermann Burchardt's letzte Reise durch Südarabien" (Leipzig. Story by Burchardt's Arab secretary of their last journey, 1909, during which Burchardt was murdered by bandits. Arabic text, German translation, map, 28 plates of fine photographs).
1927. ROSSI, G. B. "El Yemen ; Arabia Felix o Regio Aromatum" (Turin).
1930. RIHANI, AMEEN. "Arabian Peak and Desert" (London).
1931–4. RATHJENS, CARL and VON WISSMANN, HERMANN. "Südarabien-Reise," Vols. 1–3 (Vol. 1, 1931, by MORDTMANN and MITTWOCH, is entitled "Sabäische Inschriften" ; Vol. 2, 1932, by RATHJENS and VON WISSMANN, "Vorislamische Altertümer" ; Vol. 3, 1934, by the same authors, "Landeskundliche Ergebnisse" : these form Vols. 36, 38, and 40 of *Hamburgische Universität, Abhandlungen aus dem Gebiet der Auslandskunde.* Many references to Vols. 2 and 3 in the foregoing text of this book).
1933. ANSALDI, CESARE. "Il Yemen nella Storia e nella Leggenda" (Rome).
1936. COON, CARLETON S. "Measuring Ethiopia and flight into Arabia" (London. Second part relates the author's personal experiences in the Yemen while conducting the anthropological investigations referred to in my Chapter xviii).

SHORTER ARTICLES

Out of many articles, the following earlier ones are of special interest to British readers :—

1838. CRUTTENDEN, CHARLES J. (Indian Navy). "Narrative of a Journey from Mokha to San'a by the Tarīk-esh-Shām, or Northern Route, in July and August, 1836" (The *Journal of the Royal Geographical Society,* Vol. viii, pp. 267–89).
1843. PASSAMA, —. "Observations géographiques sur quelques parties de l'Yémen" (*Bulletin de la Société de Géographie de Paris,* Vol. xix,

pp. 162-71, 219-36; a short paper entitled "Observations météorologiques" appeared the same year in Vol. xx, pp. 36-9).
1874. MILLINGEN, CHARLES (M.D.). "Notes of a Journey in Yemen" (*Proceedings of the Royal Geographical Society*, Vol. xviii, pp. 194-202).
1887. HAIG, (MAJOR-GEN.) F. T. "A Journey through Yemen" (*Proceedings of the Royal Geographical Society*, new series ix, pp. 479-90).
1906. ANON. "The new Frontier of the Aden Protectorate" [as defined by the Anglo-Turkish Boundary Commission] (The *Geographical Journal*, Vol. xxviii, December, p. 632, map).
1906. BUXTON, LELAND. "A Journey to Sanaa" (*Blackwood's Magazine*, Vol. clxxix, May, pp. 597-617, sketch-map).

Various articles from "The Encyclopædia of Islam" and from scientific and archæological journals have been cited in the text. Many more are listed in the bibliographies by other writers cited above (p. 239). The following is a list of a few quite recent articles containing general information.

1929. RATHJENS, C. and VON WISSMANN, H. "Sanaa; eine südarabische Stadtlandschaft" (*Zeitschrift der Gesellschaft für Erdkunde zu Berlin*, nos. 9-10, pp. 329-53, maps).
1936-7. DEUTSCH, ROBERT. "In the unknown Yemen" (The *Seagoer Magazine*, London, Vol. 4, No. 2, pp. 27-41. A light article with some fine photographs, notably a room-interior in San'a).
1932. PETRIE, P. W. R. "An Expedition to Ta'izz" (*Edinburgh Medical Missionary Society Quarterly Paper*, Vol. xviii, Nos. 7, 8 (Oct., Nov.), pp. 150-5, 181-5).
1939. PETRIE, P. W. R. "Some Experiences in South Arabia" (The *Journal of Tropical Medicine and Hygiene*, December, pp. 357-60. Specially important for medical information).
1941. REILLY, SIR BERNARD. "The Aden Protectorate" (*Royal Central Asian Journal*, Vol. 28, pp. 132-45. General and political information).
1939-41. SCOTT, HUGH. (1) "A Journey to the Yemen" (The *Geographical Journal*, London, Vol. 93, 1939, No. 2, pp. 97-125, plates. Appendix by E. B. Britton on the Use of *Qat*); (2) "The Yemen in 1937-8" (*Royal Central Asian Journal*, London, Vol. 27, 1940, pp. 21-44, plates); (3) "The Peoples of South-West Arabia" (same periodical, Vol. 28, 1941, pp. 146-51).

Other recent articles, purely scientific, are not cited at all here, either in text or bibliography. The scientific reports of our Expedition will appear in the official publication entitled "British Museum (Natural History) Expedition to South-West Arabia, 1937-8", of which Vol. 1, part 1 (reports Nos. 1-8) was issued in February, 1941.

INDEX

NOTE. Place-names beginning with BEIT, JEBEL, WADI are indexed under those words; but in names having the prefix AL the article is disregarded (thus AL KABAR is under K). Names of persons having the title 'AMIL, AMIR, QADHI, SEIYID, SEIF AL ISLAM, IMAM, WELI, are indexed respectively under those titles.

Some general references to natural history are included in the General Index, but all names (whether scientific, English or Arabic) of wild or domestic animals, and wild or cultivated plants, are indexed in two separate lists (pp. 256-60).

I. GENERAL

'aba, 28
'Abbas 'Abdullah, Hajji (interpreter), 137
Abbasides (Khalifs), 222
'Abdali Sultans, see Lahej, Sultans of
'Abdul Karīm (Sir), Sultan of Lahej, 27-8, 78-9
'Abdul Wahab ibn Tahir (medieval ruler), 226-7
'Abdullah ibn 'Abbas (early governor of Yemen), 222
'Abdurrahman al 'Audhali, 180, 188, 190
Abraha (Abyssinian viceroy), 128; exploits and origin of, 212
Abyssinia [Ethiopia], 6, 7, 9, 10, 14, 29, 31, 32; form of beehives in, 59; hire of pack-animals in, 63; *qāt* introduced from, 95; 100, 106; rains compared with those in Yemen, 142; 180, 187; racial composition of people, 201; early settlement of highlands from Hadhramaut, 202; Portuguese in, 227
Abyssinian occupation of Yemen: first, 210, 211; second, 161, 210, 211
Addis Ababa, 180, 182
Aden, 3, 4, 5; climate, 21-2, 25, 142; Steamer Point, Crater, Ma'alla, etc., 21-4; Seerah island, 23; " Little Aden ", 22, 24; antiquity, 23-4; the Tanks, 23, 155, 220; Government House, 76; extent of Colony, 22, 24, 25; capture by Ottoman fleet, 227; by British, 23, 228; acquires status of Colony, 230
Aden, Gulf of, 7, 23
Aden peninsula, 7, 22, 23, 220
Aden Protectorate, 3; Western Division, 21, 198, 202, 233; expulsion of Yemenis from, 47; lawless mountain tribes, 72-3; tribes in S.E. of, 202; transference to Colonial Office, 230; extent, population, 233; British policy in, 233; agricultural possibilities, 234

Adua (steamship), 190-1
Adulis (city), 212
Aelius Gallus, 210
æolian deposits, 8
aerodrome (San'a), 131, 180
Africa, see East Africa, Tropical Africa
'afrit, tales of, 74
agate, 237
Agricultural Show (Dhala), 38
agriculture: methods, 49-51, 144; possibilities, 234-5
Ahmed Feizi Pasha, 229
Ahmed Hādi (tribal guard, musician), 47, 74-5
Ahmed ibn Ja'far as Suleihi, 99
Ahmed Mahmūd (Somali), 29, 42; his description of rains, 46; 57, 59, 65; skill as collector, 71, 79; 101, 108, 116, 140, 141, 148, 185
alabaster, 125
'Alaf brook (San'a), 150
'Ali (the Khalif), 170, 222, 223, 224
'Ali Ahmed (lorry-owner), 29, 31
'Ali " al 'Askari " (tribal guard), naïveté, dislike of snakes, 47; 57, 73
'Ali ibn Fadhl (Karmathian leader), 223
'Ali Muhammad, Sheikh (interpreter), 85-6
'Ali Qasim Muhammad (preacher), 86
'Ali Qasim ar Rassi (progenitor of Zeidi Imams), 170, 224, 225
'Ali " as Saghir " (tribal guard), 47

243

Index

'Ali Yahya (major-domo to Amir of Ta'izz), 88, 90
alluvial deposits, 8
alphabet, ancient South Arabian, 205
alpine plants, 60, 108
altitudes, high, 4, 9, 60, 68, 80, 108, 110, 114, 115, 153, 155, 156, 159, 161, 181; altitude-zones of cultivated plants, 234-5
Amalekites, 205
'Amil, office of, 84; of Hujerīya (Qadhi Husein), 90; of Makhadar, 106; of San'a (Seiyid Husein), 119; of Ta'izz (Seiyid Muhammad), 84, 86-7, (hearing petitions) 87, 98; of Yarim, 111
Amir of Dhala, see Amir Haidara, Amir Nasr
Amir Haidara (of Dhala), 33-4; administration of justice, 34; 42, 44, 48, 63, 73, 206
Amir of Ibb (Seiyid Yahya), 101, 103; procession from mosque, 104
Amir of Hodeida (Seiyid 'Abdullah), 187 sqq.
"Amir al Muminin" (title of Imam), 171
Amir Nasr (of Dhala), 33-5; relations with tribesmen, 34; eastern limits of jurisdiction, 72
Amir of Ta'izz (Seiyid 'Ali), 85, 88-9; political views of, 89, 90; 96, 97
Amiri highlands, 4, 33-75 (*passim*)
Amiri tribe; dress, appearance of men, 35, 42; of women, 35-6; sense of humour, 39
(Al) 'Anad, 78
Anatolian Turk, an, 129
Anglo-Italian Agreement, 230, 233
Anglo-Turkish Boundary Commission, 66, 230, 242
antimony powder, see *kohl*
apparatus for collecting, 10, 11
'Aqil, rank, meaning, 73; on Jebel Harir, 73; at Menzil Sumara, 107; near San'a, 149
aqueducts, 221; at Ibb, 102-3; Bir Hamīd, 227
Arabia Deserta, 204
Arabia Felix, 3, 53; extent, 204; early Christian missionaries in, 211
Arabia, South, 23, 66, 147, 195; inhabitants, 200-1; cultural links with other lands, 203; Biblical and classical allusions to history, 204
Arabia, South-West, 6, 14, 32, 54, 60, 95; conjectured period of separation from East Africa, 195; early history, 204 *sqq.*
"Arabia Spinosa", 53
Arabian Peninsula, political divisions, 2; dimensions, population, 196
Arabic words, transliteration of, xii; local uses of words, 71-2, 238
archæological discovery, 13, 214 *sqq., et passim*
Arhab (Harra and district), 8, 114, 152 *sqq.*
Armenia, 200
Armenoids (racial element), 200
armies, tribal, see Tribal Guards; army of the Yemen, see soldiers
Arnaud, T. J. (explorer), 13
aromatic plants, interest of classical writers in, 14
Arussi Mts. (Abyssinia), 100
As'ad Kamil, Tubba, 161, 210
Ashkenazim, 199
'Asir, 3, 4, 228, 230, 231, 236
'*askaris* (escort of Tribal Guards in Amiri highlands), 47, 67; connected with people of Jebel Harir, 69; 73-4
aspirator, use of, 11
(Al) 'Asr, 146-9, 150
Assab, 190
astral worship, tolerated under Persians, 212; outline of, 214; emblems of, 217
atebrin (drug), 15, 84
axes, long-handled, 51
Axumites, 210
(Al) 'Azraqein, 151-2, 155
Australian aborigines (Veddoid affinity with), 202, 203

Bab, (names of city-gates) : *in Ta'izz* :—al Kabir, 82; Sheikh Musa, 81, 82, 84; *in San'a* :—al Balaga, 138; al Khusemeh, 115; al Qa', 136; al Qasr, 129; ar Rūm, 123; as Sebah, 123-4, 132, 168; ash Sha'ūb, 122, 129; ash Shegadif, 164, 165; as Stran, 123, 164; al Yemen, 122, 124, 164
Bab el Mandeb, 7, 203
Badawin, from eastern desert, 106; south of Dhamar, 113; 202; origin of camel-herding and horse-breeding, 203
Badhan (Persian viceroy), 213, 222
baggage, amount of, 12, 29, 63, 78, 98, 112
Bairam, see Īd al Fitr

Index

Bājil, 185
Baluchistan, Veddoid element in, 203
Banks, Sir Joseph, 15
Banu Ya'fur, house of, 226
(Al) Barh (west of Ta'izz), 92–3
Bartholomew (Apostle), 211
basalt, columnar, 160
Bates, G. L. (ornithologist), xi, 27, 111
" Battle of the Elephant ", 210, 212
Baurenfeind, G. W. (draughtsman with Niebuhr), 15
beehives, cylindrical, 58
Behih, 182, 183 ; huts of African type at, 185
Beit Baus, 145–6, 150
Beit ad Dawa (dispensary), 121
Beit adh Dhuyūf (Guest-House, Ta'izz), 84
Beit al Faqih, 15, 16, 183, 188
Beit al Ghofr, 158–9
Beit al Hauri, 152, 154
Beit al Mal (Treasury, San'a), 119, 148
Beit (an) N'am, 159
bells, double brass, 109, 113
Berggren (servant with Niebuhr), 15
Beth-Eden, ancient State of, 23
Biblical texts confirmed by inscriptions, 204
" Bilad Aden ", 226
Bilad Hamdan, 142 ; journey to, 151–160 ; 175
Bilad Senhan, 142 ; journey to, 160–2 ; 175
bilharziasis, 138–9
biogeographical : regions, 6 ; considerations relating to Land of Punt, 206
Bir al 'Azab (San'a), 117 ; suggested meanings, 119, 133 ; 123, 124 ; description, 133 ; foreign households in, 137–8 ; 142–4 ; gate to Jewish quarter from, 148 ; 180
Bir al Baheimi (San'a), 123, 133
Bir Hamid, 227
Bir ash Shems (San'a), 123, 133
birka (*birkat*), use of word, 161
Birka Qa' Raqqa, 154–5, 220
Birkat al Bu'r, 158, 220
blade industries (palæolithic), 196
blondness among Yemenis, 197
blood-groups among Yemenis, 199
bogaches, see bukhshas
Bombay, 15 ; Government's first contact with Aden, 228
Botta, P. E. (botanist), 15, 17, 150
Bové (botanist), 16
brachycephaly, 200 ; analysis of, in Southern Arabs, *ibid*.

brass, censers, cup-stands, trays, 107, 119 ; bells, 109, 113 ; age of brass-work, 236
bricks, sun-dried, 122 ; sun-dried and kiln-baked, 126
British Museum (Natural History), xi, 3, 15 ; views of shown, 48, 87, 104, 118, 175 ; Expedition, scientific reports of, 242
British Political Clerk (at Hodeida), 186
Britton, E. B., xi, 3, 6, 15, 29, 42, 56, 57, 66, 67, 71, 80, 87, 94, 105, 111, 118, 121, 136, 140–1, 145, 150, 152, 158, 166, 180, 181, 183
Britton, E. F., xi
bronzes, 219
bukhshas (bakhsheesh), 78, 178
bull's head, emblem of moon-god, 217 ; bull-headed waterspouts, *ibid*.
Bury, G. Wyman, 16, 207, 231
Bustan al Mutawakil Allah (palace precincts, San'a), see Al Mutawakil

Cairo, ancient mosques of, 216
calcareous deposits, 59
camel-carts, 24 ; -milk, 67
Canary Islands, insects on euphorbias in, 53 ; juice of euphorbias collected in, 156
Canneh (Pliny's Cana), 24
cannon, at sunset in Ramadhan, 75 ; at beginning of Id al Kabir, 163
Caprotti brothers, 231
carnelian, 237
cars, hired, 29, 78 ; provided by Yemen Government, 112 *sqq*., 179, 188
Caspian Sea, Zeidis formerly near, 224
castles : at Dhala, interior of, 37–8 ; on Jebel Jihaf, 44 ; Sumara, 108 ; at Yarim, 111 ; pre-Islamic, 157, 219–20
Caton-Thompson, Miss G., xi, 195, 196, 200, 205, 216
cattle-culture of South Arabia, 203 ; uncertain origin of, *ibid*.
" Caucasian " features in South Arabian peoples, 201
Cavaliere, Dr. Gino, 96
caves, limestone, 41, 59 ; sandstone, 71, 155
cemeteries, camping near, 45, 65, 70 ; iris planted in, 109 ; Jewish and Arab at San'a, 136
Ceylon, 14, 202
chaining (punishment), 91, 139
chalcedony, 237
charcoal (for gunpowder), 31

Index

Chosroes I, 212; II, 213
Christianity, introduction of, 211; spread by Abyssinians, *ibid.*
chronology, pre-Islamic, 205 *sqq.*, 213
chupatties, 69, 92, 101, 149
churches, remains at San'a (?), 128, 212; in several centres, 211
cinnamon, 14
cisterns (masonry): rectangular, 93, 152, 161; circular, 113, 154–5, 220; in crater-floor, 152; subterranean, 153; types compared, 155, 220–1; medieval construction of, 227
classical authors, allusions to South Arabia by, 204, 208, 209, 212
climate, 9 (and see Aden, San'a, etc.); changes of, 8, 9, 201, 202, 208
coffee, with ginger, 69; culture of, see plant-index
coinage, see currency
colleges (medieval), 227
conduits (subterranean), 146–7, 221
Constantius II, 211
Coon, Prof. Carleton S., 196, 197, 199; on the races of Europe, 201; 202, 203
Cooper, R. E., 14
cosmetics, see *kohl*, turmeric, henna
Cowasjee-Dinshaw steamships, 188
Cowie, Miss L. J., 118, 131, 138, 151, 180
Cramer, C. C. (surgeon with Niebuhr), 15
craters, 7; near Dhamar, 114; in Harra of Arhab, 152–3
crescent, on mosques, 124
Cretaceous system of rocks, 6, 145
cross, survival of emblem (?), 128; horned form in Abyssinia, 217–18
Crown Prince, see Seif al Islam Ahmed
Cruttenden, C. J., 16
crystalline rocks, 6
currency: small, Aden Protectorate, 29, 34; in Yemen, 78; see riyāls, rupees
Cyprus, beehives used in, 59

dagger, see *jambiya*
dances (men's): in Amiri highlands, 39–40; Jewish, 39; of soldiers in procession, 104, 132, 164; wedding, 160–1; Somali, 184
Dar en Nasr (Ta'izz), 84, 88, 97
dates (chronological), rendering of, xii
Deccan, cultural links with, 203
Deflers, A. (botanist), 15–17, 31, 149, 150, 184, 231

desert, lowland (N. of Aden), 25; coastal (E. of Hodeida), 186
desiccation, gradual, from interior, 208
Deutsch, Herr R., xvii
Dhala, 4; journey to, 29–32; Rest-House at, 33, 34, 42, 75; description, 36–8; festivities at, 38–9; surroundings, 40–1; rulers of, see Amir Nasr, Amir Haidara; first British protection of, 230
Dhamar, 5, 113–15, 237; occupied by Karmathians, 223
Dhāt Ba'dān (sun-goddess), 217
Dhu Nowas (last Himyaritic Tubba), 161, 211
Dhu Raidan (Himyaritic title), 209
Dhufar, 147, 201
diseases, 138–9
distances (by road): Aden–Dhala, 29; Aden–Ta'izz, 78; Ta'izz–San'a, 116; to Bilad Hamdan, 151; San'a–Hodeida, 180
divans, 86, 88, 107
divergence of Arabian from East African species, 9, 147
Dodekites, 224
dolichocephaly, 197, 200
Doran (residence of former Imam), 227
Doughty, C. M., 40
dove (metal), emblem on mosques, 125, 129
dress of: townsmen in lowlands, 23, 24, 28; men and women, Amiri highlands, 35–6; official classes, Yemen, 104–5; cultivators on Yemen high plateau, 107, 113; men, women, in San'a, 130–1; Jews in San'a, 135; San'anis at Festival, 166–8
Dubbiosi, Dr. E., 137–8, 144, 188
" dust-devils ", 114
Dutch East India Company, 228

earth-pinnacles, 26
East Africa: resemblance between S.W. Arabian lowlands and parts of, 184; epoch of separation from S.W. Arabia, 195; possible centre of cultural diffusion, 195–6; cultural links of S. Arabia with, 203
East India Company, 228
" Eden " (of Ezekiel), 23–4
Egypt, 14; cylindrical beehives used in, 58
Egyptian University Scientific Expedition, 8, 13, 17, 203

Egyptians, ancient, 13 ; locks used by, 52 ; pre-dynastic, racial composition of, 201 ; modern, occupation of Arabian coast-towns by, 228
Ehrenberg and Hemprich (naturalists), 16
embroidery (gold, silver), 130, 135
Eritrea, 16 ; Eritrean passengers, 190
(Al) Errein (pre-Islamic site), 158
Ethiopia, see Abyssinia
Ethiopian Region (biogeographical), 6
euphorbium (used in medicine), 156
evolution of species, 9, 147
Eyyub, see *Job*
Eyyubite governors, 226
Ezekiel (cited), 23-4

Fadhl, Sultan (son of Sultan of Lahej), 28
family names, use of, 103
Farasān Islands, 16
Faroe Islands, primitive locks in, 52
Fatima (daughter of Muhammad), 170, 224
faults (geological), 7
felej (conduits), 147
fireworks, 83
fish, sold in San'a market, 150 ; narcotised, 238
fish-poison, 238
flag (modern) of the Yemen, 84, 111 ; carried at Festival, 166 ; description of, 223 ; flags on graves, 24
flail, unjointed, 50
floras of Abyssinia and Yemen compared, 16
floss (for stuffing mattresses), 31
flower-gardens, 26, 137
flowers, wild, abundance on Jebel Jihaf, 43, 55 *sqq*. ; seasons of, 55 ; see also Alpine plants, and plant-index
folk-lore concerning insects, 118-19
football, 78, 180
forays, intertribal, frontier-, 73, 80, 236
Foreign Secretary, the Imam's, see Qadhi Mohammed Raghib
forest, patches of, 58, 183
Forskål, P. (botanist), 56, 60, 70, 94 ; death at Yarim, 15, 112 ; on drug obtained from euphorbia, 156
Foster, (Sir) William, 228, 240
Frederick V (King of Denmark), 14
French occupation of Mocha, 228
Frontier Guard, a, see Hamūd
frontier of Yemen, fear of violating, 66-7 ; crossed, 80 ; unruly tribes near, 236

Frontier Officer, the Aden, 4, 80, 180
Frumentius, St., 211
Fukam, 24
fusūs (stones reputed to cure snake-bite), 175
" futas " (garments), 23, 24, 33, 35, 165

Gabriel (Archangel), 81
Gardner, Miss E. W., 195, 200
Genesis (cited), 120, 209
geographical distribution (of animals and plants), 9, 10, 147
geology, 6 *sqq*., 17, *et passim*
Ghailima, 184
ghee (clarified butter), 42
Gheil Wakra, 146
Gheiman, 160-1, 176, 210
Ghumdan (pre-Islamic stronghold), 122, 128, 212 ; description, 219 ; ruin, restoration, final overthrow, 219-220 ; encampment of Karmathians at, 223
giant mountain-plants of East Africa and S.W. Arabia, 70-1
glacis, bare rock-, 42, 70
Glaser, E. (orientalist, explorer), 13, 145
Goitein, S. D., 238
gold, 236
gorges, 9, 41, 56 *sqq*.
gourds (as food-vessels), 42, 43, 59, 140
Government Guards (Aden Protectorate), 38, 73
Governor of Aden, see Reilly, Sir Bernard
graves, flags on, 24 ; rough (in mountains), 45 ; iris planted on, 109
Great Mosque, the (San'a), 123, 126-8, 212, 216
Greeks, few in Yemen, 187
greenstone, 43
Gregentius, St., 212
Guards, see Tribal and Government
Guest-Houses, Government (in Yemen), 84, 88, 90 ; method of payment, cost of household in (Ta'izz), 90, 91 ; at Ma'bar, 115, 181 ; San'a, 117 ; Hodeida, 186-7

Hada, 145, 150
(Al) Hādi Yahya, see under " Imam "
Hadhramaut, 195, 196, 198 ; possible settlement of Ethiopian highlands by colonists from, 202 ; Veddoid racial element in, 202-3 ; 204, 205 ; ancient kingdom, 207 ; absorbed by Himyarites, 209 ; history as

told by present inhabitants cited, 209; period of subjection to Yemen, 222; 231, 232
Hais, 15; pottery-manufacture at, 185-6
Haj' Ahmed (tea-shop keeper), 129
" Hajji Baba ", 43
Hajji Mu'tassar (Turkish shopkeeper), 129
hakīm, entomologist taken for, 108
Hakūma (Government building), 111-112, 187, 189
Halévy, J. (orientalist), 13, 236, 238
Halmeini tribesmen, 72, 73
Hamād, Sheikh (owner of horses), 148
(Al) Hamdani (historian), 220, 237
Hamilton, Capt. the Hon. R. A. B., 38, 71
" Hamitic " population, South Arabians believed residue of, 200-1; term not used in racial sense, 202; Rathjens's views on ancient culture, 205-6
Hammam 'Ali, 182
(Al) Hamra, 153
Hamūd (Aden Frontier Guard), 80
hand-axe industries (palæolithic), 195
Hanish Islands, 8
harems, social diversions in, 131
Haret en Nahsein (San'a), 124
Harib, land of, 208
harras (volcanic tracts), 8; about Dhamar, 113-14; of Arhab, 152 *sqq.*
Harris, W. B. (cited), 24, 188, 212, 222, 223, 229
harvest, on Jebel Jihaf, 49; -song, *ibid.*
Hassan (son of 'Ali), 224, 225
Hassan (Yemeni soldier, field-botanist), 136, 149, 151; burnt by euphorbia-juice, 156; 164
Haushabi tribe: village of, 30; tribesmen, 78-9
Haven, F. C. von (philologist), death at Mocha, 15
Hayyim Habshush (Halévy's guide), 236, 238
Haz, 154-5, 157-9
(Al) Hejaz, 15, 40, 162, 197, 198, 229
henna (beards dyed with), 103
Hensley, Miss M., 76
herbs, on house-roofs, 105; uses of, *ibid.*
" hide " (ambush), 73
Hidrar (near Ta'izz), 92
Hillcoat, Miss D., xi, 238
Himyar, 209
Himyarites, 110, 161, 205, 206; rise of, 209; fall, 211; antiquities ascribed to, 146

Himyaritic, inscription on cliff, 146; columns, sculptured stones, 153, 158, 162; princes, 209 *sqq.*, succession to claimed by Imams, 170, 173
Hinks, R. P., and Smith, S., 219
Hiram (King of Tyre), 198
" History of Plants ", 14
Hiswa, 25
Hodeida, 5, 15, 16, 115, 132, 175, 176, 179, 180, 184, 186-190; mixed population, 190; occupation by Turks, 228; 229, 231, 232
Hommel, F., on Minæans, 205
honey, 45, 59, 69
horse-breeding, 114
hospital, the Imam's new, 138-9
hot springs, 7; at Huweimi (temperature, etc.), 78-9; near Dhamar, 114; and thermal establishment, Hammam 'Ali, 182
houses: stone tower- (Amiri highlands), 36-7; of one storey (Wadi Tiban), 64; great (Ta'izz), 82, (Yarim), 111; tall (San'a), 125-6; Jewish (San'a), 134; Imam's country-house, 149; at Hodeida, 189; ornamentation of, 37, 85, 108, 189
Hughes, Col. E. L., xi
Hujeris (negroids, S. Yemen), 198
huqqa, see water-pipe
Huqqa, village, 143, 152-4; temple, 152-3, (plan) 215-16, (destruction of) 153, 195, 215, (local tradition of destruction) 216
Husein Pasha (Turkish, 16th C.), 83
Husein, Sheikh (of Gheiman), 160
Husein (son of 'Ali), 224, 225
(Al) Huseini (Lahej), 26-8, 184
huts: rectangular brushwood, 30; circular grass-covered, 185; of straw among large houses (Hodeida), 189
Huweimi, 78-80
Huzayyin, Dr. S. A., 8, 17, 195, 196, 203

Ibb, 5, 101-5; numerous mosques at, 102; gates, aqueduct, walls, *ibid.*; densely thronged at, 103
ibex-horns fixed to houses, 133; possible origin of custom, 217
Ibn Battuta, 239
Id al Fitr (festival), 24, 27; opening of, 77; 163
Id al Kabir (festival), 163-9
Idrisi, the, 231
Imadi (riyāl), 77

Imam Al Hādi Yahya (first Imam in Yemen), 170; full names, descent, burial-place, 224-5
Imam Ismaʻil ibn Qasim, 171, 181, 227
Imam Mansūr al Qasim, 225, 227
Imam Muhammad al Mansūr (father of present Imam), 229
Imam Yahya (present Imam), recognised as King of the Yemen, 4, 230; 21, 28, 76, 96; strict order maintained by, 139; at the Id al Kabir, 164-9; nature of his office, 169-71, 226; accession to Imamate, family, names and titles, absolute rule, 169-73, 226, 229; industry, attention to details, 173-6; 233, 235, 236
Imams, the twelve great, 224
Imams, Zeidi (of the Yemen), dynasty of, 170; succession to Himyaritic rulers claimed, *ibid.*; qualifications for office, 170, 225; rise and lineage, 224-6
incense, use in social gatherings, 69; -trees, 14; -country, 24; -trade, 207
India, 14, 15, 203
Indian influence in house-ornament, 189
Indian Ocean, 23, 203
Indians in: Aden, 23; Hodeida, 190; larger ports generally, 198
indigo, turbans dyed with, 35, 42, 108, 168; on men's faces, 35; clothing of women south of Dhamar, 113
Ingrams, Mr. W. H., 195, 204, 205, 209, 222; Mrs., 195
inscriptions, South Arabian, 204
insects, number known, 10; number of specimens collected, 10; taken at light, 30; associated with tree-euphorbias, 53; folk-lore concerning, 118; from leaf-axils of aloes, 155; attracted to isolated summits, 154, 181
'Iraq, 22; threshing grain in, 51; 224
iron, 236, 237; door-knockers of, 126
irrigation, of onion-beds, 51; of fields, orchards, 93, 143, 146; -ditches across track, 113; -works (ancient), 207-8, 220, 234
Isaiah (cited), 207
Ishtar (ancient worship of), 214
Ismaʻil ba Salaama (former Amir of Ibb), 103
Ismaʻil ibn al ʻAbbas (Rasulite Sultan), 83
Ismaʻili sect, 224, 225, 238

isolation, factor in evolution, 66
Istanbul, 178
Italian: medical men in Yemen, 96, 137-8, 231, (vaccination introduced by) 139; treaties with Yemen, penetration, 230-1; war with Turkey, 231; ambitions in Red Sea, 231-2
Izzet Pasha, 229

Jaʻfar, Mr. Salih, 186; Mr. ʻAbduljabbar, 186-7
Jacob, Harold F., 234
Jamʻa Ismaʻil (Somali head-servant), 21, 27, 29, 42, 46, 57; forecasts by a dream, 62; strict observance of Ramadhan, 74; 91, 111, 118-19, 140, 174-5
jambiya (dagger), 23, 34, 35, 39, 47, 57; sheaths decorated with green twine in S. Yemen, 80; worn on right side by *seiyids*, 86; held aloft by dancing soldiers, 104, 164; richly ornamented (Sanʻa), 130; 135, 148; flourished at marriage dance, 161
Jameson, Miss V., 76
Jamiʻ al Kabir, see Great Mosque
(Al) Janad (ancient province), 80, 222
Janadīya, mosque and legend of, 80-1
Jauf, district, 150, 206, 207
Jebel: Badan, 102; Doran, 181, 227; Fiddi, 149, 160; Gheriat Jaffa, 114; Girwan, 161; Hada, 145; Hadhur Nebi Shuʻaib, 159; Haidar al Issi, 114; Halmein, 69, (tribesmen of) 72-3; Hammam al Issi, 114; Harir, 4, 47, 67, (tabletopped form) 68, (villages on) 68-70, (night-temperature at foot) 74; Hesha, 61-2, 66, 98; Jalal, 115, 181; Jihaf, 4, 42 *sqq.*, (form of, springs) 45, (climate on) 46, (summit) 60-1, (descent of precipice from) 63-4, 67, 98; Kibūd, 114; al Kohl, 153-4; Masnah, 181-2; al Meriat, 115; Munif, 30; Nuqūm, (climbed by Deflers) 17, 122, 132, (building on) 144-5, 146, 154, 164; Reiyani, 156; Sabir, (explored by Botta) 15, 80, 82, 84, 93-4; Sheʻani, 161; Shemahé, 101; Soraq, 98; Sumara, 108-9; Taqar, 100; Zafar, 110
Jebel Tair (island), 8
Jemila ('Aqil's mother), 107-8
Jeremiah (cited), 207

Jewish quarter (San'a), 133-6 ; (Haz), 157
Jewish question in Palestine, views on, 89, 90, 121, 188
Jewish saint, tomb of, 92
Jews, South-West Arabian : in Amiri highlands, 38-9, (metal-workers) 51, 62 ; in Ta'izz, 92 ; in San'a, (plaster-workers) 125, 134, (silver-smiths, dress) 135, (observances, wine-makers) 136, 138 ; at Haz, 157 ; physical characteristics, 198-9 ; origin, 198, 206, 211
Jibla (town), 100-1
Jibouti, 190
"Jingling Johnny", 166
jinn, stories of, 74
(Al) Jiraf (town), 150
Job, Book of, 46, 207 ; reputed tomb of, 62
Joktan (= Qahtān), 120, 204, 209
Jol Madram, 78
Jourdain, John, 228
Judaism, conversion of Ḥimyarites to, 161, 210, 211 ; tolerated by Persians, 212
Jurassic rocks, 6

Ka'ba, the, 74, 128, 204, 212 ; local (at San'a and Nejran), 128, 213
(Al) Kabar pass, 155
Kairouan, mosque of, 216
"Kalis" (*ecclesia*), in San'a, 212
kalpak (head-dress), 87, 117, 140, 169, 174
Kamarān Island, 16, 237
kapok, 31
Karmathians, 223, 238
"Karmats", 238
Katabanians, 205, 208-9
Kaulat al 'Asakeir, 159
Kaulat al Hauri, 152
Kay, H. C., 100, 223, 225, 239
Keith Falconer Mission, 24, 118
Keith, Sir Arthur, 200
Khalifs, early, 222 *sqq.*
khans (wayside), 107, 151, 152, 160
Kheriat an Naqil (village), 115
Khormaksar, 21, 22, 29, 76, 78, 191
(Al) Khureiba pass, 31
Kiernan, R. H., 210, 239
Kirsh (military post), 78-9
kishr (beverage), 64, 92, 99, 107, 149
kohl (cosmetic), 36, 135, 153 ; holders for, 135
Kos (bishop), 212
Kourban Bairam, see Id al Kabir

Krogman, Dr. W. M., 200
Kufa (in 'Iraq), 224

Lahej : oasis (climate, tropical products), 25-7 ; town, 25-6 ; 225 ; occupation by Turks, 230
Lahej, Sultans of : present Sultan, 27-8, 78-9 ; death of predecessor, 230 ; first independent Sultans, 226, 228
Lake, Col. M. C., 76
lapidaries (San'a), 124, 237
laryngitis, epidemic of, 179
lava, 8, 114, 152 ; -flows, 152-4
lead-mines, 236
letters (local carrying of), 132
Leukē Kōmē, 210
lightning (over Yemen), 45
limestone : caves, 41, 59 ; pre-Islamic sculptured stones, 153, 157-8
Linnæus (as teacher of Forskål), 15
Lloyd-Triestino steamships, 188
locks and keys, wooden, 52
loess, 8 ; wells sunk in, 133
Luheiya, 237

Ma'bar, 115, 181, 182, 184
(Al) Madina, Prophet's Tomb-Mosque at, 216
Madinat al Abīd, 115, 176, 179, 180, 182-3
Mahdi, the, 224
Mahra tribes, 202
Ma'in, Kingdom of (Minæan State), 205 ; ruins of city of, 207
Maitland, P. J., 207
Makhadar, 105-7
Makran coast, Veddoid element in, 203
malaria, 15, 27, 64, 84, 111, 139, 180, 182
Malay element, in Hadhramaut, 198 ; in families of Yemen Tihama, *ibid.*
Malek al Mansūr (title of 'Abdul Wahab ibn Tahir), 226
Manakha, 16, 175, 176, 178, 179 ; end of road from, 185 ; Turkish armies' advance through, 229
Mansūr ibn al Mufadhal (Suleihite prince), 84
Mansūr, Sheikh (secretary to Amir of Ibb), 101, 105
Manzoni, R., 82-3, 238
Maqam Sharif (room in Imam's palace), 174, 176-7
Maria-Theresa dollar, see riyāl
Marib : situation, 207 ; irrigation-works, 207-8 ; destruction of dam,

208; superseded as capital, 209; 210; temple at, 214
market, country-, 106
market-gardeners (San'a), 133
marriage festivities, 160–1
Massowa, 212, 231
Mas'ūd 'Awadh (lorry-owner), 78, 87
mattocks, two forms, 50, 144, 155
Mecca, direction of, 74; ancient road from Yemen to, 210; Abyssinian march against, 212; Karmathians at, 223
Medical Survey (of Aden Protectorate), 236
Mediterranean race, 197, 198; extent and varieties of, 201
Menzil Sumara, 105, 107–9
meshhed, meaning of term, 164
(Al) Meshhed Sha'ūb, 164–5
mesocephalic (type of skull), 197
metal-work, 51, 135, 236
Meysha al Abyadh (silversmith), 135
Midian, land of, 207
mifraj (pavilion, in garden or on roof), 119, 121, 122, 125, 131, 141, 151, 180
migration, early trade (from Armenia), 200; not excluded by recent anthropological views, 202; within or from Arabian peninsula, *ibid.*
mijāl (" migyal "), use of term, 161
Mījāl al As'ad, 155, 161–2
(Al) Milah (village), 30
Millingen, C., 16
Minæans, 205, 206; raided by Sabæans, 207; and incense-traffic, *ibid.*
minerals, mines, 236
Minister of Health (Prince Qasim), 121
mirage, 113
missionaries, medical, see Petrie; Muslim, in America, 86
Mocha, burial of von Haven at, 15; road from Ta'izz to, 82, 92; decay of, 84, 228; Dutch " factory " at, French occupation of, *ibid.*
Mohammed 'Ali (of Egypt), 228
Mohammed, Mr. A. C., 86
Mongol, a, 114
monsoon, 3, 8 (see also rains)
moon-god, 214, 217; survival of emblems of, 133, 217
moonlight rides, 59, 64
Morant, Dr. G. M., xi, 199, 200
Morocco (insects on euphorbias in), 53
mortar, monolithic, 111
mosques: (*general* :—) plainness of, Dhala and district, 37; with cupolas, Jebel Harir, 69; at Ta'izz: style, names, 83, 238; at Ibb: many small Zeidi, 102; at Dhamar, 114; at San'a: number, styles, 124–5; Great Mosque, 126–8, 216; ancient types derived from pre-Islamic temples, 216; small unwalled praying-places, 221; (*particular* :—) Janadīya, 80–1, 98; at Ta'izz: Al Makhdabīya, 83, 238; Muzaffarīya (Isma'il Mülk), 83, 238; Ash Sharifīya, 83, 238; at San'a: Al Abhar, 125, 126; Al Bakiliye, 125, 129, 228; Jami' al Kabir, 123, 126–8, 212, 216; Al Madressa, 125; Mahdi 'Abbas, 124, 125; Salah ad Dīn, 129
Muhammad (the Prophet), 80, 81, 198, 212, 222, 224
Muhsin (*sais*), 136
(Al) Mukarram ibn 'Ali (medieval ruler), 99
Mulbera (steamship), 21
mule-roads, ancient paved, 99
(Al) Muriah (village), 64–5, 67, 68
museum of antiquities, San'a, 153, 216
musical instruments, 38–9, 88, 104, 166
(Al) Mutawakil (title of the Imam), 123, 171, 181, 226, 227; name applied to Palace precincts, 123, 132
(Al) Muzaffar (Rasulite Sultan), 83, 226

Nabatæans, 210
Naji (chief tribal guard, Amiri highlands), 47, 57, 67; " Naji II ", 73
naqil, meaning of, 110
Naqil Isla pass, 94, 115, 181
Naqil Sumara, 110
Nasr Yahya (servant of Amir, Ta'izz), 90, 97
Natural History Museum, see British Museum (Natural History)
naturalists (earlier), 13–17
" Neanderthaloid " racial elements, 201
neck (volcanic), 149, 158
necropolises, desert, 207, 214
negritos, 202
negroes, in sea-ports, 198; woodmen, 52
negroid affinities in lowlands, 185, 190, 198
Nejd, 40
Nejran, 210; early Christian centre, 211, 212; local Ka'ba at, 213; bronze lion's head from, 219; centre of Isma'ilis, 224
nets (for collecting), 10, 11

New Moon, beginning of Ramadhan, 74; of Id al Fitr, 77
Niebuhr, C., 13, 14; deaths of companions, 14–15; agricultural implements described by, 50; 80; his plan of Ta'izz, 82; Ibb described by, 103; 112, 114; plan of San'a, 123; use of term "Yemen" by, 225–6; 236, 237
Nobat Dakim, 30, 78
Nordic races, comparison with Mediterranean, 197
Norman architecture, resemblance to, 37
nostril-stoppers, 152

oasis, of Lahej, 25–7; oases at edge of San'a plain, 150
Obādi (watchman), 47
'Obal, 184–5
obsidian, 196
"Old Ta'izz", 84
Old Testament, 23; allusions to South-West Arabia, 205, 207
'Oman, Sultanate of, 147, 221; racial types in, 200, 202; included in *Arabia Felix*, 204
'Omar Isma'il (Somali servant), 29, 42, 57, 59, 108, 140, 160, 238; nimbleness as collector, 147, 182; received by the Imam, 174, 175
'Omarah al Hakami (historian), 100
Omeiyad Khalifs, 222, 224
onyx-stone, 237
orchards, San'a district, 143 *sqq.*; terraced, 146; at Wadi Dhahr, 149
Oriental Region (biogeographical), 6

Palæarctic Region (biogeographical), 6
palæolithic culture, 195
Palestine, Arab views of British policy in, 89, 90
Pantænus, St., 211
parasitism, probable case of, 92
parchment scrolls, 134
Parsees (Aden), 23
Pashas as Turkish Governors-General of Yemen, 227, 228, 229
Passama, useful plants noted by, 16, 31
passes, mountain-, to Ibb, 99; see also Al Kabar, Al Khureiba, Naqil Sumara, Naqil Isla
Perim I., 8, 231, 233
Persian rule in Yemen, 212–13; castle of Ghumdan rebuilt during, 219; Tanks at Aden assigned to, 220; possible influence in construction of conduits, 147, 221

petitioners, heard by 'Amil of Ta'izz, 87; by Seif al Islam Ahmed, 132
Petra, 210
Petrie, Dr. Eleanor, 118, 131, 138, 151, 180
Petrie, Dr. P. W. R., 81, 118, 121; work at Imam's hospital, 138; 139; a Minister of the Scottish Church, 140; 150–2, 156, 158, 169, 180, 235
Philby, Mr. H. St. J. B., 195, 207, 213
Philostorgius (historian), 211
Phœnician, South Arabian alphabet related to, 205; conjectured origin of nation, 206; early voyages, 211
phoresy, possible case of, 92
photographs, methods, exposures, xvii, xviii; number taken, 10; restrictions on taking, 87, 164
plaster-work, see under "houses"
Playfair, R. L., 220, 222, 226
Pleistocene period, 8, 195, 201, 202
Pliny, 24, 209
plough, simple, 50; followed by men turning soil, 50, 144
ploughing, winter-, 113, 144
pluvial phases, 8, 202
Political Officers, 38, 73
polygamy, infrequency of, 172
ponds, on Jebel Jihaf, 54; summit of Jebel Harir, 70; warm (Huweimi), 79; partly artificial (ancient), 157, 220
pools, deep, 41, 56, 61, 71, 80; shallow rain-fed rock-pools, 54, 61
porters (for transport), 63, 70, 160
Portuguese, fort at Aden, 23; in Abyssinia and South Arabia, 227, 239
postage stamps (Yemen), xii, 132
postmen (San'a), 132
pottery, ancient, sherds on sand, 25; made at Hais and San'a, 185–6
pre-Arabic languages (Mahra, etc.), 203
pre-Islamic: emblems, 128, 133, 217; remains, 214 *sqq.*; at Huqqa and Haz, 153, 157–9, 216; rectangular and circular buildings, 206, 214; circular tombs, 207; see also cisterns
pre-Islamic kingdoms, 205 *sqq.*; influence on religious thought, 214
presents, indirect payment by, 90
Prime Minister (the Imam's), see Qadhi 'Abdullah
princes (sons of the Imam), 172–3
processions, at Ibb, 104; the Imam's at San'a, 164 *sqq.*

Index

Procopius (historian), 212
pumice-stone, 23
Punjabi pilgrims, 185
Punt, land of, 13, 14, 206

qaʻ, meaning of, 110
Qaʻ al Hagle, 110
Qaʻ al Yahūd (Jewish quarter, Sanʻa), 123, 133-6, 148
Qadhi ʻAbdullah al ʻAmri (Prime Minister), 117-18, 160, 168, 174, 179
Qadhi of Ibb, 101, 104
Qadhi Mohammed Raghib (Foreign Secretary), 120; reminiscences of, 120-1; views on Jewish question, 121; 168-9, 172, 174-7, 178-9
Qadhi of Saiyani, 99
Qahtān (descendant of Shem), 120, 204, 209
Qara, mountains, 147; tribes, 202
qat, drugs isolated from, 95; practice of chewing, ibid.; "parties", 95, 131; 148; see also plant-index
Qaʻtaba (frontier town), 61, 75
Qataban (kingdom of), 14, 207, 208-9
Qureish (tribe), 212

Raidan, 209
rains: summer, 8, 21; violent storms, 34, 45; ending, 45-6; autumnal drizzle, 68; winter storms in highlands, 142, 181; shower in foothills, 185
Ramadhan, 24; beginning of, corporate prayers in camp during, 74; 75; end of, 77
Ras Dhurbat ʻAli, 233
Rasell, Miss N., 76
Rassite dynasty of Imams, 170, 224, 225
Rasulite Sultans, 83, 226
Rathjens, C. (and von Wissmann, H.), 13, 16, 17, 50; meeting with, 96-7; 143, 145, 165, 198; ideas on pre-Islamic history, 205-6; excavations at Huqqa, 215, 217; 219, 221, 234
Raudha (town), 143, 150-1
real, see riyāl
red ochre, use of, by the Imam, 173, 209
Red Sea, 3, 5, 6, 7, 8, 14, 106, 186, 189, 206, 210; Turkish ambitions to control, 227; first visited by British and Dutch, 228; 233
Reilly, Sir Bernard xi, 4, 38, 39, 76
religion, ancient Arabian, see astral worship

rifts (geological), 7, 9
rivers (flowing), 8, 65, 78, 81, 150, 183-4
riyāls (dollars), occasionally current in Amiri highlands, 34; unit of currency in Yemen, fluctuating value, 77; effigies on, ibid.; 174
rock-sepulchres, 217-18; empty sepulchre at Wadi Dhahr, 150, 217
rock-staircase (natural), 60
rosary (used by the Imam), 172
route (Map 2), 20
Royal Air Force, 38
Rukheba (military post), 80
rukhsa (written permit), 91, 151, 153, 154
Rumāda (near Taʻizz), 92
rupees, 29, 34, 42

Saad (Aden chauffeur), 22
Saba, Kings of, 207; title assumed by Himyaritic princes, 209
Sabæans, 205-6; raiding Minæans, 207; wars with Katabanians, 209
sacrifices, at Mecca during pilgrimage, 163; at Sanʻa, 168
Saʻda, early Imams at, 170, 226; burial-place of first Imam, 225; iron-mines in district of (?), 237
Saiyani, 98-9
Saiyida binta Ahmed (Lady), 99-100
Salah ad Dīn (Saladin), 226
Salif, 237
Salih, Sheikh, and his brother (Taʻizz), 90-1
salt, obtained from sea-water, 24; camel-caravans of, 106, 109; rock-, 237
sambuq, embarkation in, 190
Sanʻa, 5, 14-17; description of, 122-36; population, 122; plan, 122-4; walls, gates, 123; dry watercourse through, 123; citadel, 122; altitude, climate, 122, 142-3; mosques, number, styles, etc., 124-8; suqs, 129-30; water-supply, 133; Jewish quarter, 133-6; occupation by Abyssinians, 211-12; provincial capital under early Khalifs, 222; occupied by Karmathians, 223; residence of later Imams, 225; 226, 227; sieges of, 229
Sanʻa, Treaty of, 4, 230, 231
sandhills (coastal), 25, 186
sandstones (Cretaceous), thickness, 6; massif, 68; 145; cliffs, 149; 154, 160

254 Index

sanitary arrangements and service (San'a), 126; primitiveness of (Huqqa), 152
Sapphar, 110, 209
saqiya, 51
Sa'udi Arabia, 3; Arabs from, 106, 152, 196; relationships with Yemen, 230, 231
schoolboys in march-past, 166
Schwartz, Dr. O. (botanist), 17
Schweinfurth, G. (botanist), 16
Sclater, Mr. W. L. (ornithologist), xi, 16
screes, 57, 59
scribes, professional, 132
scriptures, the Jewish, 134
sculptures, pre-Islamic, 219; of Hellenistic type, *ibid.*; built into Great Mosque (San'a), 128, 219
Seager, Capt. B. W., 4, 21, 22, 29, 129, 180, 186, 188
seals, of the Imam, 173–4, 209
Seetzen, U. J. (botanist, etc.), 15
Seif Allah (title of 'Ali), 222
Seif al Islam (title of Imam's sons), 172, 223; 'Abdullah, 165; Ahmed, 132, 140–1, 161; Husein, 131; Qasim (Minister of Health), 121, 141, 151, 165
Seif al Khulifah (title of early ruler of Yemen), 222
Seiyid: 'Abdullah ibn al Wazir, see Amir of Hodeida; 'Ali ibn al Wazir, see Amir of Ta'izz; Husein 'Abdul Qādir, see 'Amil of San'a; Muhammad al Basha, see 'Amil of Ta'izz
seiyids, lineage, 86, 197; outward mark of, 86; 118, 130–1
Seligman, Prof. C. G., 200
semi-precious stones, 124, 175, 237
"Semites", 200; southward extension, 202; 206
Sephardim, 199
serfs, as origin of negroid elements, 198
sergeant, see *shawūsh*
Shabwa, 195, 208
Shafe'i Muslims, 172, 188; districts of, religious centre of, 225
Shahara tribes ('Oman), 202
Shahārah (northern residence of Imam), 170, 171, 229
Shaif, Sheikh, 64–5
sharifs, 86–7
Sha'ūb (suburb of San'a), 143, 164
shawl (worn over shoulders), 87
shawūsh (sergeant), commanding escort, 91, 93, 101, 108, 111, 112; with caravan to Bilad Hamdan, 151, 153, 159; 160, 161, 180
Sheba, biblical references to, 24, 207; possibility of reclaiming desert in, 208
sheepskin coats, 107, 113
Sheikh 'Othman, 24–5
Sheikh Sa'id, 231
sheikhs, tribal and village, 197
Shem, traditional descent from, 120, 209
Shems (sun-goddess), 214
Sherara "place" (San'a), 124, 137, 168, 180
Shi'ahs, 170; subdivisions of, 224
Shom Pen (race), 202
shovels, for men or ox-drawn, 50, 51
sickle, form of, 50
sieves (for collecting), 11
silver, silver-work, 135, 236
Sin (moon-god), 214
singing, high-pitched, 47, 74; of harvesters, 49; of soldiers (San'a), 132, 164–5; of camel-boys, 133
sledge-shaped stones, 50
slings, 48, 57
smallpox, 139
snake-bite, reputed cure of, 175
snake-catchers, 72
Socotra, 2, 203
Solbi, the (San'a), 134
soldiers: of Lahej army, 79; of Yemen army, 80, 83, 88; character, 91; dancing in processions, 104, 132, 164; 111, 124, 130; march-past, 166
Solomon, maritime enterprises of, 198, 206
Solubba (racial group), 202
Somaliland, 31, 95, 201
Somalis, in sea-ports, 21, 23, 198; aptitude for entomological work, 29; 136
Southern Rhodesia, 214
sowing (of cereals, etc.), 50, 157
Spain, Northern, 51; Southern, 109
specimens, number collected, 10; methods, 10–12; transport of living, 179
spinning, 136
springs, sacred, 61; at foot of mountains, 150
stacks (of *dhurra*-stems), 49
stalactitic formation, 41
Stark, Miss Freya, 195
statuettes, pre-Islamic, 219
step-formation (geological), 7, 32, 110, 155
stirrups, Arab, 44; lack of, 59, 67

stone implements (palæolithic), 195
stones, semi-precious, 124, 175, 237
story-tellers (professional), 129
straw-hats (of lowland tribes), 23, 79, 184
Subeiri family (Jewish), 136
subterranean vaults, 51
Suez Canal, 228
(as) Suleihi, Suleihites (dynasty), 84, 99, 226
Suleiman the Magnificent, 227
sulphur, near Dhamar, 114 ; formerly exploited, 237
Sumara, pass, village, 105, 108–10
sun-goddess, 214, 217
Sunnis, 170, 172, 188
Suq al 'Asr, 149 ; as Sabt, market at, 105–6 ; al Wadi, 149, 160
surveillance, close, 85–6, 91, 108, 111, 188–9 ; motive for, 236
sword, the Imam's, 165, 172, 174 ; of 'Ali, 223
synagogues, 134
Syrians, in San'a, 120, 137, 166

Tahir, see 'Abdul Wahab
Taiba (walled village), 160
Tāif, 150
Ta'izz, 5, 15, 16, 49, 76 ; journey to, 78–81 ; situation, gates, mosques, 82–3 ; Al 'Urdi (barracks), 83, 88, 90 ; trade, 84 ; Amir's palace, 88, 97 ; 98, 142, 179, 187, 188, 226, 227
Tamna, 208, 209
Tanks, the (Aden), 23, 155 ; conjectured age of, 220
tanks, wayside, 84, 99, 111, 221
Taslal, 213
tea, mint-flavoured, 101
temperate and tropical species, mingling of, 9
temples, 214–16 ; see also Huqqa
tents (double-fly), 45, 64, 97
terracing, of mountain-sides, 45, 61, 94, 99, 109 ; characteristic of land of Punt, 206
Tertiary time, 6, 7
Thabad (ruined city), 84
Theophilus (bishop), 211
Theophrastus, 14
Thomas (Apostle), 211
Thomas, Bertram, 147, 200
thorns, prevalence of, 53, 59
threshing, 50 ; in several countries compared, 51
Tihama, 3, 8, 110, 185–6 ; racial composition of inhabitants, 198

Timna', 208
Toala (race), 202
tobacco-pipes (Amiri highlands), 42–3
" Tom Sawyer ", 119
tombs, circular Sabæan, 207 ; see also graves, rock-sepulchres
torrents, sudden rise of, 30
tracery, window-, 85, 117, 122, 125
trachoma, 138
transliteration of Arabic words, xii
transport, methods, 12, 63 ; costs, 42
trap (rock), thickness of, 7 ; detached slab of, 145 ; 161
traps (for foxes), 144
Treasury (San'a), see *Beit al Mal*
treaties, Sa'udi Arabia and Yemen, 230 ; Italy and Yemen, 230, 231 ; 233
Treaty of San'a, 4, 230, 231
trenching (with mattocks), 144, 155
Tribal Guards, 38 ; see also *'askaris*
tribesmen (of highlands), physical characteristics, 35, 196 *sqq.* ; character, disposition, 203, 236
Tropical Africa, 66 ; see Ethiopian Region
Tropical African, flora, 9 ; butterflies in Yemen, 93
Tubba (title of Himyaritic monarchs), 161, 210, 223, 226
Turan Shah (brother of Salah ad Din), 226
turbans, indigo, white, 35, 42, 107, 108 ; of many colours, 24, 65 ; green not worn, 87 ; set afire, 132 ; herbs worn in, 105, 160, 184
Turkish : officers in Imam's service, 120 ; barracks, 124, 131 ; periods of dominion, 170–1, 227, 229
Turks, rebellions against, 171, 229 ; policy of, towards Yemen, 229 ; agree frontier with British, 230 ; withdraw from Yemen, 229, 230
turmeric (cosmetic), 36
" Twelvers " (Dodekites), 224
Tyre, Kingdom of, 23, 198

ulcers, Yemen, 139
umbrella, carried by *shawūsh*, 153 ; the Imam's state, 165 ; umbrellas at country-market, 106
Usaifira (near Ta'izz), 93
Uz, Land of, 46, 62, 207
Uzal (son of Joktan), 120

Varthema, Ludovico di, 227, 239
Vedda (race), 202
Veddoid racial type, 198, 202–3
Venus, see Ishtar

"verdant Yemen", the, 110, 234
vermin, 157
villages, mountain-, 43 sqq. et passim;
   shouting between villages, 47
vineyards, 143, 151-2
volcanic activity, 7, 8; dying signs of,
   114; conjectured destruction of
   buildings by, 153, 195
volcanic glass (obsidian), 196

Wadi 'Amd (Hadhramaut), 200;
   temple at, 216, 217
Wadi: 'Aqqan, 78; 'Asr, 146; Bilih,
   30; Dareija, 41; Dhahr, 149-50,
   160; Hammam 'Ali, 182; Hardaba, 31; Jaira, 183; Kabir
   (branch of Tiban), 25, 26, 78;
   Kharid, 150, 238; Leje (Jebel
   Jihaf), 53, 55-60; Makhris, 99;
   Markha (ancient irrigation works
   at), 208; Masnah, 181-2; Milah,
   30; Natid, 78-80; Rima, 183;
   Sabir, 93-4; as Saghir (branch
   of Tiban), 25, 78; Siham, 183-5;
   Suhul, 105, 109; Thabad, 94-5;
   Tiban, 4, 25, 26, 30, 45, 61,
   (altitude, climate in upper) 65-6,
   (forks into two) 25, 78; Zabid, 106
wadis (dry), 9
Wahriz (Persian viceroy), 212
War Minister (the Imam's), 120
waterfalls, 8, 32, 41, 56, 58, 59, 94
water-pipes (tobacco), stands for, 64;
   brass framework of, 119; 131
water-raising apparatus (Amiri highlands), 51; at Ibb, 102-3; (deep
   wells, San'a), 133
watershed, 9, 100
water-storage, ancient contrivances for,
   220-1; see also cisterns, ponds, tanks
Wavell, A. J. B., 229, 231
weaving, 136
Weli Isma'il, qubba of, 65

Weli Shebazi (Jewish saint), 92
welis (saints), flags on graves of, 24;
   tombs of, 37, 65, 69, 227
wells, 51; deep (San'a), 133, 180
wine (made by Jews), 136
winnowing, 50; methods compared, 51
wireless sets, 89, 131
Wissmann, H. von, see Rathjens, C.
Wyman Bury, G., 16, 207, 231

Yafa, view over, 69; Sultanates, 72, 73
Ya'fur, Banu, 226
Yahya Hamid ad Din (grandfather of
   present Imam), 229
Yarim, 5, 15, 105, 109-13, 228
Yemen, Kingdom of, 3, 4, 230, 233-4;
   extent, 226; population, 171, 226
Yemen, the, meaning of name, 5, 204;
   North-Eastern, 206; extent at
   different periods, 204, 225-6;
   under earliest Khalifs, 222 sqq.;
   rise and fall of dynasties, 226
Yemenis, physical characters, racial
   composition, 196 sqq.

Zabid, 16, 183, 188; religious centre
   of Shafe'is, 225; formerly independent of San'a, ibid.; foundation
   of, 226; 227
Zafar (Sapphar), 110, 209, 211, 237
Zeid (great-grandson of 'Ali), lineage,
   martyrdom, 224
Zeidi sect: plain mosques of, 102;
   university of, 114; 165; spiritual
   headship, 169, 171; peculiar tenets,
   170; rise, tenets, 223 sqq.; formerly two bodies, 224; influence
   on architecture, 225
Ziad (Ibn), Ziadites (dynasty), 226
Zimbabwe, comparison with buildings
   in Arabia, 214
Zubair Islands, 8
Zurei'ites (princes of Aden), 226

II. ANIMALS

Abdini's Stork, 27
Abyssinian Roller, 185
Acræa, 54
Alectoris melanocephala, 182
ant-like beetles (*Anthicidæ*), 158
ants, destroying specimens, 12; winged
   female, 30; under stones, 155
Auripasser euchlorus, 106

baboon, 41; robbing *dhurra* fields, 48;
   54, 61

barbel (*Barbus arabicus*), 150
bark-beetles (*Scolytidæ*), 144
Bath White (butterfly), 145
bats, 10; in cave, 71; fruit-eating,
   144
bed-bugs, 157
Bee-eater, Little Green, 27, 143
bees, 10, 11; honey-, 58
Bilharzia, 138
"bizza" (call to cat), 71
Black-headed Chikore, 71, 182

Boædon lineatus arabicus, 72
branchiopods, 54
Bulbul, Arabian, 27, 48
burnet-moths, 182
bush-shrike, 79
bustard, 186
butterflies, 9, 10, 11; northern, 61, 145, 154, 181; tropical, 54, 93, 106, 183; attracted to *Pluchea*-bush, 79

caddis-flies, 56
Calandra, 157
camels, 38, 42, 63; for milking only, 67; mountain and desert breeds, 109, 235
Caprimulgus nubicus, 27
cat, wild, 71; domestic breeds, words for, 71-2
cattle, humped, 38, 51, 106, 163, 235; uncertain origin of, 203; straight-backed (Socotra), 203
centipedes, 10
chamæleon (*C. calyptratus*), 48
Charaxes hansali, 147
Chat, Arabian Pied, 49
chats, various, 49, 110
Chlamydotis undulatus, 186
cicadas, 31
Cinnyris habessinicus, 58
click-beetles (*Elateridæ*), 183
Clouded Yellow (butterfly), 145
Cobra, African, 48, 72
cockchafers, 30
cony (*Hyrax*), 93-4
Coracias abyssinicus, 185
Corvus corax ruficollis, 48
crustaceans, 54

dhabi, 137
dimm, 72
Dineutes, 56
dogs, in mountain-villages, 48; scavengers (San'a), 126
donkeys, 38; pack-, 63-4; finding way in darkness, 67; strong individuality, 68; at cisterns, 113; 151, 235
Dove, Laughing or Little Brown, 49
dragonflies, 31, 93
duck (various), 25

egrets, small white, 25, 27
Egyptian Vulture, 126
Eidolon helvum, E. sabæum, 144
Eurytela dryope, 93

fairy shrimps, 54, 61
fish (freshwater), 66, 150; narcotised before capture, 238
flamingo, 24
flies, 11, 26, 37, 117; riding on millipede, 92; spread eye-disease, 138; 162
flying-fox, 144
fox, 144
fritillary (butterfly), 154
frogs, 10, 93; green tree-, 162

Garra, 66
gazelle, 136-7, 140, 159, 182
giraffe, reputed former occurrence of, 206
Glossina tachinoides, 66
Glossy Starlings, Red-winged, 49
goats, 38, 40, 235
Golden Sparrow, 106
grain-weevils, 157
grasshoppers, 10, 11; brilliant hind-wings, cryptic colouring, 40; long-horned, 54
Grey Shrike, 182
Greyling (butterfly), 145, 181
ground-beetles (*Carabidæ*), 158, 183

hammerhead, 65, 71
hare, mountain-, 48, 182
hawks, various, 49, 110
herons, 25
Hoopoe, 100, 143
Hornbill, Arabian Grey, 31
horned viper, 25
horses, in mountains, 42, 44, 63; for Government Guards, 46; bred at Dhamar, 114; operation on a, 139; at San'a, 147-8
hūbara, 186
hyæna, 48, 93, 132
Hyla arborea, 162

ibex (horns fixed to houses), 133
Ibis, Glossy, 111; Hermit (?), *ibid.*

kestrel, 110
kite, 48, 126

ladybird-beetles, 181
Lanius excubitor arabicus, 182
larks, 49
leopard, 93, 132, 140
lion, former occurrence of, 206
Longicorn beetles, 144
Lophoceros nasutus, 31
lynx, 71

Melitæa didyma, 154
Merops orientalis, 27
millipede (carrying flies), 92
Milvus migrans ægyptius, 48
Monticola rufocinerea sclateri, 49
mosquitoes, 64, 79, 84, 184
moths, 10, 11, 30, 181, 182
mules, 64, 88, 98, 136, 151

Neophron hercnopterus, 126
nightjar, 27
Notonecta, 155

Œnanthe bottæ, 100, 110 ; *Œ. lugubris*, 49
Onychognathus tristramii, 49
Oriole, Black-headed, 49
Oriolus monacha, 49
ostracods, 54

Painted Lady (butterfly), 145, 154, 181
Papilio demodocus, 147
Papio hamadryas, 48
Paradise Fly-catcher, 27
Passer domesticus indicus, 48
Phoridæ, 92
plant-bugs, 11
Plegadis falcinellus, 111
Ploceus galbula, 49
Pompilid wasps, 40
Puff-adder, 72, 238
Pycnonotus xanthopygos, 27

Rana cyanophlyctis, 93
ratel, 71
ravens, 48
rhinoceros, reputed former occurrence, 206
rhinoceros-beetle (*Oryctes*), 30
Rockthrush, Little Yemen, 49

sand-flies (*Phlebotomus*), 27
Scopus umbretta, 65
scorpions, 10, 54, 150, 155
Scymnus (beetles), 181
sheep, 38, 40 ; fat-tailed, 163
shells, land- and freshwater-, 10, 12, 61 ; sub-fossil, 100

Small Copper (butterfly), 61, 158
Snake, Brown House-, 72
snakes, tribesman's dislike of, 47 ; Arabic words for, 238 ; local distribution, 72
solifugids, 54-5
sparrows, house-, 48
Sphenorhynchus abdinii, 27
spiders, 10, 12 ; paralysed by Pompilid wasps, 40 ; cave-haunting, 71
Staphylinidæ (beetles), 183
storks, white, black, 27
Streptopelia senegalensis, 49
sunbird, Abyssinian, 58, 100
swallow, 49
Swallow-tail butterflies, 147
swift, 49

Tchagra senegala percivali, 79
Tchitrea viridis, 27
Tettigoniidæ, 54
tiger-beetles (*Cicindela*), 31
tortoise, 71
tsetse fly, attempt to rediscover, 66
turtle-doves, 49

Vespa orientalis, 66, 72
vultures, 126

Wall-Brown (butterfly), 61
warblers, various, 27
wasps, 10, 11 ; chewing tamarisk-bark, 66 ; sting of, *ibid.* ; swarm to snake-carcases, 72
water-beetles and -bugs, in rain-pools, 61
" water-boatman ", 155
weaver-finch, Arabian, 49
weevils, black (of northern affinities), 154, 158, 181
wheat-ears, various, 49, 61 ; large brown, 100, 110
whirligig beetles, 56
white wagtail, 110
woodlice, 10

Zygænidæ, 182

III. PLANTS

acacia : forest-trees, 57, 60, 183 ; thorn-scrub, 64, 79, 184 ; wood as fuel, 144
acanthus-bush (*A. racemosus*), 41
'adan-tree (*Adenium obesum*), 66
Ajuga bracteosa, 61
aloe, pole-stemmed (*A. sabæa*), 41, 98 ; fibre from leaves, 57 ; 155

'*amq*-tree, 43
Antithrixia abyssinica, 181
apricot, 132, 143-5 ; giant trees, 146 ; 235
Arenaria, 154
'*Aüd adh Dhib*, 184

banana-tree, 26, 83, 94, 235

Index

Barleria-bushes, 55, 58 ; *B. Hildebrandtii*, 58 ; *B. trispinosa*, 55
barley, 43, 49, 50, 144, 234
beans, field-, 145, 235
bokar-grass, 186
buckthorn, 41
Buddleia polystachya, 100
bugle, white and blue, 61
bulrush-millet, 31, 234
buttercup, 100, 111

cactuses, absence of, 43
Calotropis gigantea, C. procera, 31
campanula, edible (*C. edulis*), 60, 108
Campanula rapunculus, 60
campion, 159
cannas, garden-, 26
Carica papaya, 235
carob-tree, 94
Catha edulis, 94, 235 (see *qat*-tree)
Caylusea, 154
Celastraceæ (Order), 94
Centaurea maxima, 70
centaury, 64
chick-peas, 43, 235
chicory, 150
chives, 114, 235
Cichorium bottæ, 150
Cissus quadrangularis, 40
citrus-trees, 26, 28, 107, 235
clematis (wild), not in flower, 55 ; in full flower, 95
coffee, 107, 183, 234-5
Compositæ, bush-, 110, 158, 181
cotton, 235
cranesbill, 107, 111
Crassulaceæ, 55
custard-apple, 26
cypress, 114, 144

date-palm, cultivated, 25, 26, 79, 92, 235 ; wild bush, 65, 71, 184
dhafar, 238
dhurra (*Sorghum*), 32, 40, 43, 49, 57, 61, 67, 70, 94, 144, 183, 234 ; -stubbles, 144, 148
Dianthus uniflorus, 60
dukhn (*Pennisetum*), 31, 32, 234
dūm-palm (*Hyphæne*), 25, 235

Epilobium hirsutum, 70
Erythræa, 64
Euphorbia Ammak, 43, 106
euphorbia-bushes (cactus-like) : low, 40 ; tall candelabra-like, 43, 44, 106 ; outward resemblance to cactuses, 43 ; insects associated with, 53, 54 ; varied and luxuriant, 92, 96, 98
Euphorbia officinalis, cushion-form of, irritant juice of, 156
Euphorbiaceæ, 43
everlasting flowers, 108

Felicia abyssinica, 158
ferns, 56–7, 61, 70, 94 ; maidenhair-, 56
fig trees, wild, 41, 43, 59, 94, 183 ; cultivated, 143, 146, 152, 235

garden-flowers, various, 26, 137
Geranium (true), 107
gladiolus, wild, 55
grape-vine, 143, 235

Helichrysum, 108
hibiscus, low (*H. meidiensis*), 55
Hyphæne, 25, 235

'*ilb*-tree, 40–1, 67, 70, 79 ; rising from hedges, 81 ; 94, 235
indigo-bushes, wild (*Indigofera*), 66, 184, 235 ; cultivated, 235
iris (*I. albicans*), 9, 109

jasmine, white (*Jasminum officinale*), 55, 181
juniper-trees, 94 ; -bushes, 115, 181

Kalanchœ, orange-flowered, 55 ; orange and yellow, 106
khardal, 235
knapweed, bush-, 70

Labiate herbs, mixed, 55, 100
Lavandula atriplicifolia, 154 ; *L. pubescens*, 115
lavender, 115 ; rare yellow-flowered, 154
lime, sweet, 149
lucerne, 43, 144-5, 235

maize, 234
mango-tree, 26, 92, 235
meadow-rue, 60
Micromeria biflora, 154
mignonette, wild, 154
millet, bulrush-, 31, 234 ; highland or white, 32, 234, etc. ; see *dukhn, dhurra*
Minuartia filifolia, 154
mustard, mauve-flowered, 93, 235

Notonia obesa, 111

Ocimum basilicum, 105
onions, 43, 93, 114, 235
Opuntia, 44, 144
orchis, 55
Osyris abyssinica, 147

Pandanus odoratissimus, 26, 184, 235; flower-heads worn at festivals, 184
Panicum turgidum, 186
pawpaw-tree, 26, 83, 235
peach-tree, 145, 235
pear, 235
Pennisetum, 31, 234 (see *dukhn*)
Phagnalon, 110
Phœnix reclinata, 65, 184
Pluchea indica, 79
plum, 235
pomegranate, 26, 143, 146, 235
potentilla (*P. viscosa*), 9, 100
prickly pear, 44, 144
primula (*P. verticillata*), 9, 56, 100
Pteris vittata, 57; *P. dentata*, 70
Pterocephalus (section of *Scabiosa*), 159

qat-tree, 40, 88, 92, 94, 145, 149, 235
quince, 143, 146, 235

rampion, 60
Ranunculus multifidus, 100
rock-pink, 60
roses, wild (*Rosa abyssinica*), 94; garden-, 26, 137
rue, 105

Salvadora persica, 147
scabious, field-, 100; creeping, 159
schörur, 156
screw-pine tree, see *Pandanus*
Sedum, 60
Selaginella, 60

Senecio, bush-, 55, 70
sesame, 235
shaddock, 107
Silene, 159
Sorghum, 32, 234 (see *dhurra*)
southernwood, 105
spurges (euphorbias), 43
Stapelia, 156
stonecrop, white, 60
Suæda, 186
sugar-cane, 26
Sweet Basil, 105; worn in turbans, 105, 160
sweet-potatoes, 26
Swertia polynectaria, 60, 70

tamarind, 235
tamarisk, 27, 31, 144, 150, 161, 184; bark chewed by wasps, 66; lofty trees, 78, 183
Tephrosia Apollinea, 238
Terminalia-trees, 26
Thalictrum schimperianum, 60
thyme, 154
tobacco, 43, 235
tomatoes, 93, 235
tulh (acacia-wood), 144

Vernonia, 55
vine, fleshy wild-, 40; grape-, 143, 235

walnut, 143, 145, 146, 235
water-dock, 162
water-mint, 147, 149
wheat, 43, 49, 50, 144, 183, 234
willow, 143
willow-herb, 70

Zizyphus spina-christi, 41, 67, 235; see *'ilb*

For Product Safety Concerns and Information please contact our EU representative GPSR@taylorandfrancis.com
Taylor & Francis Verlag GmbH, Kaufingerstraße 24, 80331 München, Germany

www.ingramcontent.com/pod-product-compliance
Lightning Source LLC
Chambersburg PA
CBHW052143300426
44115CB00011B/1497